W O R D S

W I T H O U T

M U S I C

Born in Baltimore in 1937, Philip Glass studied at the University of Chicago and the Juilliard School. The composer of operas, film scores and symphonies, he performs regularly with the Philip Glass Ensemble and lives in New York.

Further praise for *Words Without Music*:

'Glass's style of writing is devoid of pomposity or fake intellectualism. *Words Without Music* is informal, chatty and self-aware . . . an amiable and entertaining book.' *Financial Times*

'A lively, absorbing read that makes Glass's rarefied cultural sphere wonderfully accessible.' *Publishers Weekly*

'An unpretentious and often funny account of the life of a remarkable man.' *The Economist*

Philip Glass

WORDS
WITHOUT
MUSIC

A MEMOIR

FABER & FABER

First published in the United States in 2015
by Liveright Publishing Company,
a division of W. W. Norton & Company, Inc.,
500 Fifth Avenue, New York,
New York 10110

First published in the UK in 2015
by Faber & Faber Ltd,
Bloomsbury House,
74–77 Great Russell Street,
London WC1B 3DA

This paperback edition published in 2016

Printed and bound in the UK by CPI Group (UK) Ltd, Croydon CR0 4YY

The right of Philip Glass to be identified as author of this work has been asserted in
accordance with the Copyright, Designs and Patents Act 1988

A CIP record for this book is available from the British Library

ISBN 978-0-571-32374-6

2 3 4 5 6 7 8 9 10

FOR MY CHILDREN

JULIET   CAMERON
  ZACK   MARLOWE

CONTENTS

PART III

OPENING

"F YOU GO TO NEW YORK CITY TO STUDY MUSIC, YOU'LL END UP LIKE your uncle Henry, spending your life traveling from city to city and living in hotels."

That was my mother, Ida Glass, when she heard of my plans. I was sitting with her at the kitchen table in my parent's house, in Baltimore, having come back home after graduating from the University of Chicago.

Uncle Henry, a cigar-smoking bantamweight with a heavy Brooklyn accent, was married to Aunt Marcela, my mother's sister, who herself had escaped from Baltimore a full generation before me. Uncle Henry was, in fact, a drummer. He had dropped out of dental school shortly after the end of World War I to become an itinerant musician, playing for the next fifty years mainly in vaudeville houses and holiday hotels, and with dance bands all over the country. In his later years he played in the hotels of the Catskills, known then and actually still now as the Borscht Belt. He was probably playing in one of those hotels—Grossinger's, I'd bet—at that time in the spring of 1957 when I was planning my future.

In any case, I liked Uncle Henry and thought he was a pretty good guy. Truth be told, I was far from horrified by the prospect of "traveling from city to city and living in hotels." I was rather looking forward eagerly to that—a life filled with music and travel—and completely thrilled with the whole idea. And as it turned out many decades later, my mother's description was completely accurate. As I begin this book, that is precisely what I am doing—traveling from Sydney on my way to Paris by way of L.A. and New York, and playing concerts all along the way. Of course that's not the whole story, but it is a significant part of it.

Ida Glass was always a pretty smart woman.

As a young man, incautious and curious, my head full of plans, I was already doing what I would always do. I had started playing the violin at six, the flute and piano at eight, begun composing at fifteen, and now, having finished college, I was impatient to start my "real life," which I had known all along would be in music. Since I was very young I had been drawn to music, felt connected to it, and I knew that it was my path.

There had been musicians in the Glass family before, but the general view in my family was that musicians were somehow living on the fringes of respectability, that the life of music was not the life an educated person would pursue. People didn't make a lot of money playing music back then, and to spend your life singing songs in a bar was not considered a serious undertaking. In my parents' minds, there was nothing in what I was proposing to do to indicate that I *wouldn't* end up singing in some bar. They weren't thinking about me turning into Van Cliburn, they were thinking of me turning into Uncle Henry. Furthermore, I don't think they had any idea what people actually did in music school.

"I've been thinking about this for years," I said, "and this is what I really want to do."

The fact was, my mother knew me. I was a very determined young fellow. When I said I was going to do something, I simply did it. She knew I would not take her objections seriously, but she felt like she had to say it, in a dutiful way. Neither of us thought what she said was going to change anything.

The next day I took the bus to New York, which already for decades had been the country's capital of culture, finance, and ingenuity, to try to enroll as a student at the Juilliard School. But . . . not so fast. I had a handful of compositions and I could play the flute decently, but I wasn't sufficiently accomplished in either to merit admission to the school.

Nonetheless, I auditioned for the woodwind faculty at Juilliard, this being three professors who taught the flute, clarinet, and bassoon. After I played, one of them, in an astute moment, kindly asked, "Mr. Glass, do you really want to be a flutist?"

Because I wasn't *that* good. I could *play* the flute, but I didn't seem to show the enthusiasm that I would need to succeed.

"Well, actually," I said, "I want to be a composer."

"Well, then! You should take the composition exam."

"I don't think I'm ready for that," I said.

I admitted to having a few compositions but declined to show them. I knew there was nothing of interest in that early work.

"Why don't you come back in the fall and register in the Extension Division of the school," he said. "They have courses in theory and composition. Spend some time writing music and then on the basis of that you'll have an audition for the composition department."

The Extension Division was run as an "adult education" program by an excellent teacher, Stanley Wolfe, himself an accomplished composer. The plan was to spend a year preparing for a proper audition as a composer where my work would be evaluated and my application considered. Of course, this was exactly the opportunity I was looking for. I agreed to their suggestion and followed it to the letter.

But first there was the "material" question. I would need cash to get started, though I fully expected to get a part-time job after settling in at the school. I took the Greyhound bus back home and applied for the best job close to Baltimore, which was thirty miles away at a Bethlehem Steel plant in Sparrows Point, Maryland, an already aging and tired relic of early-twentieth-century industry. Because I could read, write, and knew arithmetic (not common in those days at Bethlehem Steel), I was given a job as a weigh-master—meaning I operated a crane and weighed huge bins of nails, keeping a good tally of everything produced in that part of the plant. By September, I had saved more than $1200, which in 1957 was a fairly good sum. I returned to New York and registered for Stanley Wolfe's composition class.

But before going into those first years in New York in the late 1950s, I need to fill in a few missing pieces of my story.

PART ONE

IDA GLASS WITH SHEPPIE, PHILIP, AND MARTY.

BALTIMORE, MARYLAND, 1941.

BALTIMORE

WAS THE YOUNGEST OF THE THREE CHILDREN OF BEN AND IDA GLASS. My sister, Sheppie, was the oldest, then my brother, Marty, then me.

My mother was a dark-haired, attractive woman who always had a certain clarity to the way she looked. She began her life as an English teacher and then became the librarian of the school that I later attended, beginning in 1950, Baltimore's City College, which was actually a public high school.

Ida was not an ordinary mother. Born in 1905, you could argue, and reasonably so, that she was an early member of the feminist movement, though she would never have described herself that way. Her understanding of the issue of gender in our society came through her own intelligence and the depth of her thinking. As she came to know the world, she was not content with the conventional role of the woman in America, the old German *"Küche, Kirche, Kinder"*— kitchen, church, children. Ida knew the value of education and she applied those values to herself, and as a result she was far more educated than anyone else in the family. She used some of the money she earned as a teacher to continue her studies, going on to get her master's degree and working at the doctoral level. From the time I was six, and Marty and Sheppie were seven and eight, we were shipped off to summer camp for two full months while Ida took courses. I remember she even went to Switzerland to study after the war and came back with Swiss watches for all of us. They probably didn't cost very much money, and mine didn't last very long, but we were delighted to get them. My brother and I used to compare our watches endlessly.

While my mother was away studying, our dad, Ben, was left alone to look after his record store, General Radio, at 3 S. Howard Street in downtown Baltimore. He liked my mother's sense of independence, and he supported her efforts.

Ben was born in 1906. His first job, when he was in his late teens, was working for the Pep Boys automotive company, going up into New England and opening up their stores. He became a self-taught mechanic and was good at fixing cars. Later, when he came back to Baltimore, he opened up his own auto repair shop. When they started putting radios in cars, the radios naturally began breaking, so he began fixing them, too. After a while he got tired of working on cars and just did radios. Then, as a sideline, he began selling records. Gradually the records took over the shop. There used to be just a six- or eight-foot space for records in the front of the store but eventually there would be thirty feet of records, deep into the store, as more and more people were buying them. His little repair shop ended up being just a bench in the back with him and one other man, named John.

My father was very physical and muscular: about five foot ten and 180 pounds. A dark-haired, rough-cut handsome man, he had several different sides to him: a gentle side, a tough side, a self-made businessman side. His gentle side showed in the way he looked after children—not just his own, but other people's children, too. If the fathers were absent, he would go over and spend time with the kids in the family, so much so that for a long time my cousin Ira Glass thought that Ben was his grandfather, because when Ira's grandfather wasn't around Ben would go over and play grandfather. To many of the children in our extended family, he was Uncle Bennie.

His tough side came out in the way he could run a record store in a low-rent area of downtown Baltimore, a part of the city near the waterfront that was home to both Jewish delicatessens and burlesque joints. Even though this was a rough area, he did not have any problems. He could take care of anybody who threatened him or the store, and he could pulverize them. And he would.

Ben had been in the Marines twice, once in Santo Domingo in the 1920s (U.S. troops were in the Dominican Republic for eight years, in a military occupation now mostly forgotten), and then in the Second World War, when, at the age of thirty-six—almost at the upper age limit for service, thirty-nine—he reenlisted and went off again to boot camp. He had had tough Marine training and he wanted to teach Marty and me how to take care of ourselves in extreme situations. Once he told us about the time muggers had set up a trip wire on South Howard Street near the store.

"I'll tell you what happened," Ben began. "I was coming out of the store one night after closing, about nine thirty. I hit this trip wire and fell on the ground, and I knew exactly what it was."

"What did you do?" we asked.

"I waited for them."

When they got close enough, he grabbed hold of them and beat the crap out of them.

The way he said, "I waited for them," we just thought, Yeah, he was ready.

Indeed, Ben was ready for anything. There are always shoplifters in bookstores and these kinds of record stores. You'd be amazed what kinds of things they can put into their pants and under their shirts. This was in the days of LPs, but even so they were still putting them under their shirts. Marty and I were supposed to tell him if we saw anybody doing that.

"If you see anybody shoplifting," Ben instructed us, "picking up something and putting it under their clothes, just call me."

Well, we didn't call him, because of what would happen when he would catch one of the shoplifters. He would take the guy outside and beat him until he was senseless. Our dad had no interest in calling the cops. He wasn't interested in teaching any kind of civic lessons. He just wanted to make sure they never came back to the store, and they didn't. But once you, as his kid, had witnessed that, you didn't want to see it again. I distinctly remember seeing one young fellow taking a record and putting it into his pants, and I just let him go. It would have been too upsetting to see what would have happened.

Ben the businessman would work from nine in the morning until nine at night. One time when I was still very young, I asked, "Daddy, what keeps you going here at the store?"

"All I have is this store," he said. "And what I want to do is to use this one store to be as successful as I possibly can."

"What does that mean?"

"I want to see how much money I can make. My satisfaction is in making this thing work." He really meant it. He worked tirelessly and he ended up with a fairly good business.

Ben was typical of the generation that didn't have a higher education. I don't even know if he finished high school. He was one of those young men who just went to work at a certain point. His two older brothers became doctors, but he didn't. When he was young, he and his brothers would stand on the street corners of Baltimore selling newspapers, I guess it would have been when they were twelve or thirteen. While they stood there, they played mental chess. They also played mental checkers, which is harder, by the way. At least with mental chess you know what the pieces are. With mental checkers, it's harder to visualize the board because the pieces, apart from their red or black color, are all the same.

My father taught me to play mental chess, too. I would be with him in the car and he would say, "Pawn to King 4" and I'd say, "Pawn to King 4." He'd say, "Knight to King's Bishop 3" and I'd say, "Pawn to Queen 3." We went through a game together and I learned to visualize chess. I was probably seven or eight years old and I could already do that. Years later when I was learning to do exercises in visualization, I discovered I had developed this aptitude when I was very young. In some of the esoteric traditions that I have engaged with, working with visualizations is a routine exercise. Part of the exercise is to develop a terrific clarity, so that you can actually see everything. I discovered that many people couldn't see anything, but I could see right away, and that was a big help. For instance, if I were looking at a Tibetan Buddhist meditational figure, I could see the eyes, I could see the hands, I could see what the hands were holding, I could see the whole thing. I had a number of friends who said they were having trouble visualizing and I realized that I didn't have any trouble. When I wondered why I didn't, I remembered those chess games that Ben and I used to play.

During the Second World War, every eligible male member of our family was in the armed forces. I was about to turn five years old when America went to war, and there were no men in the family living in Baltimore at that time. My mother had to go off to work all day at school, so Maud, the woman who was helping raise us and to whom we were very close because she spent a long time with us, would dress us in the morning. My mother would come back in time to cook dinner, and then she would go downtown and work in the store until nine o'clock at night. Ida ran the store all the years my father was away. During the day there were employees, but she was there at night and on weekends to take the money out of the cash register, examine the accounts, and order new records. She didn't know what Ben knew, but she knew what needed to be done. She wasn't the only woman doing that. If you think back, the women's liberation movement could well have come out of the Second World War, when women, given the labor shortage, took over many jobs formerly done by men. When the men came back from the war, their wives were working, and a lot of those women did not want to give up their jobs.

After the war, when the first televisions were made and sold, Ben sent away for a build-it-yourself television set. He built it and from that moment on he began repairing televisions. Marty and I were supposed to learn that, too, and to a degree we did, but I don't think we ever got really good at it. We didn't have the motivation that he had.

The only television signal we got in those early days was from Washington, D.C. It was a test pattern. There was a lot of snow, as we used to say. After a while, professional football games started being shown on Sunday afternoon. By 1947 or '48, more programming was needed, so an early version of what came to be known as television producers would go into the schools and get the kids to play music. They would often do live broadcasts directly from the schools, so when I was ten and eleven years old, I was on television playing the flute.

SHEPPIE, MARTY, AND I ALL BEGAN with music when we were quite young. Shep and Marty had weekly piano lessons from a piano teacher, who traveled from home to home giving children lessons, but I had chosen to study the flute. Beginning at age six, I had taken some violin lessons given as group classes at the Park School, my first elementary school. For some reason the violin didn't "take," which is odd to imagine, given that I've written so much string music—solo, quartets, sonatas, symphonies—since then.

I do recall, though, that there was a boy a year older than me at my school who had a flute. I thought it was the most beautiful instrument I had ever seen or heard, and I wanted to do nothing more than to play the flute. I wound up playing it until I was thirty. In fact, even in my first professional concerts, I was playing the flute as well as keyboards.

I soon learned that when I took my flute with me to school, I would sometimes have to fight my way home. Back then the joke was "Hey, how would you like to play the skin flute?" That was considered very witty. The skin flute, haw-haw-haw. In the semidetached houses of northwest Baltimore, the young boys were experimenting with being macho. They were terrified of being considered gay. Anything that seemed effeminate to them was horrible, and the flute to them was a feminine instrument. Why? Because it was a long thing that you blew on? It's a vulgarization of a stupid idea.

My brother would set up the fights. He said, "Okay, we're going to meet over here and you're going to fight this kid."

In a funny way, I was supposed to be the sissy. When I think about it now, I think Marty was doing me a favor. He said, "Why don't you just have a fight with this kid? Just show him who you are."

So we went to the park, and that kid didn't particularly want to fight with me, either. I was a little smaller than him, but I knew I was going to stomp him. I don't know how I did it, because I didn't know anything about fighting. I just put my fists up and beat the crap out of the kid. They finally pulled me away. I was maybe nine or ten. I wasn't especially brave, and I didn't like fights, but I felt that I had been corralled into it. The kid could have been six feet tall and I still would have beaten him, it didn't matter. After that, no one bothered me about the flute.

When my dad came home from the Marines in 1945 the family moved from the center of town to a neighborhood of semidetached and duplex homes out on Liberty Road where the old #22 streetcar line ran. The #22 streetcar would play an important part in my life until I left for the University of Chicago in 1952. I had been permitted to have flute lessons but there was no teacher in the neighborhood. But the #22 streetcar ran all the way downtown to Mount Vernon Place, home to Baltimore's Washington Monument, which faced the Peabody Conservatory. The streetcar had yellow wicker seats that were dirty most of the time. Its metal wheels ran on tracks, and it got its electricity from overhead cables. There was one man in the front who was the driver, and there was another man, a conductor, who took the money, ten or twelve cents. I don't even know if I paid at all for the first few years, since I was under twelve years old.

The fourth floor of Peabody had a long corridor with practice rooms on either side, with benches where I waited for my teacher. There was no flute teacher in the Preparatory Division of the Peabody, so I was admitted to the conservatory and had my lessons from Britton Johnson, then first chair flutist with the Baltimore Symphony. He was a wonderful teacher and had been himself a student of William Kincaid, the first chair flutist at the Philadelphia Orchestra, who was widely considered one of the great flutists of all time. So I had blue-blood lineage when it came to flute playing.

Mr. Johnson, who now has a memorial prize named after him, was round, two hundred pounds for sure, but not tall, maybe forty or fifty years old, and still, when I began my studies, at the height of his play-ing. He liked me a lot. He complimented me, saying that I had a great embrasure—which meant my lips were built for the flute. But, at the same time, he knew that I wasn't going to be a flutist. I don't know how he knew that, but I think he figured I was a kid coming from a kind of struggling middle-class family that was never going to allow their son to become a musician, and that whatever talent I had was not going to come to fruition.

Mr. Johnson would look at me, and he would sigh and shake his head, at least a few times after my lessons. Not because I was a bad flutist, but because he believed I could become a really good one. And he was right, I had the potential but it was never fully realized. I don't know if Mr. Johnson ever found out what happened to me. I doubt it. He might have known, but he would have been surprised. Mr. John-son was quite right about the family pressure, in that everyone was constantly pushing me in quite a different direction. But ultimately he was wrong, because I was not going to let myself get pushed around that way.

In fact, I really wanted both piano and flute lessons. Though they were opposed to the idea of music as a profession, Ida and Ben both considered music education basic to a fully rounded educational pro-gram. But my parents were far from well off. On her schoolteacher's salary, my mother actually earned more than my father. Still, with whatever money they earned, we were given music lessons. However, the economy of our family could allow for only one lesson per child, and the flute became my instrument.

Not to be deterred, I would sit quietly in the living room during my brother's piano lessons and follow his lessons with absolute atten-tion. The moment the lesson was over and the teacher out of the house, I would dash over to the piano, which had miraculously appeared in our new home shortly after we arrived there, and play my brother's lesson. Of course this upset Marty no end. He was convinced I was "stealing" his lessons. At the very least I was pestering him by play-ing better. He was half right. Though I *was* a first-class pesky younger brother, I was simply there to "steal" the lesson—no more, no less. Marty would chase me off the piano and around the living room and give me a few good knocks along the way. For me, this price of admission was cheap and easy.

In retrospect, what was quite remarkable was that I would, at the age of eight, take an afternoon streetcar ride to downtown Baltimore alone, and, after my one-hour weekly lesson, take the same #22 streetcar back home. In the dark, I would alight from the streetcar at Hillsdale Road and run the six blocks to our house as fast as I could. I was truly terrified of the dark. Though ghosts and dead people were the images that pursued me, it never occurred to me, my parents, or my teachers that I had anything to fear from living, real-life monsters. But in 1945 Baltimore they wouldn't be encountered anyway. Besides, all the streetcar conductors soon knew me, and I was made to sit near them at the front of the streetcar.

Eventually I was allowed to take additional music lessons, so on Saturday afternoon I studied with Mr. Hart, the head percussionist of the Baltimore Symphony. This was not solo instruction but a class for six to eight children, and it was a particular joy for me to play the timpani. I write today with great pleasure for all percussion instruments, but then there were also classical score reading and ear training classes, which I detested for no particular reason. As a grown-up and, now, even as a mature musician, I have noticed something odd about the way I hear music. I can't put my finger on it. It must have been something about hearing that was not, well, common. Nadia Boulanger, the great teacher with whom I would spend more than two years studying in Paris, worked tirelessly on "hearing" exercises for me. I suppose the problem was solved, though I never really understood what it was in the first place. And now there is no one left to ask.

MY BROTHER, MARTY, AND I STARTED WORKING at the store when we were eleven and twelve years old. Our job was to break—*actually break*—78 rpm records so that Ben could collect the "return privilege" allowed for broken records in those days. In the late 1940s, the big record companies paid retail dealers about ten cents a record for goods damaged on the way to the stores, or really for any reason whatsoever. To collect the money, the broken records had to be segregated by company and have at least the label intact. Marty and I were given boxes and boxes of records that simply didn't sell. And they were not all from General Radio, our dad's store, either. He made a second business by buying up unwanted stock from other small stores all through Maryland, Virginia, and West Virginia. I remember he bought them, still whole but unsold, for five cents a record. Marty and I broke them, repackaged them in boxes by company—RCA, Decca, Blue Note, Columbia—and Ben sold them back to the companies for ten cents, doubling his money and keeping us quite busy and reasonably happy. Marty and I were almost always in the basement of the store, either sorting records or breaking them or else working with John in the radio repair department testing tubes, trying to be some help in the repair of those old tube radios.

Ben also had clients who listened to what we called "hillbilly music." He advertised his record store on Appalachian radio stations in West Virginia and people would write him and he would send them records. I don't think he particularly liked that music, but he knew about it, and I knew about it, too.

One summer, when Marty and I were not much older, he opened up a storefront in the African-American part of town and my brother and I spent that summer selling R & B records to other kids not much older than we were. I listened to all of the popular music coming out at that time. I liked the vitality of it, I liked the inventiveness of it, I liked the humor of it. Later on, when musicians like Buddy Holly came along in the mid-1950s, early rock 'n' roll sounded to me like versions of Appalachian music. I think that's where it came from. Electric guitars replaced banjos and electric basses, along with off-beat drum playing, built up the bass lines. I loved the raw power of it.

At home my brother and I shared a room. We had a walk-in closet where we kept our clothes, we had two beds separated by a little night table, and we had a window that opened onto the steps that led to the second floor of our duplex house. It was very easy to go out at night and not be seen, so we would sneak out to buy Good Humor bars—we could hear the ice cream man with the little bell going down the street. When we got older we did more mischievous things. One of our gang had a BB gun and we'd shoot out lights going down the alley. Then we would sneak back into the house. I don't think we were ever caught.

My sister, Sheppie, had older friends, and the difference between twelve and ten seemed very big at the point when she was in high school and we were still in junior high. Also, Sheppie was much more sheltered and supervised than Marty and me. She stayed in private schools and she had her own social life until she went away to Bryn Mawr for college.

I saw Sheppie more when we went to Quaker summer camp in Maine. The place wasn't really a camp so much as it was a big old house with six or eight bedrooms in it. They would take kids from the age of twelve to eighteen, and I was among the youngest. There were no real counselors, but there were three or four older Quaker women who looked after us and it was like a big family. We played tennis, we went boating, and we went to the Grange dances every Thursday night.

The school we went to when we were very young had some Quaker teachers, and Ida liked them a lot, as her Quaker friends were involved in education. They were pacifists, of course, and very socially conscious. I don't remember ever having attended a Quaker meeting, but I knew something about what the Quakers believed in, and I was always sympathetic—as Ida and Ben were—to those ideas. They were committed to social responsibility and being connected to the world.

The Quaker philosophy is consistent with ideas that developed in me later. I never wanted to be a Quaker, but I did send my first two children to a Quaker school in Manhattan, Friends Seminary on Fifteenth Street off Second Avenue. I liked their philosophy of life, work, and spirit. Bedrock ideas of social responsibility and change through nonviolence came to me through the Quakers. When people's lives reflect ideas like that, their behavior becomes automatically part of a bigger picture.

Going to the movies every Saturday was part of growing up in Baltimore in the 1940s. We would see a double feature and previews and newsreels. This was how we learned about the war. After the Germans were beaten, when I was eight years old, I remember clearly seeing newsreels of American soldiers entering the concentration camps. The images the cameramen had filmed were shown in movie houses all over the United States. No one thought anything about it—there were no warnings that you might be upset if you watched it. In those films you actually saw skulls and piles of human bones. You saw what the soldiers saw when they walked in, because right behind the soldiers were the cameras.

The Jewish community had known that there were extermination camps in Germany and Poland. They knew because they were getting letters and messages from people who were getting out now and then, but it was not commonly known or believed by others in America, nor was it addressed by the government. After the war, refugees were arriving in America and my mother immediately began to help. By 1946 our house had become a halfway house, a place for the survivors who had no place to go. We had any number of people who would come and stay for a few weeks and then they would be resettled. As a young child, I was frightened. They did not look like anyone I knew. These were men who were skinny with numbers tattooed on their wrists. They couldn't speak English, and they looked like they had come back from hell, which is literally what had happened. I knew they had survived something terrible. We had seen what the camps looked like in the newsreels, and then we met the survivors who came from those very places.

My mother had a vision of society, much more than almost any of the people that were near her. Others were not inviting these people into their homes, yet Ida became very involved with resettlement of refugees who were pouring out of Europe. She developed educational plans for them so they could learn English, develop skills, and make a place for themselves in America. Both of my parents embodied values of kindness and caring—values that were passed on to their children.

My sister, Sheppie, has spent most of her professional life doing the same work. For many years she was with the International Rescue Committee, which responds globally to humanitarian crises. More recently, she's worked with KIND—Kids in Need of Defense, which is responding to the current immigration crisis on the southern border of the United States.

Like many other secular Jewish households, there was no religious instruction in our home, though we might occasionally go to a relative's house at Passover. Our neighborhood was a Gentile one. At Christmastime, there were Christmas lights on the trees in front of the houses, as well as Santa Claus and his reindeer on the roofs. My classmates were not Jewish, and whenever I would visit their homes during the holidays, I envied them because they had Christmas trees and stockings.

There were parts of Baltimore where people had signs up in their yards that said, "No Dogs, No Jews." As a kid, I didn't know what it meant that people had such signs in front of their houses. But if I took the city bus that went from southeast Baltimore to where we lived in the northwest, going across a large swath of the city, I would pass through Roland Park. This upper-middle-class neighborhood not far from Johns Hopkins, with nice, big houses with nice, big lawns, was a place I saw such signs. It didn't make any sense to me, but prejudice like that never did.

Thinking back, we did know a lot of Jewish people. In fact, not one person came into the house who wasn't Jewish. It was a very close-knit community, not that we were observant or spoke Hebrew—no one did. But every Sunday morning my father would say, "C'mon, kid, we gotta go get some bagels," and we would drive down to East Baltimore to some of the old delis and buy bagels, sauerkraut, and pickles out of the barrel to bring home. My mother's brothers wanted us to go to Hebrew school, so Marty and I went a couple of days a week until we were thirteen. But instead of attending the classes, Marty and I—Marty being the ringleader—spent most of those afternoons at a pool hall a block from the temple, playing pool until a quarter till six, when it would be time to go home. My mother was in the school library, my father was in his record store, and nobody knew what we were doing.

The Yiddish or Hebrew words we did know we had learned from our grandparents. My mother's family came from Russia and my father's family came from Latvia. My mother's family lived on Brookfield Avenue at number 2028, and we were at 2020, so they were very close by, and my mother would often visit her parents. As far as I remember, they weren't observant either, but they spoke Yiddish to one another, and if we were in the room, that's what we heard. In fact, I never heard them speak English. During the years when I knew them, and that would have been when I was very young, I understood everything they said.

My mother's father had started as a ragpicker, which was very common in those days. They'd go out on the street and pick up anything of value. Later on, Ida's father began making cinder blocks from a mold and selling them, and that turned into a building-supply shop. Then he began selling plywood. By the time he died, it had become a business. He started with a little store and by the time I was grown up, his sons, my mother's brothers, owned property and had become businessmen.

Most of the musicians in the family were on my father's side. My cousin Cevia studied classical music as a pianist, and there were other people who were in vaudeville. Some family members were classical musicians, and some were in the world of popular music. My father's grandmother, Frieda Glass, was Al Jolson's aunt, so there was a bloodline there. The Glasses and Jolsons were cousins. I discovered this when, years later, I was playing in Cincinnati and a well-dressed man gave me his card. His name was Jolson, and he was a dentist.

"I'm one of your cousins," he said.

"Oh, you're one of the Jolsons," I said.

"Yes."

"So the Jolsons and Glasses really are related?"

"Yes, we are."

On my mother's side, as I indicated, they really didn't like musicians. To them, the fame of Al Jolson was no big deal. Baltimore wasn't like New York, where the whole Lower East Side was filled with Italians and Jews, and one of the ways of getting out of the ghetto was the entertainment business. It reached all the way to Hollywood, where entertainers like Eddie Cantor, Red Skelton, and the Marx Brothers were symbolic of that generation.

When my father started to sell records, he didn't know which were the good records and which were the bad. Whatever the salesmen gave him, he would buy. But he noticed that some records sold and some records didn't, so as a businessman he wanted to know why some of the records didn't sell. He would take them home and listen to them, thinking that if he could find out what was wrong with them, he wouldn't buy the bad ones anymore.

In the late forties, the music that didn't sell was by Bartók, Shostakovich, and Stravinsky, the modernists of that time. Ben listened to them over and over again, trying to understand what was wrong, but he ended up loving their music. He became a strong advocate of new music and began to sell it in his store. Eventually, anyone in Baltimore who wanted to buy new music would have to go to there. He would walk them through it. He would give people records and say "Look, Louie, take this home. Listen to it. If you don't like it bring it back." He was converting people. They came in to buy Beethoven and he was selling them Bartók.

My father was self-taught, but he ended up having a very refined and rich knowledge of classical, chamber, and contemporary music. Typically he would come home and have dinner, and then sit in his armchair and listen to music until almost midnight. I caught on to this very early, and I would go and listen with him. Of course, he had no idea I was there. At least, at that time, I didn't think so. Until I was nine years old, we lived in one of the row houses with the marble steps that were the rule in the downtown Baltimore residential neighborhoods. The children's bedrooms were only one floor above the living room where my father sat for his evening music listening. Somehow, I would find myself awake and would quietly sneak part way down the stairs behind him and, sitting there, join him in listening. My childhood nights were spent with him in this way from a very early age. For me, those years were filled with the music of the great Schubert string quartets, the Opus 59 quartets of Beethoven, piano music of all kinds, and quite a lot of "modern" music as well—mainly Shostakovich and Bartók. The sounds of chamber music entered my heart, becoming my basic musical vocabulary. I thought, simply, that was how music was supposed to sound. That was my base, and quite a lot of everything else eventually became layered around it.

Always concerned about our education, my mother put us into the best places she could. My brother and sister went to private schools, but I don't think they could afford a third private school, so I went to a public high school, City College. Baltimore, in its day, was quite progressive in its ideas about public education, and I was registered in an "A" course, an enriched education program emphasizing math and language. City College is what today would be called a magnet school. Apart from the fact that it was racially segregated, as all public schools in Baltimore were, it was very forward-looking in its thinking. Graduates of the "A" course would often enter college or university as sophomores, not freshman. The point is that I was already in a high-quality educational program before the question of an early entrance to the University of Chicago ever came up.

Since my mother was the librarian in my high school, I would stay in the library after classes were over. If I had no other plans, I would wait for her to close it up for the day and get a ride home with her from school. While waiting, I passed the time browsing through college catalogues. I dreamed, of course, of escaping Baltimore and knew that my ticket out would be connected to a college. Eventually,

I stumbled on to the University of Chicago catalogue and discovered, to my delight, that a high school diploma was not required, and one could be accepted by simply passing their entrance exam. This had been put into effect by the then-president, Robert Hutchins, who was regarded as one of the most progressive educators in the country. Besides this unusual entrance requirement, he had also initiated a "Great Books" program at the College of the University of Chicago. This idea came from Mortimer Adler, a philosopher and educator who had identified the one hundred great books that an educated person should have read to earn a university degree. It was a formidable list—Plato, Aristotle, Shakespeare, Newton, and so on. In fact, in those days, not surprisingly, a large part of the College curriculum was based on the list.

I suppose that this loophole in admission policies which allowed bright and ambitious young men to enter college without having completed high school may have had something to do the end of World War II and the fact that thousands of GIs returning from Europe and Japan were taking advantage of the GI Bill that helped them go to college. By the time I came along, it was already in place, offering a way to skip over the last two years of high school and begin the exciting years of education that a big university could offer.

My high school adviser thought taking the exam would be great practice. It never occurred to him that I might pass. The test was a comprehensive measure of education: math, essay writing, and history. I didn't consider it very hard, which is partly a credit to the quality of the courses I was taking. I passed the exam and was accepted as an "early entrant" to the school, but passing the entrance exam was only the first hurdle. The real question was: Would my parents allow me to leave for a big university and live far away from home at such a young age?

One evening, shortly after I was accepted, two alumni from the Baltimore Alumni Association of the University of Chicago came to visit our home. I was sent to bed early that evening, and I have no idea what was discussed or what assurances were given, but at our usual breakfast of oatmeal and hot chocolate the next morning my mother said, "We had a meeting last evening and it was decided you can go to Chicago."

I was completely surprised. It never occurred to me that a decision would be made so quickly, but I was elated. It was as if the top of my head exploded. I knew I had completely outgrown Baltimore and I was ready to pack a few bags and leave my childhood, family, and home behind to begin my "real life" (whatever that was).

As always, with Ida, she didn't show a lot of emotion. It was there, but somewhat concealed. An odd coincidence is that my mother had herself graduated from Johns Hopkins at the age of nineteen. In fact, she was their first woman graduate, and this at such an early age, and she was made an honorary member of the faculty club. Did she, therefore, have some special insight about what a university education could mean for me?

Outwardly, both my parents' reactions were guarded. They were hesitant to even talk about it. My sister, Sheppie, told me later on that my father was the one who was doubtful, and the one who was determined that I would go was my mother. This was the opposite of what I thought at the time.

"You went there because Ida wanted you to go there," Sheppie said. "She wanted you to have the best education possible."

If my mother was proud of me for having been accepted, she never showed it. Nor did she let me know of her anxiety and understandable apprehension. After all, in 1952, I was just fifteen years old.

CHICAGO

THE OVERNIGHT TRAIN TO CHICAGO WAS RUN BY THE OLD B&O RAIL-road, which left every day in the early evening from downtown Baltimore and arrived in the Loop in Chicago early the next morning. That, or a long drive through western Maryland, Pennsylvania, Ohio, and Indiana, was the only way to get from Baltimore to Chicago. In 1952, very few people took planes, although commercial airlines were beginning to offer an alternative.

I was on my way to college with two friends from high school, Sydney Jacobs and Tom Steiner, both of whom I knew quite well. But our going out to the Midwest together was unplanned, sheer chance. They were part of a local, self-made club they called the Phalanx—a group of superbright, geeky teenagers who banded together for mutual company and entertainment. I knew them from the Maryland Chess Club, though, being several years younger, I was tolerated to a degree but had never been a part of their highly introverted and intellectual group. But I liked them all—they and their friends: Irv Zucker, Malcolm Pivar, and Bill Sullivan. Poets, mathematicians, and techno-visionaries of an order very early and remote from anything going on today.

The three of us were on the train together, bonding easily for the first time. I was extremely excited to be on my way and had barely noticed the lectures, warnings, and assurances from Ben and Ida that in the end came down to letting me know I could come home anytime I needed to if things at the University of Chicago didn't work out.

"We can arrange with your school that if you come back from Chicago before Christmas, you can go back into your grade at the high school," my mother said. Of course, I knew there was zero chance of that. They considered the three months until Christmas a trial run. For me, though, it was every kid's dream—the Great Escape.

I didn't sleep at all that night. Soon after leaving the station, the lights were out. It was just an old passenger train from Dixie to the Midwest, with no amenities of any kind. No lights, no reading, nothing to do but make friends with the sounds of the night train. The wheels on the track made endless patterns, and I was caught up in it almost at once. Years later, studying with Alla Rakha, Ravi Shankar's great tabla player and music partner, I practiced the endless cycles of 2s and 3s that form the heart of the Indian *tal* system. From this I learned the tools by which apparent chaos could be heard as an unending array of shifting beats and patterns. But on this memorable night, I was innocent of all that. Oddly enough, it wasn't until almost fourteen years later, when I was on my first voyage of discovery in India and trains were the only way to travel, that I did some serious train travel again, much as I had as a boy on my many journeys between Baltimore and Chicago. The facts of travel were similar, at times almost identical. But my way of hearing had been radically transformed in those years. One might think that the trains from *Einstein on the Beach* came from a similar place, but no, that wasn't so. That train music came from quite a different place altogether, which I'll get to later. The point was that the world of music—its language, beauty, and mystery—was already urging itself on me. Some shift had already begun. Music was no longer a metaphor for the real world somewhere out there. It was becoming the opposite. The "out there" stuff was the metaphor and the real part was, and is to this day, the music. Night trains can make those things happen. The sounds of daily life were entering me almost unnoticed.

RIGHT AWAY, CHICAGO HAD MUCH MORE of a big-city feel than Baltimore. It had modern architecture—not just Frank Lloyd Wright but the landmark Louis Sullivan buildings that were a bit older. It had a first-class orchestra—the Chicago Symphony conducted by Fritz Reiner; the Art Institute of Chicago, with its collection of Monets; and even art movie theaters. Chicago was a real city that catered to intellectuals and people with serious cultural interests in a way that Baltimore couldn't. Chicago was also a place where you'd hear jazz that you wouldn't hear in Baltimore (I didn't even know where the jazz clubs were in my hometown). If you wanted to go to a good Chinese restaurant in Baltimore, you had to drive to Washington, but in Chicago we had everything.

The university stretched from Fifty-Fifth Street to Sixty-First Street on both sides of the Midway, which had been the center of amusements and sideshows at Chicago's 1893 World's Columbian Exposition. Fifty-Seventh Street was built up with restaurants and bars, and the South Side jazz clubs, like the Beehive, were on Fifty-Fifth Street. Of course I was too young to get into some of the places I wanted to go, since I was fifteen and looked fifteen. By the time I was sixteen or seventeen, I had gotten a little bit bigger, so I was able to go to the Cotton Club, nearby on Cottage Grove, and also the clubs downtown. Eventually, the people at the door got to know me because I would stand there—just listening—looking through the window. Finally, they would say, "Hey, c'mon kid, you come on in." I couldn't buy a drink, but they would let me sit by the door and listen to the music.

The first day of freshman orientation, I walked into a room and the first thing I noticed was that there were black students. You have to look at it from the point of view of a kid who had grown up in the Dixie South—because that's where Baltimore was. There hadn't been any African-American students in any school I'd ever attended.

I had lived in a world where segregation was taken for granted and not even discussed. This was my conversion from being a kid from a border state, a Dixie state, whatever you want to call it, which was segregated top to bottom—its restaurants, movie houses, swimming pools, and golf courses. I think it took me less than a minute to realize that I had lived my whole life in a place that was completely wrong. It was a revelation.

The College of the University of Chicago was quite small in those days—probably fewer than five hundred undergraduates, counting all four years of the usual program. However, it fit into the larger university of professional schools—business, law, medicine— and divisions devoted to science, humanities, social science, theology, and the arts, as well as the Oriental Institute. The relationship of the College to this large university was surprisingly intimate, and quite a number of the university faculty taught in the College. It was thought of then as a kind of European system, though I have no idea whether that was actually true. Classes were small, consisting of twelve or fewer students with one professor—we were never taught by graduate students. We sat together at a round table and talked through our reading lists—a classic seminar format. There were a few lecture classes, but not many, and in addition, there were lab classes for science.

Very often when the seminars were over in the classrooms, the debates that had begun initially with the teachers would be continued among ourselves in the coffee shop on the Quadrangles at the center of the campus. That actually was the idea. The seminar style was something that was easy to reproduce in a coffee shop, because it was practically the same thing.

There were some sports at the school, but at that time we didn't have a football, basketball, or baseball team. I wanted to do something active so I went to the physical education bulletin board and found out they really needed some people for the wrestling team. I had wrestled in high school, so I volunteered, weighing in at about 116 pounds. I did pretty well with the team until my second or third

year of competition with nearby schools. Then some farm boy from
Iowa beat me so soundly and quickly that I gave up wrestling for life.

The University of Chicago was renowned for its faculty members.
I remember vividly my freshman course in chemistry. The lecturer
was Harold C. Urey, who had won the Nobel Prize in Chemistry. He
had chosen to teach the first-year chemistry class to seventy or eighty
students, and he brought an enthusiasm for his subject that was electrifying. We met at eight a.m., but there were no sleepyheads in that
class. Professor Urey looked exactly like Dr. Van Helsing from the
Tod Browning 1931 movie *Dracula*—the doctor who examines one of
Dracula's victims and says, "And on the throat, the same two marks."
Now, when would a freshman or sophomore kid get to even be in the
same *room* with a Nobel Prize winner, let alone being lectured on the
periodic table? I think he must have thought, There must be young
people out there who are going to become scientists.

Professor Urey lectured like an actor, striding back and forth in
front of the big blackboard, making incomprehensible marks on the
board (I couldn't figure out what he was doing—I only knew it had to
do with the periodic table). His teaching was like a performance. He
was a man passionate about his subject, and he couldn't wait until we
could be there at eight in the morning. Scientists on that level are like
artists in a way. They are intensely in love with their subject matter,
and Urey was one of them. In fact, I don't remember anything about
chemistry. I just went to see his performances.

In my second year I had a small seminar class in sociology taught
by David Riesman who, along with Reuel Denney and Nathan
Glazer, was the author of *The Lonely Crowd*, a very famous book in
those days. I suppose it might seem a little quaint today, but in the
1950s it was very new thinking. The thesis of the book was simple:
there are three kinds of people, inner-directed, other-directed, and
tradition-directed. These became personality types. The inner-
directed is someone like Professor Urey, or like an artist—someone
who doesn't care about anything except the thing that he wants to do.
The other-directed has no sense of his own identity other than that

which came from the approval of the world around him. The tradition-directed are concerned with following the rules that have been
handed down from the past. When you read these books, you immediately understand that the inner-directed people are the people that
are the most interesting.

Dr. Riesman would have eight or ten students in the class—no
more than that—and I liked him immediately. He was, like Urey, a
brilliant man, part of a new generation of sociologists who, coming
after anthropologists like Margaret Mead and Ruth Benedict, brought
methods of anthropology to bear on an analysis of modern urban life.
My connection to Dr. Riesman extended well beyond the classroom.
Twenty-five years later, his son Michael Riesman, who was about five
years old at the time I was taking his father's course, became the music
director of the Philip Glass Ensemble.

When the ensemble played at Harvard in the 1970s, Dr. Riesman
was teaching there. Michael came to tell me, "My dad is here at the
concert."

"Oh, I've got to see Dr. Riesman," I said.

"Dr. Riesman, do you remember me?" I asked when I met him.

"Of course I do," my onetime professor said.

I didn't really see any reason that he would have remembered me
after all that time, though I had, in fact, caused a bit of a fuss with
him once by challenging his ideas in the seminar. I had told him that
I thought the three categories of people that he was suggesting were
very much like the endomorph, ectomorph, and mesomorph types
that had been proposed by an anthropologist who was studying the
human body.

"Do you think so?" he had asked me.

"I think it's absolutely the same," I said.

He looked at me like I was nuts. It's funny, whenever I got an idea,
if I thought I was right, I could not be talked out of it, and maybe
that's why he remembered me. I was a sophomore in college, sixteen
years old, and he was in his midforties at the time. Why wouldn't I
keep my mouth shut? In truth, I never did. The same sort of confron-

tation I had with David Riesman was repeated with Aaron Copland a number of years later, when he and I got into an argument about orchestration.

In the summer of 1960, four years after I had graduated from Chicago, Copland was a guest of the orchestra at the Aspen Music Festival and School, where I had come from Juilliard to take a summer course with Darius Milhaud, a wonderful composer and teacher. The orchestra was playing some of Copland's pieces at the festival, and through Milhaud's class, Copland invited students to meet with him one-on-one to show him their compositions. I took him one of my pieces, a violin concerto for solo violin, winds (flute, clarinet, bassoon), brass (trumpets, horns, trombones), and percussion.

Mr. Copland looked at the first page. What I had done was to pencil in a theme for the violin—it's so similar to what I do today, I'm surprised that I had even thought of it then—and every low note of the theme, I had played on the French horn. So the violin went da-da, da-da, da-da, and the French horn outlined the bottom notes, which became the countermelody. I thought it was a very good idea.

Mr. Copland looked at it and said, "You'll never hear the French horn."

"Of course you will," I said.

"Nope, you'll never hear it."

"I will hear it."

"You're not going to hear it."

"I'm sorry, Mr. Copland. I'm going to hear it."

Mr. Copland got extremely annoyed with me, and that was pretty much the end of my lesson. He'd only seen the opening page of the piece! We never got beyond the first eight or ten measures.

What's wrong with me? I thought. Mr. Copland was much older than me. He was a *real* composer, a famous composer. He'd invited students to show him their compositions—a wonderful opportunity—and I had totally blown it. I had one lesson with Aaron Copland and we had a disagreement and he basically kicked me out.

As it turned out, I *was* right, at least that time. On a student recording the next year at Juilliard, sure enough, there was that French horn line, outlining the countermelody to the violin theme. You could hear it clear as a bell. I am sorry I didn't keep in touch with Mr. Copland, for I would have sent him the recording.

THE IMPACT OF SUCH ORIGINAL AND PROFESSIONAL researchers and academicians on our young minds was enormous. This level of leadership was everywhere—in philosophy, mathematics, classical studies. Oddly, though, the performing arts were not represented at all. No dance, theater, or music performance training was to be found. On the other hand, there were parts of the University of Chicago that were involved in studies so radical that we barely knew what they were up to at all. One of its graduate programs, the Committee on Social Thought was one such group. To graduate from the College and enter the Committee as a graduate student—to be accepted, as it were, by the Committee—would have been their greatest dream for some. Its faculty consisted of writers, scientists, and thinkers. These were men and women that some in the College—including myself— deeply, almost fiercely admired and attempted to emulate as best we could: in those years, Saul Bellow, Hannah Arendt, and Mircea Eliade, among others.

Bellow's big novel at that time was *The Adventures of Augie March*, the story of a man's life and search for identity from childhood to maturity. I was a big reader, and the two writers from Chicago who interested me were Bellow and Nelson Algren, author of *The Man with the Golden Arm*, about a heroin addict's struggles to stay clean, and *Walk on the Wild Side*, in which Algren tells us, "Never play cards with a man called Doc. Never eat at a place called Mom's. Never sleep with a woman whose troubles are worse than your own."

What I admired about Bellow and Algren was that they took absolutely colloquial language—and not just colloquial language but vulgar language—and used it as a medium of expression. Until then, I had been very taken with writers like Joseph Conrad, who wrote in a very eloquent early-twentieth-century prose, but these new writers were using the vernacular of the street.

I never saw Bellow on campus, but we all knew about him. Both he and Algren were idolized by the young people in Chicago because they *were* Chicago. They were not New York, they were not San Francisco. When I went to Chicago, I picked up Chicago writers, I picked up Chicago jazz, I picked up Chicago folk music—people like Big Bill Broonzy and Charlie Parker and Stan Getz. All these people worked in Chicago.

As often happens around a great school or university, the University of Chicago projected its aura well beyond its Hyde Park neighborhood and, for that matter, the rest of the South Side. Writers, poets, and thinkers would come to live in the shadow of the university. This larger world included theater groups and cutting-edge bebop jazz clubs, like the Beehive or the Cotton Club on Cottage Grove. There was even a rumor, and perhaps a true one, that Alfred Korzybski, the scholar and author of *Manhood of Humanity* and *Science and Sanity*, had lived and worked in Hyde Park. He was an early proponent of the study of semantics and a radical thinker who, for some reason, appealed to me. Perhaps it was his ideas about history, time, and our human nature I was drawn to—he originated the concept of time-binding, that human culture is the result of the transmission of knowledge through time. I haven't seen his books in years or even heard tell of him. Perhaps just another great soul, an American Mahatma, if you will, to be found somewhere in our libraries and collective memories.

As I learned early on, the academic arrangements made for the College were especially striking. We were assigned to courses (there were, famously, fourteen courses, each three quarters long—Fall, Winter, Spring). However, attendance was not required or even noted. There were quarterly exams that students could take. These exams were strictly optional, and the grades given were not counted toward failure or success in the course. The courses that were considered the core of the curriculum consisted of three levels each in science, sociology, and humanities. Five other courses made up the fourteen. Completion of these were the only requirements for graduation.

There would be, though, a "comprehensive" exam for whatever courses the student had registered for at the end of the year, in May. Each of these exams would take an entire day and include at least one essay to be written in the examination room. Needless to say, the subject of the essay would be unknown to the students before the exam, so of course this could be, and often was, a terrifying experience. However, the reading list for each course was available at the beginning of the academic year. The readings themselves were to be found at the U of C bookstore, either as individual books or as a collection of readings in a syllabus.

Now, the simplest and most straightforward way to prepare for the comprehensive was to buy the books and syllabus for each course and simply attend the seminars, lectures, or laboratory classes in the normal unfolding of a three-quarter course. To be truthful, I never once followed that path. Perhaps there were some who did, but in all my years there I never met them.

There were several problems that made the ideal plan difficult to follow. The biggest problem was embedded in the culture of the university itself. It was like this: though we were assigned to specific seminars, we were free to "audit" any course in the College we liked and even many courses in the university. To audit a class, you simply asked the professor for permission to attend. I never heard of a request being refused. Of course, we were encouraged to attend our registered courses, but it was not required, and in the end, the only grade earned and which actually counted was the comprehensive exam. So, in theory, one could skip all the classes and exams and just take the comprehensive. But almost no one did that, either. I think many of us took a middle road. We emphasized our regular course work, but freely "grazed" through much of the university curriculum.

Along around late March or April, when we discovered we had fallen behind in our reading lists, we started frantically reading the missing texts. It could be helpful, too, if you could find someone who had taken good notes of classes missed and was willing to share them, but this was not likely. Basically, I did a lockdown. I would go to the bookstore and buy the books, and I began reading them *slowly*. I read everything. The advantage was that when I went into the exams, everything was fresh in my mind. I hadn't forgotten anything because I had barely learned it to begin with. So I never failed the exams. My very first year, I had four exams, and I got an A, B, C, and D. My mother was horrified, but I pointed out that actually that was a B-minus average

The next year everything resolved into As, Bs, and Cs. I got rid of the Ds, but I never got all As. I wasn't that kind of student. I wasn't concerned with having a good grade point average. I wasn't going to medical school—what did I care? I didn't think the grades mattered. They weren't a systematic appraisal of what I knew. I was more interested in hanging out with someone like Aristotle Skalides, a wandering intellectual and would-be academic who wasn't a student but who liked to engage young people in the coffee shop in discussions about philosophy. Spending an hour with him at the coffee shop was like going and spending an hour in the classroom. I was more interested in my general education than the courses. It almost didn't matter to me whom I studied with, as long as I found the right teacher, and that was pretty much my attitude. In fact, I think that has persisted. I've found teachers all through my life, people I knew who were otherwise unknown.

Another distraction from the regular course work was that there were some professors who offered informal classes, usually in their homes, on specific books or subjects. For these classes, no registration was required, no exam was given, and no student was turned away. This practice was, I believe, understood and tolerated by the university itself.

Now, why would you spend your time as a student (or professor, for that matter) this way, when there were reading lists that needed to be completed? Well, the answer is that some of the classes were unique and otherwise not available. They were not offered officially, were known by word of mouth, but were quite well attended. I went to an evening class entirely on one book—Homer's *The Odyssey*—once a week for at least two quarters, taught by a classics professor named Charles Bell. These kinds of "private" courses given within the university community, though not generally known, could be sought after and found. That in itself probably accounted for their appeal.

A third distraction, and perhaps the biggest one of all, was Chicago itself. For example, during its season the Chicago Symphony Orchestra offered Friday afternoon concerts to students for a fifty-cent admission price. From the South Side, it was a quick ride on the Illinois Central train to downtown Chicago. I had been a regular concertgoer to the Baltimore Symphony practically from childhood. The editor of the Baltimore Symphony concert program, Mr. Greenwald, taught at my mother's high school, and he often gave us free tickets. The Baltimore Symphony was quite good, but the Chicago Symphony was in a class by itself.

Fritz Reiner, the famous Hungarian conductor, was fascinating to watch. He was somewhat stout, hunched over with round shoulders, and his arm and baton movements were tiny—you almost had to look at him with binoculars to see what he was doing. But those tiny movements forced the players to peer at him intently, and then he would suddenly raise his arms up over his head and the entire orchestra would go crazy. Reiner knew the classical repertoire, of course, but he was an outstanding interpreter of Bartók and Kodály, both countrymen of his. Of course, Bartók's music was already familiar to me through my father. There was also the Art Institute of Chicago, the Opera House, which I only occasionally visited, and the downtown jazz clubs, which, for a time, were still off-limits to me because of my age.

I mentioned earlier the influence of the Great Books of the curriculum, but it extended far beyond that. Whenever possible, which turned out to be all the time, the books we studied would be first-hand, primary sources. We were never given summaries to read or even commentaries, unless they themselves rose to the level of a primary source. So, for example, we read Darwin's *The Origin of Species* in the biological sciences, and we reperformed Mendel's fruit fly experiments. In physics we reenacted the experiments with rolling balls and inclined planes of Galileo. We also read Newton and followed physics up to and including Schrödinger, while in chemistry we read Avogadro and Dalton.

So the study of science became the study of the history of science, and I began to understand what a scientific personality could be like. This early exposure would be reflected in *Galileo Galilei*, which I composed forty-five years later, in which his experiments become a dance piece—the balls and inclined planes are there. I found the biographical aspects of scientists intensely interesting, and the operas about Galileo, Kepler, and Einstein pay tribute to everything I learned about scientists and science that came out of those years.

The same primary-source method was carried out in social science, history, and philosophy. Learning American history meant reading the Federalist Papers and other late-eighteenth-century essays by the men who wrote the Constitution. Of course, humanities meant theater and literature from ancient to modern. Poetry, same thing. The effect on me was to cultivate and understand in a firsthand way the lineage of culture. The men and women who created the stepping-stones from earliest times became familiar to us—not something "handed down" but actually known in a most immediate and personal way.

At this time, I became comfortable with the university's Harper Library, where I learned to research events and people. The work I later took up in opera and theater would not have been possible without that preparation and training. My first three full-scale operas— *Einstein on the Beach*, *Satyagraha*, and *Akhnaten*—were made with collaborators—Robert Wilson, Constance DeJong, and Shalom Goldman, respectively—but I fully participated in the writing and shaping of the librettos for all three. I could do this with complete confidence in my academic abilities. In fact, I now see clearly that a lot of the work I chose was inspired by men and women whom I first met in the pages of books. In this way, those early operas were, as I see it, an homage to the power, strength, and inspiration of the lineage of culture.

AFTER SPENDING THE SUMMER IN BALTIMORE, I returned for my second year at the University of Chicago in September 1953. It would be my last year living in the Burton-Judson dormitory, located on the south side of the Midway, formerly the southern boundary of the University, an area that included the prefab housing where young men with families stayed. These were families who were there thanks to the GI Bill, still very much part of the landscape.

So there I was, in the corridor outside my dorm room, when I saw a young man with a fencing mask and sword prancing around practicing his moves. The minute he saw me, he pressed a mask and sword on me. After quickly showing me some of the basics, we began fencing. His name was Jerry Temaner, and I would say that first encounter was emblematic of a friendship that has continued into the present.

He, like me, was sixteen, but was a native of the place, having grown up on Chicago's Great West Side. He was skinny, with horn-rimmed glasses, the same size as me, five foot eight, with long dark hair.

The remarkable thing about Jerry Temaner was that his father was in the same business as mine. Jerry's dad, who was called Little Al, used to run a number of record stores in Chicago. Since his father's store was called Little Al, he and I would call my father's store Big Ben. At our first meeting, we discovered not only that we had both grown up in record stores but that our experiences were, in many ways, identical—we learned music from the stores, we worked in the stores, and we knew the same records. It was through Jerry that I discovered Chicago and, actually, a lot about the university, for he also introduced me to the bebop jazz clubs on Fifty-Fifth Street, where I heard Bud Powell and saw Charlie Parker for the first time.

Charlie Parker was the great genius I had admired most in my youth. I saw him many times through the window of the Beehive before I was ever allowed to get in. To me, he was the J. S. Bach of bebop: no one could play like him. His alto playing was beyond superb.

The next person who, for me, came along and had that power in his music was John Coltrane, who could take a melody like "My Favorite Things" and pull out harmonies that one would never imagine were there. That gave him a freedom—both melodic and rhythmic—but also the harmonic freedom to explore implied harmonies. These he could outline in his playing to a point that was breathtaking. You almost never knew where he would go, because he could take it so far, and yet he was never really that far away. He was another great bebop player of our time.

In addition to Parker and Coltrane, there were other great players in Chicago: saxophonists like Jackie McLean and Sonny Rollins, as well as piano players like Thelonious Monk and Bud Powell—the great players of the forties and fifties. I came to know and love their music, and beyond that, I understood it. I heard it as a variant of baroque music. It is even organized in the same way. Jazz relies on a song's chord changes and the melodic variations that the changes inspire. Furthermore, the song has a bridge—an ABA form—and jazz solos will follow the same pattern.

Singers like Ella Fitzgerald, Sarah Vaughan, and Frank Sinatra were able to expand the performance of popular song by using techniques of the great jazz players. Louis Armstrong is an example of a singer who began as a trumpet player and "crossed over" to popular music from the jazz side. Years later, I came to appreciate the skills of these great musicians.

What I learned from that music became part of my own language. I've become very comfortable combining melodic material with harmonic material that does not *at first* seem to be supported. The melodies may not be part of the harmony, but the ear accepts them as alternate notes. They're extensions of the harmony and can even sound as if the music is in two keys at once. That way of hearing melodies certainly comes out of listening to jazz, and I hear that in my music when I'm writing symphonies and especially operas.

What was interesting about the pianists Bud Powell, Monk, and Red Garland was that they had developed a playing technique that didn't at all resemble the way classical music is performed. They punched out the tunes, almost the way a boxer would punch out and use his fists. I found that especially with Bud Powell. He would attack the piano. He was a fantastic player and he became my favorite because of his personal orientation toward the piano. He and the piano weren't adversaries, but he was able to physically pull the music out of the instrument. He had a rough style of playing, which at the same time was extremely sophisticated. Art Tatum was a more accomplished pianist, however, Bud Powell was, for me, the more emotional player.

Jerry Temaner and I also visited the Modern Jazz Room in the Loop, where you could often hear Stan Getz, Chet Baker, and Lee Konitz. It was through Jerry that I was introduced to the finer points of modern jazz. Of course, I was already a musician, with at least the beginnings of a music education as a student at Peabody, but Jerry was coming to jazz from a different place. He was really a connoisseur and, after playing a record for me, he would test my knowledge of a full array of the jazz talents he expected me to be familiar with. After a year of his tutelage, one afternoon he gave me his usual "blindfold" test, playing a saxophonist who was new to me. I had to measure the degree of his talent and explain what I liked. In fact, I liked the music very much and made a strong case for it. My mentor was very pleased. We had been listening to the tenor saxophonist Jackie McLean, though until then I hadn't heard his music.

Besides knowing music, Jerry was also very knowledgeable about film, and it was he who introduced me to the classics at the Hyde Park movie theater, which specialized in European films with subtitles. That's where you could see the films of the French director René Clair, the stark, almost morbid work of the Swedish master Ingmar Bergman, or the neorealist movies of the Italian director Vittorio De Sica. Nothing like them had been shown in Baltimore. In fact, films with subtitles were then unknown in that city. For that you would have had to go to Washington, D.C. So all of this was a revelation to me. It was in Chicago that I saw *À Nous la Liberté*, *The Seventh Seal*, and *The Bicycle Thief*. When I moved to Paris a decade later, I found myself in the middle of the formidable 1960s cinema revolution, la Nouvelle Vague (the New Wave), championed by Jean-Luc Godard and François Truffaut. By that time I had a solid background in European art films and absolutely knew what I was seeing.

Of all these films, the ones dearest to my heart were those of Jean Cocteau—in particular, *Orphée*, *La Belle et la Bête*, and *Les Enfants Terribles*. During my years in Hyde Park these films appeared several times. They must have become lodged in my mind, safe and whole, because in the 1990s, when I undertook a five-year experiment to reinvent the synchronicity of image and music in film, I chose these three films of Cocteau that I knew so well.

Jerry introduced me to other aspects of Chicago life. Besides the bebop of the South Side, there were the "big bands" you could hear—Stan Kenton, Count Basie, Duke Ellington—as well as singers Billie Holiday (I heard her at the Cotton Club on Cottage Grove on a double bill with Ben Webster), Anita O'Day, and Sarah Vaughan. So many great musicians were then coming to Chicago. When I moved to New York City in the late fifties, I became familiar with the jazz world there in the same way. As a Juilliard student I would write music by day and by night hear John Coltrane at the Village Vanguard, Miles Davis and Art Blakey at the Café Bohemia, or Thelonious Monk trading sets with the young Ornette Coleman, who was just up from Louisiana playing his white plastic saxophone at the Five Spot at St. Marks Place and the Bowery.

Years later, I got to know Ornette. He had a place on Prince Street with a pool table in the front room. A good spot to hang out and talk about music. I met numerous musicians there of all kinds, including members of his ensemble, especially James "Blood" Ulmer, who had his own band as well. Ornette gave me a piece of advice that I have pondered ever since. He said, "Don't forget, Philip, the music world and the music business are not the same."

———

SO FAR I HAVE WRITTEN ABOUT TWO TRADITIONS that became sources of the music I was later to compose. The first was the "classical" chamber music, which I learned about through my father, both from listening to music and from working at his store Saturdays and, especially, holidays. Christmas was a peak season for record sales—Ben told me once that 70 percent of his income came between Thanksgiving and New Year's. By age fifteen I had become the classical music buyer of the store, continuing to look over the stock whenever I was home from school. In those days the big companies would send lists of new releases and older catalogues, and I would check off the items and quantities that we needed. When Columbia released the complete string quartets of Arnold Schoenberg, performed brilliantly for the recording by the Juilliard String Quartet, I was thrilled. Now, buying records of classical or "art" music is a whole lot trickier than buying Sinatra, Streisand, or Presley. Often only one or two, maybe three copies at the most of the standard classical repertoire would be enough for a Baltimore record store and would easily be sufficient for a few months, or until the next buying period came up. However, carried away by my enthusiasm for the music, I ordered four sets of the Schoenbergs!

About two weeks later the box arrived from the distributor. That was always an exciting moment. Marty and I would be joined by Ben, who also enjoyed the moment. In those days we didn't know what the covers looked like—the order books provided just lists of names. But these were the early days of LPs and artists and photographers had a field day with twelve-by-twelve-inch covers. With great anticipation we tore open the box, and there were the four Schoenbergs.

Ben's jaw dropped in amazement.

"Hey, kid, what are you doing?" he roared. "Are you trying to put me out of business?"

I explained that these were the new masterpieces of modern music, and that we needed them in the store.

Ben looked at me for a long, silent moment. He was shocked by my naïveté. After all, I had been in the record business almost four years, and he couldn't believe I had been that dumb.

"Okay," he finally said, "tell you what I'll do. Put them on the shelves with the regular classical stock and let me know when we've sold the last one."

For the next seven years I would come home to Baltimore, stop by the store and check on them to see how we were doing. Finally, near the end of my Juilliard years, I came home and found they were all gone. I was elated and showed Ben the empty space where they had been.

"The Schoenbergs . . . they're gone!"

Ben, always patient in moments like these, quietly said, "Okay, kid, did you learn the lesson?"

I said nothing. Just waited.

"I can sell anything if I have enough time."

It was just as Ornette would tell me many years later—the music world and the music business are not the same.

And so we learn. Ben taught Marty and me many, many things, but, like this one, not every lesson was easily learned.

The actual sound of Central European art music, especially the chamber music, was a solid part of me from an early age but maybe not audible in my music until almost five decades later, when I began to compose sonatas and unaccompanied string pieces as well as quite a lot of piano music. Though I did write a few string quartets for the Kronos Quartet, and some symphonies besides, these works from my forties, fifties, and sixties didn't owe that much to the past. Now that I'm in my seventies, my present music does. It's funny how it happened this way, but there it is.

It was also a long time before I began to realize how jazz had entered my music. Because it is a form that is mainly improvisational, I didn't connect it at all with my work. Only quite recently, while reflecting on my own history with jazz, I was surprised by what I found. In the last few years, Linda Brumbach and her Pomegranate

Arts Company put together a new production of *Einstein on the Beach*. Since parts of the *Einstein* music have been part of my ensemble's repertoire for years, I have mainly been involved with performing the music. Recently, though, I was listening to some early recordings of the "Train" music from Act 1, scene 1. Suddenly I was hearing something that I had failed to notice for almost forty years. A part of the music was almost screaming to be recognized. I began looking around in my record library and I came upon the music of Lennie Tristano. I knew this music very well. It was from my early listening years with Jerry. At that moment, in fact, I recalled that when I arrived in New York, I had somehow gotten Tristano's phone number and called him up. I was in a phone booth on the Upper West Side near Juilliard, and to my total surprise he, Tristano himself, answered the phone.

"Mr. Tristano, my name is Philip Glass," I managed to say. "I'm a young composer. I've come to New York to study, and I know your work. Is there any chance I can study with you?"

"Do you play jazz?"

"No, I don't."

"Do you play the piano?"

"A little. I came here, really, to study at Juilliard, but I love your music and I wanted to be in touch with you."

"Well," he said, "thank you for the call, but I don't know that there's anything I can do for you."

He was very kind, almost gentle. He wished me luck.

Now fifty years later, listening to Tristano's music again, I found what I was looking for. Two tracks: the first, "Line Up" and the second "East Thirty-Second Street." I listened to them and there it was. No, the notes weren't the same. Most listeners would probably not have heard what I did. But the energy, the *feel*, and, I would say, the *intention* of the music was completely and accurately captured in the "Train." It doesn't sound like him, but it shares the idea of propulsion, the self-confidence, and the drive. There's an athleticism to it, a nonchalance, an "I don't care if you listen to it or not—here it is."

These were Tristano's one-hand improvisations and were, for me, his most impressive achievements. He would record, slowly, a steady flow of sixteenth notes, then afterward speed up the tapes. That gave the music a tremendous buoyancy and an electric energy that was completely unique. Once you hear these driving piano lines, you know who is playing. I don't know that Tristano ever became very well-known. He was well-known to me because I found his records and I admired him. I never heard him play live—I don't think many people did. He might have been known as a teacher among some jazz players, and he certainly was a teacher to me. He died in 1978, but he remains an icon in the jazz world, though still largely unknown. However, he was without a doubt a master.

When I look back on it, I was also very influenced by the raw power of bebop music. Above all, I was interested in this kind of drive—a life force that was in the music itself. And that's what I heard in the music of John Coltrane and Bud Powell as well as Tristano. That's what I heard with Jackie McLean—it goes on and on. Charlie Parker, same thing. I'm talking about a flow of energy that seemed unstoppable, a force of nature.

And that's where I knew I wanted to be. For the music I wrote in the late 1960s—in particular, "Music in Fifths," "Music in Contrary Motion," "Music in Similar Motion," and *Music in Twelve Parts*—this flow of energy had to be an important source. Clearly, the inspiration for one of the major themes of *Einstein* came from that piano work of Tristano's. I sometimes hear about work described in terms of "originality," or "breakthrough," but my personal experience is quite different. For me music has always been about lineage. The past is reinvented and becomes the future. But the lineage is everything.

In this vein, I recall something Moondog, the blind poet and street musician, told me. He was highly eccentric and very talented, and in the early 1970s he lived at my home on West Twenty-Third Street for a year.

"Philip," he said, "I am following in the footsteps of Beethoven and Bach. But really, they were such giants, and their footsteps were so far apart, that it is as if I am leaping after them."

IT WAS DURING MY FIRST YEAR IN CHICAGO that I seriously began my piano practice. I had befriended Marcus Raskin, a fellow student a few years older than myself who was very bright and had been a young pianist at Juilliard. He had given up the idea of a music career and was then at the College aiming for a career in law. (As it turned out, he was later a founding member of the Institute for Policy Studies in Washington.) When I met him he was still quite a good player and knew, besides the classical repertoire, modern music as well. He played the Alban Berg Piano Sonata, op. 1, and helped acquaint me with that part of the new music world, the school of Schoenberg, Webern, and Berg. In those days, we called it twelve-tone music. Later, it was called dodecaphonic music, but twelve-tone was probably more accurate because it followed the music theories of Schoenberg, where you had to repeat each of the twelve tones before using a particular tone again, the idea being to create a kind of equality of tonal center so that no melody could belong to one key.

I asked Marcus for help with the piano, and he became my piano teacher. With him I started on a real piano technique, and he was serious about my progress. As I mentioned, the university wasn't much help in developing my music interests. There was a small music department run by a musicologist named Grosvenor Cooper, whom I met several times and who was encouraging to a point, but there was nothing there of interest for me. In those days, musicologists studied the baroque period and the romantic period, but they were neither equipped to teach nor interested in teaching composition.

My love of the piano began at an age so early I can't even recall exactly when. As a child, I was often at the family baby grand when I wasn't playing the flute. When I came home from school, I'd run straight to the piano. But my real piano technique began with Marcus, who instructed me on scales and exercises and urged me to play Bach. Later, when I was studying in Paris with Boulanger, Bach's keyboard music was my syllabus, but in the years 1952 and 1953 Marcus gave me a good start, for which I will always be grateful.

The curriculum of the College was a great adventure, as were my classmates. Though most of them were a bit older, I didn't notice the age difference much, nor was I treated very differently. It wasn't long before I had learned to drink coffee and even smoked a bit. At the University of Chicago, social life didn't revolve around fraternities. In fact, I barely noticed that they were there at all. The social hubs for me were Harper Library, the main coffee shop on the Quadrangles, various theaters (including the already mentioned Hyde Park movie theater), and some of the local restaurants.

The coffee shop was open from morning until early evening, and people were there constantly between classes. I always went to see if my friends were there. My dormitory was a few blocks away, but I didn't go back to it, since you had to walk across the Midway to get there. The Midway was two blocks wide, with named streets running through it, and could be dangerous at night. You'd see students walking to school with baseball bats because they were afraid. Nothing ever happened to me, but I learned to be careful.

I didn't study in my room that much—mostly I studied in the library because that's where the girls were. Going out with girls maybe a bit older than me was quite informal. A "date" at the library was common. There were a handful of younger people my age—it was a policy of the school to admit "early entrants": fifteen-year-olds, or even fourteen-year-olds who had passed the exam—and the older students, rather than ignore us, would take us out to eat and talk with us like older brothers and sisters.

Naturally, it was through the older kids that I was initiated into the mysteries of sex. It was very friendly and it was all arranged. When my friends discovered I had never had sex with a woman, a young woman I knew and whom I liked quite well miraculously missed her last bus home and had to spend the night on the South Side of Chicago. By this time, I had my own apartment with another student.

She asked whether she could spend the night at my house and one thing led to another. I learned later that it was all completely orchestrated by other people—everybody knew it was going to happen. My older friends considered it important. Though I didn't particularly look at it that way, I liked the fact that it had happened, and that it wasn't with a person my own age who likely would have been just as ignorant. It was tender, and it was sweet, and there was no embarrassment. I can't think of a better way it could have happened.

In Chicago in the early 1950s, the people I knew did not do drugs. In fact, there were scarcely any drugs around, not even marijuana. Maybe there was a little of what was called Benzedrine—there was one fellow who was supposed to be taking drugs, and it turned out that he was taking speed. But everyone I knew thought he was completely degenerate.

The people in my crowd were interested in politics, not drugs. In the fall of 1952, during my freshman year, we were inspired by Adlai Stevenson, who was running for president against Dwight Eisenhower. One must remember that these were the McCarthy years, and the University of Chicago was considered to be a hotbed of communism. It is true that we studied Marx and Engels, but it was in the same way that we studied any theory of economics. The very fact that it was taught at all would have made it seem to others that we were all Communists, but, in fact, very few people had radical politics of that kind. Our idea of radical politics was Stevenson, who lost the election to Eisenhower, which was considered, in my day at Chicago, a huge tragedy. We thought it was the end of the world.

In retrospect, those years, far from being all work and no play, seem to have been mostly play and very little work at all. Besides the classes, which I mainly found entertaining, there were all sorts of diversions, especially concerts at Mandel Hall, the small, cozy concert hall on the Quadrangles. There were regular chamber music concerts there—the Budapest String Quartet, for instance, but you could also hear Big Bill Broonzy, Odetta, and a whole raft of fifties folksingers. It must seem that I was just having a lot of fun and, truthfully, that's just about the way it was. I would say that the rhythm of my life was then, as it is today, not just active but quite intense. I had acquired, in those Chicago years, the habit of a 24/7 schedule—meaning I didn't recognize holidays or weekends—and I suppose it suited me well then, as it does now.

As an undergraduate, I made regular visits to Baltimore during Christmas and Easter. My parents and I also had a Sunday phone call scheduled every week. In those days we thought a five-minute phone call—long distance to Baltimore—very expensive, even though it was actually half price because it was Sunday. When I got home that first Christmas, my parents asked me if I had had trouble making friends, because the other students were older. "Absolutely not," I told them. In fact, it seemed to be easy to make friends. The University of Chicago was a very gregarious place.

Besides our weekly phone call, Ida wrote me a letter every week. Often it would be barely a page long, with hardly any family news at all, just whatever she was doing that day. Some thirty-five years later, when my own daughter, Juliet, was away at Reed College, I did exactly the same thing. I had learned from Ida that the content of the letter really didn't matter at all. It was the fact of the letter itself and its regularity that bound us together.

WHEN I FIRST BEGAN COMPOSING MUSIC during my freshman year, I was hardly prepared for the task that would become the focus of my life. I had already been playing music for years and was well acquainted with practicing and performing, starting with my lessons at the Peabody Conservatory, where, at the age of eight, I was told I was the youngest student to have been enrolled there. In school I had played in amateur musicals and in bands and orchestras, as well as in a marching band, where I was also the leader of a fife and drum corps. When I was ten, I had played with a church orchestra that performed Bach masses and cantatas. Coming from a Jewish family, I remember that I was actually terrified to be playing in a church. I don't know what I was afraid of—perhaps it was simply that the ambience of the church seemed so unfamiliar. It's probably a good thing I got over my fears at that time, because in my years as a performer I've played in churches all over the world countless times, and even once was married in one.

My reason for beginning to compose at all was very simple. I had begun to ponder the question "Where does music come from?" I couldn't find the answer in books or from musician friends, and perhaps it was an irrelevant question to begin with. However, that didn't stop me looking for the answer. I thought then, in my freshman year, that if I began composing music myself, I would somehow find the answer. I never did find the answer, though over the next six decades I found that the question needed to be changed from time to time. Finally, many years later, I arrived at what seems now as a reasonable answer to a reformulated question. But, first, I need to go over "the beginning."

From my days in the record store I knew something about modern music, but that was mainly about Schoenberg and his school. On reflection, even though Schoenberg's music was no longer "new" (that music would have been new when my grandfather was still a young man), it was quite a good place to begin. The only person I knew who had hands-on experience with this music was my piano teacher, Marcus, and he was enthusiastic about it. So I went to Harper Library and, sitting at one of the long tables, plunged into the scores of Schoenberg, Berg, and Webern.

At the time, there were only a handful of recordings to help me. The Webern Opus 21 orchestra music had been recorded on Dial Records, and I also was able to find a recording of Berg's *Lyrische* Suite, a string quartet. I remember that I found some Schoenberg piano pieces, which I could manage on the piano, but at a very reduced tempo. If I could find a recording of the music as well as the score, I could compare the score to what I was hearing, so that helped a little bit. Just to add to my difficulties, I had been urged by one of my friends to listen to Charles Ives, the early-twentieth-century American composer. For that purpose I checked the *Concord* Sonata out of the library. I could barely play any part of the Ives, but I took an immediate liking to the music. Ives's work was full of popular melodies. He didn't mind if his pieces had tunes in them—that was not foreign to his practice at all. His music was polytonal and it could be dissonant and, at the same time, it could also be very beautiful. Dissonance and beauty are, of course, not actually very different from each other.

Berg, the Austrian composer who had been a student of Schoenberg's, was my favorite. I became very familiar with his music, which had a more romantic feel and much more of an emotional sweep. It was beautiful music, and not as strict as Schoenberg (Webern was even more strict). Most of this music did not have a strong emotional effect on me. It was very easy for me to set it aside, but I was interested in it because there was a method of composition, which anyone can use if you can count to twelve.

These first encounters with "modern" music, none of which was written near my lifetime, were overwhelming. It took a huge effort just to visualize it, even with the help of a piano—which was in the common rooms of the Burton-Judson dormitory and pretty much ignored by the other residents—because it lacked a familiar tonality and the usual modulations. When you listened, it was hard to remember the melody because it was hard to remember the harmony. It didn't mean that it wasn't lovely music. It could be gorgeous. For example, composers like Karlheinz Stockhausen later on would create more modernist versions that were very beautiful.

Still, I was able to get the idea of how twelve-tone music was put together. I bought some blank music paper that found its way into the university bookstore and composed my first music—a string trio in one movement. I wrote it in my dormitory room. Since I didn't have a piano with which to test the notes, I played it on the flute. I could play all the lines on the flute, and I could try to imagine how they sounded together, and over the course of two or three weeks I actually completed a composition seven or eight minutes long. I knew how to make it sound modern because I avoided triadic harmony. I avoided anything that sounded consonant. I wrote all the parts so that nothing sounded like it was connected to anything else. I think it sounded rather like any ordinary piece of twelve-tone music. No one ever played it, but I could play all the parts and I could hear them, without knowing what I was hearing. The ability to hear with clarity and judgment came only through real practice and study, and most of that was accomplished later, partly at Juilliard and then completed with Boulanger.

My string trio wasn't particularly good or bad, but it was my first composed music and that was good enough. I have no idea where that music is today. I thought it might have been in a box of early compositions that had ended up in my brother's house in Baltimore. But about ten years ago he delivered to me a box of music he found in his basement and this composition wasn't there. What *was* there were Juilliard pieces that I had long ago forgotten.

In any event, that was where I began, in the library at the University of Chicago, studying the scores, and in my dormitory room, struggling to put together my first composed music. I had as yet no teacher of composition, but I found two sources of instruction. The first was a harmony book by Schoenberg. I had heard that there was such a book, but couldn't find it in any bookstore. I finally sent away for it, and it arrived several weeks later by mail. It turned out to be a very clear, well thought-out book on traditional harmony. Not at all what I expected, but actually what I really needed. From that book I began learning music "theory," as it is called.

Then, following my freshman year, I worked in Baltimore as a lifeguard at a summer camp for children and spent my entire pay, perhaps two hundred dollars, on my first real music composition lessons, which I took from a Baltimore composer, Louis Cheslock, whose name I had gotten from the Peabody Conservatory. He was a real, living composer and even had his symphonic music played, though only occasionally, by the Baltimore Symphony. At Mr. Cheslock's home, he would give me harmony exercises and counterpoint exercises, and that was my introduction to real music training. He was quite a good teacher and easily answered questions that had arisen from my initial understanding of the Schoenberg book. With him I felt at last that there was solid ground under my feet.

In the early 1950s, the only door that appeared to me to be open for a composer was to carry on in a European tradition of modernism, which really came down to twelve-tone music. Now, I didn't know about other modernists who were not using the twelve-tone system, among them Stravinsky, the French composer Francis Poulenc, and the Czech composer Leoš Janáček, not to mention the Americans Henry Cowell, Aaron Copland, and Virgil Thomson. These tonalists were related in one way or the other to the folkloric roots of classical music. For example, the first three ballets of Stravinsky—*The Firebird*, *Petrushka*, and *The Rite of Spring*—are all based on Russian folk music. I knew this because in my early years at Juilliard I used to exchange music with a pen pal in Russia. He sent me a collection of Russian folk music that was arranged by Rimsky-Korsakov, and in that book, I found all the melodies of *The Firebird* and *Petrushka*.

I had heard some of the music by these tonalist composers in Chicago—because Fritz Reiner played Bartók—so it wasn't so much that I didn't know their work, it was more that their work was not considered in academic circles to be important. Of course, it wasn't long before I became acquainted with other kinds of alternate new music, including, among many others, Harry Partch, John Cage, Conlon Nancarrow, and Morton Feldman.

AN INFORMAL GROUP OF US SPENT SIGNIFICANT TIME just listening to music. This might have merely been casual listening, but it turned out to be surprisingly significant later on. My listening companions were, among others, Tom Steiner and Sydney Jacobs—my pals from Baltimore—as well as Carl Sagan, the future astrophysicist and cosmologist. This group undertook a superserious study of recordings of Bruckner and Mahler. It should be remembered that in the early 1950s, this school of music was virtually unknown outside of Europe. In the next decade conductors—especially Leonard Bernstein—would make their work widely popular in the States, but that was yet to come. In any event, we spent hours and hours together listening to recordings of Bruckner and Mahler symphonies, comparing recordings—often difficult to obtain even in Chicago—by Bruno Walter, Jascha Horenstein, and Wilhelm Furtwängler.

Of these three, Furtwängler, a tall, magisterial conductor, was the master of SLOW. He could find gaps between quarter notes that were almost unimaginable. He pushed dynamics and tempos and imposed his predilection for certain kinds of extremes in music. He forced it right onto the music, and you either liked it or you didn't. His Beethoven was considered highly controversial, because it was so different from conventional interpretations. Toscanini, in contrast to Furtwängler, was very fast. In their readings of Beethoven's Fifth Symphony, they could be twenty minutes apart in terms of the timing of the piece. It was astonishing how different they could be.

The other master of SLOW, whom I would know years later, was our own Bob Wilson, my collaborator on *Einstein on the Beach*. In many ways Furtwängler's Bruckner and Beethoven prepared me for Wilson. With Bob it was a visual tempo that he played with, but in the end it comes down to the same thing. With both Furtwängler and Wilson, the metronome clicks plunge down well below the comfort level of the human heartbeat. And what these truly great and profound artists reveal to us is a world of immense, immeasurable beauty.

With Bruckner and Mahler, I was interested not only in the orchestration but also in the extreme length of the pieces. They could be two hours long, or an hour and a half long, easily. I liked the scale of it. It was extreme in a certain way, but it was a very big canvas that they painted on in terms of time. There were things that, in retrospect, I didn't like so much: a lot of it was based on folkloric concert material, which I wasn't very interested in. Mahler was especially like that. Bruckner, on the other hand, composed symphonies that were epic, almost baroquelike edifices of symphonic music. Huge granite objects, but in music. The music reminded me very much of the church and I learned later that he had been a church organist. In his symphonies it was as if he had made an orchestra sound like an organ. He had mastered the orchestra to that extent.

One major, and unforeseen, benefit of the Bruckner expertise I acquired came when my longtime colleague and friend, the conductor Dennis Russell Davies, who had been the conductor of the Vienna Radio Orchestra, became, in 2002, the music director and conductor of the Linz Opera and the Bruckner House Orchestra. Through Dennis, my symphonies were played in Austria. I went to Linz for the first time with the poorly conceived idea that my music would sound better played by an American orchestra, because they would understand the rhythms that I was composing.

To my surprise, the Bruckner Orchestra played these compositions better than American orchestras. Somehow, Bruckner's sound had gotten lodged in my psyche. I had taken those pieces and digested them whole, and they had remained in my memory. When I was writing the opera *Satyagraha*, I found myself doing a similar kind of orchestration: all the strings played together in blocks, all the winds played together in blocks, and I took these blocks and managed to move them in new ways. I wasn't consciously trying to emulate Bruckner, but it was only when I heard the live Bruckner Orchestra, an Austrian orchestra, playing my music—my Sixth, Seventh, and Eighth Symphonies as well as other pieces—that I said, "Oh, this music sounds right." Then I realized that the reason it did sound right was that there were remnants of the Bruckner symphonies I'd heard many years before still in my mind.

The Austrian players were amazed that I knew that literature and cared for it so passionately. It smoothed the way for us in our composer-player friendship. And I absolutely loved the way they made my symphonies sound—quite a few were composed for them. This became clear to me through Dennis's interpretations and their beautiful performances. My connection to these musicians, their conductor, and the orchestra altogether formed for me an empathetic link to my own history—my present and, surely, my future. I doubt whether many other American composers would have had that experience.

MY MOTHER'S BROTHER, UNCLE WILLIE, had often talked to me about becoming a part of his business. He owned a company with my other uncle, David, which had been started by my grandfather, the rag-picker. They had taken over, and it became a very successful business called the Central Building Lumber and Supply Company.

Uncle Willie had no children. He hadn't liked my idea of going away to college in Chicago and, like the rest of my family, he wasn't in favor of my going to music school. He wanted me to come back to Baltimore and eventually take over his half of the business. When I told him I wasn't interested, he said, "Do you think you could think about it?"

"I'll think about it," I said, "but I'm not interested. That's not what I'm going to do."

Uncle Willie didn't want to give up the idea. "Why don't you go to Paris this summer, take a course in French, have a look around, and think about what you really want to do."

It was the summer of 1954, and I was seventeen.

"Okay," I said. "I will."

So, the summer after my sophomore year, I found myself on the *Queen Mary* on my way to France. In 1954, that's how you traveled to Europe. No one took the plane. There was a French-language summer class given for Americans in Paris, and that was where I was headed. The *Queen Mary* docked in Le Havre in the morning. I got on the train, and by three in the afternoon, I was in Paris. After leaving my bags at the dormitory, I went to register at the school and then I was ready to go out to see something of the city. At registration, I met a girl my age named Karen Collins and I said, "Karen, let's go get a drink," so we went to a café. It was about nine in the evening.

While sitting at the café, we suddenly saw a mob of people in costumes walking down Boulevard Montparnasse.

"What is this?" I asked.

"This is the night of the Bal des Artistes," someone sitting next to us said.

We were told that every year the École des Beaux Arts had an all-night party for graduates, current students, and, indeed, anyone who had been part of the École des Beaux Arts—a huge range of people: some artists, some kids, but also older graduates in their forties and fifties.

When this fantastically costumed group saw us—two kids really, a very nice young woman from Kansas and a nice young man from Baltimore—they must have seen something that said, "These are our children, and we need to take them with us." It was all very high-spirited and good-natured. They were having fun playing around with us. They pretended to speak English but of course they couldn't, not really. They just grabbed us and took us with them. I knew very little French at that time, but Karen and I were whisked away with these people and taken to a huge armory like the Grand Palais.

We arrived at ten or eleven o'clock, and basically we were with them until eight the next morning. The artists at the Beaux Arts were considered to be very rowdy, so at a certain point the gendarmes came and locked the doors and no one was allowed to leave. The reasoning was simple: they were afraid all these people would go running amok all over Paris. So the doors stayed closed until sometime after dawn, and once the celebration was over, there was a grand parade through the streets of Paris. This was my introduction to the bohemian life of Paris, and it was quite an introduction.

First of all, we had to have costumes. The armory had been set up in such a way that there was a big open space in the middle, and along the sides were large rooms, where each *atelier* had its own party with its own wine and food, mostly bread and cheese and fruit. At different times, the various groups would all come out from these rooms and congregate in the big open space in the center for all kinds of communal activities. But the first thing they did was take me to one of the studios where they took all my clothes off, painted my body completely red, and gave me a piece of gauze to put on around my waist.

It was almost nothing to wear, but I wrapped it around my body as best I could. They did the same thing with Karen in a separate studio, and when we came out, both of us were red. We stayed painted and "dressed" like that for the rest of the night.

There were set events throughout the evening, contests for the best costumes for men, and a separate one for the women. They also had to elect a king of the ball and a queen of the ball. A jury made up of some of the older people made the selections, and the winners of each event were greeted with tremendous enthusiasm by the crowd.

In between these "public" events you could hang out with the crowds in the open hall, or, for a little rest and recuperation, retire to your own *atelier*. The *ateliers* corresponded to the classes and year of the École des Beaux Arts itself, and it was considered proper to remain mostly with your own *atelier*. For Karen and myself, though we had just been thrust among them, they had become our friends and companions for the evening.

It was a wild, wild party, with a lot of nudism, and the crowds flowed constantly between the *ateliers* and the main hall. The main events were always punctuated by a finale of sorts. The chosen winners, including the king and queen, were seated on a camel—a real live one!—and paraded around the circumference of the hall, waving and blowing kisses to the rest of us, their approximately eight hundred enthusiastic admirers.

A small, highly energized ensemble played music throughout the night, the main music (and in fact, I remember no other) being the "Triumphal March" from Verdi's *Aïda*. I remember a clarinet, trumpet, trombone, violin, and a trap set for percussion. There must have been replacement players throughout the evening, for the music never stopped. I saw something similar years later when visiting south India in the town of Cheruthuruthy, when I was present for an all-night performance of the Kathakali—one of India's dance-theater traditions. There, too, the music was uninterrupted from evening until dawn, with drummers and singers alternating throughout the night, thereby sustaining a continuous musical presence. That summer of

1954, in Paris, the music of Verdi was played in a stately manner—perhaps a shade slower than you would hear in an opera house. It filled the hall and never stopped until the doors were unlocked from the outside by the gendarmes in the morning. The celebration concluded with a parade through the streets. When we came near the corner of Boulevard Montparnasse and Boulevard Raspail, Karen and I recognized our dormitory and we quietly slipped away. When the concierge saw us walking in like this, she knew right away.

"So," she smiled, "where did you come from?"

"We've been to the Beaux Arts Ball."

"Of course, of course!"

My hair was red, and there were people at that time who thought I was a redhead because I couldn't get it out of my hair. I don't know what—paint of some kind—they put on us, but it didn't come off very easily. For that summer, I remained a redhead.

That was my introduction to Paris. The rest of that summer was spent roaming around the city and studying very little. Paris is an easy city to walk around. I met artists, writers, and all manner of travelers. Ellie Childs, a student at my school, introduced me to Rudy Wurlitzer, another American who was also coasting around Paris. Rudy and I were to become lifelong friends, and when I arrived in New York City several years later, he was among the first people I knew. Later we bought property on Cape Breton in Nova Scotia together, and over the years we began working together as well, with Rudy writing librettos for two operas, *In the Penal Colony* and *The Perfect American*.

So many seeds were planted during that summer sixty years ago. In the mid-1970s, I met Ellie Childs's younger sister, Lucinda Childs, whom Bob Wilson and I saw performing at Washington Square Church with her dance company and invited her to work with us on *Einstein on the Beach*.

On my way home from Paris, I stopped in London for a few days. While I was there, a new play by a then little-known Irish playwright was being presented at a London theater club. It was Samuel Beckett's *Waiting for Godot*. I wasn't able to get a ticket but I remembered the name and found the play in print not long after I returned. A decade later, when I had returned to live and study in Paris, I began to compose music for Beckett's plays. Eventually, I contributed music to eight of his works.

One of the most important moments for me in Paris that summer was the realization that I would have to return to live there at least for a few years. That plan began to take shape in my mind at that time, and it was settled for me, even before I went to Juilliard.

I initially took the events of my first evening in Paris as an omen, but now I see it as something more definite, in fact as an actual marker—a line of demarcation that I had crossed. In retrospect, I think those people dressed in costumes walking up Montparnasse must have seen something before anybody else did. When they looked at me and said, "This guy comes with us," I think it wasn't just an accident, it was as clear a sign as I would ever get that I was going to enter the life of the artist. I was going to disrobe myself, I was going to put on a new identity, I was going to be somebody else. It took much longer for that transformation to take place, but in time it did happen. I returned home to the United States feeling for the first time the wind at my back. I suppose it had been there for quite some time. But this time I felt it for sure.

Back in Baltimore, I saw my Uncle Willie.

"Well, what'd you think?" he asked.

"Still going to music school," I replied.

NEWLY GRADUATED FROM THE UNIVERSITY OF CHICAGO, I SPENT the summer of 1956 working with my brother, Marty, for Uncle David and Uncle Willie, unloading boxcars of plywood for their lumber supply company in industrial downtown Baltimore. Working at Central Building Lumber and Supply was a mild preview to my work in the steel mills in that the workers were mostly Southern and poor, but this was a family business, which separated us automatically from the other laborers.

In the fall, I went right back to Chicago. I needed to think things over, and I felt freer to do that in a place where I had been living independently for some years already and was far away from any parental influence. Even though I registered for a few philosophy classes at the university, most of my time was spent planning my entrance to New York.

I had settled on Juilliard as my goal. Marcus Raskin, my piano teacher, had studied there, but he hadn't told me much about it. I picked the best music school in America and decided I was going to go there. I applied to only one school, and it was the best I could find. I made no second application. I made no third application. I already had an academic degree from one of the best universities and I had no further interest in academic pursuits. I was really looking for a trade school, and that was Juilliard par excellence.

Young as I was, I had a tremendous confidence that I could do what I wanted. Still, when I thought, I'll go to New York, I didn't *quite* know how to do it. I wrote away and found out when the auditions were held. Back then, arrangements like these were not made by phone. You would write a letter and you'd get a letter back. My appointment for an audition was for the flute. At that point, I didn't want to show them my first compositions. I knew they would not be good enough. By then I was already past my early twelve-tone Alban Berg–inspired music. I don't think I was particularly good at it. The aesthetics were foreign to me. It sounded like overcooked German expressionism and far too abstract to stimulate my own imagination. In time, and much later, I came to love the music of Stockhausen, Hans Werner Henze, Luigi Nono, Luciano Berio and even Pierre Boulez, but in 1957 I was listening to Charles Ives, Roy Harris, Aaron Copland, Virgil Thomson, and William Schuman.

Once my audition at Juilliard was scheduled, I left Chicago by train for Baltimore, where I had the conversation with my mother in which she warned me what I was getting myself into—a life of traveling and living in hotels—and took the bus to New York. As I described earlier, the audition took an unexpected turn and resulted in my accepting the suggested plan—that is, I would spend one year in the Extension Division in Stanley Wolfe's composition class, and in the following spring of 1958 I would reaudition as a composition student. Then, if accepted, I would be able to enroll as a composition student that fall.

The only problem to solve was, as always, the material question, so I went back to the Port Authority Bus Terminal at Eighth Avenue and Forty-First Street in Manhattan and bought a ticket back to Baltimore, with Bethlehem Steel as my goal.

IN ITS HEYDAY IN THE 1950S, THE NIGHT SKY at Bethlehem Steel in Sparrows Point was a splendid sight. I would drive from my parent's home in Clarks Lane, off Park Heights Avenue, to the steel plant. Ben and Ida had finally arrived close to the suburbs after twenty-five years of struggling to be out of downtown Baltimore. Driving from their house, I would bypass the city, going southeast to Sparrows Point. From a good fifteen miles away, the sky glowed from the light of open-hearth furnaces, where iron ore was melted and rolled out into thick steel slabs. At first the light would be seen as a shimmer—less colorful than a sunrise, more like an inverted sunset, gradually filling the night sky with a fiery white light.

I was working a swing shift, meaning that in the course of three weeks my workday shifted from 6 a.m.–2 p.m. to 2 p.m.–10 p.m. and then 10 p.m.–6 a.m. The night shift was my favorite. I would borrow the family car, a pale blue Simca, leaving home at nine, and after about forty minutes I would see the first sign of the furnaces. It never failed to thrill me. The air was filled with light and power, only out-shone by the morning sunrise, hours away. It didn't matter whether it was raining or clear. The white heat of the open hearth prevailed.

That's where I wanted to work, but the job I landed next door was different. I was running an overhead crane, guided by rails hung to the ceiling, in the nail mill. My work was to pick up full bins of nails, weigh them on a giant scale, and deliver them to the door of the mill to be packed and labeled. The floor of the mill was lined with row upon row of machines that took steel wire cable and punched out nails at an astonishing speed. It was noisy and dirty as hell.

This was piecework, which meant that the machine operators were paid according to how much they produced. Effectively, they left their machines idle as little as possible. These were very tough men in their thirties, forties, and fifties looking for good-paying jobs who had come up to Baltimore from the Carolinas, Florida, Alabama, and Louisiana. Sparrows Point was the first heavy-industry stop on their way north, unless they had taken the route to Chicago. They were all incredibly strong and hardworking. One man—tall, lean, and all muscle—was said to be from Florida and was known to have wrestled alligators. He didn't talk much, so I never actually heard it from him, but I believed it. He was one of the ones who could stand at his machine and work nonstop for a full eight-hour shift. Another was famous for building a small hunting lodge in the Maryland hills, using exclusively materials he took home from the plant—boards, wire, nails, even broken windows. He was a well-known "hero" in the plant.

I must have been quite a sight to these men: slim, with a barely shaved fresh face and a ready smile. And why shouldn't I have been smiling—I wasn't paid as well as them but it was a hands-down easy job. I would have intense periods of less than an hour when I was weighing and recording the nails produced in the nail mill. In between, I would sometimes have two hours while I waited for the bins to fill up again.

Despite my youth, the workers were very friendly to me. I suppose being the weigh-master assured me of a friendly greeting throughout the mill. The only untoward event that happened to me occurred on my very first day at work, when I mistakenly walked into the "colored" bathroom. I was promptly and bodily thrown out amid a roar of hooting laughter. It wasn't mean or vengeful, just, to them, very funny. Anyway, I got the point. All in all I got along pretty well with the men in the mill, though they were unlike any of Ben's employees or customers in the record store. I guess that fewer than half of them had more than a grade school education.

In the rural South there were plenty of young men leaving school to go to work as soon as they were able. These men were, most of them, not even working-class, but right off the fields and farms that not that long before had been part of the Confederacy. I was curious about them and they were curious and friendly to me. By gender, it was all men and by race, mixed—black, brown, white. They wore rough clothes, some with long hair, some short. The amazing thing to me was the parking lot—full of new cars and a surprising number of big Cadillacs, complete with radio aerials, leather seats, and huge fins in the back. It would be some years later before I too drove a Cadillac—not until my film-score-writing days in L.A., when I would pick up a Cadillac as a car rental. I'm sure the Bethlehem Steel parking lot was still in my mind. Not unlike those fellows I had known long ago, it gave me a quick, easy feeling of accomplishment to command a big car like that.

Luckily for me, I never minded earning money as best I could, and I actually enjoyed working at the mill. It's a good thing, too, because I would not make a living working full-time as a musician-composer until 1978 when, at the age of forty-one, I was commissioned to compose *Satyagraha* for the Netherlands Opera. Still, all the years of day jobs—twenty-four years—never bothered me. My curiosity about life trumped any disdain I might have had for working. So if this was a reality check, then I had happily signed on at a fairly early age.

After five months of working at the mill, I had saved $1200. Ida and Ben now knew of my plans and though dismayed, didn't in the least attempt to dissuade me. There was also no discussion of help, either. After all, they had already helped me through the university. Now, on my own, I went to New York to begin my music studies in earnest.

MY FIRST HOME IN NEW YORK was a small room on the fourth floor of a brownstone on Eighty-Eighth Street and Columbus Avenue. It cost six dollars a week and had a small bed, a dresser, and one lightbulb hanging from the ceiling. More humble conditions would have been hard to find, but the price was right.

At least for the first few months, until I had a part-time job and a bigger home, it meant that I had no piano, but the Juilliard practice rooms were available. Since I was not a piano major or even, as yet, a matriculated student, it meant I could not reserve a regular time for using a piano. I would have to find an empty room and hold on to it until evicted by its assigned occupant. There were plenty of rooms, but there also were plenty of pianists, singers, and conductors. I was hard at work improving my piano playing and using the time to play through my compositions and exercises, but finding a room was not easy. As the Juilliard school building was open by seven a.m., my solution was to get there early and find whatever piano I could, since the good ones were so much in demand. With luck I could manage to get about three hours free, often changing rooms as the scheduled occupants arrived. Juilliard students are as driven a group of young people as you can find, and unused practice rooms would sometimes not be available.

I had registered in October, a month late, but it didn't make any difference in the Extension Division. At the same time, I began taking other classes as a nonmatriculated student in music theory and history, known at Juilliard as L & M—Literature and Materials of Music. You were allowed to take the regular courses of the school, so I could do everything I wanted, except I didn't have a private teacher in composition, as I was not officially in the school. In fact, I was in the adult education department, which provided a possible entrance to the school even without an undergraduate music degree.

In the late 1950s, before the construction of Lincoln Center, Juilliard was located in a building at 122nd Street and Claremont Avenue, backing onto Broadway. The first and second floors were ringed with practice rooms, above a big cafeteria on the ground floor, while the dance studios were up top. There were a number of classrooms that could hold fifteen or twenty students, with big blackboards that had the staves with five lines on them for writing music. Someone might be teaching how, say, the German sixth worked, and they would write it on the blackboard so everyone could see it.

While I was living on Eighty-Eighth Street, I found a little diner on the corner where in the evenings I could sit at a table with a cup of coffee and fill notebooks with harmony exercises and my own music. The owner and waitresses liked me, and I was left alone there to do my work.

One night I noticed an older man, perhaps in his sixties, in another booth doing the same thing—writing music! He was often there when I arrived and remained when I left. I don't think he ever noticed me, so absorbed was he in his own work. After a while my curiosity got the better of me and I quietly approached him, looking over his shoulder to see what he was writing. It was a piano quintet (piano plus string quartet) and, from my few quick glances, it looked very well thought out and "professional." That was a most remarkable thing for me to stumble on—an older man composing in a coffee shop exactly as I was doing.

Now, here is perhaps the most remarkable part of the story, and something I didn't understand until many years later: I wasn't at all upset by this nonencounter. It never occurred to me that, perhaps, it was a harbinger of my own future. No, I didn't think that way at all. My thought was that his presence confirmed that what I was doing was correct. Here was an example of an obviously mature composer pursuing his career in these unexpected surroundings. I never knew who he was. Perhaps he was there, escaping from some noisy domestic scene—wife, kids running around, too many guests at home. Or, like me, perhaps he was simply living alone in a single room. The main thing was that I didn't find it worrisome. If anything I admired his resolve, his composure. It was inspiring.

My first "day job" in New York—found through the placement service at Juilliard—was loading trucks for Yale Trucking, an outfit on Fortieth Street and Twelfth Avenue, facing the Hudson. The business isn't there anymore, but for a long time, if you drove down the West Side Highway, which was elevated at the time, you would see an actual truck suspended in the air in front of a billboard that said "Yale Trucking."

It was a very good job. I worked from three p.m. to eight p.m., five days a week. The setup was simple: they had bays with trucks in them, and each truck would go to a different place. I was given the Orange, Connecticut, truck; someone else had the one to Boston; someone else had the one to Stamford, or wherever. My only job was to take care of all the freight that went to Orange, Connecticut.

I was told that I needed some training, so for the first two hours on my first day, I was trained by an older worker. I was young and strong, so I didn't have any trouble moving the stuff around. "Okay, son, this is how we do it," my trainer explained. "This is your truck. You start loading it in the afternoon, and you're done when the truck is full." The instruction continued: "The first thing you need to know is you got to put the big, heavy things on the bottom, because if you put the light things on the bottom, the big, heavy things'll start chasing you out of the truck. There'll be a wall of boxes falling down on you, and you got to get out of there."

He watched me load the heavy boxes until they were stacked almost chest high.

"Okay. Now you got the heavy ones on the bottom. You look strong, so take this one"—he picked up a smaller, lighter box—"and you see the back wall there?"

He pointed to the far back wall of the inside of the truck.

"Throw it as hard as you can at the back wall."

He showed me how to do it—*whack!*

The box bounced off the wall and landed with a dent in it. He looked me straight in the face and said, "We don't give a damn."

That was my training.

I never did throw the boxes into the back of the truck. I didn't get that big of a kick out of it. I just loaded the Orange, Connecticut, truck and went home. I had that job for a year, and that was how I made a living my first year in New York.

I found my first music friends in Stanley Wolfe's composition class. It appeared that anyone was welcome. The class was, in fact, fairly small, and we soon knew each other quite well. There were a handful of serious and aspiring young composers like me who hoped to use the class as a way to enter the composition department of the school, but there were also amateurs, some quite elderly, who were there to pick up whatever skills they could for their composing. One man, clearly retired, was only interested in waltzes. The class was run in an open seminar fashion, with students bringing their music for comments and advice from Mr. Wolfe and reaction to their work from fellow students. I was impressed by how seriously all of the students' work was addressed by our teacher. The "waltz man" brought in a new waltz for every class and was offered serious and good advice.

Mr. Wolfe, tall, with black hair and eyebrows and a thin face, was an excellent teacher, and by the following spring, when my audition before the composition department came around, I had composed ten to twelve new pieces that the faculty composers looked at. I was anxious more than nervous. Stanley Wolfe had already let me know that I was doing pretty well. He had really guided me in what I should be doing in order to prepare for that audition, which was, in effect, an entrance audition.

The letter of admission didn't come for about ten days, but when it did, not only was I admitted to the school, I was also given a small scholarship. It was very encouraging: in other words, they wanted me to come. This scholarship was a special nod of approval that let me know that I didn't get in by the skin of my teeth. From then on, I had part scholarships, part fellowships, and, somewhat surprisingly, a little bit of money from Uncle Willie, who finally relented and began sending me a couple hundred dollars a month, which was a big help.

I knew by then that moving from the Extension Division to the regular school curriculum was not at all common, but I had worked very hard that year and had been able to make a good case for myself to the composition faculty. I was accepted as a regularly enrolled student in the composition department for the fall semester of 1958. Once admitted, I took only music courses and worked directly toward a diploma, which I accomplished in two years.

William Bergsma was my composition teacher. No more "classes." One-on-one instruction was available now that I was in the department. Bergsma was still a young man when I knew him. He had made a name for himself with an opera *The Wife of Martin Guerre*, as well as a host of orchestra and chamber works. Bergsma and I got along well and I was soon absorbing everything I could in the school—the L & M classes, a second major in piano, and regular attendance at the orchestra rehearsals, as well as permission to audit conducting classes taught by Jean Morel, who was a regular conductor at the Metropolitan Opera in New York and himself a superb musician.

Bergsma was considered an up-and-coming composer in the Americana school of Aaron Copland and Roy Harris. I was already a tonalist by then, so he was the right teacher for me at that time, and was highly encouraging. He showed me what he called tricks, which often were very simple things, like how to set up a page of music so that it was easier to read, and how to review a piece by taking all the pages, putting them on the floor, and standing on a chair and looking down at the whole piece at once. That way you didn't have any page turns. I had a great affection for him because he took it so seriously. In fact, I would compose my first string quartet with him.

We would decide together what I would write, and then I would work on it until it was complete. Then we would go on to the next piece. With him, I was composing a piece every three or four weeks. There was one student at the school, a dedicated dodecaphonist, and he could spend a whole semester writing two pages of music. He almost got kicked out. At the end of the year, you were supposed to hand all your pieces in to a jury of composers, and you could flunk out at that point. It was impossible for me to flunk out—I had written too much music. I had the naïve but probably correct idea that if I wrote enough music, I would start to get better.

My compositions at Juilliard sounded rather like those of my teachers. In the late 1950s and early 1960s, composers had to make a big decision, whether they were going to write twelve-tone music or tonal music. I had already made that decision in Chicago, so it was no longer an issue. I was not going to write twelve-tone music any longer. I had done that already. As far as I was concerned, I was over it. Now I was interested in the music of Copland, Harris, Schuman, and Thomson. They were very good composers who dominated the American music scene at the time, and they were my models. Their music was tonal the way a popular song would be. It had melodies that you could sing. It could be beautifully orchestrated and have surprising harmonies in it—it didn't use routine harmonic phrases. It could be polyrhythmic and polytonal, but it was always meant to be heard and remembered, which was very hard to do with the European twelve-tone style of music.

During the period I was coming of age, these two schools—the American tonal school and the European-American twelve-tone school—competed for dominance. There were bitter arguments fought out in the academies, magazines, and concert halls. For a while, it appeared that the twelve-tone school had prevailed. However, almost any young man or woman now writing music in the new millennium has embraced an openness and tolerance to fresh and new musical styles that make those earlier battles seem distant, quaint, and ill-conceived.

Though I was a very busy and dedicated music student, that wasn't all I was up to. I had become quickly engaged with discovering New York City. After moving out of my Eighty-Eighth Street room, I ended up moving all over the Upper West Side, usually within walking distance of Juilliard. Soon, I was spending twenty dollars a week for a larger room with a small kitchenette. Along the way I met a young man the same age as myself working as a super on West Ninetieth Street. Michel Zeltzman had just emigrated from France with his mother and (new) American stepfather. As a young Jewish boy with red hair and blue eyes, Michel had spent the war years hiding in a Catholic boarding school somewhere in the South of France. His stepdad was an American soldier who had been stationed in Paris after the war. His own father had been deported from Paris by the occupying German army and sent to die in one of the death camps set up to exterminate Jews, gypsies, and other "undesirables." In exchange for putting out the garbage and keeping track of the people in the building on Ninetieth Street, Michel had gotten the ground-floor apartment there free.

We became friends on the spot. He was then an undergrad at Columbia with an aptitude for acting and a love of literature. Michel had an inborn reverence for culture, history, and art, and it was a very European point of view. He began teaching me French right away, so that by the time I went to Paris seven years later I had a working knowledge of the language. He would also introduce me to the work of Louis-Ferdinand Céline and Jean Genet, both of whom used a French so rich in *argot* that I never was able to read them in the original. Besides French and literature, Michel and I discovered all sorts of things together—motorcycles, yoga teachers, vegetarianism, anything to do with India or music, as well as many new friends who were musicians, dancers, actors, writers, and artists. For a time he worked at the French Cable Company down on Wall Street. It was a night job and during countless evenings we roamed around lower Manhattan before he was off to work at midnight.

From the time I moved to New York in 1957 until I left in 1964, Michel was part of my life. Whenever I talk about the things I was doing during that period, he was always there. During the time I was away from New York, from 1964 to 1967, living in Paris and traveling to India, Michel moved to Baltimore to work as an assistant to my cousin Steve, by now a young doctor doing research on fish brains. After some time, Michel decided to become a nurse and began taking courses. It was only years later that I found out that part of Michel's nursing education was taken care of through the organization that my mother, in the years just after the war, had become involved with, working to resettle families, mainly Jewish refugees, in the States. This organization provided scholarships for children of the emigrants for university education. Michel and his family weren't emigrés from the war years, but came a bit later. Ida never mentioned her involvement to me, but my sister, Sheppie, knew about it and later told me of the connection. Then I remembered that Ida would frequently ask about Michel, wanting whatever news of his life I could give her.

After he earned his degree, Michel would spend the rest of his life as a nurse in a pediatric cancer ward at Johns Hopkins Hospital, working with children that had cancer.

I asked him once, "Michel, after all the work you've done, why don't you just become a doctor?"

"If I became a doctor, I wouldn't be able to work with the children" was his reply.

He wasn't interested in being a doctor, he was interested in doing the work.

"What's it like?" I would ask him. "You must lose kids all the time."

"I lose them all the time and it is very, very hard."

Michel and I knew each other for fifty years, and his life, and his recent death, made a deep impression on me. In his seventies, Michel himself became sick with cancer. The illness lasted long enough so that he would go in and out of chemotherapy, which could be debilitating. But when he came out, as soon as he was able to work again, he would go back to the hospital and resume working with the children. As long as he could move, he continued his work at the hospital. I have met only a few people in my life who had the same awareness and tireless, active compassion as Michel.

SOON AFTER MEETING MICHEL, I became more adventurous regarding my housing. Over the next few years I left the Upper West Side to live all over Manhattan. I was, like Michel, even a super in an apartment building in the East Sixties close to the Central Park Zoo. In the late 1950s and early 1960s apartments were not expensive, and they were plentiful all over the city, not as it is now. Rents were low and the subways dirt-cheap. When I first arrived a token was fifteen cents, the same price as a slice of pizza. A truism known probably only to New Yorkers is that the price of a subway ride and a slice of pizza would always be the same. Or they play tag with each other so closely that you would have to suspect that somewhere behind the scenes the prices of these two New York City staples are inextricably bound together—fixed, as it were. Odd facts like this abound in New York City and can keep the place endlessly interesting.

Today a young musician or dancer will have a much harder time finding an affordable place to live and work. Even part-time and occasional work was easy to find in those days. I could manage quite well working as few as twenty to twenty-five hours a week—in other words, three full days or five half days. Even after I returned from Paris and India in the late 1960s, and well into the 1970s, I could take care of my family by working no more than three or four days a week.

It wasn't only that living was cheaper and work easier to find. Back then the city was considerably less violent. On an early summer evening it was common for my friends and me to walk down Central

Park West from 110th Street to Times Square, have a $1.50 dinner at Tad's Steakhouse on Forty-Second Street, go to a movie for $1.25, then stroll back up the length of Central Park West. If it was a warm night, in the time before air-conditioning, there would be people sleeping in the park.

My last two apartments on the Upper West Side were both on Ninety-Sixth Street. By then my rent had climbed to $69 a month and, finally, a high of $125 a month, and I was ready for a change— and it was a big one. In 1959, I moved all the way downtown to Front Street, just a block away from the Fulton Fish Market. It was the beginning of the years when artists and some musicians were making over industrial lofts into living-work places. My loft was on the second floor of a building that backed onto the building on South Street that housed Sloppy Louie's, a seafood restaurant. Between the fish market and the restaurant, there was a pervasive aroma of fish in the air—fresh, salted or cooked. The fish market itself seemed to be 24/7. I don't remember ever seeing it completely closed, though it could slow down in the afternoons.

My first loft was an unheated square room and very large compared with what had been my standard apartment until then. It had a toilet and a cold-water basin. My neighbors and friends, there being only artists in the building, initiated me into loft living. First, I learned how to use a potbelly stove, installing it on a metal plate and connecting it with stovepipes through the top of a nearby window, then loading it with wood. The wood itself was easy to find and plentiful in that part of the city. It was almost entirely from the wooden pallets that were used to haul around materials, manufactured goods, and sometimes fish. After being used they were abandoned in the streets. You could go out with a hammer and saw and bring back armfuls of broken planks in way less than an hour. However, that was only when we didn't have coal. In our building there was an empty elevator shaft and a few of us got together and had a half ton of coal dumped right into the shaft from the ground floor. From there we would bring soft coal up to our lofts a pail at a time.

I learned how to stack the coal so it could burn eight to ten hours without having to touch it. First you would make a good bed of embers with wood. Then on top of that you would stack the coal in a half-pyramid shape up to the top of the stove. In this way, the coal would slide down into the embers as it was burned. At that point you would shut down all the dampers and air inlets of the stove. These were not the airtight stoves, the beautiful ones from Vermont you can buy today, but they were tight enough. I kept a pail of water on the stove at all times and that was my hot water for washing and cleaning up. If you got it right, the stove could go all night. In the morning I would shake down the ash and replenish the coal. It was quite common to keep the stove burning sometimes continuously for a week, letting it go out only long enough to completely clean out the ash and start over. If you needed really hot water, you just had to open the air vents at the bottom of the front door and open the damper on the stovepipe leading out of the stove, and in twenty to thirty minutes the stove would be cherry red. I sometimes lit it up like that for company just to show off.

The stoves were easily found. A lot of hardware stores downtown would have them right out on the sidewalk for forty or fifty dollars. Then there was always Lee-Sam's, a plumbing supply place on Seventeenth Street and Seventh Avenue. They always had a few stoves out front. The only trouble with the stove system was that this was soft coal, not anthracite, and a fine but persistent dust settled throughout the entire loft. Not many years later, living in Paris, I had a coal stove once again. Of course I was a complete expert by then, and I loved the hard anthracite that would come delivered to our *atelier* in a huge burlap sack carried on the back of a local workman. It was a much cleaner burn, but not as easy to maintain and even harder to start.

The rent for my loft on Front Street was $30 a month, and I soon learned that the other artists in the building were furious with me, because they were paying only $25. They were sure the landlord had taken advantage of my naïveté and, by charging me more, would use this as an excuse to jack up everyone else's rent to $30. In fact, I don't think that actually happened. I paid my rent every month to a company in Long Island City named Sterling Real Estate. I sent them a $30 money order and I don't remember ever signing a lease.

The other tenants were all artists. John Rouson, a painter from London just a few years older than me, became a great friend. It was mainly John who tutored me in the details of loft living as we knew it in the late 1950s. He showed me how to stack the coal in the stove; he rolled his own cigarettes, which I also learned to do; and he showed me how to read the *I Ching*. He was short and slim and wore thick glasses. He spoke rarely and with a Cockney accent, to great effect. His judgments about painting, politics, poetry, and women were clear and crisp, if sometimes a bit harsh. By then Michel and I had taken up with a yoga teacher, Yogi Vithaldas, and John didn't think much of that at all. I think his whole *I Ching* connection had more to do with the fact that John Cage used it as a compositional method than it had to do with Chinese philosophy—though he did know a bit of that, too. John was a beautiful, beautiful painter. His work was quasi-realistic—still lifes and landscapes.

John Rouson was a deep fellow, no question. He knew what it was to be an artist and live without money. He would periodically take a job at a tobacco shop near Wall Street, because he liked getting free, loose tobacco and, after a few weeks or a month, he would have a bit of cash put aside, quit work, and go back to painting. I don't remember him ever selling a single painting. He, like Michel, had a childhood disrupted by the war. In his case, John had been sent out of London to avoid the Blitz bombing that was visited on the city. I think he missed London but didn't miss the bombs.

Eventually, Michel and John came to know each other quite well and the three of us shared a huge appetite for new painting, dance, and performance. We would travel around the East Village and lower Manhattan seeking out the latest new and unusual artistic experiments. In 1961–62 I remember going with John to Claes Oldenburg's "The Store" in a first-floor railroad apartment on East Second Street. In each room—they were strung out one after the other, like railroad cars—was a happening or an installation, or both. In one room you might encounter a long-legged girl in fishnet stockings handing out marshmallows and hugs to the spectators who wandered casually and carelessly between the rooms. Or perhaps a room of mirrors with flashlights and candles. These were the early days of happenings. I loved everything about them, the weirder the better. And, I must say, I feel the same way today. I like all kinds of art/performance, but I love it the most when it's fresh out of the can, not even reheated.

John was a great music lover, too, and insisted on hearing everything I wrote. By then we were no longer living on Front Street. He was in Hell's Kitchen, and I was in Chinatown. I would go over to his place, another cold-water flat, and he would hand-grind some strong coffee in his coffee grinder, and I would put on a new tape of my latest compositions. He would peer at me, as if smiling through his thick glasses, and quietly nod his head. At times we also listened to Elliott Carter and the early recordings of Cecil Taylor.

Michel would be with us sometimes, but often quite odd people would be visiting as well, like Roland and his girlfriend, Jennifer. Now that was a pair. He was dark and as handsome as they come and had a half-closed right eye. He was always well dressed—usually a suit, shirt, and nice shoes—and Jennifer was a stunning young woman, always and forever beautiful. I had no idea who they were or what they did. They rarely spoke. I usually saw them at John's and occasionally at a concert of mine. They seemed to drift in and out of our lives—like snowflakes lost from some storm that we had somehow missed. Over the years I've thought of them from time to time, but after I left for Paris in the fall of 1964, I never saw them again.

It was during this period, in the early 1960s, when I went for the first time with John and Michel to Yoko Ono's loft on Chambers Street. In those days, Yoko was presenting some of the earliest performance art to be seen in New York City. In the company of only a handful of other spectators, we were present for some of La Monte Young's seminal, quite early performances. One involved a pendulum, a pointer, and a piece of chalk. Hard to describe, but in the course of several hours La Monte drew an ever-thickening white chalk line on the floor, measured by the pointer attached to the swinging pendulum. Of course the whole affair was either maddening or mesmerizing depending on your point of view. For me, it was the latter.

Another piece was called "Piano Piece for David Tudor #1" (aka "Feeding the Piano"). There would be a piano, and La Monte would come on and put a bucket of water and an armful of hay by the piano, and then he would go sit down with the audience, really only a handful of people. We would sit there with the piano and the water and the hay, and after a while, when La Monte decided that the piano had eaten enough, he would pick up the hay and the water and he would leave.

But that wasn't all La Monte did. He also composed music that was a sustained, low-pitched, quiet tone that rumbled at the low end of what was humanly audible. Later, he studied Indian vocal music with the Indian master Pranath and also became an accomplished singer-composer. Not long ago I visited his Dream House, on Church Street, just below Canal Street in New York City, for a Sunday afternoon concert. The small loft was packed with young people. La Monte still performs wonderfully.

JOHN ROUSON USED TO PAINT A SELF-PORTRAIT on every birthday.

"How long will you continue this?" I asked him once.

"Not much longer," he said. "Because I won't live to be more than thirty."

I took that as a strange, but not serious, comment. I didn't think he was asking for my solicitude. How would he know? He seemed to be healthy. He didn't have a terminal illness of any kind—he was completely well.

A few years later, when I was living in Paris, John and Michel were sharing a bike on a cross-country ride. They had just stopped for the night at a motel on the road, and John said, "I'm going to take a little ride on the bike."

Michel called me on the phone in Paris.

"John just died," he said.

"What happened?"

"We're in Wyoming, and he got on the bike, and he wasn't going very fast—in fact, he was going rather slow—and the bike fell over and he died."

"Did he hit something?"

"No, the bike simply fell over."

"Did he have a helmet on?"

"Yes."

"How did he die?"

"We don't know. He was on the bike, the bike went down, and he was dead."

It happened about fifty or sixty feet from the motel, with Michel watching. It was John's thirtieth birthday.

A little later, another odd thing happened. An actor named David Warrilow, who was a member of a theater company we formed in Paris (later, in New York, we named it Mabou Mines), called me from London. I was just back from India and Paris and living in New York again.

David had been in touch with some medium or psychic in London. He was into that kind of thing, though it didn't mean much to me. Anyway, David said his English psychic friend had a message for me from a painter who had known me. I told David that, yes, I had such a friend and he had recently died.

I'm sure that David had never met John. I knew David from Paris and John from New York. Anyway, the message from John was that he had been present at some recent concerts of mine and wanted to tell me what he thought of the music.

For me that was the end of the conversation. I told David that I had a message for John, and would he please pass it back to him through the psychic. My message was that I had no interest at all in talking to dead people. Any more conversations would have to take place in some future time when, perhaps, we might meet. I never heard from the psychic or John again.

BESIDES JOHN, THERE WERE A NUMBER of other artists in the Front Street building. One with whom I became most friendly was Mark di Suvero, who occupied the space directly above me, on the third floor. I met him soon after I moved in. I was at home working one afternoon and heard a loud clanking moving up the stairs. I went to the door and saw a wiry young man with a reddish, scraggly beard being carried up in a wheelchair by a couple of men. He seemed very pleased to meet me, so I invited him in for some coffee. I found out then that he was a sculptor and had recently had a crippling accident— he had fallen down an empty elevator shaft. It had obviously slowed him down but he was far from stopping. He was delighted to find a musician-composer living just below him, and we had a great time together. On his way home, he would often stop at my place, and we would talk and sometimes listen to music, beginning a friendship that has lasted until the present.

At that time, when Mark was just back from the hospital, I heard some pretty heavy work being done above me. However, until the afternoon when Mark invited me up to his loft, I didn't know what to expect. After all, this was someone in a wheelchair, so what could it be? What I saw were a number of very large, bold pieces made from giant beams of wood formed into freestanding sculptures, accented throughout with huge iron chains. I think I almost fainted. It was very strong, it was abstract, and near overwhelming, crammed into a studio that, though twice the size of mine, could barely accommodate the work. Mark sat there in his wheelchair with a huge grin on his face. He couldn't have been happier when he saw my amazement.

I knew he was getting ready for a big show uptown at Dick Bellamy's Green Gallery. I went to Mark's opening and was again impressed. At the time, Dick Bellamy was also a young man, slim and soft spoken, and known for having a great "eye" for young artists and new work. I would not meet him again until almost ten years later, when I was working for Richard Serra as his studio assistant and Bellamy was one of the first people to notice and appreciate Richard's work.

It would not be until 1977, though, that Mark and I finally worked together, when I contributed the music for a film made by François de Menil and Barbara Rose about Mark and his sculpture. The film follows him making a number of large outdoor pieces, and my job was to compose music for each of the works that were a subject of the film. It eventually became one of my early recordings under the title *North Star* (*Etoile Polaire* being the original name of one sculpture in the film). But all that happened almost twenty years after we first met. Once the film was completed and the music I had composed was available on LP and tape, Mark told me that he took particular pleasure in listening to that music with headphones while he was in his crane working on new sculpture.

I would stay on in Front Street for another year before moving into a small house on Park Street in Chinatown (that whole block is gone now, having been absorbed into a parks development project across from the Tombs—the affectionate name New Yorkers give to the temporary jail set up across from the city's criminal courts building). Before then, in the late 1950s and early 1960s, all manner of artists lived near the Fulton Fish Market. Rumor had it that Jasper Johns and Cy Twombly had lofts down there, though I never saw them in the neighborhood. I recently read that Robert Rauschenberg had been on Front Street in the mid-1950s, after his Black Mountain College days. I didn't meet him there, but did so only a few years later when he was on Lafayette Street, just above Houston Street. By then (and this was much later, in the mid-1980s), I was nearby on Second Avenue, while Robert Mapplethorpe and Chuck Close were on Bond Street, Robert Frank and June Leaf were on Bleecker Street, and Jasper was in the Bank on Houston Street.

In short order, I had adopted the living style of the artists I knew, and this as early as 1960. I learned an enormous amount about art, performance, music, dance, and theater from being part of that world and, when I returned from Paris in the spring of 1967, that was the world I returned to.

My real introduction to that world had happened years earlier, while still at school in Chicago and visiting Baltimore in the summertime. During that time, Bob Janz, a young painter, and his wife, Faye, were living in downtown Baltimore. I met them through Bill Sullivan, a poet who had been part of the Phalanx group. Janz was an American born in Belfast. I suppose he was largely self-taught, but he was able to talk about paintings—their structure, content, and history—in a most articulate way. He is still painting today and living in New York.

When I first encountered him, I was only fifteen years old and Bob was four years older. I often joined him when he made regular visits to Washington, D.C., which was only forty miles from Baltimore. He would find someone to drive us or we would take a bus—either way it took an hour. Our destination was the Phillips Collection, which was located in a large private home near Dupont Circle. The Freer Gallery, a part of the Smithsonian, with a collection mainly of traditional Chinese and Japanese paintings, was also nearby. Janz could also speak quite elegantly about the Asian paintings at the Freer, but the paintings at the Phillips were the main attraction for us. Duncan Phillips had built up a private collection during his lifetime that turned out to be a most remarkable selection of contemporary work, ranging from the impressionists and early Picasso to ground-breaking work by American painters of the fifties and sixties. Besides a roomful of paintings by the Swiss artist Paul Klee, the Americans included Milton Avery, Arthur Dove, and Georgia O'Keeffe, all of whom I admired. The painters, however, whom I loved and who were wonderfully represented in the collection were Morris Louis, known to us as a Washington painter, as well as Kenneth Noland, and Mark Rothko.

For me, Rothko was a revelation. There was a small room at the Phillips that had three of his beautiful paintings. These did not resemble the dark paintings he would make later for the Rothko Chapel in Houston, but were huge amorphous squares, one above the other and only two to a canvas. They were painted in warm shades of orange and red. The effect was of an organic pulsating canvas. I could, and did, sit in front of these paintings for long stretches, bathing in their strength and wisdom.

The works of other younger Americans such as Jackson Pollock, Willem de Kooning, and Franz Kline were not easily seen in Baltimore and Washington. I didn't see full, life-size paintings of theirs until after I came to live in New York in 1957. Though the Phillips did have a few small paintings of Franz Kline, they were not on the scale of the large dynamic works I saw later.

Janz knew the work of these young abstract expressionists, and he made sure that I knew them as well, even if only through catalogues and reproductions in art books. I was entranced. Janz, himself an accomplished and sensitive painter, tried some action painting of his own. He would take a large roll of brown wrapping paper, lay out a six-by-four-foot piece of it on his studio floor, paint his body red, and lay down, twisting left and right until he had made a good impression on the paper.

About that time the *Baltimore Sun* had gotten wind of Pollock's revolutionary painting techniques, dripping and squeezing oil paint over an entire canvas. The art critic of the paper, like many people in those days, was shocked and outraged by this latest affront to Art. He went to the Baltimore Zoo and somehow got permission to work with one of the chimpanzees in the monkey house. The chimp was given a large canvas and tubes of oil paint. It didn't take long for him to squeeze the paint onto the canvas. This was photographed and put on the front page of the newspaper with a headline that read something like "Baltimore's Own Jackson Pollock Is Alive and Well and Is a Chimpanzee in Our Own Zoo." This kind of thing was going on all over the country, especially among art lovers. Usually it was left as a simple claim such as "My two-year-old daughter can paint better than Pollock."

I rushed over to Janz's studio to show him this latest attack on Art—on the front page of my hometown newspaper, no less. He studied the newspaper photo for a while. Then in a calm and dismissive manner he said, "The trouble with the paintings is that the chimp is not a very talented painter." The humor of that moment calmed me down.

I remained a great fan of these abstract expressionist painters for a long time. However, a show at the Museum of Modern Art in New York during the winter of 1959–60 titled "16 Americans" made me, once again, rethink the limits of modern painting. The exhibition included works of Jasper Johns, Bob Rauschenberg, Frank Stella, and Louise Nevelson—a long and excellent list.

When I saw Stella's paintings in the show, I was at first deeply shocked. After all, my head was still filled with Pollock and de Kooning. The next moment I had a deeper realization: the rate of change in the visual arts world was far, far quicker than could ever happen in the music world. The world of painting expected innovation and new ideas, but in the world of music, which was a much more conservative environment, there was no cachet at all in having new ideas. The music world was still obsessed with "new music" that was more than fifty years old. This was a liberating moment for me.

Modern jazz and experimental music *did* offer examples of change and dynamic development. The gifted geniuses of jazz—Charlie Parker and Bud Powell, to mention only two—were, like their counterparts in the abstract expressionist world, playing their music of deep expression with energy and at high speed. In the late 1950s we began to hear the new "cool jazz" as played by Miles Davis, Gerry Mulligan, Bob Brookmeyer, and Chet Baker. It was equally complex but in a very different aesthetic—sometimes more reflective and laid-back and always more distant. On the other hand, Ornette Coleman, a younger player, was working in a more abstract harmonic language than most jazz, yet he maintained a drive to his music in which you could hear blues and contemporary jazz at its root. In this way, he was the most radical.

In experimental music, John Cage, along with Morton Feldman, Christian Wolff, and Earle Brown were offering a music also cooler in feeling and springing from different principles than the twelve-tone school of Boulez, Stockhausen, and Berio. Later I got to know John and his music friends quite well, but that would not be until the late 1960s.

Apart from jazz and experimental art music, it was largely the art world that gave permission to a younger generation to change the rules by which we worked. The difficulty was that at that moment I simply didn't have the technical musical skills to make the work I wanted to make. It was a lack and a need that I was determined to address. And as soon as possible.

AT THE SAME TIME AS I WAS SETTLING INTO the sometimes overstimulating art scene, I was up at Juilliard every day pursuing my music education and training. Those Juilliard years lasted until the spring of 1962—five years of determined and intensive work. At the beginning, with my first year in the Extension Division, I was painfully aware of how defective my basic skills were. Whatever I had accomplished in playing the flute or piano, and especially in composition, was the result of youthful enthusiasm. In fact, I had a very poor grasp of real technique.

The school was quite remarkable in one way, bringing together a brilliant, accomplished faculty and an extremely talented and competitive student body. It was very clear to me from the outset that everyone at Juilliard—faculty and students alike—was extremely busy with his or her own work. The environment was ideal for work, but short on real guidance and direction. It seemed in those days that the strategy of the school was to find really talented young people, throw them together for four or five years in a kind of musical pressure cooker, and then to summarily graduate them into the "real world." We were not given any education courses at Juilliard, and so we weren't qualified to teach in any New York state schools. But we were in New York City, a real-life sink-or-swim environment. In other words, Juilliard had a very high-standard entrance exam and a rather casual graduating process. The funny thing is, given the pas-

sion and eagerness of the students and the example of a highly successful faculty, that the system actually worked as well as it did.

I had two things in my favor. First, I had just come from the University of Chicago—a whole universe of extremely smart, hardworking people. Second, there was nothing else I truly wanted to do. I
never decided to become a musician, I simply followed the only path
that was available to me, and therefore I accepted a lot of hard work
and a lot of what other people would call deprivation. It didn't bother
me at all, because I was so focused on the work itself.

I realized right away that I needed to quickly develop impeccable
work habits. In that regard, the University of Chicago hadn't helped.
Though it was similar to Juilliard in having a very bright group of
youngsters thrown together, the system of exams-at-the-end-of-the-
year didn't encourage disciplined work habits.

I approached my problem in several different ways. First, I needed
to improve my piano playing very quickly. Though Marcus Raskin
had been a really excellent piano teacher, the fact that I started with
him when I was fifteen, not five, meant I had a lot of time to make
up. By my first full year at Juilliard, I had a regular piano teacher and
I was in the practice rooms early every day. I needed the sounds of
others practicing to goad me into practicing myself. I could get in several hours a day that way, which was all the time I had for that part
of my work.

I now had my own piano at home. While living in the West
Ninety-Sixth Street apartment I found upright pianos, free to be
taken away, in a local Buy-Lines (a popular "for sale" newspaper). All
that was needed was a small rented truck for a few hours and three or
four friends. We only had to wrestle the pianos down several flights
of stairs, onto the truck, and when we arrived at Ninety-Sixth Street,
up six more flights. I recall now that after a few months I was offered a
better piano, and we did the same thing again, ending up stacking the
second piano in front of the first. The problem was that my place was
a railroad apartment and the hallway, being part of the rooms, was
quite narrow. So a double stack of pianos was as far as you could go.

The discipline needed for composing was a different matter altogether and required more ingenuity. My first goal was to be able to sit at a piano or desk for three hours. I thought that was a reasonable amount of time and, once accomplished, could be easily extended as needed. I picked a period of time that would work most days, ten a.m. to one in the afternoon. This allowed for my music classes and also my part-time work at Yale Trucking.

The exercise was this: I set a clock on the piano, put some music paper on the table nearby, and sat at the piano from ten until one. It didn't matter whether I composed a note of music or not. The other part of the exercise was that I didn't write music at any other time of the day or night. The strategy was to tame my muse, encouraging it to be active at the times I had set and at no other times. A strange idea, perhaps, undertaken as an experiment. I had no idea whether it would work.

The first week was painful—brutal, actually. At first I did nothing at all during those three hours. I sat like an idiot without any idea of what to do. When the three hours were up I bolted for the door and practically ran out into the street, so relieved was I to be away from the piano. Then, slowly, things began to change. I started writing music, just to have something to do. It didn't really matter whether it was good, bad, boring, or interesting. And eventually, it *was* interesting. So I had tricked myself into composing . . . something.

After a few weeks I found the transition from near madness and frustration giving way to something resembling attention. It probably took a little less than two months to get to that place. I wouldn't say it was easy, but it was pushing me toward a place I wanted to be. From then on, the habit of attention became available to me, and that brought a real order to my life.

The second part of my plan worked as well. That is, I was never tempted to compose outside of times I set for myself. At the beginning I was not at all flexible about my work times. For example, if I would wake up at night with the thought of writing music, I simply declined to do so. This somewhat strange habit persisted as part of my working life for more than forty years. Only recently have I begun to work in a more casual way—sometimes going to my music room in the dead of night for a few hours of unscheduled work. And now I no longer follow any particular schedule at all. In terms of my overall productivity, I haven't noticed any change whatsoever. As far as I can tell, the amount of music produced and the general quality is about the same.

Once I was accepted in the composition department, I began to make friends all over Juilliard. There was a very active dance department led by the Martha Graham Company as well as by José Limón, developer of the "Limón technique," who was often present in the school. The resident teacher of choreography was Louis Horst, a most renowned dance personage. On a number of occasions I contributed music, playing the flute for his dance composition class. He would sit curled up in an armchair, wearing a rumpled beige suit, not looking at all like a dancer. I quickly learned that young dancers are always in need of new music and I eagerly began writing for them.

In the same way, Conrad Sousa, a young composer just my age, began leading me toward writing music for theater productions. He was well connected on the West Coast and also contributed music for theater productions at the McCarter Theater in Princeton, New Jersey. Once, when he was occupied with other work, he sent a job my way: to write music for Molière's *Scapin*. I was paid a total of twenty-five dollars, and I had to compose and record the work myself. I was delighted to find, even during my first student years at Juilliard, that theater and dance people wanted and needed music in a way that no one else did. In this way, a rhythm of work and collaboration began to take root in me at this early stage.

These works were outside of the regular composing I did with my first Juilliard teacher, William Bergsma, and my second, Vincent Persichetti, with whom I continued after my diploma in 1960, until I completed my master's degree in 1962. I don't remember ever showing them these works for dance and theater.

Persichetti was a very lively teacher, much sought after by the young composers. He was a short, muscular man, brimming with talent and energy. Unfortunately he had a habit of taking an unfinished piece that I would bring him and demonstrating to me, with his marvelous piano technique, how it could be completed. I soon stopped bringing him "unfinished" pieces, which was not good for either of us. It meant he didn't get the fun of finishing them for me and I wasn't able to benefit from his suggestions—which he was not generous with anyway. Apart from that, Vincent, as he liked to be called, and I got along very well. In my last years at Juilliard, he steered several pieces of mine to the small music-publishing company, Elkan-Vogel, where he was the editor. That firm eventually became part of the Theodore Presser publishing company and those early works—juvenilia, really—are still there today.

Persichetti was a formidable pianist who often played concerts of his own music. Yet at Juilliard there was a division between music theory and music practice. Once I was officially in the composition department, I was told I wouldn't need to play the piano anymore, as there were very good players at the school who would perform my music for me. I was given a piano teacher for several years, but no one in the composition department was in the least interested in the possibility that I might want to be a composer-performer. I have no idea where the notion came from that performance need not be an essential part of a composer's skills. Making the practice of music and the writing of music separate activities was poor advice. It's a misunderstanding about the fundamental nature of music. Music is, above all, something we play, it's not something that's meant for study only.

For me, performing music is an essential part of the experience of composing. I see now that young composers are all playing. That was certainly encouraged by my generation. We were all players. That we would become interpreters ourselves was part of our rebellion.

THE CAFETERIA AT JUILLIARD WAS THE PLACE to meet people and make new friends. My fellow student composers were all young men—at this point, there were scarcely any women composers around, in or out of school.

Peter Schickele, a year older than me, was one of my best friends there. He was a hilariously funny guy as well as being a very talented composer. It was at Juilliard that he developed his alter ego, P. D. Q. Bach, the illegitimate twenty-second son of J. S. Bach. Every spring at the Juilliard end-of-the-year concert Peter would appear on stage in period costume and wig and play his baroque, Bachesque compositions. He always made sure that they were well written and well thought out, and if you knew anything about music, they were doubly funny because he did it so perfectly. It wasn't just that he sounded like Bach, or like a version of Bach—P. D. Q. Bach was clearly gifted, and Peter *was* P. D. Q. Bach.

Peter's brother, David, was a filmmaker, and David and I would help build the invented instruments Peter used in his concerts. Peter would come up with the title of a piece and then write the piece. For example, in New York there used to be a chain of automats called Horn & Hardart, where the food was dispensed from behind small coin-operated glass doors. You'd put in a nickel or a dime, you'd turn the handle, the glass door would open up, and you would take out your coffee, sandwich, or dessert. I ate there all the time because they had a thirty-five-cent lunch special.

Well, Peter wrote a Concerto for Horn & Hardart. We knew what the Horn was, but no one knew what a Hardart was, so David and I had to build the Hardart. Peter decided that the Hardart looked like a keyboard, but the keyboard would be made of toy instruments: little whistles and harmonicas and accordions and triangles—whatever could make pitches. Each note would be made from a different toy, but Peter could look at the keyboard and see what the note was: it would be an F or a G or a C, but it might be coming through a whistle or a claxon or a horn.

"Okay, you guys," he said. "You build the Hardart. I'm going to be in this room over here writing the piece for it." He would run in and look at what we were building, and then he would run back and write in the other room.

Peter was full of such jokes, but we were full of jokes, too. We made a two-octave chromatic instrument that looked like a keyboard, but we didn't tell Peter that it was a transposing instrument. We did not use a common transposition, like a French horn in F, or a trumpet in B flat. We chose a transposition to an imaginary instrument in E. That meant a C would sound as an E, and an F would sound as an A, and so on.

"It doesn't work!" Peter exclaimed when he finally tried to play the Hardart.

"Peter!" I said. "You didn't ask us. It's a transposing instrument. It's in E."

"Oh my god," he exclaimed.

So not only did he have to play the Hardart, he had to transpose it at sight, during the performance. That was one of the funnier things that we did with him.

Peter later developed P. D. Q. Bach into full-length concerts, and he toured the country. Within two years, he was actually making a living with it. Long past our Juilliard days, after my opera *Einstein on the Beach* had appeared in New York, Peter called me up and said, "Look, Phil, would you be offended if I did a piece called *Einstein on the Fritz?*"

"No, no, Peter, absolutely not. Go ahead and do it."

"Would you come and hear it?"

"Of course."

What I didn't reckon on was that Peter reserved me a seat in the center of the audience at Carnegie Hall, where everyone could see me. And then he had a spotlight on me. So not only did he do *Einstein on the Fritz*, but I was there, and everybody knew I was there, and everyone was watching. The music turned out to be a concerto in three movements that Peter made sound like P. D. Q. Bach's music, but a minimalist version of it. And the piece itself—would you believe it—kept repeating itself. It seemed to never be able to get past the first measure.

THE STUDENT BODY AT JUILLIARD WAS NOT VERY LARGE, numbering perhaps five hundred students. This included instrumentalists, pianists, singers (mainly in the opera program), and conductors. The dance department was not that large, with certainly no more than sixty students at any time. The composers never numbered more than eight in any year and the conductors perhaps a few less. There were always enough players for several orchestras, and the chorus was made up of singers, composers, pianists, and conductors.

For us, the chorus was a two-year requirement. That meant there was a pretty good-sized regular chorus available every year, and it allowed the school to prepare three or four large choral works with chorus and orchestra. This could, and did, include complete performances of the Verdi *Requiem*, Masses by Mozart, Beethoven, and Bach, and usually several modern pieces. I also first heard and performed the music of Luigi Nono, the son-in-law of Arnold Schoenberg, and Luigi Dallapiccola, both Italian modernists. As well, we often read through new works by the faculty composers and even William Schuman, the school's president.

At first I resented the three chorus rehearsals every week. I soon got over that and began to take a keen interest in the music we were singing. I was in the bass section but, as there was plenty of rehearsal time, I passed the hours also singing the soprano, alto, and tenor parts, displaced by an octave as necessary. Nobody seemed to mind, and in this way I came to have a complete understanding of vocal writing for a full chorus.

Abraham Kaplan was our young, charismatic conductor. As he often segregated vocal parts when working on the intonation (pitch), I was able to hear very clearly how the voice movement and part writing was realized. These were the great choral classics, mind you, and all in all some of the best training to be had at Juilliard. However, you had to know this and pay attention to benefit from the rehearsals. Almost twenty years later, when I was composing the choral music for *Satyagraha*, I became gratefully aware of those lessons. By then I knew absolutely how to make a chorus "sound," where to "divisi" the voices, how to support them with the orchestra—all manner of techniques of a necessary and deeply musical nature. All the choral music I made for operas—*Einstein on the Beach*, *Satyagraha*, *Akhnaten*—symphonies, and a cappella (voices alone) choruses grew out of those experiences during my Juilliard chorus years. I had acquired, without intending to, an early and reliable knowledge of basic vocal writing. The skills and craft of writing for solo voices was something I learned later and with the help of the singers I worked with. Vocal writing is not easily learned. Time and quite a lot of coaching and practice were necessary for me to arrive at a reasonable degree of ability.

I began another lifelong study—writing for orchestral instruments as soloists or as players in chamber or full orchestra. In this case, I did have personal experiences playing in orchestras, from playing in church orchestras or in high school musicals. Most of that was flute-playing, which I could handle pretty well. During my two years of high school, I had also played in marching bands—my way of getting into football games and having a very good seat at the games themselves. I was not big enough to make the team, so music was my form of participation. In the marching bands I sometimes played a bass trumpet—a one-valve instrument probably only used in bands of that kind. However, that did give me a physical, real-life experience of playing in a brass ensemble. That kind of firsthand contact with an instrument is invaluable and really can't be deeply learned or duplicated in any other way. Writing for percussion instruments, all of them, came easily to me, as I had been part of a percussion ensemble from the age of eight, when I was studying flute at the Peabody Conservatory in Baltimore. That left the string sections—double bass to violin. Being able to write well for string instruments was high on my list of skills I needed to acquire, though this list was made by and for myself.

At that juncture, I had no idea what kind of composer I wanted to become. My instinct was to cover everything I might need. As it turned out, that broad training I was seeking eventually proved to be essential. For string writing, there was only one solution. I borrowed a violin from the school and began to take violin lessons. By accident or, perhaps, by design, I found myself sitting next to a pleasant, beautiful young woman in my L & M class. Her name was Dorothy Pixley, soon to become Dorothy Pixley-Rothschild, as she was engaged to be married the next year. We soon became friends and I asked her for violin lessons, to which she happily and easily agreed. I found, in general, that my fellow students at Juilliard were always very kind in matters like this. It was easy to get help and I often consulted friends for any information or assistance I might need. So, I began playing scales, developing some rudimentary skills in fingering and bowing. I also started writing music for Dorothy—string quartets, a trio, and even the concerto for solo violin, winds, brass, and percussion that I composed when I was at the Aspen Music School studying with Darius Milhaud in 1960.

Though I never became even a decent violinist, I learned what I needed to write well for the instrument. Since then I have composed seven string quartets, two violin concertos, two cello concertos, and a double concerto for violin and cello. Of course, all ten symphonies and almost all the operas have string parts. Like the voice, string writing is a study of a lifetime. I've always worked closely with string players and feel confident now when I compose for them. Still, there are plenty of challenges left. Writing solo music for the double bass, for example, is not easy. The finger positions on the fingerboard are very far apart, as required because of the range and size of the instrument. Double-stops—playing two notes together—have to be understood very well when including them in double bass parts. Composing skillfully for any instrument is full of such details, all of which have to be learned and mastered through application and practice. Fortunately, that was the kind of thing I liked to do.

In the end, the biggest subject for me was the orchestra itself. Oddly enough, we had no separate orchestration class when I was a student at Juilliard. Details like this, as well as a real understanding of counterpoint, harmony, and analysis, were left to the L & M course. For pianists, singers, and instrumentalists, that could be fine. For composers and conductors, it was simply inadequate. The benefit of studies in the actual technique of music composition is not acquired through the casual absorption of information, but through rigorous practice. For me, that kind of study would have to wait until 1964, when I went to Paris to work with Nadia Boulanger. In the meantime, I found several ways of improving my technique and understanding.

I began attending the orchestra rehearsals led by Jean Morel. He himself had been thoroughly trained in the French system of solfège, figured bass, and harmony, and I assume, being French, he had also had the usual studies in strict and free counterpoint, analysis, and orchestration. He was a fine conductor and an excellent musician who was a tremendous inspiration and influence on the many Juilliard students who came his way. In my case, I asked him if I could audit his conducting class as well as attend his rehearsals, to which he agreed. He was kind to me, and he conducted and recorded my graduation piece with the Juilliard orchestra. I did find that my ideas about orchestration sometimes differed from Morel's, but, unlike my previous experience with Aaron Copland, I kept my mouth shut.

During my years at Juilliard, Morel covered the standard repertoire as well as early modern and contemporary music. I would arrive at the rehearsals with the scores borrowed from the library and follow the rehearsals, paying particular attention to his many comments to the players as well as to his own conducting students. His instructions were clear and illuminating. I attended these rehearsals many, many times. Besides the orchestra players, all of his own students were there, but surprisingly very few composers (apart from the occasional faculty member who happened to have a work of their own being performed). The conductor Dennis Russell Davies became a student of Morel's about the time I was leaving Juilliard. Since his first performance of *Satyagraha* in Stuttgart in 1980, Dennis has been a constant supporter of the music I have been composing, and I don't doubt that our very close music collaboration was facilitated by his deep connection to Morel.

My second study of the orchestra came through a time-honored practice of the past but not much used today—copying out original scores. In my case I took the Mahler Ninth as my subject and I literally copied it out note for note on full-size orchestra paper. Mahler is famous for being a master of the details of orchestration, and though I didn't complete the whole work, I learned a lot from the exercise. This is exactly how painters in the past and present study painting—even today, some can be seen in museums making copies of traditional paintings. It works the same way in music. This business of copying from the past is a most powerful tool for training and developing a solid orchestration technique.

The person who set up this task was, for me, the most influential musician whom I met at Juilliard, a fellow student named Albert Fine. It was he who interceded so that I was allowed into Morel's class, something very rarely done. Morel permitted it because I was a friend of Albert's—Morel preferred to speak French when he could, and he and Albert talked about Proust together. It was Albert's encouragement that got me to the rehearsals, and he also started me on the detailed study of Mahler that was at the core of the copying exercise.

One could easily wonder how such a young man could have made such an impression on me. The answer is that he was simply the most highly developed musician I met at Juilliard. The fact that he was close to my age made no difference at all. And I wasn't the only one who thought so. One evening, Albert and I were having a dinner at the Tien Tsin, then a popular Chinese restaurant at 125th Street and Broadway. At one moment William Schuman who was also dining there, approached our table and said to Albert, "Hi, Albert, I have a question for you regarding the bass clarinet part in a new symphony of mine. Do you think you would have time to look at it for me?" I was totally shocked to discover that Albert's opinion would be so openly solicited by the president of Juilliard.

Another time, once I was a regular student of his and had a private lesson from him every week, I was in Albert's apartment and saw a score by Vincent Persichetti on his kitchen table. I remember very clearly it was his Symphony no. 5. I knew this would be Vincent's new symphony, only recently completed. I asked Albert how it came to be in his house. Albert told me that it was being prepared for publication and that Vincent had asked him to "look it over" before it went to press. I asked Albert whether he had found anything amiss. He said it was fine but he had found one mistake: in the last movement a theme from the first movement had been incorrectly quoted by either Vincent or the copyist. He also told me that the editor later confirmed that it was an error.

I had met Albert when I was first registered as a composer. He was in his early twenties then, a very striking young man, with a round face and long blond hair brushed to one side. He was always elegantly dressed, in a jacket and ascot, and always had a volume of Proust's *À la Recherche du Temps Perdu* in his hand. He conversed with Morel only in French and he quickly became a friend of Michel's after I introduced them. Once I became aware of his very high level of musicianship, I begged him for lessons. He agreed to give me a weekly lesson at no charge, provided I followed his teaching regimen to the letter. "Of course," I agreed. None of my other teachers knew about this. But I soon discovered he had one other "secret" student in the school. It was the singer Shirley Verrett, soon to be a famous opera singer in her own right. I saw Albert regularly for several years and one day asked where he got his training. He was born in Boston, where his mother was a music teacher, but his real training came from Nadia Boulanger. I discovered later, when I was her pupil, that many of the exercises that I had learned from Albert were a regular part of her teaching.

Among my Juilliard friends, Albert was the only one who shared my interest in the downtown art world. Indeed, he would in time become known as one of the founders of the Fluxus movement that was then taking shape. He eventually developed his own circle of friends that overlapped with mine. He knew John Rouson and Bob Janz quite well, and through him I met a host of interesting and unusual people. Among the most striking was Norman Solomon, a very unusual painter, not well-known today, who specialized in a personal kind of calligraphy, making large black and white paintings, but not at all like Franz Kline.

The most memorable of Albert's friends was Ray Johnson, who is still known today as the founder of the New York Correspondence School. Then, and again in the late 1960s, when I was back from Paris, Albert would bring Ray to visit me. He was a most enigmatic character and very quiet. You might almost think he was shy. He was slim, of medium height, and completely bald, with bright clear eyes. When he did speak, he would make puzzling, outrageous pronouncements, which I have never forgotten.

Once, during one of those strange visits, and after not having spoken at all, he said, "There is so much time, and so little to do."

The New York Correspondence School seemed to be mainly Ray Johnson himself. He would send out postcards to his friends, usually just images or some enigmatic remarks. Really, it could be most anything. I didn't reply to him, I just collected the postcards, and they would arrive always unexpectedly.

Ray died in 1995, an apparent suicide. He was last seen swimming out to sea off of Sag Harbor, Long Island. I heard about his death and was very surprised to hear he had taken his life. I knew him as a good friend of Albert's, a latter-day Dadaist and one of the founders of the Fluxus movement. Though I didn't know his art all that well, I thought of him as a quintessential artist of our time.

Albert had also developed a taste for the most avant-garde, cutting-edge work. He was well versed in John Cage's writings and music, both of which had made a deep impression on my circle of friends. Albert, John Rouson, Michel, and I had all been immersed in Cage's *Silence*, the Wesleyan University Press collection of writings published in 1961. This was a very important book to us in terms of the theory and aesthetics of postmodernism. Cage especially was able to develop a very clear and lucid presentation of the idea that the listener completes the work. It wasn't just his idea: he attributed it to Marcel Duchamp, with whom he was associated. Duchamp was a bit older but he seemed to have been very close to John. They played chess together, they talked about things together, and if you think about it that way, the Dadaism of Europe took root in America through Cage. He was the one who made it understandable for people through a clear exposition of how the creative process works, vis-à-vis the audience.

Take John's famous piece 4' 33". John, or anyone, sits at the piano for four minutes thirty-three seconds and during that time, whatever you hear is the piece. It could be people walking through the corridor, it could be the traffic, it could be the hum of the electricity in the building—it doesn't matter. The idea was that John simply took this space and this prescribed period of time and by framing it, announced, "This is what you're going to pay attention to. What you see and what you hear is the art." When he got up, it ended.

The book *Silence* was in my hands not long after it came out, and I would spend time with John Rouson and Michel talking and thinking about it. As it turned out, it became a way that we could look at what Jasper Johns, Robert Rauschenberg, Richard Serra, or almost anybody from our generation or the generation just before us did, and we could understand it in terms of how the work existed in the world.

The important point is that a work of art has no independent existence. It has a conventional identity and a conventional reality and it comes into being through an interdependence of other events with people. Later on, when I would be talking with students, I would ask them, "What do you have in the library here?"

"Music books," they would say.

"No, but what is it?" I would ask again.

"It's music," they'd say.

"No, it isn't music. It's pages with lines and dots on them, that's what it is. Music is what you hear. Those books aren't music, they're just the evidence of somebody else's idea. Or you can use them as a way of making music. But they're not actually music."

The accepted idea when I was growing up was that the late Beethoven quartets or *The Art of the Fugue* or any of the great masterpieces had a platonic identity—that they had an actual, independent existence. What Cage was saying is that there is no such thing as an independent existence. The music exists between you—the listener—and the object that you're listening to. The transaction of it coming into being happens through the effort you make in the presence of that work. The cognitive activity is the content of the work. This is the root of postmodernism, really, and John was wonderful at not only articulating it, but demonstrating it in his work and his life.

I immediately abandoned any idea I had that music had some kind of eternal existence, an existence that was independent of the transaction that happens between the performer and the listener. What John was focusing on was that transaction. Later on I understood that the performer has a unique function in terms of what I call this transactional reality which comes from being in the presence of the work: that the interpreter/player of the music becomes part of that. Until then, I had really thought of the interpreter as a secondary creative person. I never thought he was on the same level with Beethoven or Bach. But after I had spent some time thinking about all that and began playing myself, I saw that the activity of playing was itself a creative activity and I came to have a very different idea about performance and also a different idea about the function that performing can have for the composer.

The activity of the listener is to listen. But it's also the activity of the composer. If you apply that to the performer, what is the performer actually doing? What is the proper attitude for the performer when he is playing? The proper attitude is this: the performer must be listening to what he's playing. And this is far from automatic. You can be playing and not pay attention to listening. It's only when you're engaged with the listening while you're playing that the music takes on the creative unfolding, the moment of creativity, which is actually every moment. That moment becomes framed, as it were, in a performance. A performance becomes a formal framing of the activity of listening, and that would be true for the player as well.

When I'm playing a concert now, I know that what I must do is to listen to the music. Now, here are some curious questions: When does that listening take place? Does it take place in the present? Do you listen to what you're playing, or do you listen to what you're about to play? I don't really have a prepared answer, except my intuition is this: the best-case situation is that I'm playing, and I'm almost hearing what I'm about to play. And my playing follows that image. In other words, it's like a shadow that precedes the object, rather than follows it. If you start playing the piano, and you're thinking *that* way, and you're hearing *that* way, you have a very different engagement. You're not just playing a piece because you practice it—there are pieces that your fingers can play for you, everybody knows that. You can train your fingers so that you can even find yourself thinking about something else, which is not a good way to perform. The ideal way of performing, to my way of thinking, would be when the performer allows the activity of playing to be shaped by the activity of listening, and perhaps even by the activity of imagining listening.

ALBERT FINE DIED IN 1987, one of the early victims of AIDS in those years when there was no known treatment. His musical legacy was left in the hands of others, like myself, who were inspired and deeply influenced by him. He was trained as a conductor at Juilliard, but I saw him conduct only once and, then, with a student ensemble.

Albert once described his whole life to me in the following sentences: "I began playing the clarinet when I was six, the piano when I was eight, composing when I was twelve, conducting when I was sixteen. Then I gave up conducting, then composing, then piano and finally clarinet." Such a strange story in one way, but in another way, genuine and all too believable.

Albert's death was a personal tragedy for all his friends. It was also part of what was really a worldwide tragedy. The world I knew well and lived in and worked in—the world of dance and music theater, as well as the world of painters, composers, writers, and performers of all kinds—was decimated. During the 1980s it was as if the loss of life and talent were an unrelenting wave of pain and death to a degree that was literally unimaginable to most of us. I will give a simple list of irreplaceable artists whom I knew well, and some of whom I worked with. It is meant to represent the depth and breadth of the disaster and, though small, might help to illustrate:

Albert Fine, musician and artist, died 1987, age fifty-four
Robert Mapplethorpe, photographer, died 1989, age forty-two
Charles Ludlam, playwright/director/actor, died 1987,
    age forty-four
Ron Vawter, actor, died 1994, age forty-five
Jack Smith, filmmaker/playwright/actor/performer, died
    1989, age fifty-six
Arthur Russell, composer/musician/performer, died 1992,
    age forty
David Warrilow, actor, died 1995, age sixty

I was personally close to four of them—Mapplethorpe, Fine, Russell, and Warrilow—sharing music and music projects together. I also knew Ludlam, Smith, and Vawter, but did not work with them. The quality of their work impressed me and had become part of the downtown theater landscape where I thrived. No doubt, if you asked anyone working in the arts during those terrible years, they would give you seven completely different names. The amount and depth of the talent lost was continuous throughout every day, week, and month of that decade. It was as if a reign of terror had been inflicted on a generation—really, it was cross-generational— of performers and art makers. It was a catastrophic time, for sure. Slowly, slowly, medicine and therapies began to appear to ease the worst of those days, and now, AIDS seems far less the death sentence it once was.

The AIDS epidemic blunted the tremendous surge of the fifties, sixties, and seventies, which had been an incredible period of sustained growth and innovation in the arts. It could not have been otherwise. Too many artists and too much talent had been lost to the disease. The loss of idealism and energy that came with the lives lost became a decisive fact. The gay community suffered most heavily. Progressive art-making has always been the haven for non-conformists and innovators, and not surprisingly the gay community has contributed splendidly and with terrific commitment to the arts.

In books of this kind, stories about talented and clever, famous and charismatic people are expected. Yet, some of the most important people to us may never have lived long enough to become famous or generally known. And perhaps they didn't care for that kind of fame anyway. Leaving that aside, I knew so many people who died too young, and not only from AIDS, though sometimes it could have been that. John Rouson, Ray Johnson, the writer Kathy Acker, the artist Gordon Matta-Clark, and many more were like that for me. Some readers may have heard of some of them, but others remain entirely unknown. I do miss them all the same.

AT THE END OF EACH ACADEMIC YEAR Juilliard gave out prizes to its students. As there were very few composers in that department—eight at the most—and as there were numerous annual prizes set up by former students and successful musicians, it was almost a cinch to get a prize or two. That meant $500 to $1500 every May or June. I suppose we were meant to use the money to allow for a summer of work and practice, but I didn't always do it that way. At the end of my third year as a full-time student, when I won a $750 prize, I immediately went to a BMW motorcycle shop in the Eighties on the West Side and bought a used BMW R69 500-cc motorcycle, all black and, though used, in great shape. I must have learned to drive it on my way home that very day. I don't remember ever having any lessons. For me, the bike offered a quick way of getting around the city and also a recreational escape from the intense job of preparing for an uncertain future.

I was living in Chinatown by then and I had a basement in the tiny house I rented. It was really only two rooms, one on top of the other and a basement big enough for the bike. I found a wide, heavy wooden plank that I would lay down on the basement steps that led to the sidewalk. I would start the bike in the basement and leave it running in neutral, then run up the steps to the sidewalk to make sure it was clear of pedestrians, then run back to the bike and ride it up the plank to the sidewalk, park it at the curb, and go back to lock the basement door. From there I drove to West Street and onto the West Side Highway. I could get to the 125th Street exit to Juilliard in twenty to twenty-five minutes.

Some of my Juilliard friends had also taken up an interest in motorcycles, and during the academic year, we kept our bikes in shape with fairly regular evening runs from 125th Street in Manhattan to Coney Island. The route was highway all the way to Ocean Parkway—West Side Highway, the tunnel to Brooklyn, and then the Belt Parkway. Except when there was snow or ice on the road, we made the trip all through the winter, though, with the wind in your face, it could be quite cold. Once in Coney Island, we would stop at Nathan's near the boardwalk and park our bikes with the other motorcycles that lined the curb. On many nights there could be fifteen or twenty bikes parked there. Everybody had a hot dog and a Coke but me—I had a knish and a Coke because I was already a vegetarian by then. The way out was maybe thirty-five minutes, max. Then, a brief walk on the boardwalk after our stop at Nathan's and the return ride would bring our outing to less than two hours. The regulars were Peter Schickele, Bob Lewis (a Russian language major at Columbia but practicing to become a professional oboist), and me. Sometimes we were joined by John Beal, an excellent double bass player, then a student at Juilliard.

We mainly had German bikes but there were a few British (BSAs) and Italian (Moto Guzzis) bikes among us. For no particular reason, no Harleys. But for sure the BMWs were great road machines. Nothing could be better for the long flat American highways than a BMW 500-cc or 600-cc. I made the cross-country trip—New York to San Francisco, out and back—twice in the next two years. Going out I favored the northern route—the turnpike from New York to Chicago and then pretty much Route 80 straight across Iowa, Nebraska, and Wyoming (staying on Route 80) then heading down through the top of Utah, straight across Nevada on Route 40 and, finally heading south for San Francisco.

The way home was a little different. We called it the southern route. We would pick up Route 70 just east of Los Angeles and stay on that through Arizona, New Mexico, and the panhandle of Texas. Then we headed northeast on Route 66 through Oklahoma and into St. Louis. Starting from Route 40 out of St. Louis, we would drive northeast until connecting with the Ohio, Pennsylvania, and New Jersey turnpikes. I made the journey with Michel for the first time in 1962 and the second time in 1963 with my cousin Steve.

On those long drives we always wore helmets, leather jackets, and boots, because if you fell down and you were in your shirtsleeves, you could lose the skin off your arms. The leather jacket was offered as a sacrifice to the demons of the asphalt streets that were waiting to devour you. Same thing with the shoes: the boots were to protect your ankles and your legs. If you went down and you ended up with a bike on top of you, which could happen, the leather boots would protect your feet. It would have been crazy not to wear the gear, and we weren't crazy people. We liked riding bikes, but we were going fifty, sixty miles an hour on the highways. Basically, you're traveling through space on nothing, really, and if the bike goes down and you go hurtling off by yourself into the ditch, you better have the right clothes on. We didn't even consider not being equipped like that.

I only went down twice during those years, both on wet highways, and, luckily, just sliding into a ditch. The bike was not so big and, with a little help, I pulled it out and, in a few minutes, was on the highway again. We would ride for about two tanks of gas. You stopped and filled up once and you went another two hundred miles, so you could do about four hundred miles in a day. That could be about six or eight hours.

On the Road by Jack Kerouac had just been published, in 1957, and we all had read it and no doubt were inspired to make the journey ourselves. You got a sense of the vastness of the country from the extreme distances that you had to travel. The *huge* lacunae—hours and hours and hours of empty landscapes—and the power and the beauty of the American landscape were what we were involved with, much more than the kind of people that Kerouac was writing about. His book is full of interesting characters, but that's not what happened for us. We weren't interested in having those kinds of experiences, we were out and abroad in America, consuming the country visually and experientially by driving through it.

On the way out we would stay in the little hotels that follow the Pacific Northwest Railroad. They were always near the train station and so were easy to find. A completely clean, decent room could be had for ten or fifteen dollars a night, or we would just stay in the town park. In those days, every Midwestern and Western town had a park, and when we came to a small town, we found out the best thing to do was to go to the police station and say, "We're traveling across the state and we camp at night—where do you recommend we stay?"

They would say, "It's good that you came and told us you're here. Just go to the town park. No one will bother you there."

The southern route on the return wasn't so easy. The deserts were cold at night and not as inviting, but Route 70 had plenty of little motels, gas stations, and diners. Going out we would take two days to get to Chicago, two or three to get to the Rockies, and from there about two days to get into San Francisco—six or seven days in all and the same thing going back.

I HAVE SO FAR WRITTEN ABOUT TWO important threads that were central to my learning before I went to Paris. The first was the downtown world of art and performance. The second was the uptown conservatory world of Juilliard. The third thread was no less significant for me.

During the spring and summer of 1957, when I was working at Bethlehem Steel, I would have intense periods of less than an hour when I was weighing and recording the nails produced in the nail mill. In between I would sometimes have two hours or so while I waited for the bins to fill up again. During that five-month period I read all the works of Hermann Hesse that were available in English. These included *Siddhartha, Steppenwolf, Journey to the East*, and *The Glass Bead Game*.

The late 1950s produced an important literary and cultural moment in time. As I mentioned, *On the Road* was published in 1957, with Cage's *Silence* coming in 1961. I knew the Kerouac and Cage books almost from the day they were published, and I was far from alone in reading Hesse, who had won the Nobel Prize for Literature in 1946. These were all staples of the beat generation poets, readers, and activists. And, in their own way, they were also deeply connected to the music world of the time.

I want to go over this literary background because it is essential in understanding the intellectual and emotional world in which I lived. Alfred Korzybski and Immanuel Velikovsky (the iconoclastic thinker who wrote *Worlds in Collision* and *Earth in Upheaval*) were authors, for example, whom I read while still only fifteen or sixteen. By 1957 I had become an avid reader of Kerouac, Allen Ginsberg, William Burroughs, and Paul Bowles. The work of Hesse, a Swiss German writer, had, however a huge, though generally unnoticed, impact on the young Beats.

It was a time of awakening. The culture encouraged you to make a profound change in your life through the way you saw the world. The reason Hermann Hesse was so interesting was his vision of a transcendental life. He was in between the East and the West, and he was talking about a path, a way of life, that took you beyond the visible world.

Up against the suggestions of transformation and transcendence to be found in Hesse's work, there were only two other European movements worth acknowledging. The first was led by the existentialist writers, known popularly through the writing of the French authors Jean-Paul Sartre and Albert Camus. Their work was heavily nihilistic and oddly narcissistic, and these sentiments simply did not play well to the aspirations of a new and powerful generation of Americans who came up after World War II. Their books struck me as full of self-pity and despair at the meanness of their lives and their inability to find value therein, and my generation was impatient with all that. Though they were known and even somewhat admired, they were, like the romantic but gloomy films of Ingmar Bergman, simply too dark and hopelessly lost for the new American spirit that was about to make itself known.

The second and quite formidable influence following the war was the work of Bertolt Brecht, often accompanied by the neo-cabaret music of Paul Dessau and Kurt Weill. I don't mean to be dismissive of these composers. They are both wonderful, and very little theater music today can match the expressivity and power of their music. I am referring to their largely mannerist style, which, though very popular, sets a limit to its emotional range. In any case, Brecht, in my opinion, was largely misunderstood. His idea of epic theater was always fundamentally political in nature. His main characters in *Mother Courage* or *Rise and Fall of the City of Mahagonny*, for example, were not meant to be heroic figures, but poor, lost victims to the unfeeling power of a capitalistic state. Brecht, who died in 1956, never lived to see the failure of his own Communist ideology as it played out in Eastern Europe and China. It's a strange irony that his most popular works in the States, *The Threepenny Opera* and *Mother Courage*, themselves ironic in nature, are now presented as triumphs of the human spirit. I truly don't think that was what Brecht had in mind.

The more radical authors—in particular, Jean Genet and Samuel Beckett—were a different matter altogether. I would get to know their work much better in Paris, but I had already been reading them in New York. By the end of the 1950s I already knew Beckett's novel trilogy of *Molloy*, *Malone Dies*, and *The Unnamable*, and his plays *Waiting for Godot* and *Endgame*.

What I liked about Genet, author of *Our Lady of the Flowers* (a novel) and *The Balcony*, *The Blacks*, *The Maids*, and *The Screens* (plays), was his exuberance and his complete disdain for all things conventional. There was a vitality in his writing that appealed to me, and it was certainly true as well of Beckett, an Irish writer who was the most dire, the very grimmest of the modernists, but even so, had a joyfulness about him. What you found in Beckett that was so refreshing was a clearing of the decks. He wasn't interested in any kind of artifice or pretense at all. What you ended up with was a joy in his writing that I *loved*. It was also very, very funny. What I embraced was the way he swept past the cobwebs of so-called modernism and just got rid of it. Dumped it. Cleaned the table off and said, "Okay, what's really here?"

In spite of my constant reading, I wasn't a literary person. I didn't study books and I didn't take courses in literature. I pursued literature as a personal refreshment. My opinions didn't need to be authenticated or verified by anyone else. I read books for pleasure and their transformative power.

For me, Beckett's and Genet's worldview was much closer to Hesse's—being more radical in intent and closer to Hesse's ideas of transformation and transcendence. Though there was a strong political dimension to the Beats' activism, it was, at heart, a philosophy of "going beyond" the ordinary world and, at its root, a strategy for transformation. As Hesse is not read much these days, the impact on young people some fifty to sixty years ago may be largely unknown. But missing his profound impact on that moment is missing a vital part of that story. And that is my story as well.

Michel and I were very much in the sway of these ideas, so fresh at the time. We were eager to make them an active part of our lives, to begin our own "journey to the East." Accordingly, we decided to take up the study of yoga. The problem was that in 1958 there were simply no public yoga studios in New York, let alone reliable teachers of any competence. From time to time, starting after the World's Parliament of Religions in 1893 in Chicago, where Swami Vivekananda had created a sensation with his opening speech, there had been visiting swamis and yogis in North America. But few schools had emerged, and no reputations had been established. Better known, perhaps, was

Yogananda, whose *Autobiography of a Yogi* appeared in 1946. It was a wonderfully accessible book but, again, in terms of a wide audience, largely unknown at the time. However, it is probably Yogananda's book that Michel and I had read and had led us to search for a practicing yogi in New York.

Finally, after having had no success in finding such a teacher, I had the idea to look in the white pages of the New York City telephone book under the letter *Y.* There we found one entry—Yogi Vithaldas! We called him, made an appointment, and a few days later were at his apartment door in a high-rise on the Upper East Side. We had no idea what to expect. "Yogi" at that point was just a word to us. We had no idea what a yogi did or how or where one might live.

Yogi Vithaldas answered the door, a man in his late forties, barefoot and in loose-fitting Indian-looking clothes.

"Ah, my *chelas* have finally arrived," he said when we walked in, greeting us with open arms.

Chelas means "students" or "followers," but Michel and I didn't know that at the time. He marched us into his living room and gave us our first yoga lesson on the spot. In time I came to realize that his clients were mostly Upper East Side ladies looking for an exercise program, so he was delighted to have us as his students.

It was a decisive meeting. We both now had a yoga program we followed every day. Yogi Vithaldas was a teacher of hatha yoga—the yoga *asanas* or positions—which was the only branch of yoga most people would have known about. After our lesson, he invited us into his kitchen and begun instructing us in vegetarian cooking. My conversion to a vegetarian diet was immediate, and it has been a cornerstone of my personal life ever since. Only years later did I discover that Yogi Vithaldas was the main yoga teacher of the famed violinist Yehudi Menuhin.

My second teacher was Dr. Ramamurti S. Mishra from India, who was at that time a resident psychiatrist at Bellevue Hospital. Dr. Mishra taught raja yoga, normally taken to mean, simply, meditation. Michel, Albert Fine, and I found him a few years later, perhaps 1960, teaching a small class in his apartment on Twenty-Eighth Street near Second Avenue. He was quite a handsome man, in his forties, extremely gentle, with dark penetrating eyes. The classes were detailed instruction on meditation practices, bringing the mind to a point of clarity and steadiness. Mantric repetition of sacred syllables and *pranayama* (breathing exercises) were a normal part of the training. I was not a close student of his, but I was a regular one. Albert, on the other hand, became very involved with Dr. Mishra as his meditation teacher, and he went much further in his practice than either Michel or I. Soon Albert was going on solitary retreats in the country, and sometimes, in New York, he observed long periods of absolute silence.

Some years afterward, I came across Dr. Mishra's book *The Textbook of Yoga Psychology*. Firmly based on Patanjali's *Yoga Sutras*, I do not know of a better book or a more fully outlined account of the Indian yoga system and its philosophy. Just remembering his intelligence and the depths of his attention to his students is a warm thought for me.

AS MY YEARS AT JUILLIARD WERE WINDING DOWN, I told Albert I wanted to go to Paris and study with his teacher, Nadia Boulanger. He agreed that it was an excellent plan, and he offered to write a letter recommending me. I applied for, and received, a Fulbright to study with her in Paris, but at the same time I had applied for a fellowship from the Ford Foundation under a program for newly graduated composers to become "composers in residence" in U.S. public school systems. The program involved no teaching by the young composers, only composing for the orchestra, vocal ensembles, and instrumental chamber groups in the school system.

About ten young composers a year were awarded these positions in cities like L.A., Pittsburgh, Seattle, and St. Louis, and when I was chosen I decided to accept. The Fulbright committee informed me that I would have to reapply, and the next year I did just that, reapplying for Paris while spending that academic year of 1962–63 in Pittsburgh.

I found a loft–living space on Baum Boulevard in a lower-middle-class to middle-class neighborhood not far from downtown. Pittsburgh reminded me of Baltimore. Both towns were close enough to the South that there was a strong presence of Southern culture, with Baltimore not that far from Virginia and the Carolinas while Pittsburgh was in close proximity to Appalachia. The cities were similar in size, and both had good schools and universities, large Jewish and Catholic populations, and Bethlehem Steel plants. Living in Pittsburgh revealed almost nothing to me that I didn't already know from growing up in Baltimore.

The city of Pittsburgh had an administrator for instrumental music and one for vocal music who were responsible for all the music in all the schools. I had just come out of Juilliard, and now I was given basically a school system with tens of thousands of children, a huge number. I wasn't teaching, I was only composing. There were orchestras all over the town, there were brass bands, there were string quartets, there were choir ensembles—they played everything. Being the early 1960s, this was the heyday of music programs in public schools. You could be a kid with not a dime in your pocket and you could go to a school in Pittsburgh—or, in fact, most big cities in the United States—and they would give you an instrument and you would start to take music lessons. Public schools in those days had instruments and conductors, and we had people coming out of high school and going right into conservatories. It was a tremendous time for music education in America. These days such programs have pretty much been gutted. Some public schools may provide them, but the money usually has to be supplied by the parents in order for music teachers to be hired.

In Pittsburgh, I wrote some music for children in grade school and some for high school orchestras. These were young people who could actually play. I wrote a huge amount of music when I was there. I usually completed a piece in three weeks, then I'd follow up with yet another piece. I would go to the rehearsals and performances, too, because that was part of my duties. I had a car and what I thought was a huge salary in those days, which was probably around $7000 a year—maybe $600 a month. But you have to remember, you could get a good apartment for around $80 or $90 a month at that time.

We never forced music on anybody. Stanley Levine, the administrator of instrumental music, would say, "There's a high school in South Hills and they've got a woodwind quintet. Could you write a piece for it?"

"Sure," I'd say.

Or I'd go to a high school football game and sit in the stands and listen to the marching band play the march I had written for them. At the end of the year we had a big concert, where all the music I had written was played. It was very satisfying. Here I was, twenty-six years old, and I was having a complete concert of my own music.

In the spring of 1963, near the end of my first year in Pittsburgh, I reapplied for the Fulbright and was awarded it a second time. However, the Pittsburgh school system asked me to stay a second year and I accepted. But before starting the 1963–64 academic year, I made my second cross-country motorcycle trip. In San Francisco I met up with my friend Jerry Temaner, whom I hadn't seen since our college days. Jerry was in the Bay Area visiting JoAnne Akalaitis who, like us, was a University of Chicago graduate.

When Jerry introduced us at a coffeehouse, I was immediately enchanted by this young woman. JoAnne was then twenty-six years old, very beautiful, and very, very smart. She was working in San Francisco with Alan Schneider, a charismatic new theater director famous for championing the work of Samuel Beckett in the United States, and who was leading a small company of young actors.

After barely thirty minutes of the three of us talking over coffee, I asked JoAnne, "Do you want to ride on my bike?"

She said yes, and we got on the bike, and we then drove up and down and around San Francisco's hills. By the time we got back to where we were having our coffee, she had told me that she was on her way to New York with some other actors.

"I'm going to be living in Pittsburgh," I said, "but I have the bike and I'll drive to New York and come and see you."

And that's what I did.

In fact, this was the first great romance of my life. It led to a marriage two years later in Gibraltar, our two children—Juliet and Zack—and, even after the end of our marriage, a lifetime of theater work together. In time, JoAnne's skills as a theater director and author would enable her to play a leading role in the new theater that would emerge in New York City in the seventies, eighties, and nineties, but already in 1963 both of us were working in the theater. I had been writing theater music and dance music since I was twenty, so I was very interested in the work she was doing. Within two years we would take part in forming our own theater company in Paris and be working directly with Samuel Beckett.

Once I got settled again in Pittsburgh, I commuted to New York by motorcycle. I would spend the weekends with JoAnne in her place in Little Italy, not too far from Chinatown, where she lived with her dog, a beautiful boxer named Gus. I did what I used to do in my steel mill days in Baltimore, when I used to work a swing shift, putting in ten days in a row and then having four days off. I thought that was an admirable schedule. I could get to New York in about eight hours, and then I had two full days there before I had to head back. JoAnne and I went to the theater and movies and hung out with my friends John Rouson and Michel Zeltzman, who thought JoAnne was fantastic. She and I were both interested in experimental theater, but at that time, in 1963, there wasn't that much to see. Many of the people who would become part of the explosion of theater and performance in New York as the sixties progressed were still too young and hadn't yet begun to do their work.

At the close of my second year of residency in Pittsburgh, in the spring of 1964, I reapplied for the Fulbright and was awarded it a third time. Now it was time to go to Paris. As JoAnne and I had become serious about each other, I said, "I've got a fellowship to go to Paris. Why don't you join me there?"

"It's interesting that you said that, because I've been thinking about going to Paris. Peter Brook is there, the Living Theater is there, and Grotowski is nearby in Poland."

These innovators in the world of theater—Jerzy Grotowski, the Polish experimental theater director and author of *Towards a Poor Theatre*; Brook, the English director; and the Living Theater, the experimental theater group founded by Julian Beck and Judith Molina in New York, but at that time working in Europe—were the models for the kind of theater JoAnne wanted to study and practice. At that point, she had already been working with her friends Ruth Maleczech and Lee Breuer. All three, who had come from Alan Schneider's Actors Workshop in San Francisco, were heading for Europe, and wanted to go to Paris. Genet was in Paris, too, and so was Beckett. Paris looked to us like the place where modern theater was happening.

At this stage, my commitment to becoming a composer was complete. The only risk I had was that I might die before I could become one. The immediate difficulty was, though my commitment was complete, my actual musical technique wasn't. In order to be able to produce work of any quality, I needed to improve my ability to handle some basic materials of music—harmony and counterpoint. Even after Juilliard, I still didn't feel I had truly mastered them. That's why I wanted to study with Nadia Boulanger. I felt that I needed an absolute paragon of musical technique to be my teacher.

I had put off the trip to Paris for two years. Now I was finally free, and I was setting out to do the work for which I had been preparing. I had a premonition that important events were on the way and that I was finally setting my feet in the right direction.

After taking my motorcycle back to the BMW dealership at Eighty-Fifth Street and Amsterdam Avenue and trading it in for cash, I was ready for the next big step. In the fall of 1964 I left for Paris.

BEFORE LEAVING THE STATES, I WROTE TO CARLISLE READY, A poet friend in Paris, whom I knew from New York. Carlisle had been close to John Rouson and they had sometimes stayed at my house in Chinatown. She had left New York before me and had since married Jonathan Nicole, an English painter.

When I wrote her I would be coming to Paris, she answered, "What a pity. We're just about to leave. By the way, would you like to buy the studio?"

I didn't even know what that meant. "What do you mean?" I wrote back.

"It's called a buy. It's a lease. In France, a lease can be bought and sold. You just register the legal documents at the *mairie*," she replied, referring to the town hall of that district (*arrondissement*) of Paris.

In short order, we came to an agreement, and when I arrived, I found my new lodging was an *atelier* on a little street in the Fourteenth Arrondissement, Rue Sauvageo, which has since been swallowed up by the new Gare Montparnasse. At that time it ran parallel to and just south of Avenue du Maine.

The Fourteenth was a marvelous part of Paris. It wasn't packed with tourists or students as was the nearby Sixth. It had very much its own character—domestic, but with artists' studios scattered throughout. I was told that Constantin Brancusi, the expatriate Romanian sculptor, once had a studio nearby, and that Samuel Beckett was still in the neighborhood. It was only a few blocks from the Gaîté subway, near the Café les Trois Mousquetaires on the corner of Avenue du Maine and Rue de la Gaîté, and a short walk to the big brasseries and cafés of Boulevard Montparnasse. The *atelier* itself had once been a small carriage house, then a garage, and had been finally made into a "stand-alone" two-room studio. The bathroom-kitchen was, even by my standards, a little primitive, but the main living room was big enough for an upright piano and a combined living room–bedroom. There was a coal stove in the large front room and a big window facing the courtyard, where I placed my desk. I was very comfortably set up there from September 1964 until April 1967, when I returned to New York.

It was in Paris where my formal training was completed, my professional music life began, and a number of very important friendships were made. A few months after I settled in, JoAnne joined me. Apart from the eight to nine hours of study that my work with Mademoiselle Boulanger demanded each day, JoAnne and I spent all our time together, absorbing the Parisian culture and language and working on theater projects, principally Brecht and Beckett in those first years. We were both free of professional responsibilities, and it seemed a time of almost unlimited growth and freedom.

Our main and always pressing problem was that we had very little money. The Fulbright allowed only 700 francs a month ($140). However, the *atelier* was practically paid for when I bought the lease. The maintenance costs were another $18 a month. At the beginning of the month when I got my stipend of 700 francs, we bought a couple dozen tickets for the student restaurants. These were scattered throughout the city, so even though the menu hardly changed, at least the location did. For 2½ francs (roughly 50 cents) you could have a meal (with almost no variation) of noodles, bread, a piece of camembert, a *quart de rouge* (a small carafe of red wine), and an orange. You could live on this regime, but it wasn't much fun. At any rate, we didn't use the tickets until the very end of the month when we were close to broke.

Throughout our stay in Paris, JoAnne was very energized and organized. My music lessons and language lessons were all paid for, and also, thanks to Michel, I had a good beginning with my French. I was not entirely fluent, but I could handle the language fairly well. I supplemented my knowledge with private lessons at the Institut Phonétique. JoAnne signed up immediately at the Alliance Française and within six months had quite a good working knowledge of the language. There was a large daily market nearby our house on the Rue de l'Ouest, and it wasn't long before she could negotiate quite skillfully with the vegetable, fruit, wine, and cheese merchants—not an easy task for any foreigner. We almost never ate out in normal restaurants, though there were some *prix fixe* restaurants where you could still eat for four or five francs.

Besides the student restaurants, the city of Paris provided all kinds of discounts for students, theater and movie tickets being therefore extremely cheap. The French government had a strategy, and a very good one. If you were a foreign student in Paris, you could eat, live in student housing and get a French education very cheaply. The idea was to attract young people from all over the world—Europe, Africa, Asia, Australia, and North and South America—to Paris, where they would absorb French culture, language, and general French points of view on politics and art. These young people would then go home taking with them a French bias about almost everything. Even today it is possible to find in Africa, Asia, and the Americas people, though mostly men, in positions of authority and influence with a true French education. And that certainly happened to me. My music for my entire professional life has been influenced by the French musical pedagogy. And I am sure I benefited from it.

There remained, however, another problem. As a foreign student in Paris it was very difficult to make friends among the French. Foreign students are a subculture—almost "untouchables" in French society. So, apart from the American and English theater friends with whom JoAnne and I worked, we mostly spent time with young people from Africa, other parts of Europe, and North and South America. Our common language was French. JoAnne and I did become very good friends with a man named François Kovaks, who had left Hungary in the 1940s. He had managed to escape from the Nazis when, as a prisoner being transported to jail, he evaded the guards and ran into the woods. Over a period of several months, he then worked his way across Europe to France. He seemed to me to have been completely integrated into French society, though he complained, somewhat bitterly, that after all his years in Paris, he was still referred to by his neighbors as *le Hongrois* (the Hungarian). It wasn't until the early 1970s, when I came back to Europe with my ensemble, that I made my first real "French" friends, Daniel and Jacqueline Caux, and was invited to their home. He was a music broadcaster at France Musique and she was a documentary filmmaker.

The mid-1960s were a marvelous time to be in Paris. The Nouvelle Vague (New Wave) cinema was led by Jean-Luc Godard (*Band of Outsiders, Pierrot le Fou, Masculine Feminine*) and François Truffaut (*The 400 Blows, Jules and Jim*), who were working then at a furious pace. Every few months, and often more frequently than that, there would be a new film playing in Paris. You could feel the excitement among the young people at the screenings. At the same time, Pierre Boulez, the French composer and conductor, was presenting the latest in European music at his "Domaine Musical" concerts, which were musical highlights of my years in Paris. I found many of these new works stunning, especially the music of Karlheinz Stockhausen, the German composer who had once come to Juilliard to meet with the composition department when I was still there. Just talking about his music, he hadn't come across well as a person. His self-importance was alienating to most everyone. However, when I came to know his music during the years when I was living in Paris, I found it quite easy to put aside his personality problems. In the presence of his powerful music, those issues just faded away.

I learned from that experience to separate the work from the social and even musical/political problems that artists sometimes bring with them. The never-ending insistence on the seminal, historical quality of the "dodecaphonic serial" school was easily overlooked. And in fact, this overstatement of their importance doesn't in the least take away from the very real beauty of some of their music. Writing about this now in the early years of the twenty-first century, we can clearly see that music and the arts have moved in a direction far different from what one might have expected thirty to fifty years ago. Still, the music I heard in Paris during those years was exciting, if not altogether so new, and retains all its qualities today, no more but no less. The way things changed during my professional lifetime is, in part, the subject of this book.

The Paris theater world had a great producer in Jean-Louis Barrault at the Théâtre de l'Odéon. He and Madeleine Renaud, his wife, presented *Oh les Beaux Jours* (*Happy Days*) by Samuel Beckett in 1964. It's a "two-hander," as it is called in the theater world—just those two on stage with a gorgeous set. Other works were produced there, more by Beckett and also by Genet. JoAnne and I were there during the premiere performance of *Les Paravents* (*The Screens*), Genet's play set during the French-Algerian war, and we witnessed an actual police riot in front of the theater at the Place de l'Odéon.

The TNP (Théâtre National Populaire) was also busy presenting more traditional work as well as the work of Bertolt Brecht, the East German playwright. Between the Théâtre de l'Odéon, the TNP, and other smaller companies in Paris, JoAnne and I were able to get a good idea of what was happening in contemporary European and progressive theater. This was so far and away different from the American "naturalist" theater we had grown up with—the works of Tennessee Williams, William Inge, and Arthur Miller—that this new theater was a kind of culture shock, and refreshingly so. JoAnne, along with Ruth Maleczech and Lee Breuer, was already moving in the direction of a new theater, much more in alignment with the works of Peter Brook, Grotowski, and the Living Theater, as mentioned before.

As part of our immersion in the European theater modernists, JoAnne and I went to Berlin to see the work of Brecht as produced by his original theater company with his widow, Helene Weigel, still at its head. In 1965, Berlin was in fact two cities. We took the train from

Paris and spent almost two weeks there (it must have been during one of the rare holiday breaks that Mlle. Boulanger allowed during my years with her). In any case we stayed in an inexpensive hotel in West Berlin and, late every afternoon, we passed through Checkpoint Charlie to enter East Berlin. The tension between East and West Berlin was very high in those days, and passing through that checkpoint could be quite scary. These were the days when people escaping from the Eastern bloc countries would routinely try to cross the no-man's-land between East and West Berlin. The East Berlin police were there in their sentry towers, eager and ready to shoot them down. It made a normal visit on a one-day pass feel very uncertain. But we persisted and, in a short period of time, saw four or five original Brecht productions that included *The Caucasian Chalk Circle*, *Mother Courage and Her Children*, and *The Resistible Rise of Arturo Ui*. There happened to be a production of Brecht's *Galileo* in West Berlin during that same time, and we also took that in.

While in Paris, JoAnne and I would go to London from time to time. JoAnne would take the train-ferry-train, and I would *auto-stop* (hitchhike) the train parts of the itinerary. *Auto-stop* was very common in the sixties. Many young people—students all—would travel throughout Europe regularly in just that way. Often JoAnne and I would be on the same ferry crossing the Channel together, then separate again for the last leg of the journey to London. When we arrived, we would find a bed-and-breakfast for very little money (not much more than a pound a night), and then go to the Royal Shakespeare Company (RSC) and queue up on the all-night line, which ended in midmorning when standing room tickets would go on sale at the box office. This most thoughtful and generous plan set up by the RSC allowed a limited number of students to see these productions for little more than a few shillings apiece. While in London we also saw memorable performances by Laurence Olivier in Shakespeare's *Othello* and in Strindberg's *Dance of Death*.

Our third theater pilgrimage was to the South of France, this being the summer of 1965. That first summer I didn't study with

Boulanger—she was in Fontainebleau, teaching a summer school program. We had August off, like the rest of France, so we put together a few hundred dollars, bought a wreck of a VW Bug, and drove south. First we headed to Spain to visit an American painter friend, Dante Leonelli, who had a place in Mojácar. His adobe house on the beach was primitive by any standards. I don't even believe there was running water in it.

After Mojácar, we continued our trip, driving west to Gibraltar.

"You know," JoAnne said, "we can get married here for five pounds."

We were both twenty-eight years old. Both of us had artistic agendas—hers as committed as mine. She was always very clear about her commitment to her life in the theater and her work in the theater—that was never in doubt. Both of us also took getting married and having children very seriously. I knew that there were sacrifices that would have to be made and I knew that we would both have to make them. JoAnne was not the kind of woman who was going to stay home while I went out to work. But whatever was going to happen, we were going to be partners—it didn't even have to be discussed. What we were talking about was sharing a family and working together. In the end, our professional relationship has lasted over fifty years.

We took our five pounds to the civil office of a Mr. Gonzalez, and that's where we were married. It only took about ten minutes. Mr. Gonzalez wore a herringbone suit with a tie, I was wearing the clothes I was traveling in—a light shirt, sandals, and jeans—and JoAnne was in a summer dress with sandals and sunglasses. It was a real marriage, with a legal Gibraltar marriage certificate. Afterward we celebrated in an inexpensive way—we had very little money and almost never ate in a real restaurant in those days, but that night we splurged with a meal and a little champagne, then we found a room for a few dollars, and that was our wedding night.

From Gibraltar we traveled back to France to see the Living Theater in Avignon. In Europe the company was known simply as "the

Living," a most appropriate name. Led by Julian Beck and Judith Molina, they were performing *Frankenstein*. JoAnne and I were bowled over by it. The work was written and produced collectively by the company, arrived at through a process of improvisation and editing. It was very much the way our own new company, just being formed, wanted to develop.

Frankenstein was an imagistic, stream-of-consciousness work that was lyrical, dynamic and, to our eyes and ears, completely fresh. We met Julian and Judith afterward. They were both around forty then, though the other members of the company were, generally speaking, far younger. Julian was tall, slim, and very alert. He had the air about him of a Talmudic scholar—bright-eyed and intense, but without the yarmulke. Judith was altogether different—short, round, and with a bristly, Afro-like halo of hair.

I'm sure meetings like this were common for them. Starstruck young people like us, willing to give up everything to be part of an ecstatic theatrical environment. For some it was a young adult version of running away to join the circus. JoAnne and I had not gone that far, but were pretty close to it all the same. Julian and Judith were warm and sympathetic as they listened to our dreams of a new theater company. In the end they encouraged us to go off on our own, which was what we had meant to do all along. I appreciated their kindness, even to spend that small amount of time with us. That kind of support, especially as given by the older ones to the younger, I found to be generally present among the new generation of experimental theater groups.

AFTER JOANNE AND I RETURNED TO PARIS, I sent my parents a letter telling them that we had gotten married. Even though I was from a Jewish family and JoAnne was from a Catholic one, I didn't think very much about it because my father's two brothers, Lou and Al, had both married Gentile women. Half of my blood cousins, those on my father's side, were Protestants.

In the return mail I got a letter from my father that was very brief and to the point: "You are not allowed to come into the house again."

I was shocked. Basically my father had said, "You can never come home."

I didn't say anything to JoAnne. I read my father's letter twice, and then I destroyed it. I thought that was the right thing to do, because after that I forgot the details and just retained the gist. I also destroyed it because I thought it was a letter my father would be sorry he had written. I wanted it just to disappear.

Thus began a long silence between my father and myself.

Silence can be a strange business. At the time, it didn't make sense. My father and I had been very close. I didn't know the reason, and I never could understand why my father didn't talk to me.

Nine years later, in 1974, I was living in New York. I had two children by then—my daughter Juliet, born in 1968, and my son Zachary, born in 1971. During all that time, my father and I hadn't seen or spoken to each other at all.

One day I got a phone call from my cousin Norman, who along with his two sisters and mother—Aunt Jean, my mother's sister—had lived upstairs from us on Hillsdale Road.

"It's time for Ben and Ida to meet their grandchildren. Come to Baltimore."

Norman arranged everything. When I got to my parents' house, Ben met the kids and immediately loved them. He always loved kids. He was happy, and relieved, to see me, too.

"Hey, kid," he said. "Let's go for a walk."

We got about halfway around the block before he said anything. "Look, you remember that letter I wrote you?"

"Yeah."

"Let's forget it."

"I already have."

That's all we ever said. We didn't discuss it. That was the whole conversation.

Two weeks later, I was back in New York. I got a call from my brother, Marty, saying that Ben had been running across the street in downtown Baltimore and had been hit by a car. He was in the hospital. He had been hit by one of those drivers who liked to beat the lights. He was sixty-seven, still a relatively young man even for those days. He just couldn't run as fast as he thought he could.

About three hours later, I got another call from Marty. Ben had died.

After our meeting, I had expected that we would be seeing each other more, but that never happened. Sadly, he never saw a public concert of mine. Had he lived two more years, he could have been at the Metropolitan Opera and seen *Einstein on the Beach*. After his death, when I went down to the store with my brother, I found that Ben was carrying my first album on the shelves. He hadn't said anything about it when we met that last time. He never said to me, "I have your record in the store." I was looking to see whether he was keeping up with new music, and there was *Music with Changing Parts*, the album I had recorded in 1971, on the shelf in the classical section.

Soon after my father's death, I began a psychoanalysis that lasted nine years, trying to understand why he had stopped talking to me. At a certain point I said to my analyst, "You know, I don't know what happened, but I don't care anymore. I've been talking about it for years and years and I'm bored with the whole topic. Let's just forget it."

My analyst was a Freudian, so he, of course, didn't say anything.

Many years later I was in Washington, D.C., to hear a piece of mine that was being performed by the National Symphony. Afterward, I was walking back to my sister's house with my cousin Norman as well as some of the younger children. My nephew Michael Abramowitz, my sister Sheppie's son, said, "Uncle Phil, I hear that you and Grandpa didn't talk to each other for a while. What was wrong?"

He was just fourteen or fifteen, and he was understandably curious.

"I really don't know," I said.

Norman, who was walking alongside us, said, "I know."

"What?" I replied.

"I know why he wouldn't talk to you."

"You know? How could you know this? Please tell me, because I have to tell you, I spent nine years in psychoanalysis trying to understand it and I never succeeded."

"I'll tell you," Norman said. "What happened was this. When your uncles Lou and Al got married to Gentile women, your mother wouldn't allow them into the house anymore. So Ben wasn't able to see his brothers in his own home. That was a big blow to him because he was very close to them, but that was the rule and they never did come to the house again. When you got married some years later, it was your father's chance to get even. It was as if Ben were saying that if he wasn't allowed to see his brothers, he was going to make sure that she couldn't see her son. When you married JoAnne, a Gentile woman, it was your father's turn."

On those Sunday mornings, when my dad would say to me, "Come on, kid, let's go get some bagels," he was actually using that time to go see his family. He always made up a reason why we had to leave the house, as if we were supposed to be at the store doing inventory or something else, but the real reason was that we were visiting his brothers. I knew that, but no one else did. I was the one my father used to take with him. My sister and brother rarely went. For some reason, he liked to take me along, and I, of course, liked going, and I got to know them all, my uncles and my cousins. But they never came to our house. It was clear that something was wrong, but I didn't know what.

What made my father's letter so incomprehensible to me, and probably why I didn't understand it until Norman's explanation, was that neither my father nor my mother had much interest in traditional religion. Atheism was a way of life in our family. As far as I know, my father only went to Temple twice—to see my brother and then me do the bar mitzvah rites. The fact is that the trouble in our family was not about religion. But it was the kind of dispute that sometimes happens within a family, and unfortunately it happened in mine.

Years later, in 1987, I wrote a violin concerto for Ben. I knew he loved the Mendelssohn violin concerto, so I wrote it in a way that he would have liked. In his actual lifetime I didn't have the knowledge, skill, or inclination to compose such a work. I missed that chance by at least fifteen years. But when I could, I wrote it for him anyway.

ONCE RUTH MALECZECH AND LEE BREUER arrived in Paris, our as-yet-unnamed theater company began to take shape. I was automatically the resident composer and we now included two other performers—Fred Neumann and David Warrilow. Fred and the rest of us were Americans, but David was an Englishman, bilingual, and the editor of a Parisian *Vogue*-type magazine called *Réalités*. He was an incredible actor, but I don't know if he had professional training. I think he had been an amateur actor in college. He and Fred had formed a kind of an American-in-Paris theater company at the American Church. They were going to be permanent expatriates, living in Paris and having their small English-speaking theater company. Ruth, Lee, and JoAnne, coming right out of San Francisco and Alan Schneider's theater, represented a cultural adventure that was unknown to them. They were very attracted to the intensity of the commitment to a pure kind of noncommercial theater—to an art theater. We were doing Beckett and Brecht but they didn't know that work. What they knew was commercial theater and movies, yet both of them eventually pulled up stakes and came to live with us when we went back to New York.

Fred and David had already found a livelihood in Paris, working in films as actors, doing *doublage* (dubbing English onto the lips of French actors in movies) or *figuration* (being extras in French films). A few hours' work would mean seventy-five francs, which, when you were living on seven hundred francs a month, seemed more than adequate. JoAnne and the others joined them and did quite well. Although I had no problem synchronizing my spoken words to the image on the screen, since I was not even an amateur actor I was only hired once for *doublage*. Still, occasionally I could get work as an extra. Those were my very first experiences working in film and now, looking back, I am very glad for it. I learned many things about filmmaking just by being a small part of it. Some were useful, others just curious. Years later, when in my fifties I began writing film scores, it all came back to me. One of the odd things I learned was that doing *figuration* was considered an actual *métier* (profession or craft). There were more than a few people in Paris who made a living doing only that. They usually had their own costumes and complete wardrobes so, when they were called for a job, they would show up all dressed and ready to go. Although I was a complete interloper in their world, they were usually quite friendly to me and, because I was a composer, considered me an artist, though a young and very poor one. That was one of the things I loved about France and the French. As an artist in that country, one was respected and routinely well treated.

I soon learned another of the not so well-known tricks of *figuration*. If the day's filming began with a crowd scene, and it usually did since that's why the extras were hired, the best thing was to not be in the picture during the first (or "master") shot. If you were caught in the picture, then you had to be in all the shots thereafter. If you were not in the master shot, then you could spend the rest of the workday in the canteen, drinking coffee and reading or even writing music if so inclined. Truthfully, it was dead easy *not* to be in the first shot. All the professional extras in their beautiful costumes were gently shoving their way into camera range. It's what they lived for. I never once ended up in the picture. Though I was paid at the end of the day, I still had to wait it out in the canteen. *Figuration* paid better than *doublage*, but that was the real price you paid—a day in the canteen.

Our little company began by spending an enormous amount of time on *Play* (*Comédie*), a work of Samuel Beckett. Our form of collaboration depended on collective work as well as direction by Lee and music by myself. The immediate by-product of this was to develop a personal connection to Beckett. David Warrilow became the main conduit for our discussions with Beckett. He was quite willing to work closely with one of us (David) in the exchange of ideas and direction, but he was not at all interested in meeting and talking with the whole company. In any case, Beckett actually lived in our neighborhood and actively participated with suggestions of his own.

As a company and individually, we were involved in Beckett's work from 1965 until well past his death in 1989. Among these works were *The Lost Ones, Mercier and Camier, Endgame*, and *Play*. Some were actual plays, others adaptations from his narrative works. He remained in touch with us and was aware of all of our productions of his work. Some years later, when we were all back in New York, Fred was adapting and directing *Company*, which would premiere at the Public Theater in 1983. I was asked to write music for the production. By then Fred had established his own relationship with Beckett and I asked him to inquire whether the author had any thoughts about the placement of the music. Beckett's reply, though perhaps puzzling, was quite precise: "The music should go into the interstices of the text, as it were." And that's exactly what I did. That particular piece of music—four short pieces for string quartet—was later published with the same name, "Company," and has been performed as a concert piece, sometimes with a full string section, countless times since then.

The most emphatic and long-lasting effect of the theater work I was doing in 1965 in Paris began with the music for *Play*. The play itself is the story of the love affair and death of one man, his wife, and his mistress. The story is told by all three characters—played by JoAnne, Ruth, and David—each with a strikingly different version of the tale. The telling of the story begins when a spotlight shifts from the face of one character to another. These shifts appear to be random in sequence and in length of time. We, the spectators, see only the heads of the actors appearing on three large funeral urns that are supposed to be holding their ashes. As the light falls on each character, he/she begins speaking as rapidly as he/she can, and each actor begins to tell the story of the triangle. Clearly, Beckett, who was always among the most radical theater writers, was in this work unmistakably "breaking the narrative," by using the light to disrupt the normal story line. In that regard he was close to, if not identical with, what the earlier Dadaists—and later on, the writers Brion Gysin and William Burroughs, who would take a narrative piece, cut it up with scissors, and then paste it back together again—were doing in making his art out of cut-ups. This jumble of plot and character produced an instant abstract art form, leaving the spectator with the problem (or privilege) of completing the work. Beckett, Gysin, and John Cage, with his 4 minutes and 33 seconds of silence—a strange family of artists working out an artistic strategy, in tandem with each other, probably unknowingly.

For me, the exercise of combining this theater work with a new music pushed me into what became my first really original music. *Play* itself provided no clue as to what the emotional shape of the music might be, and what the response of the audience could be. As the composer, I was thereby liberated from the necessity of shaping the music to fit the action, or even to *not* fit the action. I think that I had stumbled my way into a situation similar to the one in which the choreographer Merce Cunningham and John Cage found themselves during their collaborations—often making the dance and music separately, without a particle of reference between them.

I learned of all this later, but even so, I saw the situation then for what it was, and, considering my age and inexperience, I responded quite well and, perhaps, even elegantly. I wrote a series of short, twenty- to thirty-second duets for two soprano saxophones. Each instrument had only two notes for each segment, and they were played in repetitive and unmatched rhythmic phrases. The effect was of an oscillating, constantly changing musical gesture. I composed about eight or ten of these and then recorded them. From these short pieces, and allowing a five-second break in between, I strung together a composition that was the length of the play. The music began when the first light was seen in the play and continued until darkness had been completely restored. The volume of the music was low, but always audible. As it turned out, it worked extremely well in providing music aligned to the stage action, text, and lighting.

After the first series of performances were completed, I took the tape home and listened to it many times. I needed to teach myself how to hear the music. What I noticed during the run was that, from one night to the next, my experience of the theatrical event was substantially different, depending on how my attention was functioning. The epiphany—the emotional high point—came in different places, due to the disruption of the narrative. I had found the music that would fit with that, and that became the third element: there were the actors performing the text, there was the light, and there was the music.

The music functioned as an accomplice in triggering a moving epiphany. The way the play and the music worked together had become a strategy for tempering the attention of the spectator—making the attention solid and focused. In this way, the flow of emotion experienced by the spectator was both dependent on and independent of the theatrical event.

The musical solution I had found formed the basis of a busy stream of new music that I began to produce. The very next work I composed was a string quartet in which I applied the same technique of structure and discontinuity as the basis of the piece, but this time for four string parts. This was recorded as my String Quartet no. 1 by the Kronos String Quartet almost thirty years later.

Clearly this new music was born from the world of theater.

"If you're not a minimalist, what are you?" many have asked over the course of my career.

"I'm a theater composer," I reply.

That is actually what I do, and what I have done. That doesn't mean that's the only thing I ever did. I've written concertos, symphonies, and many other things. You only need to look at the history of music: the big changes come in the opera house. It happened with Monteverdi, with his first opera, *L'Orfeo*, first performed in 1607. It happened with Mozart in the eighteenth century, Wagner in the nineteenth century, and Stravinsky in the early twentieth century. The theater suddenly puts the composer in an unexpected relationship to his work. As long as you're just writing symphonies, or quartets, you can rely on the history of music and what you know about the language of music to continue in much the same way. Once you get into the world of theater and you're referencing all its elements—movement, image, text, and music—unexpected things can take place. The composer then finds himself unprepared—in a situation where he doesn't know what to do. If you don't know what to do, there's actually a chance of doing something new. As long as you know what you're doing, nothing much of interest is going to happen. That doesn't mean I always succeeded in being interesting. Sometimes I did and sometimes I didn't. But not surprisingly, I found that what was stimulating to me came out of trying to relate music to the theater work of Beckett. That would not have happened if I hadn't been working in the theater.

RAVI SHANKAR

DURING MY SECOND YEAR IN PARIS, I BECAME FRIENDLY WITH AN English photographer named David Larcher, a young man with tons of energy and a camera. I can still see him in my mind's eye, leaning out the back of one of the old buses in Paris with an open back deck, trying to take a picture of himself taking a picture of himself.

It happened that David got a job with a film producer to do the stills for a movie. That was routinely done to keep a running record of location, scenery, costume, and weather. It was a film being made by a young American, Conrad Rooks, titled *Chappaqua*—the name of a small town just north of New York City. One day David came to see me, very excited because Conrad had asked him to find a music person to help with the music production. What they really needed was a music producer, but Conrad—himself not much older than me and out to make his first film—didn't know any better. I must have looked okay to him, and I actually was. My spoken French by then was quite good, I could read and write music, and I knew something about the music that Rooks himself liked. I was hired on the spot.

The first thing Conrad did was to play an Ornette Coleman score that had already been composed for the film. I thought it was a masterpiece and said so, though I knew it might well mean that I would soon be out of a job. Instead, Conrad insisted that Ornette's score wasn't what he wanted. He had settled on Ravi Shankar to be the composer of a new score. It was an excellent choice. Raviji, as he was known to friends and colleagues, was becoming very well-known at that time through his long-term efforts to find a European and American audience. He had a strong working relationship with the outstanding violinist Yehudi Menuhin and was also beginning to work with Jean-Pierre Rampal, the French flutist. Furthermore, his recent friendship with George Harrison of the Beatles was becoming generally known, which led to him being recognized worldwide. Besides being a superb soloist in the great tradition of Indian concert music, he was also known as a composer who worked with both Indian and European musicians. And, finally, he had extensive experience as a composer of film music, though almost entirely of Indian films. However, his participation in the Monterey Pop Festival, the Woodstock Festival, and the Concert for Bangladesh hadn't happened yet, and the simple fact was that though I knew of him by name only, I had never heard his music or any Indian music—popular, devotional, or concert music—at all.

It was very common in the 1960s for Western musicians, even composers, to be completely ignorant of global, or world, music. It was certainly not taught in conservatories, though it was considered an interesting subject of study for musicologists—they called it ethnomusicology. Even in as prestigious a school as Juilliard there would not be more than a handful of relevant recordings. In the school's library there were some books by A. M. Jones, including his studies of African music that were published as early as the 1940s, but I don't remember anything as well-known as that in the field of Indian music. When I found I would be working with Ravi Shankar, I simply went out and bought a record of his—easy to find in Paris. At my first listening I couldn't make heads or tails of it. At twenty-nine, I was completely ignorant of any non-Western music.

Things were moving quickly with the film—Conrad was well past the rough cut, and he needed the music as soon as possible. Straight away I was off to meet Raviji at his hotel. He was forty-five years old, a strong handsome man, not big by Western standards but clearly muscular enough to handle the sitar, the famously demanding principal instrument for concert music in north India. He was bursting with energy and was delighted to meet me. He told me he had met Mlle. Boulanger and was very pleased I was her student. There were endless cups of tea and a lot of talking about music, but no concrete discussion of the score that we were about to record.

By the end of our first meeting, I learned that there would be no score. Indian film music was never prepared that way. Raviji expected to see a loop of film of each scene that needed music. Then, on the spot, he would compose the music on his sitar. My job would be to notate all the parts for the small ensemble of French musicians who would be sitting there waiting for their completely notated parts. Now, my first encounters with Indian classical music had been very recent and not very encouraging. I heard my first recording of Raviji playing a concert and I had no idea what he had been doing. It could have been a moment of panic, but instead I asked—begged, actually—if perhaps we could start ahead of time. We had a whole week before the first session and I hoped to get a handle on the job before the reality of the actual recording kicked in. Raviji readily agreed and told me to be at his hotel every day at eight a.m. and we would get started.

I was greatly relieved. But the problem wasn't resolved because, though I was there every morning at eight, there was a continual stream of friends and admirers, as well as tours and projects that needed his attention. They were lively and entertaining mornings, but nothing was accomplished regarding *Chappaqua*.

Finally, with no mornings left, I begged him again if we could get started. He, of course, agreed and asked me to be at the studio an hour early and we would have a little time together. I was there the next morning and Raviji was there, too, and not even very late. He spent the next forty-five minutes coaching me on how to play the tamboura, the stringed drone instrument that would accompany the music. He also assured me that, as he had worked with Western musicians many times before, he would retune his sitar from its customary F-sharp key, down a half step, making it F-natural, and therefore far easier for Western musicians. Soon the musicians arrived and arranged themselves just below the screen on which the film loops would be projected. It was an ensemble of nine players—a small string section and woodwinds. The plan was very straightforward: Raviji would view the segment that needed music, he would then play each instrumental part, one by one, and I would notate the part for each of the players. There would not be a complete orchestral score, only the parts the musicians actually played. I would conduct the players for a first recording while Raviji watched the film at the same time. After the ensemble was recorded, Raviji would record a solo sitar part, accompanied by Alla Rakha, his longtime tabla player (the tabla is a set of two hand drums that underscores all the music and is responsible for its rhythmic structure). I would accompany him on the tamboura. A good plan and it worked fine, once I had understood how to notate the music.

Alla Rakha was the one who caused me the most anxiety but also, in the end, provided the solution. The "problem" occurred with the very first piece we recorded. Immediately Alla Rakha interrupted the playback, exclaiming very emphatically that the accents in the music were incorrect, to which Raviji quickly agreed. I had already set the metronome to the tempo Raviji wanted and I began writing out the parts again, grouping and regrouping the phrases to get the accents the way they were supposed to be heard, a very tricky business.

Each time, Alla Rakha would interrupt and, shaking his head, say repeatedly, "All the notes are equal."

I then tried moving the bar lines around.

"All the notes are equal," he declared again.

By now the musicians had joined in and the session was becoming chaotic, with the players shouting and playing suggestions to solve the problem. In the midst of all this and in desperation, I simply erased all of the bar lines, thinking I would just start all over again. There before my eyes I saw a stream of notes, grouped into twos and threes. I saw at once what he was trying to tell me.

I turned to him and said, "All the notes are equal," and his response was a warm, big smile.

A few moments later I saw there was a regular sixteen-beat cycle that governed the whole of the music. Later I learned from Alla Rakha that this was called a *tal* and that this *tal* in sixteen beats was called *tin tal* and, finally, the very first beat of the *tal* was called a *sam* (downbeat). All this is something any world music class would learn at the beginning of the first class on Indian classical music. But learning it at such a public, high-pressure event gave it a special, unforgettable meaning. I didn't realize at the time the effect it would have on my own music, but at that moment in the recording studio on the Champs-Élysées, I now had the conceptual tools that were needed to carry out the work.

The rest of the week went by quickly. I notated all of Raviji's music for the players accurately, conducted them during their actual sessions and even contributed some wildly dissonant music (just bits and pieces) for places in the film that Conrad wanted to sound incoherent and scary. About a year and a half later, I would study with Alla Rakha in his private percussion class in New York City and come to understand in more detail about how the *tal* and raga (melodic system) work together, which is very much the way that harmony and melody work in traditional Western concert, popular, and commercial music.

It was altogether a wonderful and inspiring week with Raviji. During the breaks in the film-scoring work we were engaged in extensive discussions on Western modern concert music. His curiosity was deep and his musical intelligence so highly developed that he easily grasped the principles of harmony, tonality, atonality, and orchestration. In addition to all that, by the end of the week he was so fluent in the solfège system—whereby musicians, especially in France, can verbally and with accurate pitch sing a melody—he then could communicate directly to the players, though I was still needed to write it out in standard—though bar-less—notation.

I kept in touch with Raviji. Soon after working on the film, I was in London again on one of my short visits, and Raviji was there playing concerts in a club setting, which he didn't like very much. It was at the beginning of his time with George Harrison, which was very important to him, but there were also parts of the pop culture world that were anathema to him and which he never got used to. The casual drug use by young people particularly upset him. Sometimes he would lecture me about drugs, and I had to remind him that I was drug-free.

After the concert, I went to visit Raviji in his hotel room. He was sitting cross-legged on his bed and I was in a chair. I asked him the same question I had asked myself when I first began to compose, the question that I had long thought about and was most interested in what the answer would be.

"Raviji, where does music come from?"

Without hesitation he turned to a photograph on his bedside table. It was of an elderly Indian gentleman, dressed in traditional clothing and sitting in an armchair. Raviji folded his hands and bowed deeply toward this man.

"Thanks to the grace of my Guru, the power of his music has come through him into me."

It was a stunning moment. The simplicity and directness of the answer made a deep impression on me.

Over the next decade I spent a lot of time studying and experimenting with the ideas, new to me, that I learned during the time with Raviji. Some things very soon became incorporated into my music. When only a few years later, in 1968, I began writing for my own ensemble, I dropped completely the practice of composing a full score before writing out the individual parts for the players. I could easily keep a composite "sound picture" in my head without having to write it out. So even the longer, complex works composed in the early and mid-1970s were composed as individual parts that I handed out to the players. That included some very long pieces as well, such as *Music in Twelve Parts* and *Einstein on the Beach*. As a general practice, as these were all performance works for the ensemble, I would write out my own part first and then compose the other music or individual parts for the players. Later scores were made by other people who made a composite from all the parts. I am not alone in working this way. I suppose that could easily have been a Renaissance and baroque practice as well, though I don't have any solid information about when and where it might have happened. However, it is well-known that Schubert's *Trout Quintet* for piano, violin, viola, cello, and double bass was composed in just that way. It certainly is convenient for the composer, as it eliminates a whole step in the process (composing a "master" score), which may be unnecessary. I thought of the music I was writing in those years as being for performance or, perhaps, recording only. It never occurred to me that someone else would want to look at the score. It wasn't at all a matter of being overly modest. It seemed to me, as a practical matter, that all the effort of producing a score simply wasn't worth the time.

The second thing I brought away from *Chappaqua* was a new way of looking at possible rhythmic structures in music. I had seen right away that even complex patterns of music could be understood as groupings of 2s and 3s. Virtually any compound pattern can be reduced to a succession of 2-note and 3-note phrases. On reflecting on this recently, I see that Raviji's 2s and 3s are, in fact, a binary language and identical in structure to the 1s and 0s in a digital language. Not too long ago, I was in Zurich giving a public talk with the Indian tabla player Trilok Gurtu. I suggested to him that the long history of a binary musical language was a part of the tradition of today's Indian concert music. He understood and quickly accepted the idea.

REALIZED FROM MY FIRST MEETING WITH HER IN HER APARTMENT IN THE Rue Ballu that Mademoiselle Boulanger was certainly one of the most remarkable people I had ever met. I would know only two of the rooms in her house, but both had the imprint of who she was—a renowned teacher in the world of concert music, ancient and modern. Her waiting room was a small library with music scores and books lining the walls from floor to ceiling, and when I had the good luck to arrive early I would be free to browse through the music. Among the scores were any number of original manuscripts signed over to her by the composers. Stravinsky was prominent among them, and I remember seeing there the original piano score, written in his hand, of *Petrushka*. Stravinsky, I knew, had written three of the pieces—*The Firebird*, *Petrushka*, and *The Rite of Spring*—that changed the way a lot of people thought about modern music. He had given the score of *Petrushka* to her and she had bound it into a book. What I was holding in my hand was the first draft of the ballet that to this day is considered a masterpiece of music. It was a humbling moment.

There was also an abundance of literature, many in first editions. I noticed, however, that there was not much there that was modern and certainly very little literature that came after André Gide, the renowned writer, or Paul Claudel, the poet. No Beckett and certainly no Céline or Genet. I suppose that would have been true of the music scores as well. She always dressed the same way—floor-length dresses, all handmade for her. She told me once that as a young woman she would submit to whatever was the fashion of the time. Then, in the 1920s, she found the style of clothing that suited her. From then on all her clothes were made especially for her and, frozen in time, never advanced past that period.

Her music studio was quite large. It had a small pipe organ and a grand piano. On Wednesday afternoon there was a class that was open to all her current students, whose presence was required. In addition, any former students who lived in Paris or happened to be there were welcome. It was customary for the room to hold up to seventy people on most Wednesdays. There would be one topic for the whole year. During the two academic years I was there, we studied all of Bach's *Preludes and Fugues, Book 1,* in the first year, and the twenty-seven Mozart piano concertos in the second. We were also expected to learn and be able to perform the "Bach prelude of the week." Typically the class would begin with Mlle. Boulanger calling out, without as much as looking up, the name of the one chosen to perform that morning. "Paul!" "Charles!" "Philip!" God help you if you weren't prepared or, even worse, not present. If she was expecting you to be there and you didn't show up, you probably would just have to leave town. She would say, "I think you should come to the Wednesday class. Of course, it's voluntary." But of course, it wasn't voluntary. You had to be there, and you had a week to get ready.

"Next week we'll be playing Concerto no. 21. Please be ready to play the third movement," she would add, and if someone said, "Mademoiselle Boulanger, I'm not a pianist," she would say, "It doesn't matter, play it anyway." People who were violinists or harpists or whatever would have to sit down and demonstrate that they had learned it. If they couldn't really play it, if the person didn't have a piano technique, the notes would still have to be in the right place. It wouldn't be a good performance by any means, but you were supposed to overcome the difficulties.

The first day I met Mlle. Boulanger, she ushered me into her music studio and took the handful of compositions I offered her. These were the very best ones out of the forty or fifty I had written in my five years at Juilliard.

She set them on the music rack of the piano and proceeded to speed-read her way through them, silently without comment—just very quickly working her way through page after page. Finally she paused and, stabbing one measure of music with her long pointed finger, proclaimed triumphantly, "Ah, this was written by a real composer!"

That was the last compliment I heard from her for the next two years. I left that day with an assignment to write a fugue and return in a few days. We hadn't practiced composing fugues at Juilliard, but I wrote one anyway, practically overnight. When I returned two days later, she glanced at my poor effort and set a very rigorous agenda for me. I would have one private lesson with her a week and we would begin with first-species counterpoint—that is, the very beginning of the study of counterpoint. Then I would come to the public Wednesday analysis class, another private lesson with her assistant, Mademoiselle Dieudonné (for Renaissance music, sight reading, and solfège) and, finally, every Thursday morning, a class with five or six of her other private students. During the private lesson, when time allowed, she would herself take care of training in figured bass.

I was expected, within the first month, to master all seven clefs, and thereafter I should be able to transpose music from and to any other key at sight. I accomplished this through brute memorization. I read music using all the clefs over and over again until it seemed easy. Moreover, another weekly exercise was to thoroughly learn a four-part Bach chorale in open score. That involved three or four clefs already, so only three clefs were left to learn from scratch, as it were.

The lesson in counterpoint also required a high level of preparation. For example, if the lesson was first-species counterpoint—and I was made to begin with that, all my Juilliard years and earned degrees notwithstanding—I was expected to bring in twenty pages of completed exercises for each weekly lesson. First-species would cover "note on note" (two lines of music). Normally, four weeks of exercises would be required before graduating to second-species, which introduced the practice of alternate entrances of lines. Then, you would continue the process with third-species, fourth-species, etc., until you reached eight lines of music, maintaining as much as possible the independence of each line. The baroque period is replete with examples of this kind of composing, Bach's *Art of the Fugue* being perhaps the most famous example. As a compositional technique, it continues to be used up to the present day, including the third movement of my own Symphony no. 3.

Studies in harmony, figured bass, and analysis would be carried out in similar ways, but with special exercises and emphasis depending on the topic. In Mlle. Boulanger's training there was no disconnect between foundation studies and professional achievement. Through her students, she changed the very way music was taught in the United States. Virgil Thomson had studied with her and famously remarked, "Every town in America has a drugstore and a student of Boulanger." Indeed, she had thousands of students, though perhaps only a handful became well-known for their music. Her enduring gift to American music must include the many fine teachers she trained, Albert Fine being one of them.

I would describe it this way: If you wanted to be a carpenter, you would learn how to use a hammer and a saw and how to measure. That would be basic. If someone said, "Here, build a table," but you had never done it before, you would pick up the tools and maybe you could build a table but it would be shaky and probably a mess. What Mlle. Boulanger taught was how to hold a hammer, how to use a saw, how to measure, how to visualize what you were doing, and how to plan the whole process. And when you had learned all that, you could build a really good table. Now, she never thought the "table" was itself music composition. She thought her training was simply about technique. Basically, when you left her, if you had studied with her diligently, you would end up with a toolbox of shiny, bright tools that you knew how to use. And that was a tremendous thing. You could build a table, you could build a chair, you could put in a window— you could do anything that was needed.

There were countless other musical chores I was meant to accomplish. For example, I was supposed to "sing" (from the bass up) all the possible cadences in all their inversions from any note. This little exercise, once learned, could take up to twenty minutes to accomplish when going at top speed.

Her students began coming for their hourly lessons at 7:30 a.m., and she would continue teaching straight through the day until early evening. Mostly Mlle. Boulanger spoke to me in English, which she knew perfectly from having taught in that language for fifty years. When she did speak to me in French, I mostly answered in English, as my French was not yet fluent. The worst lesson time was at 12:30 p.m., her lunchtime, and I had that time slot for a few months, until I found someone innocent enough to trade lesson times with me. The problem was that, even during her lunch break, she didn't stop teaching. She would balance her plate on the keyboard, which, of course, was in constant danger of crashing to the floor. While pecking at her food she would be reading and correcting the counterpoint exercises on the piano's music rack. Though she worked at being kind and considerate, the effect was of a powerful musical personality who stayed pretty much in the range between intimidating and terrifying. She was not a tall woman, but to us she seemed tall. She was slight of build but she was *physically* very strong. Mlle. Dieudonné was quite the opposite: she was a round woman, and a more gentle personality, but relentless in her efforts to improve my skills in score reading, sight reading, and ear training. She gave me things to do and she insisted that I do them. She was very firm about it, but she wouldn't assault me verbally for being lazy and wasting her time with my lack of attention. I was never scolded by her, but I could definitely be scolded by Mlle. Boulanger.

For sure, the most difficult class was the Thursday morning encounter (among ourselves, we referred to it as the Black Thursday class). There were six or seven of us expected each Thursday. We were convinced she had assembled both her best students and her worst into one class. The problem was that the pedagogy was so ruthless that we couldn't tell, any of us, in which group we should be counted. A single example will be enough. We all arrived one Thursday to find a simple melody written out in tenor clef on the piano. It was suggested to us that it was the tenor part of a four-part chorale. We were all familiar with the Bach chorales, having been expected to master one of them each week. That meant being able to sing any one part and play the remaining three. But this exercise was different. The first of us chosen would, looking at the tenor part as a reference, sing an alto part that would fit. Then the next one chosen had to sing the soprano part that fit with the given tenor part and the alto part which had just been sung, but not written down. Finally, the last one chosen had to sing the bass part that fit with the given tenor part and also fit with the alto and soprano parts, both of which had been sung but not written down. Mlle. Boulanger always said, before any of us tackled the bass part, that this was the easy one, since the notes of the other three parts had been already determined. Of course, it was "easy," provided you remembered, as well, all the other sung parts.

It goes without saying that all the rules of voice leading applied. No parallel octaves or fifths were allowed, either open or "hidden." The ultimate objective of counterpoint is to combine different voices in ways that preserve their independence, while at the same time following a strict protocol in terms of interval relationships. Parallel moving octaves or fifths, either open or hidden, are not heard as independent voices, but as functionally identical with each other. That destroys the sense of independence, whereas real counterpoint ensures it.

There were a seemingly endless series of exercises of this kind waiting for us each Thursday. The three hours set aside for the class never seemed enough. After the class most of us went to the café opposite Mlle. Boulanger's home for a coffee or beer. The amount of effort we had expended in the class invariably left us shaken and silent.

Apart from my three classes with Mlle. Boulanger and the one with Mlle. Dieudonné, I had a significant amount of work to do at home. For Mlle. Boulanger that was many, many pages of counterpoint each day, hours of work with figured bass and score analysis. For Mlle. Dieudonné there was sight reading and ear training. If I began at seven in the morning, when it was still dark during the Parisian winters, I would be quite busy until seven in the evening. I found time for the theater work in the evenings. That was also the time of day for going to concerts, films, and theater events. It made for extremely full days.

It was all the more difficult because of the very high standard by which we were measured. That was made completely clear during my first weeks with Mlle. Boulanger. One afternoon I arrived with my usual stack of counterpoint—at least twenty very dense pages. She put them on the music rack of the piano and began to speed read her way through them. At one point she stopped and caught her breath. She looked at me steadily and calmly asked me how I was feeling.

"Fine," I replied.

"Not sick, no headache, no problems at home?" she continued.

"No, Mlle. Boulanger, I am really fine."

But now I was getting worried.

"Would you like to see a physician or a psychiatrist? It can be arranged very confidentially."

"No, Mlle. Boulanger."

She paused for only a moment, then, wheeling around in her chair, she practically screamed at me, while pointing to a passage in my counterpoint, "Then how do you explain this?!"

And there they were—hidden fifths between an alto and bass part. I was deeply shocked by this whole maneuver. It was then quickly upgraded to a complete denunciation of my character, with special reference to my lack of attention, general distraction, and even my commitment to music. That was the end of my lesson for that day.

I went home and pondered the problem. What I needed was a method by which errors could be spotted before I got to Rue Ballu. I came up with a system where, when an exercise was completed, beside each "voice," I listed the intervals in all the parts below and/or above. I began with the bass and worked up to the soprano part. Now it was very easy to see what was going on. Two 5s or 8s in a row meant that there were parallel fifths or octaves. Two 3s, 4s, or 6s were okay. 2s and 7s rarely happened and could be avoided. The next week I went to my lesson with the usual stack of pages. But, besides the usual lines of music, the pages were filled with columns of numbers beside each vertical line of notes. I was very curious to see her reaction. And I was disappointed. She looked through the pages—all the music completed and numbered—and she said . . . nothing. Absolutely nothing. It was as if she had not seen the numeric proof at all. On my side I knew I had a foolproof system to produce a perfectly correct result. It seemed to me that, even in the face of her complete silence on the matter, I had no choice but to continue in that way. And that is what I did for the next two years.

When I arrived in France at age twenty-seven, I was older than many of her private students. I was aware that she gave me a great deal of work to do and was unrelenting in her demands that I make my very best efforts in her work. Our relationship was very intense. "*Il faut faire un effort*" ("It is necessary—mandatory—to make an effort") became her mantra for me and I heard it countless times. I knew that I had come late to her and she had made up her mind, it seemed, that I would come away from her with the best she could offer. It was never spoken, but I accepted nonetheless and worked unfailingly and daily to that end.

I never studied composition with her. Once I asked her whether that could or would be part of my training and she told me that she had such respect for composers and their vocation that she dared not advise them on their compositions. She was afraid, she said, that she might unintentionally misadvise or otherwise discourage them. So she concentrated on pure technique. Though, personally, I have to say that it was much more than that. Even as I admired her and was often terrified of her, I stubbornly refused some of her demands—those which seemed to me to be irrelevant to the true matters between us. Her younger sister, Lili Boulanger, long deceased, had been a gifted composer and winner of the Prix de Rome—given annually to an up-and-coming composer in France. Mlle. Boulanger produced a concert of Lili Boulanger's music every year in a church in Paris. All her students were expected to be there. I'm told she would sit at the door, silently counting their attendance. I was not in the least interested in the music of Lili Boulanger and I never attended the concerts. At my next lesson after the concert I said nothing about it at all—no lies, no excuses. And, on her side, she made no comment. There were numerous topics—social, political, religious—we never discussed, and I felt better for that.

Slowly, over those two years, her teaching began to take root in me and I began to notice a marked difference in the way I could "hear" music. My attention and focus became heightened and I began to hear music in my "inner" ear with a clarity I had never had until then, or even suspected was possible. I became able to have a clear audio image in my head. I could hear it, I knew what it was, and also—something a little bit more difficult than that—in time, I could hear something I hadn't heard before, and I could find a way to write it down. That is actually quite hard to do and a major accomplishment by itself.

There were countless times when she brought me to a deeper understanding of music. And, besides, she kept one more surprise for me, which came at the end of my second year. One afternoon in the late spring of 1966 I brought her a fairly long and complicated harmony exercise. She paused at the end of her usual reading and told me that the resolution of the soprano part on the tonic (or root) of the chord was incorrect. By then I knew the rules of harmony top to bottom (or, rather, bottom to top). I insisted it was correct. She reiterated that it was wrong. I persisted. Then, before my eyes, she performed an amazing feat of musical erudition. She reached behind the music rack of the piano, picked up an edition of Mozart's piano music (which just "happened" to be there). She turned to a middle movement of one of the piano sonatas and pointed to the upper note in the right hand. "Mozart, in the same circumstance, resolved the upper note on the third, not the tonic." I couldn't believe what I was hearing. After two years of solid application to the rules, they had suddenly been set aside. Well, not exactly. There was actually nothing wrong with my solution. It was just that Mozart's was better.

We sat quietly for only a moment and I understood, suddenly, that somewhere along the way, she had changed the point of the exercise. I had thought she was teaching technique—the how you "do" or "not do" in music. But that was over. She had raised the ante. Now we were talking about style. In other words, there could be many correct solutions to a musical problem. Those many correct solutions came under the rubric of technique. However, the particular way a composer solved the problem, or (to put it another way) his or her predilection for one solution over several others, became the audible style of the composer. Almost like a fingerprint. Finally, to sum this all up, a personal style in a composer's work makes it a simple matter for us to distinguish, almost instantly, one composer from another. So we know without doubt or hesitation the difference between Bach and Bartók, Schubert and Shostakovich. Style is a special case of technique. And then, almost immediately, we know that, beyond a shadow of a doubt, an authentic personal style cannot be achieved without a solid technique at its base. That in a nutshell is what Madame Boulanger was teaching. Not as a theory, because theory can be debated and superseded. She taught it as a practice, a "doing." The realization came through the work. Her personal method was to just bang it into your head, until one day, hopefully, you got it. That's how, in the end, I understood my work with her.

In fact, I was only a handful of years away from realizing a personal style of my own. When it happened, back in New York in the late 1960s (and even before, in Paris, when French colleagues refused to play my music because it was "nonsense"), I was often taken by surprise by the anger over the new music I was writing. I was widely considered a musical idiot. I found this unexpectedly funny. The thing was, I knew what I knew and they didn't.

This fixation on me as a kind of musical dunce continued well into the 1970s. Once, in 1971–72, when I was touring with my ensemble, I was playing in an art gallery in Cologne run by a very smart man named Rolf Ricke. There was a radio station in Cologne that was famous as a promoter of modern music—in fact, it was Karlheinz Stockhausen himself who was the guiding force behind the aesthetic principles of its programming—and I went there with a few scores for a hastily arranged meeting with a young music programmer. We were in his office and he sat nervously looking at my scores. Finally, in a gentle and really kind way, he asked me if I had ever considered the possibility of going to music school. Somehow, I wasn't surprised. I thanked him for his suggestion and time spent with me and left. Some years later I was back in Cologne, again performing with my ensemble, in a beautiful large new concert hall. I met that same music programmer again, but he clearly didn't remember our first meeting. At least neither of us mentioned it. And he liked the music—this time, very much. That kind of monkey business went on for years.

After my first year with Mlle. Boulanger, I had not been able to get a renewal for my Fulbright scholarship. As it turned out, Paris was such a sought-after destination that renewals simply were not available in the spring of 1965. In spite of this, Mlle. Boulanger had insisted that I stay on and continue working with her. She actually waived her personal teaching fee, which seemed enormous to me at the time.

"I won't be able to pay for the lessons," I explained.

"You don't have to pay for them. You just come and continue your studies with me."

"But how can I pay you back?"

"Someday," she said, vaguely.

A little over a year later, in the summer of 1966, my final months in Paris, I went by train every week to Fontainebleau for my lesson with Mlle. Boulanger.

Paris is very quiet in August and JoAnne and I were busy planning our upcoming India adventure. Before I knew it, early September had arrived and I went to see Mlle. Boulanger to tell her I was leaving. By then I was twenty-nine and really ready to leave my years of training and study behind. I was most eager to return to New York and begin my professional life in earnest. The India trip also had to happen before our return and I knew that leaving Mlle. Boulanger would be a battle, but I was determined not to be swayed.

She must have thought that I was coming that day for my usual lesson, so when I told her I was coming to say good-bye, she was surprised. I told her simply that it was time for me to go home and start my life again in New York. I didn't mention my India plans to her.

She stood up and there we were, face to face. "You have to stay with me for a total of seven years and, if not seven, then five, and if not five, at least three," she said very forcefully.

Standing up to her was no easy thing. But I knew what I needed to do. My student days had to be over. I had no intention of being one of those unable to leave, ending up at best teaching counterpoint in some *lycée* in Paris. I also knew that without her and what I had learned I would have not been able to do anything.

For years afterward, people would ask how she had influenced me. I had never studied composition with her, only basic musical technique, and that, endlessly. I have always replied to that question that since my studies with her, I have not written a note of music that wasn't influenced by her. I meant it then, and, even now, so many years later, it strikes me as true.

But at that very moment in September 1966, facing her in her music studio, I said, quite simply, "I am leaving."

Finally, after a long moment, she seemed to physically relax. She had let go.

To my complete surprise, she embraced me. I was not only shocked but moved. I saw a tear in her eye. Or maybe it was mine. I turned and left.

THIRTEEN YEARS LATER, IN OCTOBER 1979, I heard that Mlle. Boulanger had died at the age of ninety-two. She had still been teaching, though I am told she was almost blind by then. I had never been able to send her any money for those free lessons she had given me—in 1979 I was only then giving up my day jobs and beginning to work on *Satya-*

graha, and in the intervening years I hadn't made a nickel from my music.

I don't know whether she ever heard any music of mine. In 1971 and 1972 I was back in Paris playing pieces in concert halls—not big halls, but at least I was playing in Paris. I knew she would, if she came, be sitting in the middle of the first row. That was her favorite place to sit, and she would be unavoidably present. When I played in those places, I would look from behind the curtain at the first row to see if she was there, and I never saw her. I understood that she wasn't there.

I heard that someone asked her if she knew my music, and she said, "Yes, I know it."

It's hard to know what that means. I hadn't made the scores available, but I had made recordings by 1971 and 1972, and those recordings were circulating. I remember being in France, and they were being played on Daniel Caux's radio program on France Culture. So she could have heard it on the radio.

In the late 1990s, I was at the Maison de Musique, which was then a new venue on the north side of Paris. I had been invited to present *La Belle et la Bête*, a new opera, and after the performance, a young man came up to me and he said he had something to give to me.

"What is it?" I asked.

"I have some letters."

"What letters?"

"In the 1960s you applied for a renewal of your Fulbright fellowship and you were denied. There was no chance to get a renewal, but your teacher tried to get you one. Her name was Nadia Boulanger and she wrote a couple of letters and I have the letters."

"How did you get the letters?"

He mentioned something about working in the cultural division at the U.S. embassy.

"Can I see the letters?"

"Yes, I have them right here."

I looked, and I said, "These are the original letters. These aren't Xeroxes."

"No, you have the original letters. I made copies and put the copies back in the file. They're still there, but you have the originals."

I opened them then and there and read them. They weren't long. Nadia Boulanger was a very important and very famous person and they didn't need to be long.

What she had written so many years ago astonished me:

"I've been working with Mr. Philip Glass on music technique. My impression is that he is a very unusual person, and I believe that some-day he will do something very important in the world of music."

I was completely shocked. I had no idea. Of the many students she had at the time, I was convinced I was among the less gifted. She had given me so much work to do that I thought, Surely my case must be almost hopeless, and I can only be saved by a tremendous amount of hard work. True though that may have been, it was not what she said in the letters.

There were countless moments during my years in Paris when Mlle. Boulanger or Raviji passed on to me insights about music in particular and life in general. It was if I had two angels on my shoul-ders, one on the right and one on the left, both whispering in my ears. One taught through love and the other through fear. For sure, these were the two who brought my years of music training to its formal close. The informal close has never happened. Without both of them, I would not have been able to compose the music for which I am known today. The implementation and maturing of their music teaching has been the subtext of what I have done.

And, between teaching with love and teaching with fear, I have to say the benefit of each is about the same.

ON A TYPICALLY DAMP LONDON EVENING IN THE WINTER OF 1965–66, I found myself stuck without enough British pounds to pay for the train and ferry ticket back to France. The money exchanges had already closed, so I went to my friend David Larcher's flat near Notting Hill Gate to see if he could change some francs into pounds for me. David was happy to help and asked me to wait in his library for a few minutes while he got the cash together.

I still remember sitting on a couch in a room filled with books. I reached behind me and, without looking at the title, picked one off the shelves. When I opened it, I found myself looking at an astonishing image. The book was *The Tibetan Book of the Great Liberation* and the image was a painting (*thangka*) that was meant to illustrate some of the more esoteric passages of the book. What I saw was so powerful and beautiful that, in that moment, I knew I would have to learn everything I could about the painting and go wherever it might lead me.

"David, what does this painting mean?" I asked.

"Take the book home with you and read it," he replied.

The book turned out to be the last of four books published by Oxford University Press based on a translation by Lama Kazi Dawa Samdup, a Tibetan monk who made a living teaching English to children in a Sikkimese grade school. All four books were edited by

Walter Evans-Wentz, an American anthropologist and early pioneer in the study of Tibetan Buddhism who was responsible for the 1927 publication in English of *The Tibetan Book of the Dead*. When I left London that evening I had borrowed the *Book of the Great Liberation* and two other titles from that series—*Tibetan Yoga and Secret Doctrines* and a biography, *Tibet's Great Yogi Milarepa*. I made arrangements with David to have additional books related to the subject in a general way sent to me from London, and I also asked David for any other titles on the subject of Tibet that might interest me. David was pleased to help as he himself was most interested in anything related to the Buddhism of Tibet.

Even before this encounter, I had made up my mind to go to India. While I was working with Conrad Rooks, I had met the well-known and widely respected yoga teacher and spiritual master Swami Satchidananda, who, along with Vishnudevananda, was among the better-known students of Sivananda, the Hindu spiritual teacher who had founded the Divine Life Society in India in 1936 and the Yoga-Vedanta Forest Academy in 1948. By then I had eight years of Yogi Vithaldas's practice behind me, and I quickly added Satchidananda's program to that. He was Conrad's personal teacher and was happy to give me lessons, and I wanted to continue studying with him. When Swami Satchidananda invited me to join him at his ashram in Kandy, Ceylon (now Sri Lanka), I made a plan to visit India briefly and then continue on to Ceylon.

I had previously read books about all kinds of Indian yogis, including Ramakrishna, the Bengali saint (his teachings can be found in *The Gospel of Sri Ramakrishna*), and Swami Vivekananda, Ramakrishna's student. Now added to that were the books on the subject of Tibet available at that time, including works by Marco Pallis (*Peaks and Lamas; The Way and the Mountain*); Alexandra David-Neel (*Magic and Mystery in Tibet*); Lama Govinda (*The Way of the White Clouds*); Giuseppe Tucci (*The Theory and Practice of the Mandala*); and Theos Bernard (*Penthouse of the Gods; Heaven Lies Within Us*), whom I became especially interested in.

Bernard was an American, born in 1908 in Tombstone, Arizona. He mastered hatha yoga while still living in the States and then in the mid-1930s traveled to India to further develop his practice. In Kalimpong, a town near India's borders with Sikkim, Bhutan, and Tibet, he made contact with the publisher of the Tibetan Mirror Press, a Tibetan named Reverend Gegen Tharchin. Finally, after an intense period of study of the Tibetan language, he managed, with Tharchin as his guide and friend, to get all the way to Lhasa, the capital of Tibet. When I first came across his name, he had four books in print and David managed to find all four.

After my years-long actual exposure to yoga and once I read these books about Tibetan Buddhist practices, I expected that the kinds of esoteric traditions I was interested in would still be alive in India and in Tibet. I knew intuitively, or for reasons beyond that, that there were things to be learned in those places. JoAnne was up for the adventure, which would involve traveling across most of Europe and Central Asia. We knew that our eventual return to New York would involve, for both of us, a big investment of our time. We were in complete agreement about making our personal and professional lives in New York—we never considered anything else. In addition, we both knew that we would be starting a family soon and, if we didn't go now, a trip to India might not happen for a long time. The idea was to leave for India in the fall of 1966 and return to France the following April, at which point I could pick up my return ticket to New York and we would only have to buy one ticket for JoAnne.

Of course, there was no internet available in the 1960s, so for much of our planning we had to rely on information learned from recently returned travelers. For financial reasons and, more important, out of simple curiosity combined with a taste for adventure, we decided to take the overland route through Turkey, Iran, Afghanistan, and Pakistan. The crossing between Pakistan and India, we were informed, would be the trickiest part. In reality, that turned out not to be the case, though it would require a bit of waiting time once we arrived at the border.

Our informants on the best route and means of transportation were mainly young Australians. It was not uncommon for them, after their college graduation, to take a year off and travel to London. They would leave by boat from Perth, the westernmost Australian port, and find passage to Colombo, Ceylon, often on a commercial ship that could only accommodate a handful of travelers. From there they would make the short trip across the Gulf of Mannar to south India. Some of these Australian travelers would then go straight north to Nepal, where the hashish was almost black, pungent, and dirt-cheap. From there they could travel by bus and rail back to New Delhi, for a quick trip to Agra to see the Taj Mahal; then on to Bombay if they were continuing by ship (the Messageries Maritimes, for example) through the Arabian Sea; then up the Red Sea and through the Suez Canal, passing by Alexandria and landing in Marseille. That was the most traveled route from Australia, though not everyone wanted to go to Nepal, and it could easily be dropped from the itinerary.

We found out a lot from these travelers about travel conditions and possible problematic passages. For example, the Iranians were known for having a fear of long hair (this was the sixties, remember). Actually, it was more like a severe case of Beatle-phobia. This was still in the days of the Shah who was often chided for being too "progressive." When we left France in September, I had a new short, short haircut. Also, I didn't have a backpack, but carried a small suitcase. JoAnne was also dressed as much like a tourist as believable. Sure enough, when we did get to the Turkish-Iranian border, we were waved through. For the other young people entering Iran, there was a barber waiting for them. They either submitted to a haircut or were turned back.

Before leaving Paris, we went to the American Hospital in Neuilly, on the edge of the Sixteenth Arrondissement. We drove there on a small motorcycle that we had bought a few months earlier for a few dollars from an American student going home. It had been a great way to spend our last months in Paris. We passed by all the métro stops that we knew only as names on a map, and the city of Paris, having its glorious autumn, seemed to be showing off the best of itself. A long and sweet farewell. At the hospital, we got all the shots—tetanus, hepatitis, and so forth. In fact, we had so many I felt quite dizzy driving back with JoAnne behind me on the passenger seat.

I made only one significant purchase before leaving Europe—a small, inexpensive transistor radio. I planned to listen to music all the way across Central Asia and into India. This was soon after my work with Ravi Shankar, and my ears were, quite suddenly, wide open for whatever "new" sounds came my way. In fact, that was an extraordinary experience in and of itself. Starting in Europe, passing through Greece, and on the whole passage thereafter, I was forever tuning into whatever I could find on local radio stations. It seemed that every hundred kilometers or so, I could detect a change of some kind in the music that people there were listening to on a daily basis. The changes were slow but ongoing, providing a musical passage to accompany the local culture that we were passing through. It was all new to me, and all highly exotic.

First, we went down to Spain because the boat we were going to take would be leaving from Barcelona. We hitchhiked because we were saving for India and we weren't going to spend any money in Europe. To start off, we took the métro to the outskirts of Paris and stood on the highway that led to Bordeaux. It was very common for young people to travel that way, and we got picked up a lot by truckers. In those days, hitchhiking wasn't considered a dangerous thing to do. The consensus was that these were just young people who were trying to go home or go someplace else, so it wasn't difficult.

We would go as far as we could go and in the evening we would stop at a hotel. The hotels could cost as little as twenty francs—in those days, about five francs to a dollar—so four or five dollars. These were not particularly clean hotels. You'd hear doors opening, slamming, and shutting all night long. They were basically bordellos of one kind or another. During our time in Europe we had spent quite a few nights in places that were servicing a nocturnal crowd like that, so it didn't particularly bother us. But it didn't make for very good sleeping.

After two days on the road, hitchhiking all the way, we arrived in Barcelona. Although it was mid-September, it was still warm. We had just enough time to find the ticket office and buy our tickets for the boat to Turkey.

The ship on which we took deck passage traveled at night and anchored for the day at ports between Barcelona and Istanbul—Marseille, Genoa, Naples, Brindisi, and Piraeus. Deck passage was unbelievably cheap—about thirty-five dollars for the whole journey. It also allowed for a day in each port to get off the ship and spend eight to ten hours sightseeing. The ticket did not include any meals, so we would in any case have had to leave the ship in the daytime to buy food. The nights on deck were pleasant, and I loved approaching the ports each morning, seeing Genoa and the various other stops along the way from the sea for the first time.

On our days in these port cities we mostly went to see the places you didn't have to pay to enter, like cemeteries and cathedrals. The architecture in the Italian cemeteries was remarkable. Living in Paris we had visited the cemeteries like Montparnasse and Père Lachaise, with all the famous people buried there—chess masters, poets, musicians—but in Italy, it got even more flamboyant. Some of the tombs looked almost like chateaux on top of the plots of ground, with whole families buried in and under them. We would get off the boat and eat breakfast at a café, then have a late lunch in another café, then bring bread and cheese to eat and water and wine to drink for the night ride, returning to the boat at six or seven. At eight the boat would embark and we'd eat, go to sleep on the deck, wake up in the morning and be in the next city. It was comfortable. It was still summertime and the Mediterranean doesn't have big swells. We were traveling with other young people, most of whom were going home to Turkey, Pakistan, or India.

When we stopped in Piraeus, we traveled into Athens to see the Parthenon, and we also went to the theater at the base of the Acropolis where I later would play many concerts. We were in the land of Homer and it was, for me, absolutely thrilling to be there. We knew the history of Greece because we had studied it, so we had an academic's memory of these places, which were literally the cradle of Western civilization. We felt we had inherited more from the Greeks than from the Romans, though, in fact, I discovered later, when I was working on the opera *Akhnaten*, how much the Greeks had borrowed from Egypt. But that wasn't emphasized very much in my education. I learned that from my own reading.

Some years later, when my sister Sheppie's husband Morton Abramowitz was the ambassador to Turkey, Allen Ginsberg came with me and some other friends on a tour of Greek theaters on the Ionian Coast. I was interested in the acoustics and how they worked, so Allen would go on the stage and recite the famous W. B. Yeats poem "Sailing to Byzantium." The tourists who were around would sit down in the seats in the amphitheater and listen, because here's someone with a big head of hair who looked like a professor—I don't think anyone knew it was Allen Ginsberg—and the guards didn't stop him. He would walk to the center of the stage and recite, and it was amazing how beautiful and clear the poem would sound in that open environment.

JoAnne and I left Piraeus in the late afternoon for Turkey. I still remember slipping into Istanbul (Greek Byzantium/Roman Constantinople) two days later as the sun was setting, making the sky glow with a soft orange and red light—a warm, welcoming moment. With Istanbul we felt, for the first time, that our journey to the East had really begun. I was keenly aware that this was the gateway to the East, and it was easy to see how the city and its history, dating back to the Greeks in the seventh century BC, had the power to capture the world's imagination. Straddling the West and East all this time has given the city its special quality: coming from Europe, it appears as an Asian city; coming back from Asia, it looks like a European city. It's actually both. It's a place where everyone can feel at home yet, at the same time, the call to prayer will be heard from minarets all over the city five times a day.

Leaving the ship, JoAnne and I headed to the area around the Blue

Mosque, where, as expected, we were able to find cheap lodgings. This was a lively crossroads for young people going overland to and from India. We picked up all kinds of useful information, for example, how to make the crossing at the Khyber Pass where there were no formal travel arrangements available, or being given details of the bus that left Munich once a week and went straight through with minimum stops to Tehran—which we didn't actually take, preferring instead to travel by rail, which was not much more expensive. Even with the East so near at hand, we had trouble pulling ourselves away from Istanbul. In the end we spent almost a week there. We visited Topkapi, an extraordinary museum, the steam baths known as *hamams*, and took a sightseeing trip up the Bosporus to the Black Sea. There was also the food (a vegetarian's dream), the light, the city, and the people—all things together making it hard to leave.

We had been strongly advised not to take the short route through Iraq to the city of Basra. From there it would have been much shorter to go by ship through the Persian Gulf and straight to Bombay by way of the Arabian Sea. However, the area was considered even then far too unstable and violent for two young Americans—and one a blond blue-eyed woman at that—to safely travel there. Even so, we had to be careful all the way through Iran and Afghanistan. On the one hand, we had a "hospitality rule," which meant that whenever we met local people along the way who invited us for tea or coffee or even to their homes, we would accept—that is, providing there were no overt signs to warn us away. It seemed to us that since we were so ignorant of local customs, we should either accept all invitations or none. I've followed the "hospitality rule" all over the world since then and, with one exception, have never felt uncomfortable. This was when, while having tea in the home of some military people in Kandahar in southern Afghanistan, there was some suggestion that JoAnne and I might be separated from each other. They said, "We're going to separate you now, but we'll bring her back."

"No, you're not going do that," I replied, because I was sure I would never see JoAnne again. We got up quickly and left, without explanation. There was no resistance, they let us go. I think they were not intending to be violent, but I didn't trust the situation at all.

Except for that incident, our experience traveling through Central Asia, as well as the extended stay in India, was free of any trouble or conflict. True, everywhere we went, everybody—men and women—stared at JoAnne. It must have been shocking and provocative for them to see a blond woman lightly dressed and with her legs showing. She should have been covered. When a woman wore a burka, she was covered head to toe, and you wouldn't see anything except the flash of her eyes. Here was a woman, from their point of view, practically undressed, walking around the streets. I don't think we had any idea how we looked to them. People didn't actually follow us, but they followed us with their eyes. It shifted once we arrived in India. India had been in the hands of the English for two hundred years by then and they were used to seeing Europeans. That made a difference.

When we left Istanbul we took the train to Erzurum, the biggest city in the far east of Turkey, and from there we took a bus to Tabriz, the first big town in Iran. We crossed the border without any trouble, and after Tabriz we took buses the rest of the way to Tehran. Here we were surprised to find a fairly modern and newly built city. The Germans had a very strong business connection with Iran in those days, and in many ways had become a conduit of Western European architecture and culture. This was still before the last days of the Shah's Pahlavi dynasty, and the suspicion of all things Western, and especially American, had not yet taken root throughout the country. The powerful fundamentalist state that we know today would not emerge until after the revolution of 1979, so what we saw then in Tehran was the pro-Western culture of a country that was embracing the West and modernism.

After leaving Tehran we went to Mashhad, the last big city in the eastern part of Iran, where the same attitude did not prevail. We had been on the road now, counting from when we left Paris, for about five weeks, and our next big goal was to travel through Afghanistan and arrive at the Khyber Pass sometime toward the end of October. It was in Mashhad that we encountered the first sign of a fundamentalist reaction to our presence. In Turkey we had never seen anything of the kind. It had for quite a while been considered a secular country with a strong Muslim majority and we often visited mosques and holy places there without any difficulty. But Mashhad is considered a holy city, where saints are buried. We planned to spend a few days but soon found that whole parts of the city were closed to us. There were no signs or warnings. If we wanted to enter a part of the city that, unknown to us, was closed to foreigners, a crowd of people would quietly but suddenly block access. It was not violent, but it was decisive. We never were able to see any of the religious sites of Iran.

Apart from that, we found the Iran of 1966 surprisingly modern. Ten years later the Shah was still there when Bob Wilson and I were in the midst of touring Europe with *Einstein on the Beach*. Bob had performed in Iran in 1972 in *KA MOUNTain and GUARDenia Terrace*—a play Bob described as a "mega-structure" that unfolded over seven days—and we were both very interested in the possibility of taking *Einstein* there. We had an invitation to perform at a festival in Persepolis, near Shiraz, but by then the Shah and his government were considered too repressive, and our *Einstein* supporters at home and even some newspapers were dead-set against our going. However, Tony Shafrazi, born in Iran and well known in the New York art world, urged us to go. He insisted that *Einstein* could be like a window onto the contemporary world of performance, and our presence there would have a powerful effect. But that one voice of support was not enough to make it happen.

In the end, JoAnne and I liked Iran very much—the people, the sights, and the remaining artifacts of the ancient Persian culture, which were still very much around. We left for Herat, the first big town in Afghanistan, again by bus, and found an almost startling contrast to Iran. Years, even decades, of conflict, both internal and from abroad, had left the country largely poor, undeveloped, and difficult to navigate. There was one major road, a two-lane blacktop, which connected Herat, Kandahar, and Kabul. It had been built, we were told, by the Russians. There was a small fleet of school buses that had been supplied, in turn, by Americans, and that was the public transportation between their three major cities. Herat and Kandahar were not big cities, each numbering far fewer than 200,000. Even Kabul had less than half a million. In between was high desert country, stark and mountainous, with flocks of sheep and shepherds scattered throughout.

My memories of Herat are of a dark, somber place, a frontier city. We passed only one night there, but Kandahar was another story. Though not much bigger than Herat, it was lively, with a busy central market and many small hotels. We hadn't come for the hashish, but many others did, and that kept a small, transient population of young Americans, Europeans, and Australians very much present, and the hotels reasonably busy. It was warmer than the northern part of the country, but even so it could be quite chilly at night and in the morning. There was no heating at all in the kind of hotels we knew. The second day, we noticed that there was simply no glass in the windows. The desert breeze just blew right in. With all that, we liked Kandahar best. It was bright and sunny, but I was tiring of the food. For a vegetarian it was challenging. Lamb seemed to show up everywhere—in soup, rice, and always also by itself.

We went on to Kabul but didn't stay there long. It had an almost international look to it, with all the UNESCO and U.N. people as well as the embassies. It reminded me a lot of Washington, D.C., which I knew quite well, only this was a more or less frontier version, and quite a bit smaller. There were government buildings and government people and Afghani soldiers around. It looked like the capital of a nomadic state, which I think is what Afghanistan was at that time. But now only the Khyber Pass and Pakistan separated us from India and we were ready to complete this first stage of our journey.

Our information about the Khyber Pass was sketchy. It was known that no commercial buses passed that way. There was clearly no rail travel and whatever air transportation might have been available was far too expensive for us. The best we could find out was that there were "oilers" (big oil rigs transporting gasoline and heating oil) going through the Khyber Pass to Pakistan all the time. Travelers would wait on the main road out of Kabul until one of them would pull over. The going rate was one British pound per person, two at the most (the drivers preferred English money). It all seemed a little unlikely, but we had no choice but to try. First we changed money in the market and bought about four pounds, and the next morning we were standing on the road outside of Kabul leading to the pass. In only a matter of minutes, a big truck stopped just ahead of us. I suppose he was a Pakistani driver, as he knew a little English. Sure enough, the fare would be two pounds for us both. It was only a few hours to cross the pass, but the trip was extraordinarily beautiful. We had the name of a small town used for the border crossing, but after being dropped off near Peshawar we went on to Lahore, which would be our main stop in Pakistan. Also from here on we would be traveling by rail, where—with a few notable exceptions—travel was much more comfortable than the buses we had used since leaving Erzurum.

The British colonial regime had left behind a three-gauge rail system that served the whole of India and Pakistan, all of which it had ruled as one country before the disastrous partition of 1947. I would say that the whole governmental infrastructure, including mail and telephone, was then running quite well. Before the British, there had been another well-organized government on the Indian subcontinent, that of the Mughal Empire, which had ruled from the early 1500s until the British East India Company gradually took over some two hundred years later.

With a history of four hundred years of well-organized government as a legacy, it should be no surprise that India is considered today to be the most populous and successful democracy in the world. However, JoAnne and I were there long before the age of internet communication, and some things were not functioning in a completely modern way by Western standards. Even in a major city, like Bombay, you had to go to a telephone office equipped with rows of wooden benches in order to make an international telephone call. There, you waited for your phone connection. When you placed the call, you were given a choice of "normal," "fast," or "lightning." For an international call, "normal" would mean a wait of six to eight hours, "fast" two hours, and "lightning," half an hour. Still, everything actually worked and, considering the size of the country and the density of its population, not that badly at all.

First, though, we had to cross the border between Pakistan and India, and given the deep hostility between the two countries, we were expecting some delay. We began by taking the train from Peshawar to Lahore. Lahore is the second largest city in Pakistan and the capital of its Punjab region. It is laid out as a grand city, with wide boulevards and architecture that looks a lot like what you see in India if you visit the Red Fort in New Delhi or other buildings that have survived from the Mughal dynasties, which lasted into the eighteenth century. We found Lahore picturesque and pleasant but left after a few days for a small town nearby, which was where the actual crossing took place. The Pakistani and Indian border authorities had decided that a small fixed number of crossings both ways would be allowed. It was clear that they both would have been quite happy to shut down the border altogether, but since that was not practical, the crossings were cut down to a bare handful each day. We had to queue up and wait our turn, which in our case was about three days, not nearly as bad as we had feared. While there we were treated to all kinds of horror stories from the local hotel people and restaurant waiters about how horrible India was and how unhappy we would be there. Of course, once in the Indian Punjab we heard the same stories about the Pakistani Punjab, almost identical in sentiment and tone.

We managed to make the crossing in the morning and headed directly for Amritsar. We were now in the homeland of the Sikhs and were eager to visit the Golden Temple. All of this was quite nearby. Once we arrived at the lodgings provided for pilgrims, we were greeted and asked if we were on a pilgrimage. We replied that we were, which had the virtue of being true. We were then given two beds in a dormitory for married people and were invited to take all our meals in the adjoining dining room. We would soon find that this kind of hospitality was available throughout India. It is a wonderful system that encourages all kinds of people to travel around the country and become familiar with their own heritage. In Amritsar, the hospitality was simple, the meals always adequate and well prepared. The work of maintaining the dormitories, kitchen, and dining room seemed to be mainly volunteers. I spoke with many of them and found that they had usually traveled great distances. Their work was an offering to the temple, which they carried out with a real sense of joy. No one ever questioned our motives or right to be there. Our status as pilgrims was enough.

The Golden Temple in Amritsar is just that: a gleaming golden pavilion. It's set in a large pond with a walkway from the shore to its entrance. Services were continuous, day and night. The music part of this service—singers, string instruments (sitars, tamboura, etc.), and percussion—was most appealing to me. This was certainly the best known of the Sikh temples. True to its renown, it was beautiful and impressive, and JoAnne and I spent the better part of four days there.

After making the trip by rail from Amritsar to New Delhi, my first stop was at American Express to see if there was any mail for me. During our journey we hadn't been getting any news of the world because we didn't stay in hotels or places where it would have been available. There was no place from which I could send mail, so I hadn't been writing postcards or letters. As a result, I was out of touch with any European or American connections for most of the whole journey.

To my surprise, I found a letter waiting for me, and it was not good news. Satchidananda, whom I expected to meet at his ashram in Kandy, had decided to go from Paris to New York. He had met the artist Peter Max, a friend of Conrad's, and he had been invited to New York to open a yoga studio that Peter would sponsor. Peter, who was a well-known photographer and designer, had photographed Satchidananda many times (on my return, I saw these photographs of

Satchidananda, so handsome in his red robes and long white beard, hanging all over New York). Satchidananda was an absolutely marvelous teacher of hatha yoga and a very kind person, and my acquaintance with him had partly inspired my visit to India, which I count as having been a momentous event for me.

At that moment in the American Express office, my first feelings were of deep disappointment. But then, and very quickly, I began to feel released, even liberated. We were in India and I had no plans to go back to New York before spring. I had done a lot of reading about India and Tibet and was in an absolutely ideal state of mind to pursue all the questions that were swirling around inside me.

RISHIKESH, KATMANDU,
AND DARJEELING

N FUTURE YEARS, I WOULD SPEND WEEKS AT A TIME IN NEW DELHI, BUT most of the things I was interested in at that moment were elsewhere, so we did not stay there for long. I made a survey of places I wanted to visit in the Himalayan regions that were home to Hindu and Buddhist yogis. First on the list was Rishikesh, one of the most famous places for Hindu yoga retreats in northern India. There were supposed to be hundreds of solitary yogis living in the open or in caves in the area and, as well, there were a few well-established ashrams, such as the Sivananda Ashram that served as the headquarters of the Divine Life Society and the Yoga-Vedanta Forest Academy.

To get to Rishikesh, north of New Delhi in the foothills of the Himalayas, we went by rail to Hardwar and then took a bus the rest of the way. Until we headed back to Europe, JoAnne and I depended almost entirely on the railways to get around. For quite a while we traveled third class, which could be very rough at times, because the trains were extremely crowded. Somewhere along the way we learned that there was a tourist incentive available. With a foreign passport, you could ask for an automatic upgrade at an office in the train station. It was almost always given. From then on we traveled second class, which was almost completely filled with military or petty government officials. It made a huge difference in comfort and the degree

INDIA ITINERARY

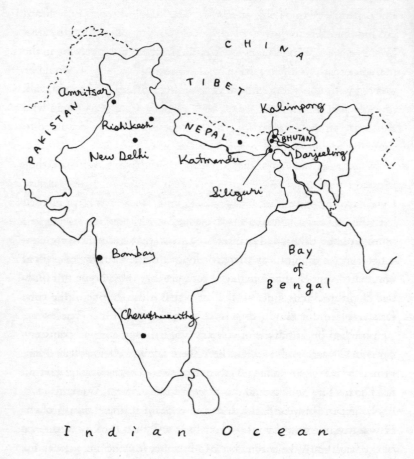

of travel fatigue. India is a very big country, but express trains are not always available.

When we arrived in Rishikesh, we went directly to the Sivananda Ashram where, as a student of Satchidananda, I was welcomed. We were given a room and meals at the ashram but we were also free to look around. It was here that I saw for the first time *sadhus* (wandering ascetics) and yogis living in the open, completely unclothed, often with their thin bodies painted and using a trident for a walking stick. Mostly you didn't see them, as they lived alone in the forests around Rishikesh. Local people claimed that the sound "*om*" could be generally heard around there due to the many, many yogis living in retreat in the area. We never spoke with the ones we would happen upon walking in the many footpaths in the forest. Instead, almost invariably, we would be greeted with a beaming smile, a very slight nod, and they would walk on right past us. I did take some yoga classes with a young man who was living in the ashram, but I already knew the *asanas* he wanted to show me, and he seemed disappointed in our meeting.

When the residents of the ashram learned I was a musician, they insisted I meet their "music" yogi, an elderly man living in the ashram. I was introduced to him, but he never spoke to me. When I entered his living quarters he was already playing a vina, a string instrument often used to accompany singers. He sang hymns and devotional songs for the several hours of my visit. He was far from the great musicians I have known, but he was clearly transported by this practice of playing and singing. I was told that most of his waking time was passed in that way.

I learned that Maharishi Mahesh Yogi, the founder of Transcendental Meditation, also had an ashram in Rishikesh, though I didn't visit it at the time. Later, on my way back to Europe and passing once again through New Delhi, I attended a big public talk he gave. I believe that this was about the time that George Harrison met him or was even visiting him. He was very "at home" with a very large crowd and easily held our attention. I never met him personally, though later I met many of his TM students.

Among my most memorable experiences was taking a refreshing dip in the Ganges. The river, though not wide at this point, is very fresh, fast-flowing, and clean. JoAnne and I found a quiet spot just outside the town, took off our clothes, and bathed in the Ganges. The sky was blue and clear, the sun unclouded and strong. Even though it was now November and we were in the foothills of the Himalayas, we weren't at all cold.

To return to New Delhi from Rishikesh, we traveled by bus and then by rail as before, but we didn't stay at the Birla Temple, where we had previously lodged and which had provided accommodations much like those in Amritsar. After weeks of traveling, we had already outgrown the Indian hospitality system, so we found a small hotel near Connaught Circle where we were close to most things of interest to us.

We decided that our next stop would be Katmandu, Nepal, in order to visit Boudhanath, an ancient massive stupa, reputed by some to be the holiest Tibetan Buddhist temple outside Tibet. That meant a train ride east from New Delhi to Patna, a major rail junction in the northeast of India. From there it was a long and bumpy bus ride to Katmandu. Nepal was (and still is) a mix of Hindu and Tibetan Buddhist culture all through. It seemed very exotic to us. Clearly this was a place that drew from far and wide. There were also more wandering sadhus, just as we'd seen in Rishikesh. We stayed at the Tibetan Blue Moon Hotel, which was modest but authentically Tibetan, and I had my first experience of the food, tea, and beer of Tibet.

Katmandu in 1966 was much smaller than it is today. It was little more than a muddy-street town, and Boudhanath was located outside of it. (These days, it's inside Katmandu itself). On our first day we took a taxi through the surrounding fields out to Boudhanath. It is a most impressive stupa, with large eyes painted on all four sides, indicating that the compassion of the Buddha is without limit. For some reason, as we were looking around, we were taken to see Chinia Lama, the director of the temple. He seemed very pleased to see us and spoke English quite well. We had tea with him and then, to my complete surprise, he wanted to know if I was interested in buying a *thangka*. Until that moment it had never occurred to me that these paintings were even for sale. He took my hesitation for a yes and showed me two vivid paintings. About sixteen by twenty inches, they were oil-based paintings on canvases sewn into a much larger brocade of Chinese silk, complete with two red ribbons that hung down either side of the main image. The paintings were not that old (perhaps ten or twenty years) and the colors were still strong. I later came to know the central images very well. One was a simple Shakyamuni Buddha and the other was a meditational deity. I was sure that JoAnne and I didn't have the cash for anything of that quality, but it turned out that we did. I told Chinia Lama I needed to think about it, and we returned the next day and paid the asking price—seventy-five dollars for both. That was the beginning of my serious interest in the art of Tibet, and by the time we returned to Europe we would be bringing home seven *thangkas*. In almost every case they were offered to me for sale or barter.

AFTER RETURNING FROM KATMANDU back to New Delhi, we began to plan the last and most important part of our Indian tour, which would take us first to Darjeeling and then to Kalimpong—our ultimate destination—both in the foothills of the Himalayas in the far northeast of the country.

After obtaining the necessary permits for traveling to Darjeeling at an office in New Delhi, we began our journey. It took five solid days on the train to reach Siliguri, the last rail station before the Himalayas. Because the upgrades to second class were all taken, we traveled the whole way in third class. Our car in the train was more like a village on wheels than a modern railroad car, with waves of people leaving and arriving at absolutely every station. But what a panorama of life, both inside and outside the train! It felt to me like the first, but not last, initiation and benediction to life in India. Days and nights were endless, one blending into another. The railroad car was filled with humanity, and the difference between sitting in a seat and on the floor was indistinguishable. A whole family could surround you completely for hours at a time and then disappear at a wayward rail stop, only to be replaced by another complete family. JoAnne and I desperately held on to our spot on the floor of the train when one of us had to leave for a comfort stop in the latrine at the end of the car or, when the train was at a station, to dash to the platform to buy tangerines or peanuts. This was without a doubt the most difficult journey I have ever experienced, before or since. The long train ride, however, had one mitigating feature. Every station of any size had a bookstall that carried the whole Penguin Books series, brought out from London. I clearly remember reading George Orwell's *Burmese Days* between Lucknow and Patna Junction, and Alexandre Dumas's *The Three Musketeers* between Patna Junction and Siliguri.

Every rail stop also had food sellers, but by then I had learned to be careful about drinking and eating in India. We confined ourselves to bananas, tangerines, and peanuts, often for days at a time and therefore never had dysentery problems. In later years I would prepare for a rail journey by buying a loaf of bread and making a dozen peanut butter and jelly sandwiches. I never drank liquids of any kind, not even hot teas, since the water usually never had reached the boiling point in its preparation. Fresh oranges or tangerines, which we were able to peel ourselves, were our entire source of liquids. Hard travel to be sure, but, for me, never uninteresting.

During the whole of my time on the trains in third class I never once saw a ticket being collected, or even a ticket collector. Perhaps the trains' functionaries kept themselves to the second and first class carriages. Years later I did take a first class train and traveled in a sleeping car. I went to sleep in the evening and was awakened in the morning to find myself on a side spur of the main track. It was the gentle knocking on my sleeping compartment door by the *chowkidar*, which seemed to be the general name for a personal servant, to let me know we had arrived. No such waking service was either available or necessary in this, our first cross-country Indian rail journey.

We descended at the Siliguri train station, quite a small place just big enough to have jeep transportation up to Darjeeling (literally meaning "the Place of the Thunderbolt" in Tibetan). Jeeps were the main transportation in the hill towns of the Himalayas. The seats behind the driver had been removed and replaced by two facing wooden benches each made to hold four persons. It was very airy as there were only open spaces where windows might have been, and every bump and turn of the road was made known to the passengers. The drivers always seemed to me to be driving too fast and too recklessly, but no one ever complained. The road climbed quickly from the plains around Siliguri, and we were soon passing through the Himalayan foothills. We would climb, in all, about 7500 feet in four to five hours, which meant a most dramatic change from the landscape of the plains to that of the Himalayan ranges.

Just before arriving in Darjeeling we stopped at Kalu Rimpoche's monastery in Sonada. In those first months in India, I sought out any number of Tibetan teachers. By then I had formed the idea that perhaps it was still possible to meet a Tibetan teacher and find out first-hand, as it were, whether the practices of Tibetan yogis were still known and followed. It may seem a strange question now, since today there are many books and teachers of the four well-known Tibetan lineages. But in 1966 it was not obviously so. When I met Kalu Rimpoche that first time in Sonada, I received from him my first spoken explanation of a Tibetan text. On the wall next to his sitting room was a painting of the Wheel of Life (Sipa Khorla). With the help of a translator, I asked for and received a detailed account of the cycle of existence as rendered in this painting.

Our next stop was at the Samten Chöling Monastery (Ghoom Monastery), fewer than five miles from Darjeeling itself. It was one of the places frequented by Lama Govinda, a German Buddhist who had written some of the first books in English about Tibetan Buddhism. He was the student of another very well-known teacher, Tomo Geshe Rimpoche—literally meaning "the Blessed Doctor of the Tomo Valley." That particular Rimpoche was known as the "former body" of the next living Tomo Geshe Rimpoche, whom I would soon meet in Kalimpong. (There is a third Tomo Geshe Rimpoche, who is now twelve years old.) I eventually got to know some of the lamas and teachers of the Ghoom Monastery. In future years, whenever I was passing through Darjeeling on my way to Kalimpong, they would send vegetarian dumplings to my hotel and, to this day, I receive a card from them on Losar, the Tibetan New Year, every February.

Darjeeling was the most beautiful of the hill stations I had seen, an old town that seemed to be a reflection and presentation of the past and present. It had once been the residence of the British raj during the long, hot Indian summer months.

JoAnne and I stayed in the Prince Edward Hotel for very little money. I ordered a bath one morning. Moments later, a ladder appeared outside our third-floor bathroom door (facing the mountains) and a young man scampered up with a full bucket of hot water. It took him eight or nine trips to fill the bath, and such was his speed in climbing up and down that, when complete, the bathwater was still piping hot.

It was in Darjeeling that I first met an Anglo-Indian community, which was quite present there some fifty years ago but is probably hard to find anywhere today. These were people who had somehow fallen between the cracks. I found them a most interesting and likable group. For years I would stay in the same place—the Prince Edward Hotel—when passing through Darjeeling. JoAnne and I were very happy there, with its ridiculously beautiful mountainscapes and its steeply winding streets full of antique shops. It was December when we arrived that first time, and I remember hearing Christmas carols being sung to us by Christian Indian carolers in a popular restaurant on Christmas Day of 1966.

We stayed longer in Darjeeling than we intended and finally needed to leave before our permit to stay there had expired. Our permits for Kalimpong, which we had obtained upon our arrival in Darjeeling, would allow us to remain in Kalimpong for only five days at a time. This meant that as soon as we arrived there, we would have to apply at the Kalimpong police station for an extension. Since the permits and extensions could only be issued in Darjeeling, our passports would be sent back there by the Kalimpong police, a process which took four days or five days. As it turned out, we would wind up staying for fifteen days during our first visit to Kalimpong, so the whole time we were there our passports were traveling back and forth between the Darjeeling and Kalimpong police stations without us.

For some reason I found the situation endlessly amusing, albeit a little nerve-racking.

I was just learning about the political and military situation in that part of India, which was the reason for these permits. The Chinese had slowly taken over Tibet in the 1950s, supposedly to liberate Tibetans from themselves. At that time, there were other major global problems, including the Cold War in the West. The problems of Tibet, a country then virtually unknown to the rest of the world, and the subsequent border problems between China and India, simply were not interesting to the rest of the world. I myself ended up practically on the border these lands shared before I became aware of their recent history. Soon I would be seeing dozens of refugee camps—Tibetans who fled Tibet with the Dalai Lama, or soon after his escape to India in 1959. The permits were necessary because of the Indian military checkpoints near the border with China (formerly independent Tibet). Crossing the Tista River on the road from Darjeeling to Kalimpong, where our permits were scrutinized, could take several hours for that reason alone.

We left for Kalimpong, doubling back on the road by which we had arrived, and, just before reaching Sonada, we headed east down a winding road that took us to the small bridge over the Tista River. It's a glorious ride going down several thousand feet in a few hours. The trees and foliage seem to change by the minute. I remember that short ride vividly with a crisp blue sky and the temperature rising as we descended to the floor of the valley.

THE BLESSED DOCTOR OF
THE TOMO VALLEY

HAD KNOWN FROM THE OUTSET THAT WE WOULD END UP IN KALIM-
pong. Kalimpong is about 3500 feet lower than Darjeeling but still
high enough to rise to a cooler temperature as we drew near. If you
look on a map, it will be just a small dot nestled between Nepal,
Bhutan, and Sikkim (now an Indian state), and easy to miss, but I
knew from my reading that for scholars, travelers, and Tibetan business families it was a major destination and junction. The goods that
left Tibet over the Nalah Pass stopped first in Kalimpong. From
there, they were sent either south to Calcutta on the Bay of Bengal
or straight across northern India and Central Asia and on to Europe.
Business families in Lhasa had homes and offices in Kalimpong, so
there was a settled Tibetan community there.

Really, everybody who was interested in Tibet passed through
Kalimpong. Sir Charles Bell, who wrote some of the earliest authorita-
tive books on Tibet as well as a handy dictionary of colloquial Tibetan
and English, had stayed there in the early part of the twentieth century. Walter Evans-Wentz met Lama Kazi Dawa Samdup either in
Kalimpong or Sikkim, and Theos Bernard met Gegen Tharchin, his
major guide and contact to Tibet, there as well. Geshe Wangyal, a
Lhasa-educated lama from Mongolia, had also spent significant time
in Kalimpong. In 1966 entering the town was like coming across a

campfire that had burned throughout the night and was still smoking in the morning. But if you got down on your knees and began gently blowing on it (and persisted) you would definitely see the flames again.

Theos Bernard described Kalimpong as the most beautiful town he'd ever seen. I didn't see it like that, but there the Himalayan peaks are very close, and the morning and evening sun make striking appearances. At 28,000 feet, the nearby peak of Kanchenjunga is the third highest mountain in the world. Many other mountains close by are easily over 20,000 feet. Yet it is never too cold, and I've often been there in the winter months. It's a much more rural place than Darjeeling, and the Friday *hat* (market) brings people in from Bhutan and Sikkim. It only takes a few visits to easily distinguish them by their clothing, each area being that distinctive, though all so close together.

When we arrived, JoAnne and I went to the Himalayan Hotel, made famous by generations of trekkers, climbers, and Indian and English officials on their way to and from Tibet. It had been built by David MacDonald, a veteran of the British Younghusband mission in 1904, which was a military invasion led by Colonel Francis Younghusband, with the purpose of countering Russian influence in Tibet. The hotel had been the family home until the family turned it into a hotel—one of the MacDonald daughters was still running it during our first stay. You could sit outside in the garden and have afternoon tea with Kanchenjunga appearing as if very nearby. It is said that Alexandra David-Neel, the French-Belgian student of Tibetan Buddhism who made it to Lhasa in 1924 disguised as a pilgrim, had stayed there, as well as Charles Bell. In 1966, I was close enough to those travelers that I felt their path not yet too distant from my own. Perhaps that is why I liked Kalimpong so much.

There were three people I met in Kalimpong whose lives and experiences made a deep impression on me. The first was the previously mentioned Reverend Gegen Tharchin, who was in his seventies and semiretired from his business, the Tibetan Mirror Press. He described himself when I met him as a lexicographer, and at one point in our friendship he gave me a trilingual dictionary he had composed in Hindi, English, and Tibetan. However, I knew him as much more than that. As a much younger man in the 1930s he had been Theos Bernard's guide and companion, friend and tutor, and, most important, the connection to the nobility and officialdom of Lhasa. Without Tharchin's support and connections, Bernard would never have gotten to Tibet. I had read all about this while still in Paris from Bernard's own accounts, and I was intensely interested in whatever details that Tharchin could (or would be willing to) provide.

Every day I would take a walk down Ten Mile Road, a dirt road that led from the main square away from the other side of town where the Himalayan Hotel was set, and I found out that Tharchin lived on that very road. Of course he was well-known locally, so he wasn't hard to find. I found the best time to visit him was right at teatime, about four in the afternoon. He had a fairly large house above Ten Mile Road, where one of his housekeepers would open the door and let me into his bedroom. He would be napping in a large bed with two or three dogs and again as many grandchildren. Once we had met, this kind of informality between us was normal. He would wake up the moment I was in the room, the dogs and children would scatter, and he would pick up a conversation we had been having the day before as if it had hardly been interrupted by yesterday's departure and today's arrival. He certainly knew a lot about Tibetan politics and history, and he had been with Bernard every minute of the latter's time in Tibet.

Tharchin added his own personal slant to what appeared in Bernard's books and journals. Bernard had disappeared somewhere in the area of Ladakh in 1947 on one of his many pilgrimages. I asked Tharchin for any details he might know. It was during the violent days following the partition of India into India and Pakistan, and it seemed clearly a case of Bernard's being in the wrong place at the wrong time. Still, there was some doubt about his death: his body was never recovered and no reliable eyewitnesses were found at the time. Tharchin told me that he got in touch with the local police where Bernard had last been seen. They claimed to have his belongings, clothes, and some personal effects, and they believed he had been killed by a weapon of some kind and his body swept away in a fast-moving nearby river. Tharchin was convinced by the evidence and left it at that. The strange thing was that Bernard had been settled in Kalimpong and planning a study period there with some *geshes*—the western equivalent would be "doctors of philosophy"—including Geshe Wangyal. He had left to avoid the rainy season, which he found disagreeable and, wandering west, had been caught by the Muslim-Hindu violence that was raging, particularly in the valley near Ladakh he had been visiting. From the beginning his life had many strange twists to it and it ended the same way.

JoAnne and I were not in Kalimpong very long before we were directed to the Tharpa Chöling Monastery (Tharpa Chöling means "the Place of Liberation"). I had been asking around if there were yogis living in the area, though truthfully, I had not as yet had much success. Still, I had continued making routine inquiries as we traveled. At the monastery we were welcomed by some of the monks to look at the wall paintings and I asked if there was a yogi residing at the monastery. We had almost no common language between us, but the word "yogi" is always understood. One monk nodded his head and pointed to a house on the road at the edge of the monastery compound.

After months of traveling around India and Nepal, I was in no hurry to knock on another door, but after a little while, I did just that. I was shown into a small waiting room and, after a few minutes, into another, larger ceremonial room to find myself in the presence of Tomo Geshe Rimpoche, a young man about my age (his birthday turned out to be ten days before mine, and in the same year) dressed in extremely simple maroon robes. He and I spent a few minutes together with barely enough words between us to talk at all, but I understood that I should come back the next day, and this time a translator would be waiting.

At that very moment I knew that my search was over. I didn't need an explanation or a sign of any kind, though perhaps there were some but not easily described. It was all very surprising and I did not know what to make of it. The young man didn't say very much to me, but I understood through the little I knew at the time that he was a practitioner of the kinds of esoteric practices and traditions in which I was interested. Finally, I had found a doorway that would open the unseen world to me.

The next morning, Tomo Geshe Rimpoche himself welcomed me in the same room and introduced his translator, a middle-aged man in yellow robes named Rinzing Wangpo. I later found out the interpreter was known in the region as "the Yellow Monk," though in fact he wasn't a monk who had any affiliations at all. He had lived an ordinary life as a layperson with a wife and a daughter and then in middle age had taken (unofficially) monk's vows and began wearing yellow robes. He was not a scholar or solitary practitioner—just a man who decided, late in life, to become a monk. He didn't even belong to a monastery. He lived alone in a one-room apartment in the town. One of the odd and unexpected parts of his story is that the Tibetans loved him—monks and laypeople alike—and I immediately liked him, too.

Rinzing Wangpo's English was quite good and over the next week we met often with Tomo Geshe Rimpoche, discussing what kind of work I could do with him. I was invited to come and stay as his guest in his home, not the monastery. Geshe Rimpoche, as I began to call him, wanted me to begin a study of the Tibetan language, and he said that he would begin to learn English. I also made a commitment to visit him regularly. He was planning his first visit to America. He told me that he expected to be in the States at some point with a traveling exhibit of *thangkas* from Tibet House in New Delhi, a combination library and cultural center.

I was slowly beginning to realize that he was far from an ordinary lama, but, instead, a man venerated by many and admired by almost all who knew him in the Tibetan community. As previously mentioned, in his "former body" he had been the spiritual inspiration and adviser to Lama Govinda and had been the very Rimpoche who was featured in *The Way of the White Clouds*, a book that I had already read. I discovered all this during the next several weeks, before JoAnne and I began our return to Europe.

"What would you like to do?" Rimpoche asked me.

"I'd like to learn from you what you are willing to teach me," I said.

Rimpoche paused as if in thought, then continued.

"Normally, you would have to be here for months and weeks, and there would be all kinds of tests of your commitment and interest. However, I understand that you've come from very far away to be here. It was a difficult journey and somehow you found your way here, and that tells me that these other preliminaries will be unnecessary in your case. We can start any time you want."

We began with very simple things, such as making a commitment to follow the teachings of the Buddha. More developed practices would follow—things that are familiar to people in that tradition such as mantras, visualizations, texts, and so forth. In order to prepare for the practices, the mind has to be settled and quiet. It has to be free of the ordinary disturbances of the day. A typical method is through counting the breath, which can be done in many ways. The Indian yogis, for example, like to bring the breath through the right nostril and to exhale through the left nostril, and then alternate by bringing the breath through the left and exhaling through the right. This very basic practice is usually the first thing that is taught. Breathing is not the only way of bringing the mind to a state of attention. Walking is another. A walk of attention can bring one to a similar state.

These practices, though very simple at the outset, when extended and developed by the practitioner will remain right up through advanced teachings. There will always be meditation; there will always be breathing; there will always be focusing of the mind; and very often, in most traditions, there will be visualizations. These techniques are not secret—they are described in detail in many books—but Geshe Rimpoche taught them to me through the power of oral transmission. It is a conviction of many traditions that transmission doesn't happen through a book but must be received in person from a qualified teacher.

Transmission is the beginning of acquiring. It can lead to strategies and even the ability to visualize this other world that I had read about. It's not an easy thing to do, and I can't claim to have done very well by it. However, people who are adept can go very far. I have had two of the very best teachers in Tomo Geshe Rimpoche and, beginning in 1987, Gelek Rimpoche, another Tibetan Buddhist teacher to whom I was introduced by Geshe Rimpoche. Even with the best teachers, and with a clear desire and commitment, what I've acquired is limited. Remember, there I was at the age of twenty-nine, almost thirty, meeting the first real teacher in that tradition. These Rimpoches are men who began training when they were six years old or younger, and to catch up to that level is a daunting exercise. It would be a great deal to accomplish in such a short time.

The eagerness I had to understand these things had led me to travel overland from Europe all the way to the foothills of the Himalayas. I had been on the road for weeks to do that, without much money, and in all I spent four months on that journey. When Geshe Rimpoche told me that because of what I had done, I had exhausted the preliminaries, he surely must have possessed some insight into my motivation.

I never thought, Oh, this is a wild goose chase, or What am I doing here? I was on the trail of something. The motivation was very deep and it had to do with, as I called it, an eagerness, a desire for understanding, and finally I had found access to it. From my first visit in January 1967, the month and year of my thirtieth birthday, I began, through Tomo Geshe Rimpoche, a relationship with another lineage of work that continues to this day. I see these many interests that I have taken up and kept alive as powerful threads—or themes, if you like—that together make up a real and recognizable totality.

Over the next thirty-five years, I made many short trips to India— probably twenty visits in all—each usually for two to four weeks. Many of them included a stop in Kalimpong, but not every one. India is a very big country, much like the United States in its size and diversity of populations. From the beginning, I knew that only by planning many short trips would I be able to develop my professional and family life in New York and, at the same time, cultivate my connection to India in general, Indian music especially, and, above all, my connection to the culture and tradition that Geshe Rimpoche represented in his own person.

In the early 1970s, when Geshe Rimpoche was getting his green card to stay in the United States, I found a lawyer who offered to donate his services pro bono. I took Geshe Rimpoche to the lawyer's office, where a very nice young man said he would fill out the papers.

"Now tell me," the lawyer said, "what is it that you teach?"

Very quietly, Geshe Rimpoche replied, "Mind training."

"You teach what?"

"Mind training."

And that's what he taught, sometimes in a very vivid way. On one occasion in the 1980s, I was visiting him at his upstate New York home and we were were sitting at the table having tea.

"Be careful of Sindu," Geshe Rimpoche said, pointing to his dog. "He's going to be under the table. Be sure you don't kick him. He fools around under there and you might accidentally kick him."

"No, no, don't worry," I said. "I'm not going to kick the dog. I would never think of kicking him."

Yet less than a minute later, *boom!* I accidentally kicked the dog.

At that very same instant, Geshe Rimpoche clutched his side in pain. He bent over as though he himself had been kicked in the ribs.

I don't know how he set this up—I actually think he and the dog had worked it out, so that virtually within seconds, I had kicked the dog.

He didn't see me kick the dog, but he was such a master of compassion that he somehow felt the dog's pain immediately.

This is very typical of how Tomo Geshe Rimpoche taught.

Through Geshe Rimpoche I made a connection to Phintso Thonden, the head of the office of Tibet in New York. Part of my commitment was to study the language, and I began with the Tibetans. There wasn't anyone else teaching, so I studied with Phintso Thonden's wife Pema, who for more than three years was my Tibetan language teacher. I had just come from learning French at the Alliance

Française and the Institut Phonétique, so I had the tools to notate the language, in terms of getting the sounds right. I had no books, however, so we did conversation. Pema would say, "How are you?" in Tibetan and I would answer, in Tibetan, "Very well, thank you." After a few years, my Tibetan, at one point, was quite passable, but in recent years and through lack of regular practice, a lot of it has been lost.

Another close friend of Geshe Rimpoche was Khyongla Rato Rimpoche, a Tibetan monk and scholar living in New York. I had the great pleasure of helping with the establishment of his teaching center, the Tibet Center, there. Also, I began making weekly visits to Freehold, New Jersey, to the teaching center of Geshe Wangyal, the same lama who had been in Kalimpong only a few years earlier. I was not one of the brilliant young American students who, along with Robert Thurman, Alexander Berzin, and Jeffrey Hopkins formed the first wave of American translators and teachers in America, though I knew them all (and Geshe Wangyal, too) from my visits to New Jersey. I was there to take lessons from Ken Rimpoche, an elderly Tibetan gentleman who had come to New Jersey at the invitation of Geshe Wangyal. My lessons were astonishing and concrete. Using the Charles Bell Tibetan-English dictionary, Ken Rimpoche gave me the task of learning the correct pronunciation of every Tibetan word in the dictionary—a most difficult but surprisingly useful, if not always illuminating, exercise. Those meetings lasted about one and a half years before he returned to India.

The last and certainly one of the most important meetings Tomo Geshe Rimpoche arranged for me was with Gelek Rimpoche, the old friend of his from Lhasa who moved to the States in the 1980s and is the founder and spiritual leader of the Jewel Heart organization. Tomo Geshe Rimpoche was what was called a "heart teacher," and there is another kind of teacher that's called a "text teacher." These kinds of teachers can teach both ways, but if you have a heart teacher, he won't teach you the text, you'll have to go somewhere else to do the texts. This is an old-fashioned way of doing it, I think, and that's how it happened with me.

Tomo Geshe Rimpoche told me, "If you want to learn the texts and study, then you have to go see Gelek Rimpoche. He can teach you that." In this way, I began studying with Gelek Rimpoche, who, for me, is one of the most brilliant minds I have ever encountered. Geshe Rimpoche died in September 2001 but I remain very close to Gelek Rimpoche.

AS I MENTIONED, MY THIRTIETH BIRTHDAY, in January 1967, found me in Kalimpong. Soon, JoAnne and I would begin our return to New York by way of Paris. While we were waiting for a jeep to take us down the hill to the railroad station at Siliguri, a young Tibetan boy wanted to show me a *thangka*. By then we were getting too low on cash to risk another purchase, but he wouldn't give up and wanted to know if I had anything to trade. He spotted my little transistor radio and said that would be fine. At first I wouldn't make the swap, because I knew the radio was on its last legs and would soon need to be repaired. He then assured me that he was completely capable of making any repairs himself. I finally relented and accepted the trade. This had all happened at his home, and then JoAnne and I returned to the marketplace. Less than twenty minutes later he ran into the square and found us in a jeep all loaded and ready to leave. He had a pair of fur-lined boots and told me that he felt very bad about getting too much the better of us in the swap. He pressed the boots on us, refusing to leave until they were accepted.

On our way to Bombay, clear across the country, there were some very long train rides. Once we arrived, we found good accommodations at the Salvation Army. For thirty rupees a day a couple could have a room and three (vegetarian) meals. If you counted the four p.m. tea—which we never missed—that made four meals. The energy and beauty of Bombay attracted us, and we decided to stay on for a few days.

By good luck, JoAnne was hired to play a part in an Indian film. No doubt her blond hair and obvious Western appearance got her the job. That went on for a week, while I happily strolled around on my own. The Salvation Army was on a little street right behind the Taj Mahal Hotel, where the Beatles were said to be staying. I was also told that Raviji was there, but I didn't look him up at that moment because there was a huge amount of security around the hotel that arrived with the Beatles. I guessed that I wouldn't even make it to the front desk. Nearby was not only the Prince of Wales Museum, which had a beautiful collection of Indian miniatures, but also a number of antique stores, where sure enough, I found a set of three *thangkas* for sale at a ridiculously low price. Nowhere in India had I found anyone who understood their value, the Tibetans being such fresh arrivals.

Once the film work was over, we booked passage on a liner from the fleet of Messageries Maritimes, a French company that had a line of ships that traveled between Vietnam and France, Marseille being the first European port. The ship had only two classes, cabin and steerage. The cabins were taken up entirely by ourselves and men who had served with the French Foreign Legion. We found them to be odd but friendly, and a hard-drinking bunch. There were no Frenchmen among them. The stories I had heard—of men escaping their past by giving up their normal citizenship and identity and joining the Foreign Legion—were, as far as I could tell, completely true. However, for the four or five days we spent together, they were very good company. The Indian passengers were all below deck and seemed to be overcome by seasickness the moment they boarded the ship. In any case, we didn't see them until, five days later, we arrived in Europe.

In contrast to our outbound voyage, the route back was very straightforward. We crossed the Arabian Sea, through the Gulf of Aden, which took us past Yemen, Somali, and Djibouti then up the Red Sea to the Suez Canal. We passed Alexandria, Egypt, and crossed the Mediterranean Sea, docking at last in Marseille. I don't remember any day stops at all on the way. From there we traveled by train to Paris, staying there only a few days to collect our belongings and repack our bags. The timing was good and we left for Le Havre a few days later, where we began, at last, our long transatlantic passage back home.

THE FREQUENT TRIPS TO INDIA LASTED UNTIL 2001, WHEN MY SECOND family of children, my sons Cameron and Marlowe, began to arrive and brought a temporary end to the journeys that had taken me all over the country. My first visit to south India had come in 1973 at the invitation of David Reck, an American composer living and studying in India, who took me to the state of Kerala to see the Kathakali, the classical Indian dance/theater. The highlight was an all-night performance of three plays from the *Ramayana*, an epic text that consists of fables and historical stories of the gods and the philosophy of ancient India. It was the first time I attended a play that began at six or seven o'clock at night and ended at seven o'clock in the morning. The next time I saw an all-night performance would be when the Brooklyn Academy of Music presented Robert Wilson's *The Life and Times of Joseph Stalin* in December of the same year—perhaps just a strange, if unlikely, coincidence.

Kathakali is what we would call multimedia theater: it is music, it is dance, it is storytelling. It is performed in several ways: one performer sings and tells the story, accompanied by a musical ensemble, and at the same time the dance company acts out the story as it's being told.

The theaters themselves were humble beyond belief. They presented the play outdoors, in the courtyard of a temple, on a wooden platform. The curtain was held up by two men holding the ends of a piece of rope. When the cast was ready, they just dropped the rope and then the performers would be seen on the stage. By the time I got to see the performances, they had electrical lighting, some of which was just neon light. It was not the most beautiful lighting—often there were people holding lights—but it was lit. There were also all kinds of torches that would give light onto the stage. The costumes were extremely colorful. They looked like paintings of traditional images of the Hindu princes and gods. To do costume changes, they would raise the curtain. Every night they told three stories, each lasting roughly three to four hours, with hardly a break between them. The show began when it got dark and would go on until morning.

In the early 1970s, there were very few Westerners present. Mostly it was village people. Everyone in the village would sit on the ground to watch the play. They didn't pay much attention to us. If you had to take a nap, you would go into the bushes and sleep for a few hours. When you came back, the performance would still be going on. We were told in advance what the stories would be. From the reading I had done in the *Ramayana* and the *Mahabharata*, I already knew a lot of the stories. But there were far too many of them, and I rarely knew beforehand the ones I would see on stage. Still, I could understand much of it. The best place to see the performances was in the Kathakali Kalamandalam's (the Kathakali academy) home village of Cheruthuruthy, which I would visit on three separate occasions over the next twenty years, staying each time for several days.

While the Kathakali Kalamandalam is a professional theater company, its members are drawn from the people in the countryside— it's hard to imagine somebody growing up in a city like New Delhi and then going to become a Kathakali singer. When you see the traditional Kathakali in India, you realize that the people who live there get their knowledge of their history through this theater: that is where it's taught, in the stories that are told and acted out, and it remains very alive to them.

When I asked if I could see how the children were taught, I was

invited to go to the music lessons. The morning after one of the performances, I went to a clearing—virtually in the jungle—and I saw
twelve or fifteen kids, all little boys, sitting down in a row. In front
of each was a big stone, and each had a stick, and they were learning
to keep the rhythm by hitting the stone. The teacher had a stick and a
stone as well, and he was teaching these very young kids—four, five,
six years old—to play the rhythms very regularly, until they got the
beat. I watched them closely for quite a while. Some of those boys
would become part of the company and would eventually learn to
play the drums, sing, or dance.

Ah, this is where it starts, I thought. The fabric of the music is
strongly percussive, with drums playing all the time, and the rhythm
is very intricate. It has to start somewhere, so they start with that. I
never saw any music lesson more arresting than those little boys with
their sticks and stones.

The Kathakali traditionally has the same four elements found in
Western opera—text, image, movement, and music, just like *Rigoletto*.
It becomes very clear how theater and opera must have evolved—by
telling religious stories in front of people, as an historical spectacle. In
this way, the tradition and lineage of these stories has been kept alive.
Every generation performs them and perpetuates them, but they do
them, inevitably, with variations.

In India, the characters in the stories of the Kathakali theater might
be Arjuna and Krishna. In villages in the mountains of Mexico, where
the Wixárika people do not speak Spanish—only Indian languages
are spoken there—they present spectacles in which they tell the stories of their gods and spirits. The storyteller, the *marakame*, is accompanied by people playing violin and guitar as he sings and acts out
the stories with his hands. Certain groups of people are designated
to wear ritual clothing—very colorful wide-brimmed hats with all
kinds of feathers and white clothes with flowers. They make all the
clothes themselves. In a country like Mexico, where fire is such an
important element, the storytelling takes place around a fire, with the
fire almost acting as the stage. There might be two or three hundred

people sitting within a fairly small area, and there might be four or five people telling different stories at the same time, dancing around different fires in a kind of stylized folk dancing. Like the Kathakali, it goes on all night, until sunrise.

Once you see how these performances are done in India or in Mexico, you understand that you are close to a tradition that has been handed down from generation to generation. We are talking about hundreds, more likely thousands of years.

MY SECOND VISIT TO KALIMPONG, IN 1969, had enormous implications for me. During my morning walks on Ten Mile Road, on my way to see Tharchin or Geshe Rimpoche, I had begun to notice a small rug shop with its owner at the door. Soon we were nodding to each other, then exchanging greetings, and finally, he invited me into his shop for tea. His name was Mr. Sarup and we struck up an easy friendship, not once referring to the rugs that were hanging down from the ceiling of his store.

One morning Mr. Sarup asked me if I had a little time for him, that he had something to show me. Our conversation had been very general about life in our two countries, and the state of the world— that sort of thing. I had no idea what he had in mind, but I agreed to come by his shop the next day in the late afternoon. When I arrived, he led me a few streets away to the local movie house. It was not very big, containing perhaps one hundred seats, and showed a film only on the weekends. Mr. Sarup told me he had arranged a special showing for me, which turned out to be a newsreel, a short piece in which a small skinny older man dressed only in a dhoti—a simple linen covering that men wore from the waist down with its ends tucked in at the waist—walked with a wooden staff toward the ocean. A huge crowd surrounded him. He waded into the ocean and dipped the ends of his dhoti into the water, then held it up for all to see. His energy and concentration were electrifying. I knew, even with his simple gestures, that something monumental was taking place.

"That's Mahatma Gandhi," Mr. Sarup said, "and this is a newsreel from the Salt March, also known as the Salt Satyagraha, in 1930. By harvesting the salt from the sea and refusing to pay the salt tax to the British raj, Gandhi was demonstrating his nonviolent protest."

I was stunned by what I saw. I was in awe of the man. Suddenly I needed to know everything I could about him. By this time I was beginning to know my way around India, so I went back to New Delhi and began my study of Gandhi at the National Gandhi Museum and Library. Over the next ten years I visited various ashrams in India where he had lived and worked, including the most well-known, Sabarmati Ashram in Ahmedabad, Gujarat. While in Ahmedabad I was the guest of the Sarabhai family, who at one time had been the owners of the Sarabhai Textile Mills and, at that moment in time, were Gandhi's adversaries in disputes over workers' rights while remaining supporters of his ashram. I came to know them through their interest in American avant-garde dance and music, learning that Merce Cunningham and John Cage had been guests as well.

On a subsequent visit, I went to Gandhi's ashram in Wigram, near Hyderabad. During that ten-year period, I was actively seeking out persons who had known him and been with him during his marches and Satyagraha activities. I managed to find one of his staunchest supporters and co-workers, Vinoba Bhave, who was then living in south India. I wanted to meet him and went to see him. He was then in his late seventies, still very alert, and most kind and helpful. It was still possible in the 1970s to meet quite a few people who had known Gandhi and who had been close to his work.

At the time it never occurred to me that I might one day turn my hand to an operatic work about Gandhi, but from 1967 until I wrote *Satyagraha* in 1979, I was in India every other year, and on every trip, there was a Gandhi element. This total immersion in Gandhi's personal history was a great help in making the opera, for which I had been, consciously and unconsciously, preparing. Almost all the details that would appear on stage could be traced back to my research over the years since I saw the film clip with Mr. Sarup. I think the fire that was lit that day had begun much earlier, with what I learned from my mother about social responsibility. I would guess that a hint of it also came from the Quakers, when I lived with them in the summer at their camp in Maine. I wasn't a Quaker, in fact, I never went to a Quaker meeting, but I knew them as highly moral people—I don't know any other word for it.

The power of morality is not something that is talked about much these days, especially among contemporary people. But when we look at it from the point of view of commitments, and when we see how the Buddhists treat making and keeping commitments as a form of morality, then we can come to a better understanding of Gandhi's work and how it continues to reverberate with us.

FOUR PATHS

OVER A PERIOD OF ALMOST SIXTY YEARS, I HAVE TAKEN UP the study and practice of four traditions: hatha yoga, following Patanjali's system; Tibetan Mahayana Buddhism; Taoist qigong and tai chi; and the Toltec tradition of central Mexico. All of these work with the idea of "the other world," the world that is normally unseen, the premise being that the unseen world can be brought into view. Though their actual strategies and practices are vastly different, these are brother and sister traditions, which reflect a common goal.

To some degree, some things can be understood, if not learned, by reading texts and memoirs of traditional practitioners. However, these uncommon kinds of studies and practices have proven to be best guided and stimulated by a direct encounter with knowledgeable and skilled teachers. In fact, developing in music follows the same pattern. Great teachers in music—and I can list personally four: Nadia Boulanger, Mlle. Dieudonné, Ravi Shankar, and Alla Rakha—teach in an identical way, that is, one-on-one sessions with their students who then have to master techniques a step at a time through intensive personal application.

It would not be until the 1980s that I would meet another yogi, Swami Bua, who in retrospect was the finest yoga teacher I have known. I'm not sure what his lineage was, though I did see a photo of him in his studio, a portrait of him and Sivananda taken in 1924, when Swami Bua was about thirty. It was my son Zack, when he was barely more than thirteen, who took me to Swami Bua's yoga class in his small apartment near Columbus Circle in New York City. As we walked into his living room studio, Swami was sitting cross-legged on the far side of the room.

"Ah, sir, you have brought your son to me," he said. "Don't worry, I will take good care of him."

"No, Swami," I said. "My son is bringing me to you, and I would like you to take good care of *me*!"

Swami was in his nineties when I met him, still giving two classes a day. By then I was in my late forties and I had no problem jumping into his program. However, it was highly developed and personal with many details that were new to me. He was always lively, though sometimes as he was nearing the one-hundred-year mark, he would doze off during a class. Ultimately, his program became the base of the yoga practice I continue to follow on a daily basis.

Swami Bua was himself a strict vegetarian. Sometimes during a class he would begin a fierce tirade on meat eating. Since he was shorter than any of us, perhaps five foot one or two, he would raise his hand with a finger in your face and very heatedly say "You're turning your body into a cemetery!"

On one occasion I was receiving the brunt of the lecture with exactly that line about the cemetery.

"But, Swami," I protested, "I've been a vegetarian for thirty years."

His face and voice softened immediately. He reached up and tapped me on the head.

"Ah, God has blessed you!"

The clearest direct link between my work with these Eastern traditions and the music work that I was doing at the same time is in the pieces that have been based on those traditions. One major work based on Indian sources is, of course, *Satyagraha*. Another is *The Passion of Ramakrishna*—an oratorio for chorus, soloists, and orchestra composed in 2006. Though sung in English, the work is based on the biography of Ramakrishna written in the late nineteenth century by

one of his disciples. Besides these two, there were several other selections from Indian religious texts that appear in my Symphony no. 5
(1999). From my involvement with Tibetan Buddhism has come the
music for *Kundun*, the Martin Scorsese film about the life of the Dalai
Lama, and "Songs of Milarepa" (1997), a piece for soloists and orchestra based on the poems of Milarepa, the Tibetan yogi and poet who
lived almost one thousand years ago.

These works never could have been imagined, let alone written,
without the kind of in-depth study and practice that came from my
direct experiences with India's and Tibet's traditions. I haven't been
back to India in some time, but my search and quest for the esoteric
or transcendent in ordinary life has continued, and in several other
directions.

I TOOK UP QIGONG, THE THIRD TRADITION I mentioned, with the Taoist
teacher Sat Hon. Born in China, Sat Hon came to the United States
with his family to live in New York's Chinatown, and then, after
graduating from Princeton University, returned to China to complete
his study of Chinese medicine.

In 1996, I began a qigong program, which is quite different from
hatha yoga. It is the parent study to tai chi, which is probably more
widely known. When I entered into lessons with him, Sat told me I
would be learning "longevity practice." I continued with the qigong
for a good fifteen years before he began to teach me tai chi. He seemed
to think I would have time to practice: the matter was urgent, but no
rush was necessary. He has told me that though I came to him at fifty-
nine years old, my forty years of yoga and thirty years of Mahayana
Buddhist studies had made it possible to begin studying with him
without any major mental or physical deficit.

It was at least ten years before Sat even mentioned the word
"Taoist" to me, at first with a few books, then with his translations
from ancient Chinese poems. Recently he has added sword and staff
training and now tai chi. I know very little about classical Taoism, but

the training continued and expanded in its detail and precision, and I have gone into it conscientiously and as deeply as I could. It's hard to say what I have learned from all this, but I have noticed a certain ease I have begun to experience in my daily life. This extends not only to living but to the subject of dying as well. More than that I am unable to say.

There have been several music collaborations with Sat as choreographer. The first was *Chaotic Harmony*, a work for flute and dancer, and a second, recently completed work, *Taiji on 23rd Street*, is a film featuring Sat Hon as performer.

MY MOST RECENT ENCOUNTER with an esoteric tradition was completely unexpected and moreover the most surprising. And it has the special quality of being wholly born in North and Central America.

Browsing through the Eastern philosophy section of the St. Mark's Bookshop sometime in 1996, I came across *The Toltecs of the New Millennium* by Victor Sanchez. It was a story of a young man who had gone on a pilgrimage with a group of Wixárika Indians from the mountains of central Mexico. The book was a revelation. At the bottom of the last page the author had printed his e-mail address.

This was close to my sixtieth birthday, and Orly Beigel, my friend and Mexican concert producer, had arranged a big party and some concerts for me at the main concert hall in Mexico City, Palacio de Bellas Artes for the year coming up, 1997. I wrote to Victor Sanchez, telling him I enjoyed his book and suggesting, if he lived in Mexico City, that we have lunch together. He wrote back that yes, he did live in Mexico City and would be happy to meet me, and by the way was I the composer by the same name? I was totally surprised that he had heard of me at all. But there it was, all arranged. Soon after, we had lunch together in Mexico City every day I had a concert, which made it five days in a row.

Victor had been a student of anthropology, but he describes himself as an anti-anthropologist. He believed that the only way to learn about an indigenous culture was to be immersed in the culture itself. Of course this was anathema to an academic, scientific point of view. The normal way of working for an anthropologist at that time was for the scientist to keep a distance between himself and the subject. But Victor instinctively rejected the idea and therefore had to leave the university, freeing him to find the tools and knowledge he was drawn to on his own. He spent quite a lot of time after that with the Wixárika people, and the book I read was a report on his work.

There was no other way to learn about this tradition than through personal involvement. It is a culture with an oral tradition but not a written one. Knowledge for the Wixárika people will not be found and read in a book. The desert and mountains are their encyclopedia. The *Poderíos*—the Powers: the sun, moon, fire, earth, wind, ocean, the Blue Deer and the "little" Blue Deer—are the teachers. The Wixárika people are the students. They have learned to listen to Grandfather Fire, and they have found the voice with which they can speak to him. There is no practice like yoga *asanas* or Buddhist texts or Taoist poetry. There is the desert, the mountains, and the *Poderíos*. However there is a little more than that, too. There is a path of discovery, a kind of technology and procedure—in this sense, meaning literally "how things are done"—that, if not exactly practiced, still has to be experienced. Along with that comes, on the one hand, a development of attention, and on the other hand, an almost Buddhist "not-doing" that is known and cultivated.

I've been with Victor now on fifteen or sixteen separate visits, each ten days to two weeks long. A lot of time was in the mountains of the Sierra de Catorce, but there were also visits to the river country of San Luis Potosí and expeditions to the monuments and pyramids of ancient Mexico in the south of Mexico and Mexico City itself, as well as the jungles of Guatemala and Honduras. This can be hard travel, usually without hotels and restaurants.

During these journeys, there is some talking in the evening but almost none during the days of climbing and trekking, usually with just four or five of us traveling together. There is no question that there are things to be seen that are otherwise not viewable. And there are other times when the ordinary world can be terrifying. These are not tourist getaways. They are deeply exhilarating experiences.

In 2011, Victor asked me to prepare a concert in honor of the new Mayan calendar that was to begin at the 2012 winter solstice. I replied that I would like to do it with Wixárika musicians—Roberto Carillo Cocío, who plays a homemade guitar, and whom I had met previously, and Daniel Medina de la Rosa, who plays a homemade violin and sings. In July 2012 we had two days of rehearsal in the town of Real de Catorce, where we began preparing music we could play together at the the Casa de Cultura, which, surprisingly, has a Yamaha baby grand piano. The final rehearsals took place several days before the concert, and on the evening of December 20, 2012, we played in front of a packed house of maybe sixty people. Over the subsequent two days we recorded the music as *The Concert of the Sixth Sun*.

IN A CLEAR WAY, WE ARE BOUND TO OUR CULTURE. We understand the world because of the way we were taught to see. That's why we become Americans, we become Indians, we become Eskimos. We see that world because that's what was installed, almost banged, into our heads when we were very, very young. But it's also possible to step out of that world.

For many years I always thought of the music as being separate from these other activities. It was only recently that I began to see it as connected to everything else. I remember talking once to Tomo Geshe Rimpoche, who invited me to spend some time at his place in the Catskill Mountains north of New York City. "Why don't you come and just do a retreat here?" he asked.

"Can I bring my music with me?"

"You're *supposed* to bring your music with you."

When I got there, he began to place me on different days in every cabin, house, and other building on the property. I wrote music everywhere—that's what he wanted me to do.

At first, it wasn't easy for me to accept the idea that my pursuits of these various paths had anything to do with music. But my friends who are professionals in this business all said, "No, no, no, it's the same thing."

I finally arrived at that conclusion, but with some difficulty. Still, even today it's an idea that does not come to me easily. However, the mental concentration and physical stamina that result from these disciplines is virtually identical to that needed in music making and performing. To this point, I can't even say which comes first. My personal experience is that they nourish and support each other. The question is not how could I have had the time and energy to pursue both personal and musical development, but how could I have done it any other way?

PART TWO

PHILIP GLASS AND ROBERT WILSON IN ROBERT MAPPLETHORPE'S STUDIO. NEW YORK, 1976. PHOTOGRAPH: ROBERT MAPPLETHORPE.

RETURN TO
NEW YORK

NEW YORK LOOKED MUCH THE SAME AS WHEN I HAD LEFT IT IN 1964, but my generation, now in its late twenties and early thirties, felt an energy that seemed to pervade the entire city. In only a few years, the Beats had become the hippies, while the dreamers had reawakened as activists. Woodstock was just two years away, and a new electric popular music set the beat for everyone. The scene at Berkeley was very much a part of our energy system, a second pole of active creativity, as it were. Looming over everything and everyone, however, was the long shadow cast by the Vietnam War. It still had years to go, and no one, either for or against it, could withstand its pull. The drug culture had not yet taken root in our lives, which, for some, meant there would be dark, dark days ahead. Some would not survive. AIDS had not surfaced, still over a decade away, and sexuality was still a playground of sorts. You could say that these were still our days of innocence.

I was thirty years old in 1967, and I was coming back from Europe with not only the instruction I had gotten from Nadia Boulanger but also the training I had received from Ravi Shankar. With these skills, I was very well equipped musically. I also had the beginnings of a new musical language that was developed to the point where I could work with it professionally. I had composed music for Samuel

Beckett's *Play*; I had applied the procedures I used in composing the Beckett music to write chamber music that had no theatrical or literary connection: String Quartet no. 1; and I had made a piece, "Music for Ensemble and Two Actresses," for JoAnne and Ruth Maleczech, in which they recited a recipe from a cookbook with my new music.

What was interesting about those early works was that from the beginning they had a musical personality. How that happened, I'm not quite sure. It may have been my approach. I was really looking for a *language* of music that was rooted in the grammar of music itself. I was working in a very foundational way, building the language of the music that I was going to be working with for the next ten years.

When our ship docked at the pier on Twelfth Avenue in Manhattan that April of 1967, JoAnne and I were greeted by a host of friends, among them Michel Zeltzman; my cousin the artist Jene Highstein; Bob Fiore, a Fulbright student of film I knew from Paris; and the sculptor Richard Serra.

I had met Richard when he had arrived in Paris a few weeks after me on a Yale Traveling Fellowship, and right away we became friends. It has been a friendship that has lasted for decades and had important consequences for me, especially after my return to New York. While in Paris, we spent a lot of time together, talking about art and absorbing the nuances of Parisian culture. Richard took life classes at the Grande Chaumière, a studio on Boulevard Montparnasse—and when we first met he was still polishing his skills in drawing, much as I was doing with the fundamentals of music. Besides that, we both had local heroes among the Europeans. I remember many afternoons having coffee with him on the terrace of one of the big Montparnasse cafés. The rumor was that both Giacometti and Beckett would frequent this particular café. Richard was hoping to get a glimpse of Giacometti and I of Beckett. We saw neither, but we enjoyed each other's company. Richard spent his second year in Florence, and, as he would be in Paris from time to time, we would often meet. I found out later that he was from Oakland and, as a youngster, had known Mark di Suvero, a strange coincidence that these two men, not very different in age (Mark being the older), would both become famous for large, monumental outdoor sculpture and had known each other practically from childhood in Oakland.

When he met me at the pier in New York, Richard announced, "Don't worry. I've got your truck."

"What do you mean, you've got my truck?" I said.

"Well, I've been moving furniture, but I just got a little teaching job, and I'm going to be working for the Castelli Gallery. I don't need to move furniture anymore, so here's the truck."

Richard had returned from Europe a year ahead of me, and he pretty much knew the ropes when it came to scratching out a living in the city.

I wound up being in the moving business on and off for the next two years. My partner in my first moving company was Bob Fiore, who in his professional life would go on to shoot and edit Richard's film *Hand Catching Lead* (1968) and Robert Smithson's *Spiral Jetty* (1970), among others, and would also work with the Maysles brothers on the Rolling Stones documentary *Gimme Shelter* (1970). Bob liked the name the Prime Mover and we used it for a while. We understood immediately that anyone reading the *Village Voice* ads would have no idea who any of the advertisers really were, so the name meant everything.

The second year I worked with my cousin Jene. We came up with a far better name, advertising ourselves as Chelsea Light Moving, which turned out to be much more successful. To me the name conjured an image of dapper young men in uniforms with white linen gloves. Of course, we were nothing of the kind. We didn't have uniforms, much less linen gloves. We didn't even have insurance, which would have been unheard of in those days. We had Richard's truck, but after a while it fell apart. After that, we rented trucks by the day.

Living in New York was still cheap, and JoAnne and I found our first loft on Sixth Avenue and Twenty-Fifth Street, on the edge of the flower district. JoAnne's job was to book the work that the ads brought in. The moving business operated as a mini-seasonal affair in

which the last week of every month and the first week of the following month were the working days. Nothing much else happened the
other two weeks, making it an ideal job for a musician or artist. JoAnne
just booked everything she could into each day, regardless of the vertical or horizontal distances the move required. We never complained
about her scheduling skills, though our clients always did. We figured
any job that was tackled and accomplished in the same day was a job
well done, though sometimes we didn't finish and the first day spilled
over to the second or the third day. We hardly ever broke anything.

When JoAnne wasn't booking our jobs, she was cleaning houses.
That was her day work, but she soon became involved as well in her
theater life. Our theater ensemble, unnamed at this point but later
to become Mabou Mines, reassembled piece by piece in New York:
JoAnne and I first, Ruth Maleczech and Lee Breuer next, and David
Warrilow, who joined us from Paris, later on. JoAnne, Ruth, and Lee
met Ellen Stewart, the founder of Café La MaMa, which went on
to become the legendary off-off-Broadway La MaMa Experimental Theater Club. These were the great early days of La MaMa on
East Fourth Street. Ellen was very interested in and enthusiastic about
what young people were doing in theater and, at that time, we were
young people. We presented ourselves as a company of five, and later
on we were joined by Fred Neumann, also from Paris, and Bill Ray-
mond, already living in New York.

Besides La MaMa, the other institutional downtown theater—
institutional in the sense that they had full-time people working
there and presenting pieces—was Joseph Papp's Public Theater. Joe
had started his New York Shakespeare Festival company in the 1950s
on Avenue C, and in 1967 moved to Astor Place. Joe once told me that
when he started his first theater, he furnished it with theater seats he
found abandoned in the street, which is believable, because later on I
adapted a loft on the corner of Elizabeth Street and Bleecker Street for
performances in exactly the same way. I always liked Joe's spirit and
I liked the fact that he had one foot in the classics and one foot in off-
off-Broadway. He loved to do Shakespeare, but he also would pick up

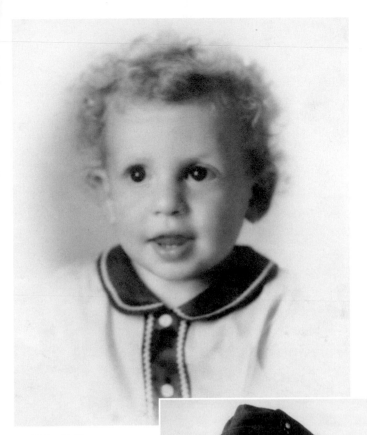

Philip. Baltimore,
Maryland, 1938.

Ben Glass.
Private in the
Marine Corps,
1943.

Michel Zeltzman.
1983.

[NOELLE ZELTZMAN]

Ravi Shankar and Philip Glass composing *Passages* together.
Santa Monica, California, 1989. [ALAN KOZLOWSKI]

Philip Glass
and JoAnne
Akalaitis on
the beach in
Mojácar, Spain.
Summer 1965.

[JOANNE AKALAITIS]

World-renowned teacher
and conductor
Nadia Boulanger
(1887–1979) at the Free
Trade Hall, Manchester,
February 27, 1963.

[PHOTOGRAPH BY
ERICH AUERBACH / HULTON
ARCHIVE / GETTY IMAGES]

Philip Glass and the score of "Piece in the Shape of a Square" set up for the performance at the Cinematheque in New York. May 1968.

Dorothy Pixley-Rothschild performing "Strung Out" at the Cinematheque in New York. May 1968.

Philip Glass Sunday afternoon solo loft concert at 10 Elizabeth Street.
New York, early 1970s. [RANDALL LaBRY]

Richard Serra and Philip Glass. New York, early 1970s.

[© RICHARD LANDRY 1975]

Richard Serra and Philip Glass installing
Splash Piece: Casting, 1969–70 at Jasper
Johns's studio. New York, 1969.

Juliet, Philip, Zack, and JoAnne.
Cape Breton, Nova Scotia,
summer 1973. [PHILIP GLASS]

John Dan
MacPherson,
patriarch of the
MacPherson
family and
close friend of
the Glass and
Wurlitzer
families.
[PHOTOGRAPHER
UNKNOWN]

Rudy Wurlitzer and Philip Glass. Cape Breton,
Nova Scotia, summer 2000. [LYNN DAVIS]

Philip Glass with Zack and Juliet in Venice, Italy, on the first tour of *Einstein on the Beach*. Summer 1976. [© ROBERTO MASOTTI]

Sheryl Sutton and Lucinda Childs in "Knee Play 2," *Einstein on the Beach,* at the Brooklyn Academy of Music. New York, 1984.

[PHOTOGRAPH © PAULA COURT]

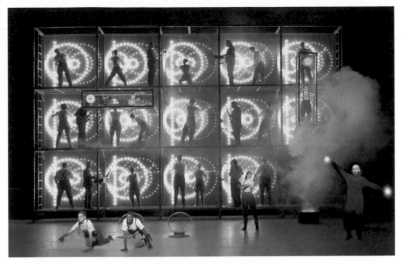

Einstein on the Beach, Act 4, scene 3: "Spaceship." The 2012 revival produced by Pomegranate Arts. [© LUCIE JANSCH]

Satyagraha, Act 1, scene 1: "The Kuru Field of Justice," with Douglas Perry singing the part of Gandhi. Directed by David Pountney. Designed by Robert Israel. Netherlands Opera, 1980.

[TOM CARAVAGLIA © 2008]

Philip Glass and Godfrey Reggio. Production meeting for Godfrey's film
Visitors. Opticnerve Studio, Red Hook, Brooklyn, 2013. [© MIKE DEBBIE]

Still from *Koyaanisqatsi*, 1982. Directed by Godfrey Reggio.
Cinematography by Ron Fricke.

Candy Jernigan.
East Village,
New York, 1986.
[PHOTOGRAPHER
UNKNOWN]

Philip Glass and
Doris Lessing at
the English
National Opera
for *The Making of
the Representa-
tive for Planet 8.*
London,
November 1988.
[DAVID SCHEINMANN]

Foday Musa Suso and Ashley MacIsaac performing in *Orion*.
Odeon of Herod Atticus, the Acropolis, Athens, Greece, 2004.

Dracula, directed by Tod Browning with original score by Philip
Glass. Performed live with the film by the Kronos Quartet, Philip
Glass, and Michael Riesman, conductor and performer.

Michael Riesman.
Rehearsal during the
Philip on Film tour, 2001.

Leonard Cohen and Philip Glass during rehearsals for *Book of Longing,* a musical theater work based on the poetry of Leonard Cohen, 2007.

Dennis Russell Davies and Philip Glass. Rehearsal of the opera
The Lost with the Bruckner Orchester Linz. Linz, Austria, 2013.

The Philip Glass Ensemble performing *Music in Twelve Parts*
at the Park Avenue Armory. Lighting design by Jennifer Tipton.
New York, 2012.

Jene Highstein
walking near his
summer home in
Cape Breton,
Nova Scotia, 2010.
[KITTY HIGHSTEIN]

Father Stanley
MacDonald.
Cape Breton,
Nova Scotia, 2011.
[REBECCA LITMAN]

Marty Glass, Sheppie Glass Abramowitz, and Philip Glass at the Metropolitan Opera performance of *Satyagraha*. New York, 2008.

Lucinda Childs and Philip Glass at a rehearsal of the 2012 revival of *Einstein on the Beach*. Baryshnikov Arts Center, New York, 2011. [PAVEL ANTONOV]

orphan companies like Mabou Mines who were doing very experimental pieces at that time. He considered it an important part of his job to give young theater groups places to work.

Joe was always an idealist and passionate about any issue of free expression and speech and experimental theater. In the early 1970s, I came across a book that contained his testimony when he had been called to appear before a subcommittee of the House Committee on Un-American Activities in 1958. This subcommittee's main power was to intimidate and frighten people, making them think that they would never work again unless they told everything that they knew. They put Joe in the crosshairs and he took the microphone and he turned the tables on them. He roasted them.

When he was asked if he used the productions of his plays to inject propaganda that would influence others to be sympathetic with the beliefs of communism, Joe replied, "Sir, the plays we do are Shakespeare's plays. Shakespeare said, 'To thine own self be true.' Lines from Shakespeare can hardly be said to be subversive."

When pressed to reveal names of people he might have known who were Communist Party members, Joe stated, "There is a blacklisting device in the theater and film industry, and the naming of people this way does deny these people the right to work, which I think is terribly unfair and un-American. I just think it is wrong to deny anybody employment because of their political beliefs. I have always been opposed to censorship." He castigated them thoroughly and let them know that they were complete idiots and beggars at the table of art. He was a man of tremendous vision and integrity.

The next time I saw Joe at the Public I told him, "I just read your testimony from the fifties, during the McCarthy days."

"You did?!"

"Yes, and you were fantastic!"

"I'm so glad you read it," he said. He seemed very moved. I think people had forgotten by then what he had been like when he was our age.

The last time I talked to Joe—he was quite sick toward the end—I was working on a piece at the Public, and he was there in the hallway. It was less than a year before he died, in 1991. I remember he stopped and looked at me. He took me aside, and said, "I'm always happy to see you in my theater, Philip." He looked me in the eye and I knew he meant it, that he wanted people like myself there. That was the kind of man he was.

NEW YORK'S DOWNTOWN THEATER SCENE in the late 1960s was alive with new companies and new work. An unbelievable amount of talent and energy was launched at that time, and significant parts of it still remain in their original homes in the East Village. Some of it was a bit obscure and hard to find, but many of the companies were reaching out to a new audience of young artists, performers, and producers who, like themselves, were beginning to move into the East Village and the newly discovered SoHo district.

Almost all the players were there when we arrived from Paris: Richard Schechner's Performance Group, Joseph Chaikin's Open Theater, Meredith Monk's the House, Bob Wilson's Byrd Hoffman Foundation, Peter Schumann's Bread and Puppet Theater (though actually based in Vermont), and our own soon-to-be-named Mabou Mines Theater. Besides that, Richard Foreman, Jack Smith, and countless other independently minded people were working, and in 1971 George Bartenieff and Crystal Field founded the Theater for the New City as a home for new plays.

The different theater companies worked in various ways. Some were built around a visionary, like Meredith Monk, Bob Wilson, or Richard Foreman. Others, like Mabou Mines or the Performance Group, were more oriented toward people working collectively. In Mabou Mines, the members were all called co-artistic directors. There was no *leader* of the company. We were proud of the fact that we worked as a collective.

All of these companies were resolutely unconventional. Most of the work had very little to do with ordinary storytelling and very little to do with Broadway, off-Broadway, or off-off-Broadway. We were off-off-way-off-Broadway. We weren't interested in the traditional theater. We didn't measure our work by those standards. In our acting and performing, we were looking for a theatrical language that was different from Tennessee Williams and Arthur Miller, the American school of naturalism with which we had grown up. When JoAnne had done summer stock before we left for Europe, there was a different play every week: it could be Shakespeare, it could be *A Man for All Seasons*, it could be a Broadway play. A lot of people who trained in that work went on into film or television, but the kind of work we were doing followed in the European tradition of experimental theater. Both JoAnne and Ruth traveled to the South of France in the spring of 1969 to study with the seminal Polish director Grotowski, working along the lines of the practices and theories he wrote about in his book *Towards a Poor Theatre*. What Grotowski meant by "poor theater" is that you didn't *have* anything. Everything had to be made by the actors: the costumes, the words— everything was built, was handmade. And it was not narrative work. It was radical, in the sense that it didn't depend on the artifice of theater. It depended on a kind of emotional truth in the acting. I still recall Grotowski's plays, and they were beautiful. Of all these new active theater companies, I believe it was Mabou Mines especially that knew European experimental work firsthand and managed to align it to an American aesthetic. In retrospect it seems natural that it should have come about in this way.

Though all of these quintessentially American companies were fully acquainted with theater history and philosophy, Mabou Mines emphasized collaborative work techniques, which eventually extended to its directors. JoAnne would become a formidable director, writing, adapting, and directing new work, as did Ruth Maleczech and Fred Neumann.

We had come to New York with a piece ready to go: Samuel Beckett's *Play*, which we had done in Paris. The theater aesthetic of Beckett's work had taken hold of the company from its beginning. The sets and costumes were uncomplicated—three urns (façades of urns, really) in which the performers would sit, while a moving spotlight set in front of them and operated by Lee would light their faces in turn. The actors' faces were plastered with a heavy coat of oatmeal, which gave them an eerie, fresh-out-of-the-grave look. The music I had composed, inspired by Beckett's text, was already recorded.

Play was presented at La MaMa on Fourth Street and was warmly received. Ellen had already put the entire company on stipend. She was like that. If she liked you, she signed you up and took a chance. She provided a regular stipend of fifty dollars a week for each member, which meant that JoAnne and I together had one hundred dollars a week. That, plus my moving business and JoAnne's occasional house cleaning (now becoming increasingly occasional as her theater work took over), was enough to keep us going. In those days, no one had health insurance and, fortunately, the need never came up.

The next work for the company would be *The Red Horse Animation*, a new original work by Lee Breuer. Its realization by the entire company occupied us for years. It was first presented at the Paula Cooper Gallery, then at the Guggenheim Museum in November 1970, and at La MaMa in June 1971. For this piece I composed a "tapping music" to be performed live by the actors on a floor that was set in four-by-four-foot modular plywood squares, each square amplified with a contact mike. Most of *The Red Horse Animation* was learned and rehearsed in New York City but the final work, including the amplified floor and a wooden wall capable of physically sustaining an actor pinned perpendicularly on its surface, was built and rehearsed in Cape Breton, Nova Scotia, not far from the company's namesake, the town of Mabou, known for its coal mine. The company by then was artistically secure and mature enough to make original and striking pieces, and in the early 1970s it embarked on a period of beautiful collaborative works. Power Boothe, who designed the floor and wall for *The Red Horse Animation*, was the first resident artist with the company, and in time was followed by others, including Jene Highstein.

In the downtown theater world we all knew each other and each other's work. It was a true community of artists. Each company pursued its own interests and we appreciated the curiosity and imagination of others. I went to see Joe Chaikin's and Richard Schechner's work, as well as Bob Wilson's, Meredith Monk's, and Richard Foreman's. We rejoiced in the diversity—it became affirmation through diversity rather than by consensus. Even so, a spectator might find himself challenged rather than intrigued. Richard Foreman's pieces, for instance, were stimulating and puzzling in equal parts. I saw everything he did for years, and I rarely understood what I was watching, nor was I supposed to understand. In fact, I would say his pieces were anti-intellectual in the sense that applying rational processes to them was discouraged and, practically speaking, impossible. Richard managed to create a flow of scenic and dramatic events on the stage that was totally arresting. At the same time, there were usually lights in your eyes, noises in your ears—everything was done to disturb the normal train of thought that you would bring to the theater. At a certain point, you began to watch in a different way. You never knew what was going happen, and it didn't matter.

The power of Richard's theater making was that it had the coherence of rationality without the logic. The emotional effect was what many people were looking for, a kind of transcendence and epiphany, an emotional high that came from being detached from the world of the rational and the dramatic. It turns out that there is a lot of room in the human mind to experience deep and transcendent emotions that may not have very much to do with ordinary subject matter. In that way, it's not so different from an exhilarating moment in a forest or watching a brilliant summer sky.

These ways of looking for transcendent emotions are not related to the theory of drama as presented by Aristotle and perfected by Shakespeare. When you look at a play of Beckett's, the epiphany doesn't come where Aristotle said it was supposed to come. It doesn't come from the fall of the hero. In *Play* and in *Waiting for Godot*, it can happen at any point in the work. When the *feeling* content is not necessarily related to the *narrative* content, and the epiphany can come anywhere, then that feeling has become unrelated to the actual material you're attending to. It becomes a different way of experiencing music or, for that matter, painting, dance, literature, poetry, or film.

Moreover, this experience itself now has the power to become transformative. It can appear as a transcendental experience, not conceptually, but because we're having experiences that don't have a preformed context. The story is gone. *Romeo and Juliet* is gone. We've gotten to the *power* of romance literature without the *story* of the romance. There's an edginess to it. Normally when we go to the theater or opera house and it's a conventional theater piece or a conventional opera, we don't have the feeling that we're on the edge of the unknown. We're wallowing in the known. We may even be rejoicing in the known. But in the alternative theater being presented by Richard and others who were suggesting a radical change in perception, the result could be a keen sense of delight and abandon. It certainly took courage, both on the part of the author and the spectator. It was either the courage of ignorance or of sophistication, but in the end, that didn't really matter.

Why did it occur at this time? It was a reaction in many ways against the modernism of the twenties, thirties, and forties. We still had plays from Tennessee Williams or Arthur Miller, but we were feeling the exhaustion of the romantic principle. We were the exhausted ones, so we had to start somewhere else. We got rid of the things that were trivial, even nauseating, to us, which meant most of the content had to go.

We did have some immediate predecessors: we had John Cage, Merce Cunningham, Robert Rauschenberg, and the Living Theater. We even had Claes Oldenburg's "The Store" and Allan Kaprow's "happenings." These artists were a little older than us, and they had begun the work of clearing the ground for a new kind of theater to take root, a theater that was not based on any kind of a story, one that was visual, emotional, and chaotic. They were already crossing the borders between the arts: the composer Cage worked with the choreographer Cunningham; the painter Rauschenberg also worked with Cunningham as well as with choreographer Trisha Brown and the Judson Dance Theater. The way the generation before us worked was very important to us. Though their accomplishments were pretty much ignored by the arbiters of culture in New York and elsewhere in America, we took them very seriously.

Because of the artists like Cage and Beckett who came before us, we didn't have to take everything apart, since it had already been taken apart. We didn't have to destroy the idea of the novel—Beckett's *Molloy* and *Malone Dies* had done that. In many ways, Cage and Beckett cleared the playing field and gave us permission to start playing again. We were the beneficiaries.

John Cage liked me personally, but sometimes we would have conversations in which he would shake his head and say, "Philip, too many notes, too many notes, too many notes."

I would laugh, and reply, "John, I'm one of your children, whether you like it or not."

In spite of his comments about "too many notes," we got along fine. He finally found a piece—my 1979 opera *Satyagraha*—he liked, and he made a point of telling me. He mentioned to me several times that it had made an impression on him.

The work I did with Mabou Mines, which went on for more than two decades, was my real apprenticeship in the theater. In time, I branched out to work with other theater directors and other companies, contributing incidental music and songs when needed. This in turn made an easy transition for me to work in film in much the same way. By then I understood not only the job of the composer but I also had some acquaintance with many of the other theater crafts— lighting, costumes, scenery—that normally would not be in the purview of the composer. I made it my business to learn whatever I could. Not that many years later, I would be working in opera houses, again not just as a composer. I took authorship of an opera seriously and my goal was to be comfortable with all its aspects.

ALONG WITH THE ARTISTS AND THEATER COMPANIES, dancers and choreographers were moving into SoHo, making the area rich in talent
and invention. The Grand Union, a contact improvisation company,
came into being. It included, at various times, Trisha Brown, Barbara
Dilley, Douglas Dunn, David Gordon, Nancy Lewis, Steve Paxton,
and Yvonne Rainer. Twyla Tharp, Lucinda Childs, Laura Dean, and
Molissa Fenley all had companies in the early 1970s. I'm citing as
many as I can remember to give a sense of the depth of talent that was
working and reinventing dance. They were emotionally, artistically,
and actually younger than the older companies—Paul Taylor, Alvin
Ailey, and Merce Cunningham—though quite a few of them came
out of Merce's company or his classes.

These dancers were taking colloquial movement—movements of
everyday life—and turning that into dance. They weren't specialized movements made for dance bodies and dance-trained people.
They were for people who could just be walking, running, or jumping around. They didn't always wear dance clothes. Sometimes they
even wore jeans. They also didn't wear dancer's shoes. They might
wear tennis shoes, or sometimes just bare feet was enough.

One of Yvonne's dance pieces began with a ladder and a pile of
mattresses. The company would climb up on the ladder and dive onto
the mattresses, and whatever happened, happened. They would let
their bodies respond to the gravity and the fall and the physicality of
the mattresses. It was like watching a study in human motion. There
were eight or ten people who would just continually dive onto the
mattresses. This was something that came out of the idea that the aesthetic content of this "dance" would be in the mind of the viewer and,
in this way, John Cage had really affected young people. In this tradition, Yvonne didn't choreograph the piece, she let the falling body
choreograph it.

I performed in 1971 with Yvonne at the Galleria l'Attico in Rome,
where the gallery director, Fabio Sargentini, was putting on a series

of performances in an apartment building garage. Yvonne built a box that was six feet high, three feet wide, and twelve inches deep that one could stand in. Yvonne just put your body into the box, and the interaction of you and the box made something happen that wasn't programmed or anticipated. The viewers could find choice aesthetic moments, if they cared to, and if you yourself were performing in it, you were in for an unknown experience, because there were no real instructions and no rehearsal. I just walked into the box and moved inside it for fifteen or twenty minutes while Yvonne was moving around on the outside. I was always curious about dance, but I came to it too late and without the discipline. Even so, I did actually perform once, and it was with Yvonne.

Who were the audiences for these theater and dance performances? We were: the musicians, actors, painters, sculptors, poets, and writers, many of whom lived and worked in the area. If Yvonne or Trisha Brown had a new work—Trisha was doing pieces that were very similar to what I was doing, using a vocabulary of repetitive movements—the artists were mainly the audience, often at events hosted by SoHo galleries. Paula Cooper Gallery on Prince Street was one of the first, and has remained the most prominent. Paula took up the idea that the gallery space could be used as a performance space, and she embraced it freely. Her gallery was home not only to painters and sculptors but to performers as well. I played there with the Mabou Mines, and I played there alone. Even today Paula presents new work in her latest location in New York's Chelsea neighborhood.

SoHo was also home to Jonas Mekas's Cinematheque and to The Kitchen, founded by Woody and Steina Vasulka, who initially rented the kitchen of the Mercer Arts Center in the former Broadway Central Hotel, hence the name. When the hotel building collapsed, they moved to a space on Broome Street. There was no money, there was nothing. In its early days, The Kitchen didn't even advertise. They simply posted the week's program on the door. John Cage, Molissa Fenley, Talking Heads, Bob Wilson, myself, and many others performed there.

In the beginning, the lofts in SoHo were dirt cheap. A large 2500 square-foot space could be found for $125 to $150 a month. The screw holes in the floor clearly showed where lines of sewing machines had once been installed. The whole area had been a factory district, and it remained so for almost another quarter of a century. Instead of coats, trousers, or sweaters, the spaces became the birthplace of new inventions in dance, music, theater, art, and film. In the early years of my soon-to-be-formed Philip Glass Ensemble, we played all over SoHo. And then there was Food, a restaurant on the corner of Prince and Wooster that featured a different artist as guest chef every night. JoAnne for a time was a regular chef there, and in my plumbing days—yet another in my long list of day jobs—I installed the radiators that heated the place.

JoAnne and I never lived in SoHo ourselves. Within a few months of our return to New York, we moved to an empty building on Twenty-Third Street and Ninth Avenue. My cousins Steve and Jene and I convinced the owner, an Irishman who owned the bar on the corner, that we would do all the work renovating the building and get a "C of O" (certificate of occupancy) from the city. In exchange we would take over the building "rent free." We knew, and our land-lord must have suspected, that there was no possibility of that actually happening. For that we would have needed architects, engineers, and a licensed electrician and plumber, not to mention cash for materials and waste cartage. There was no way we could do all that. But I think the landlord just liked us. He was always in his bar at one of his booths drinking, so he definitely knew no construction work was happen-ing. Still, we were there for almost three years. JoAnne and I took the upper two floors and the cousins the lower two. The top floor was used both for my own ensemble rehearsals and theater rehearsals when they began.

I had completed a few pieces in my new style, and I was most anx-ious to continue to develop the language I had begun after working in Paris with Raviji and Alla Rakha. By luck it turned out that in the fall of 1967, Raviji would be a composer-teacher at New York's City

College. Not only that, Alla Rakha would be with him, first of all to accompany him as needed, but also to give private lessons on his own. I was very happy to see Raviji again, but I knew from experience that he would be frantically busy. I elected to attend his classes uptown at 135th Street at the school and take private tabla lessons with Alla Rakha downtown. This meant JoAnne and I had to have a serious talk about money. The lessons were not expensive by any standards— maybe twenty or twenty-five dollars apiece—but it would make a serious dent in our weekly budget. There were no children yet, but still it seemed a lot. JoAnne, however, had only the most encouraging words for me. In those years, when there was no money and few prospects, she was always looking for long-term and future benefits. A few years later, when I began making return visits to India, she was equally supportive. That was more difficult, for by then there were two children—Juliet, born in October 1968, and Zack, born in March 1971. Not only would I have to spend money to go, but she would be left alone with our children.

The lessons with Alla Rakha were riveting and immediately rewarding. They were not dry lectures. I had to buy a pair of tabla (another seventy-five dollars) and learn everything both as a theory and, even more important, as a practice. Working directly with Alla Rakha, I began to get a real grasp of how the rhythmic structure that was at the root of his playing shaped the overall outcome of an entire composition. By then, having a solid basis in Western classical technique, I was able to quickly assimilate the theory behind the music. The elements—harmony, melody, rhythm—are present, either all together or in part, in all music. In our Western traditions, the melody and harmony interact to form the overall structure, with the rhythm usually taking on no more than a decorative role. In other words, the emotional shape of a piece of Western classical music—for example, a symphony of Beethoven's—would be determined by the development of the harmony and the melody.

With Indian classical music it's different. There the melody and rhythm form the structural core and the harmony appears hardly at all, and that makes a huge difference. The music is organized in a specific way. The *tal*, or the rhythmic cycle, is the number of beats that make up a complete sequence. It provides the ground upon which the melodic material will be heard. The coincidence of the two elements, rhythm and melody, become the main concerns of the music. The raga will have a shape to it, in the same way that a harmonic sequence would have a shape, but within that shape the sitar player or the singer will be improvising melodies. One way to describe it would be this: There is the beginning and the end of the cycle in which the melody occurs. Within a fixed number of beats—it doesn't really matter how many, as long as the number remains the same—the performer will find a phrase, which they call a "place." The place, ideally, will be a moment the listener will easily recognize—for example, an ascending interval or a whole phrase within the melody itself. The place will always occur in a specific moment of the rhythmic cycle, and part of the pleasure of listening to the music is recognizing that place in the midst of the melodic improvisation.

Alla Rakha—plump and extremely pleasant—was in his late forties and he was a fabulous player. He had short but very strong fingers. He was a master of what is called "calculation." When he played his rhythmic sequences, he could fit them into the *tal* any way he liked, and the ways of counting were endless. Within a *tal* of eighteen, there would be strings of notes, some with phrases of 3, some with phrases of 4, some with phrases of 2. In the *tal*, he always knew where he was. One of the things he liked to do was to tease the audience by pretending to come to the end of the *tal*, and then jump over the end to be in the middle of it again. He would do that four or five times, and when he finally came to the beginning of the *tal* again, when the melody came to that point and everything coincided on the first beat—which was called the *sam*—you could feel it in the audience. Together they would exhale an audible sigh of satisfaction. Part of the attraction of the music comes from this sort of playfulness.

My goal was to integrate all three elements—harmony, melody, and rhythm—into a single musical expression. The first part of this work began in 1967 and ended in 1974, a period of seven years. I knew that in New York I would have to take on the work of playing and presenting this new music myself. My first encounters with working musicians in Paris had convinced me that I would get no help from that side. In fact, they practically kicked me out of Paris. When they heard the music I'd written for the Beckett play, my French friends said, *"Mais ce n'est pas la musique."* "But it's not music."

FIRST CONCERTS

N THE FALL OF 1967 I MET JONAS MEKAS, THE DIRECTOR OF THE FILM-Makers' Cinematheque, who later went on to found Anthology Film Archives. I asked Jonas right away whether I could present a concert at the Cinematheque on Wooster Street in SoHo. Jonas could not possibly have heard a note of my music, yet his reply was to smile and say, "Of course. When would you like to make your concert?"

We settled the date on the spot, arranging the concert for May 1968. I managed to book several more concerts with similar programs around the same time, including one at Queens College a month earlier, in April. Between moving furniture, composing, and rehearsing, I would be pretty busy for the next six months, and that turned out to be a good template for the next ten years. Once the Philip Glass Ensemble began working, there were always concerts to play, and my life got progressively more intense. The cycle of music, family, my personal disciplines, and especially the day jobs was pretty much the way it would be. There was no way of getting around the constant problem of money until that moment arrived by itself.

The first concert pieces came right out of my working experiences with Raviji and my private lessons with Alla Rakha. The music, to my ear, was strongly rhythmic and with a melodic dimension that was becoming more defined. These first New York compositions were solo pieces and duets, so I needed only a handful of players for my first New York City concerts. I called Dorothy Pixley-Rothschild, my old friend from Juilliard. As a student, Dorothy had played a violin concerto of mine and a couple of string quartets. She was very happy to hear from me.

"Do you have any new music?" she asked.

"You bet I do," I replied, and she went for it right away.

A recent acquaintance, Jon Gibson, who was also a composer, joined us on saxophone and flute while I played keyboard and flute.

One of the early pieces, "How Now," for solo piano, was pretty much like the string quartet I'd written in Paris, with six or eight "panels" of sound, each one an intensely repeated structure that then interfaced with the others. "Strung Out," a violin solo for Dorothy, and *Gradus*, a solo saxophone piece for Jon, were straightforward pieces based on repetition and change. I was working with a language that, in the beginning, was simple but because of the perspective I brought, it became surprisingly interesting. In pieces like "In Again Out Again," "How Now," and "Strung Out," I was already using additive processes and subtractive processes in the course of my playing, but they were done more instinctively.

"Head On"—a trio for Dorothy on violin, myself on piano, and a cellist—was first played for a group of Dorothy's friends at a party at her house. It was really obsessive music, seven minutes long, which began with the players playing different melodies. With each development of the piece, the differences started to become eliminated, so that by the time we came to the end, everyone was playing together. At the very end of the piece, there was a collision of all this music— that's why it was called "Head On"—simplifying itself until it became a single melody.

Dorothy's husband, Joel Rothschild, a very nice man, must have thought I was insane, because Dorothy would come home with music that probably sounded like the needle was stuck in the groove—that's what people used to say. He loved his wife, and he loved music, but I think this pretty much tested his love of music. Still, he was always most interested and supportive. Dorothy was a first-class player who was already very well-known in the world of chamber music and would later become the concertmistress of the Mostly Mozart Festival Orchestra at Lincoln Center. But she had this goofy friend—that was me—who wrote this weird music, which she continued to perform.

In composing these pieces, I made the musical language the center of the piece. By "language," I mean the moment-to-moment decision made when a note of music is composed. To make that work, I had to find a music that would hold your attention. I began to use process instead of "story," and the process was based on repetition and change. This made the language easier to understand, because the listener would have time to contemplate it at the same time as it was moving so quickly. It was a way of paying attention to the music, rather than to the story the music might be telling. In Steve Reich's early pieces, he did this with "phasing," and I did it with additive structure. In this case, when process replaced narrative, the technique of repetition became the basis of the language.

There is a psychology of listening involved in this. One of the most common misunderstandings of the music was that the music just repeated all the time. Actually, it never repeated all the time, for if it had, it would have been unlistenable. What made it listenable were precisely the changes. There was a composer who was describing my music to someone else, and he said, "Here's what it is: if you take a C-major chord and just play it over and over again, that's what Philip Glass does."

Well, that's exactly what I *don't* do. He completely missed the point. In order to make it listenable, you had to change the face of the music—one-two, one-two-three—so that the ear could never be sure of what it was going to hear. If you look at "Music in Similar Motion" or any of the other earlier pieces, what is interesting about them is how they don't repeat. To miss that point is like going to a play and falling asleep but waking up for the intermissions. You miss everything if all you hear is the intermissions. You've got to hear what the piece is actually doing, and unfortunately, at first, not everyone was able to do that.

Why could we hear something, while the people who screamed,

"The needle is stuck!" could not? Because we were paying attention to the changes. The mechanics of perception and attention tied you to the flow of the music in a way that was compelling and that made the story irrelevant.

When you get to that level of attention, two things happen: one, the structure (form) and the content become identical; two, the listener experiences an emotional buoyancy. Once we let go of the narrative and allow ourselves to enter the flow of the music, the buoyancy that we experience is both addictive and attractive and attains a high emotional level.

MY MOTHER ARRIVED BY TRAIN from Baltimore for my first concert at Queens College on April 13, 1968. During my travels to and inside India, I had barely been in touch with my family. Their reaction to my marriage to JoAnne had been surprising. I had never expected such a complete rejection. When I arrived in New York, I had called my sister and brother, so Ida and Ben knew through them that I had returned. My father and I were still not speaking, but my mother was in contact. She wasn't able to have me come to her home, but that didn't mean she couldn't talk to me or see me. The rejection had come from Ben, not Ida, but it turned out that she was the one who was being punished. She had learned about the concert at Queens College and said she was going to attend. I was surprised, but I met her at Penn Station and she rode out with us to Queens in a rented car. She didn't say anything about the rift in our family, and neither did I.

I must have been a big worry to her and Ben. They weren't happy about my marriage to JoAnne, and my choice of a vocation—composing music—had never made them happy either. Once I had left for Chicago in 1952, I never again needed their permission. I didn't ask for it, and I never got it. We just left it at that.

Though the concert was beautifully played and very rewarding for Dorothy, Jon, and myself, the fact of the matter was that there were only six (six!) people in the audience—one being my mother,

Ida Glass herself. I don't believe that she, unlike my dad, had any ear for music, but she could count, and the number of heads that made up the extremely small audience must have seemed a disaster. It had been an afternoon concert, and since Ida had never planned on spending the night in New York, I accompanied her back to Penn Station. The only comment she made was that my hair was too long.

It would be over eight years before Ida came back to New York, in November 1976, when *Einstein on the Beach* was at the Metropolitan Opera. This time there was an audience of almost four thousand people—all the seats plus standing room were sold. She sat with Bob Wilson's father in a box. I gather that they were both mystified, but at least it must have seemed real to her. I always wondered what she thought of such a great change of fortune in such a short time. From that moment on, she took my occupation very seriously, and she was concerned that I was handling the business part of it properly. By then, she knew I was always going to be a musician, but now her concern shifted over to the likelihood that supporting my family would always be a struggle.

Ida was a very interesting woman. She treated each of her children differently. She had always saved every nickel she could, and she used to buy AT&T stock with it. All her savings were in AT&T stock, and it turned out to be a very smart thing to do, as it was an investment that just got better and better. When she died, in 1983, her various assets were distributed among her children according to how she perceived what kind of help she could be. For example, she had bought the building that my brother's business was in, and when she died, it turned out that he inherited the building. My sister received the securities Ida had accumulated. Her reasoning may have been something like, "A woman alone in the world will need the money." My sister wasn't alone, she'd been happily married to the same man for a long time, but Ida felt—and there were no grounds for this whatsoever—that she wanted Sheppie to have some cash just in case something happened to her family. In my case, Ida thought I would never have two nickels to rub together, that I would never have any money whatsoever, so she gave me half of her teacher's pension, which was possible in the state of Maryland. When a teacher received her pension, she could take it at a lower rate, and then pass it along to one family member. This passed-along pension was good for one generation, and I'm still getting that money. She got half for her lifetime, and I got the other half for mine.

After her retirement and my father's death, my mother moved to Florida with her sister Marcela and her husband, Uncle Henry the drummer. They had apartments in the same condominium complex. Ida had what we called hardening of the arteries (technically, atherosclerosis). The fat would build up, the flow of the blood would be constricted, and her limbs wouldn't get enough blood. She had a series of amputations, and it was really quite awful. Basically they cut until there was nothing left to cut. I don't know why anyone would think that's a good idea, but that's what was done then.

As her condition worsened, Marty, Sheppie, and I took turns going down to Florida. We worked it out so that there would always be someone there for a weekend, so every third weekend, I would be there for three or four days. This went on for a while. I remember once I was there with my brother and we were standing by the window. Ida's bed was across the room. She was in a coma—she was in and out of a coma for all of the last few weeks, I would say—and I was talking to my brother, and I said, "Do you think she can hear us?"

A voice on the other side of the room said, "Certainly!"

We were so shocked we almost jumped out of the window. I came to understand that people in comas can hear things. You have to be careful what you say, and also, you can talk to them. Later on, I got used to talking to people that were dying, because that's one of the things that life is about. Death becomes familiar. It doesn't become a secret ritual. It becomes something that happens to your friends and your family.

On these final trips—her life was winding down now, and if you went there, you might only hope to have a few words with her—I would simply stay in the hospital, have lunch in the cafeteria, and then come back to her room. On one of those visits, she was conscious as I was sitting with her. She motioned for me to come over.

"Yes, Mama. Yes, I'm here."

She nodded her head, and she motioned for me to lean down so she could talk to me.

"The copyrights!" she whispered.

"What?"

"The copyrights."

I understood that she was worried about the copyrights, that my music had taken on some value. She had come to the conclusion somewhere along the way—I suppose she had seen enough progress—that they were worth something, and she wanted to make sure I still owned the work.

I understood what she meant. I leaned down to her and said, "It's all taken care of, Mom."

She nodded.

"I've registered them all, and they belong to my company."

She nodded her head again. That was the last thing we said to each other. Right to the end, she was on top of everything. Not that she listened to the music, but she understood that I had reached a turning point in my life—I was forty-six, so not only had I written *Einstein* but also *Satyagraha*. By some impossible maneuver, I had risen from obscurity in the music world into somebody who had compositions that had monetary value. She just wanted to make sure I was taking care of it.

In the end, it was my brother, Marty, who brought her back from the hospital in Florida to Baltimore, where she spent her very last days in a nursing home.

I doubt whether Ida knew much about music. We have a cousin in Baltimore, Beverly Gural, whom I would see from time to time. In fact, to this day, she keeps in touch. Beverly had been to Peabody Conservatory as a young pianist. Later she belonged to the Baltimore Choral Society, and she sang some of my music. I think it was through Beverly that Ida had found out about my music, from the reviews that were starting to come out. The reviews were terrible, but that didn't matter. I would get letters from relatives saying, "Congratulations—hope you didn't miss this review," and there would be a review in a Chicago paper or wherever I had relatives, and it would be a *terrible*, scathing review. But they didn't care about that—the point was that it had been noticed by the newspapers. It wasn't sarcasm. They really meant "So you're now part of the music world." I had achieved a kind of fame. Even a bad review was fame, among my family.

BY THE TIME THE CONCERT AT THE CINEMATHEQUE came around in May, just a month later, there was more music ready for performance. This turned out to be a full-length concert. On the program was a duet for Jon and myself: "Piece in the Shape of a Square" (a pun on Erik Satie's *Trois Morceaux en Forme de Poire*—*Three Pieces in the Shape of a Pear*); another duet, "In Again Out Again," for one piano four hands, for myself and Steve Reich, a friend and fellow composition student from our Juilliard days who already was making a name for himself as a composer; "How Now," for me on solo piano; and Dorothy playing "Strung Out," for solo violin. As can be seen from the titles it was a "geometric" setting, the music stands and music making shapes in the performing space.

With these works I was making pieces that had a visual as well as a musical structure. For "Piece in the Shape of a Square," the sheet music was set on twenty-four music stands arranged in the shape of a square, with six stands per side. In addition, there was another square of twenty-four music stands with sheet music on the inside, so that there was a square inside a square, with two sets of music and no space between the two squares. The two flute players, Jon and I, began facing each other, one on the outside, and the other inside. While playing, each of us started moving to the right, so that as I was going in one direction, Jon was going in the other. We would meet halfway around the square, and meet again when we finally arrived at our starting places.

For the unfolding of the music I was still using additive and subtractive processes, but instead of repeating one note or a group of notes, the music continued to add notes to an ascending or descending scale until a complete scale was reached. When we were both halfway around the square, the music we were playing began to do a retrograde (going backward), repeating itself in reverse. It's as if you counted to ten, and then counted back from ten to one again. In the extreme parts of the piece, the music was at its most diverse, and as Jon and I began to approach each other toward the end, the music became more similar, arriving finally, in this way, at its beginning.

"In Again Out Again," the duet for one piano with four hands, had the same structure as "Piece in the Shape of a Square," except that Steve and I were sitting at the same piano. The upper part and the lower part of the music were reflections of each other, just as it was for the two flutes. In the middle, the piece could sound very wild, because both parts were extreme, but as it returned to the beginning, again, the parts became increasingly similar. The music went in and out and then back in, as described in the title.

With "Strung Out," the sheet music was taped to the wall, "strung out" in the shape of an L. Dorothy began to play while facing the wall, with her back to the audience. As she read the music, she walked along, and when the sheets made a right-hand turn down the side wall, Dorothy turned, too, following the L formed by the two walls.

By this time, I had become good friends with the "minimalist" sculptors, among them Sol LeWitt and Donald Judd. They were older than me, and in fact, they were the people for whom the word "minimalism" was invented. It wasn't invented for musicians like La Monte Young, Terry Riley, Steve Reich, or me. It was applied to LeWitt, Judd, Robert Morris and Carl Andre, among others. The term "minimalist music" was simply transferred to us, in spite of the fact that it referred to a generation that was, roughly speaking, eight to ten years older than us, which at that age was the difference between being twenty-eight and thirty-eight—the difference between being someone who had an established career and someone who was still loading trucks on Twelfth Avenue.

The second important part of the presentation that evening was the use of amplification. The intention was to separate the geometric shapes from the source of the sound, so that as Dorothy was walking and playing in one place, the sound of the music would come out of a speaker in another place. That was how I began working with amplified music. Those pieces didn't really need to be amplified, but I liked the quality it produced. In other words, the sound itself was amplified, but the amplification itself had nothing to do with the necessities of the piece.

When I played at the Cinematheque, Richard Serra and my other art friends loaded the truck and we moved in all our equipment. If it weren't for the painters and sculptors who were my friends, we wouldn't have had the manpower to even set up the concert. Soon thereafter, I played in Don Judd's loft. In time, I would present concerts in museums, and in this way my music became part of the art world. My friends who were painters would go to the galleries and say, "You have to put on a concert of Philip's."

"When am I supposed to do it?" the gallerists would reply.

"On Saturday, when everybody's there."

Not only did Leo Castelli, for one, agree to that, but he agreed to pay us. We were playing in the galleries first, and then we were playing museums. It was as if the artists were saying, "This is our music, too." My music had found a home, and the art world became its beachhead.

What I wanted was a high-concept music that was aligned with a high-concept theater, art, dance, and painting. My generation of people—Terry Riley, Steve Reich, La Monte Young, Meredith Monk, Jon Gibson, and another dozen or so composers—were writing and playing music for the dance and theater world. It seemed to us that for the first time, a music world that was equivalent to the world of painting, theater, and dance began to emerge. The music world now could say, "This is the music that goes with the art."

When I speak about the basics of music being the language of music, that in itself is abstract. *The* high concept of art is language— I mean specifically that. When La Monte Young was working with sound, he was working with the idea of a kind of sound—how it would work, how the overtones worked, and how it affected you emotionally. I was working with rhythmic structures and with the kind of epiphany that is associated with that music, as opposed to the Doors singing "Light My Fire." Most people prefer "Light My Fire." But, on the other hand, there are composers writing music that stands on its own. They make a base for themselves in terms of language, form, content, and process. These are all concepts, but are they concepts that are independent of feelings? No, I think they are the concepts that make transcendent feelings possible and understandable. I emphasize transcendence and epiphany because these experiences go together with language. To say you could have one without the other would be to say you could have a fire without logs and a match.

WHEN I HAD RETURNED TO NEW YORK IN 1967, I had discovered that the people around me at the time—painters and sculptors like Bob Rauschenberg, Sol LeWitt, and Richard Serra—all listened to rock 'n' roll. They did not listen to modern music. It was not in their record collections.

When I asked them, "Do you listen to modern music?" I found they weren't interested at all. *None* of them listened to modern music: Stockhausen, Boulez, or Milton Babbitt—forget it. You'd never find that music there. There was more of a connection, for example, between artists and writers. What Ginsberg was doing in poetry and what Burroughs was doing in literature were not that different from what was going on in the art world.

"Why is there a disconnect here?" I asked myself.

Consciously, or to some degree unconsciously, I was looking for the music that *should be* in their record collections. If Rauschenberg and Johns were looking at painting and saying, "What could go into a painting and what goes on in a painting?" I asked myself, "What is the music that goes with that art?"

I started going to the Fillmore East, then the current hip rock-'n'-roll venue on Second Avenue near Sixth Street (only a few steps away from where I would be living in 1984). The place was full of kids, twenty-one, twenty-two, twenty-three. I was thirty years old and felt like an old man going in. The place was packed, and it was loud, and it was juicy. I loved it. I heard big bands like Jefferson Airplane and Frank Zappa at the Fillmore, and I was totally enamored with the sight and sound of a wall of speakers vibrating and blasting out high-volume, rhythmically driven music. I knew that music. I had grown up with it. I had liked it when I was a kid, and when I heard it coming out of my own speakers, I said, "This is good." Yet I also knew that rock 'n' roll was anathema to classical music people. They would never accept music that was amplified and with the kind of bass lines I was running. I knew that was going to make a lot of people angry, and I didn't care.

Look at it from my point of view: there I was, living downtown. I'd come from Paris, where I'd been working with Ravi Shankar. There were other composers like myself in New York, and I met them soon after. But when I first came, the biggest thing I heard was amplified music at the Fillmore East. It had the same rhythmic intensity that I had heard in Ravi Shankar's concert music. That became a formal model, and I would say that the technology became an emotional model. It seemed like a completely natural progression to me, coming from Boulanger and Raviji and Alla Rakha, then returning to the United States and meeting rock 'n' roll head-on.

In terms of the *image* of the sound, the fact that no one was doing it in experimental concert music not only didn't bother me, it interested me. In Europe, what was being presented as new music at that time was intellectual—abstract, quite beautiful, but with very little emotional punch to it. I wanted music that would be the opposite of that. The early music I composed was inspired more by artists and by rock 'n' roll. Amplification added a content to the music that may have seemed alien to some people. Almost no one was going into the world of amplified music, or into the world of structural music. On top of that, amplification was a style of presentation that immediately set the music apart. If you look back, even pieces like "Music in Fifths" and "Music in Similar Motion," which I wrote in 1968, are well articulated. They work through a process of additive and subtractive music laid out almost as clearly as if in a textbook. However, a major part of the impact of the music comes through the amplification itself, which raises the threshold experience to a higher level.

Now that I was back, I was surrounded by new ideas coming from a new generation of young performers and artists. Moreover, there was the environment that I lived in: hearing Allen Ginsberg reading *Kaddish*, or being around "weird" artists like Ray Johnson, for instance. These kinds of ideas were boiling over, pulling the downtown artistic community in a multitude of directions. Without planning or necessarily trying, my work naturally became a part of it.

AT THE SAME TIME AS I WAS MAKING NEW MUSIC, I was looking for some other kind of work to bring in money. My cousin Jene had already moved into construction, and there was a lot of building going on in SoHo, where industrial lofts were being changed into living spaces and studios for artists.

The first jobs I started with Jene were putting up walls with sheet rock. This was heavy work. Then Jene and I began to do some plumbing, which neither of us knew very much about. There was a plumbing supply store on Eighth Avenue near Eighteenth Street, where we would go for supplies and advice. The guys behind the counter thought it was a joke. We'd come in and say, "Look, I have this part here—it goes into a sink, right?"

"Ah, okay," they'd say. And then they would go and get me the new part and hand it to me. They'd look at me, just laughing.

"Now what do I do?" I'd say.

"Well, you take this out, and you gotta get some washers to fit here and there, and then you put this in . . ."

They would talk us through it. I would take the part back to the sink we were putting it in, and I'd try and make it work.

We taught ourselves basic bathroom plumbing in this way. Very basic. Basins, toilets, showers, and tubs. Soon we learned to sweat pipes and hook up hot water heaters. We did whatever the guys who sold the parts could tell us. We bought pipe cutters, because in those days we were using galvanized pipe, so we actually had to cut the threads into the pipes. We spent a couple hundred dollars on a pipe cutter where we would hold the pipe and put a ratchet on the end that had a blade in it. We turned the ratchet on the pipe by hand and literally cut the threads in. If we'd had more money, we would have bought an electric pipe cutter, but that would have cost three or four hundred dollars.

We weren't good at first, but it wasn't that complicated, either. Later, with the switch over to copper pipes, it became much easier, except that the copper pipes had a tendency to leak more than the old galvanized pipes. Most people would not pay for brass pipes, which are softer and easier to work. The galvanized pipes would only last nine years—after that they would become so encrusted inside that problems with the water pressure would develop. The brass would last up to twenty years, and with the copper, there was no limit. But the copper was more delicate. If it wasn't unrolled properly, it could end up with a dent, and the damaged part would have to be removed. There were ways of getting around that, but basically it took a higher level of skill. The next thing that came along was PVC plastic, but by then I was done with plumbing.

There was a young man, Sandy Rheingold, who had a little storefront on Prince Street right off West Broadway. He was friendly enough and sat outside his place in jeans and a T-shirt. He wasn't an artist, just a young fellow who was doing plumbing. Strictly speaking, Jene and I should have been apprenticed to a licensed plumber, spent six or eight years working for him, and then he would bring us to the union and introduce us. We would be allowed to take the test and we'd be entered into the union and we would become licensed plumbers. That would have been about an eight- to ten-year process for most people. We weren't ready to do that at all.

One day Sandy saw us walking down the street carrying our pipes and said, "Hey, you guys, you do plumbing?"

"Yeah, we do."

Of course, that was only partly true.

"I've got a plumbing place here. You want some work?"

So we went to work for Sandy. I worked for him for about three years, and that's where I learned how to handle lead, which became useful later on, when I started working for Richard Serra.

Sandy taught us how to melt lead and how to set up a lead bend and install a toilet. The lead bend was a tube with a right angle. The bottom of the lead bend, which ran horizontally under the floor, fit into a four-inch cast-iron pipe. There would be a little bit of a hub where the four-inch pipe overlapped the lead bend, and within that hub, you would pack in a good amount of oakum (a fibrous material commonly used to caulk wooden ships) using a hammer and a wedge. Next you needed the snake, a rope made out of asbestos, which you would wrap around the lead bend where it fit into the cast-iron hub.

If you did it right, you would end up with a little bit of an opening there at the top of the asbestos snake. Then you would take a ladle and dip it into the pot of molten lead you had sitting nearby on top of a small propane burner, and you would pour the lead into the opening left by the snake. The lead would run around it, and the snake would keep it from dripping out of the hub. When you had gotten enough lead in there, you stopped and let it cool down. Then you would take off the snake and take your hammer and a smaller wedge, and pack the lead in all the way around. You did that about three times, until you had packed a solid lead collar around the pipe, which would give you a watertight connection.

Next, you had to connect the top of the lead bend, the vertical part, to the metal flange to which the base of the toilet would eventually be bolted. To do this, you had to trim the top of the lead bend and flatten it down over the flange. To make a solid connection to the flange, at this point, hot lead, as I learned, had to be "wiped" onto the flange itself.

Traditionally, brown paper was used for wiping, the reason being that plumbers in the 1950s and '60s would go to work with their lunch in a brown paper bag. When they got to work, the first thing they would do was to eat their lunch, at eight thirty in the morning, no less. They did that so they would have a brown paper bag with which to wipe the lead. You absolutely had to do it this way, using the brown paper bag, or you were considered a complete sissy, and even a fraud.

In short, you held the paper up and you dipped it into the lead. The lead was hot, so this all had to be done very quickly. You wiped the lead around the lip of the flange, let it cool, and then placed over it a wax gasket that would provide a seal between the flange and the base of the toilet. We never used gloves, asbestos or otherwise, to do the wiping. Maybe they sold them, but I never saw anyone use them. The brown paper bag was all that protected your hands. In the beginning, Sandy sent an older plumber out with us to teach us how to wipe the lead, but after we did a few toilets with him, we could do it ourselves.

Because Jene and I knew a lot of artists, and because Sandy lived there, we were mostly working in SoHo. One fellow wanted a big, oversized walk-in shower made completely out of lead. It was quite awkward, but we did the whole thing by wiping lead pieces together. We also connected pipes to the big water tanks that held the water on top of the buildings. But mostly we put in hot water heaters or basins. Kitchens, I learned, were easy: we would frame the kitchens, put up the walls, run the water lines from the wall risers, and run the waste lines into the four-inch drains. You could put a kitchen together in about six to eight days. I was working for a lot of people in those days who knew I was a musician, but no one held it against me.

My day jobs would continue for another twelve years, until I was forty-one. I never considered academic or conservatory work. The commitment of time and probable relocation to a far less interesting place than New York completely ruled out a teaching job. Of course, I was never offered a job anyway, and when I finally had a conversation about it, not even an offer, I was already seventy-two years old and unwilling to consider it at all.

IN THE SPRING OF 1968, JOANNE WAS PREGNANT, and she and I began attending Lamaze classes. For her first experience of childbirth, she wanted a natural childbirth, but she wasn't prepared to do it at home, so we went for months to the training sessions to develop the breathing technique. The idea was that if you did the Lamaze method, the child would be born without having to give the mother an anesthetic that would get into the child's bloodstream.

In October, JoAnne's contractions began fairly close to her due date. We were told to wait until the contractions were within two-hour periods, and that took a while. First there was a contraction, and then another one, and then maybe she didn't have another for four or five hours. There were a number of days like that, but we knew it was coming.

At that time there were not that many hospitals that would allow the husband to come into the delivery room, but we did some research and found one that would. When the contractions were coming regularly and close enough together, we went to the hospital. I had to be disinfected and dressed up like a doctor from head to toe. I stood beside JoAnne, and we began doing the breathing exercises together. By that time the contractions were coming maybe every ten minutes, but then things slowed down. We started off with no anesthetic, but as the hours went by, it was clear that the birth wasn't going to happen soon, and at some point the anesthetic was used. In the early morning the baby came out, a girl with a lot of hair on her head. JoAnne stayed in the hospital for a couple of days.

One of those mornings I came into the room and JoAnne said, "I've got the name." She'd been reading Shakespeare, and the name was Juliet. We took baby Juliet back home to West Twenty-Third Street.

Juliet was the first baby born in the Mabou Mines troupe. It goes without saying that there was a lot of excitement in the house. Not long after, Ruth and Lee had Clove, and on our first tour a couple of years later, we took both girls along, staying in peoples' homes because there was no money for hotels. It worked out fine, because the kind of people who would invite a theater group like ours to perform were equally capable of inviting us to stay with them. In 1976, when we toured Europe with *Einstein on the Beach*, both Juliet and our son, Zack, came on tour with us.

By the time Zack was born three years later, in 1971, it had become common for the father to be in the delivery room. This time we didn't do the Lamaze classes, as JoAnne wasn't so convinced that it had been that helpful. We also did not have the time. I was working full-time and so was JoAnne, who had both theater and housecleaning jobs to do. If JoAnne wasn't available, because of having a rehearsal, I would be her substitute. The pay wasn't bad, you could get maybe thirty-five or forty dollars for cleaning an apartment, and if you did two jobs in a day, it would be about eighty dollars, paid in cash. It wasn't a lot of money, but we didn't need a lot of money, either. A quart of milk was thirty cents, and if you smoked, a pack of cigarettes cost about the same.

We knew the second child was going to be a boy, and we named him Wolfe Zachary Glass, Wolfe coming from my uncle Willie Gouline, the same uncle who paid for my trip to Paris when I was seventeen and sent me bits of money during my years at Juilliard. Uncle Willie's Yiddish name was Wolfe, with Willie being an Anglicization of that.

While Zack's birth was not the same process as Juliet's, it was no less extraordinary. The beginning of a life and the end of a life are both huge transitions. There's nothing greater. I didn't know much about the ending of lives at that time, but I learned about beginnings with my children.

———

THE PHILIP GLASS ENSEMBLE, as it would come to be known, began to take shape because I needed musicians who were willing and able to play my music. No doubt I had been inspired by Ravi Shankar, who was the ultimate composer-performer. When I came back to New York, I began by calling up friends from my Juilliard days, first Arthur Murphy, and then Steve Reich. Both were composers. Arthur had come out of a twelve-tone and jazz background, and Steve, from what I knew of his recent concerts, was "phasing" musical phrases against themselves and producing extraordinary and beautiful music. He had begun working with tape machines, playing the same music on two different tape recorders. Since the recorders were playing at slightly different speeds they began drifting, and Steve heard new patterns of music emerging. Most people wouldn't have noticed, but Steve understood that something new was happening. The development of that idea became the basis of his early pieces. He did a piano phase and a reed phase. He went to Africa, and when he came back he began working with drumming. By then he was fully equipped to develop a whole body of original work.

Jon Gibson, who had played in my first concerts, was also one of the founding members of the ensemble. So now I had Jon playing saxophone and Arthur and Steve and myself playing piano. Almost immediately we were joined by Dickie Landry, another saxophonist, who arrived from Cecilia, Louisiana. A year later, Joan La Barbara, a singer with a *beautiful* voice, added her talents to the ensemble. Richard Peck, a friend of Dickie's, yet another Cajun from Louisiana, came up from the South. He became the third saxophonist and stayed with us for the next forty years. Michael Riesman, who began with us in 1974, became the music director in 1976. From then on, he was responsible for rehearsals, auditions of new players, and, in recent years, many of the arrangements of music that were taken from other works of mine. Significant additions to the ensemble over the years have included singers Iris Hiskey and Dora Ohrenstein, Mick

Rossi, Martin Goldray and Eleanor Sandresky on keyboards, Andrew Sterman, Jack Kripl, and David Crowell on winds, and Lisa Bielawa, singer and keyboards. Lisa expanded the role of the "lead singer" to include chorale preparation for the 2012 production of *Einstein on the Beach* that was produced by Linda Brumbach and her Pomegranate Arts company. Over the years Linda has taken on responsibility for booking live performances and many new productions. All the players in the ensemble have been composers in their own right. Dan Dryden, who has been mixing live concerts for the last thirty years, became the archivist of the ensemble's many concerts and recordings. Steve Erb served as stage mixer.

From the outset, the ensemble rehearsed one night a week, using the top floor of the Twenty-Third Street building as our rehearsal room. I had a very simple rule: the ensemble was dedicated to the music that I was writing. I would play the music of other composers in the group if they organized a rehearsal of their own. But any time they came to my house, there was only one music we were going to play, and that was my own. That was a very radical idea at the time. What normally happened was that three or four composers would get together and form a composers' group, and every time they did a concert, everyone had a piece on the program. To me, this was a prescription for disaster. The programs would always be the same, and there would always be hidden agendas. I was not interested in investing any time in anything like that.

With the ensemble, I realized there was a music problem I needed to address immediately: finding a concise solution to notating pieces of music of fairly long duration with as few page turns as possible. As long as I was playing by myself, it didn't matter, since I routinely memorized the music. But with an ensemble of four or five people, I needed a system of notation where the structure of the music could be represented in a more condensed way.

I solved the problem by inventing an additive, progressive system. If I had a phrase that was five notes long, I could add a multiplier—for example, ×5—next to it. Whenever the phrase was changed, either by adding or subtracting a note, I would then add a new multiplier as needed. This notational device made it possible to reduce a sixty-page piece to five or six pages. That "eureka" moment had come about because of the necessity of compressing the notation.

It proved to be a tremendous breakthrough that made it possible to compose two new pieces, "Two Pages" and "1 + 1," which were pivotal in the development of a repertory for the newly formed ensemble. "Two Pages" was an eighteen-minute work in which a line of music was pulled in and out of shape through adding and subtracting notes from an original theme, thereby determining the overall shape of the music. This was the first piece where the multiplier system was used, and therefore it was given the title "Two Pages." "1 + 1" was a mathematical expression of the idea of incremental changes through addition and subtraction.

I was doing two things at once: with "Two Pages" I was synthesizing new ideas about music; with "1 + 1," I was applying an analytic point of view by which I could extract and express a process. I always made the synthesis the beginning point and the analysis as the afterthought. This method came out of performance and intuition and the physicality of playing. This, in turn, encouraged me to develop as a performer, and that activity led automatically to further ideas of structure and process.

With three keyboards and two saxophones, and soon a singer, we needed a sound system we could all plug into. The ensemble's original four-channel sound system was put together with two University twelve-inch speakers and two Dyno-kit amplifiers that I had built for me from kits that came with instructions. We used Y connectors to fit the eight channels we needed into the four channels we had. I picked up three Farfisa electric organs for two hundred dollars each from the Buy-Lines. This kind of used keyboard was easy to come by. Usually a few weeks after Christmas they could be found for sale. I always found them, without exception, in a knotty-pine paneled basement in Queens. This gave me a total sound system for less than one thousand dollars. It was a stretch, but I couldn't get along without it.

It just meant more moving jobs or plumbing work. Not all that hard to manage.

What was missing was an actual sound-mixing person. That turned up very soon, but for the first concerts with works like "Music in Fifths," "Music in Contrary Motion," and "Music in Similar Motion," we had the charmingly naïve practice of allowing members of the ensemble simply to get up and rebalance the mixes themselves during the concert. Since we didn't have individual monitoring speakers, it would only be a few minutes before another ensemble member got up and remixed the whole thing again. A few concerts like that and civil war would have broken out. Before that happened, a friend sent a young man, Kurt Munkacsi to hear us play. He saw the problem right away, including my homemade system. When I asked him if he could help, he answered, rather modestly, "Oh yes, I think I can."

Kurt had been a botanist at college and left science for rock 'n' roll. He brought with him an aptitude for sound, electronics, and a pair of fine rock-'n'-roll ears. He was very interested in electronics and sound and had begun working at a place called Guitar Lab, where at one point he actually worked for John Lennon. I asked him if he would be the sound engineer for us. His ideas about music were developing very rapidly in those days. In fact, he was interested in almost anything that involved amplification. Since amplification had become such an important part of my music, it gave him a chance to develop. Mixing was something that we didn't know very much about, so he brought a certain level of expertise to what we were doing that hadn't existed before. I was delighted to be as far away as possible from the world of modern music with its wildly dissonant but overly polite veneer. The acquisition of a technique based both on Western and Eastern traditions gave me the confidence to imagine a music that needed no explanations or excuses.

Right after the Cinematheque concert in May 1968, I began writing three new pieces, which were completed between June and December—the aforementioned "Music in Similar Motion," "Music in Contrary Motion," and "Music in Fifths." I was able to compose each piece in a two- or three-week period. It then took the ensemble three or four weeks of rehearsal to achieve a reasonable command of the music. These were radical pieces. There was a grunginess to them that came out of the technology that was available at the time—the electric pianos and the big, oversized boom-box speakers. The pieces were loud and they were fast, and they didn't stop. "Music in Similar Motion" is a string of eighth notes that goes on for fifteen minutes or so. It's unrelenting. You could get high from it, and people did. That music *had* to be mixed and amplified. This was the technology that provided the emotional punch I had been looking for. Listening to this music was like standing in a very strong, cold wind and feeling the hail and the sleet and the snow pounding your flesh. It was definitely bracing. The music had the feeling of a force of nature. I had somehow stumbled onto a state of feeling that you can describe that way. It was not meant to be mindless, but to be organic and powerful, and mindful, too. If you listened to the structure, you could hear the phrases changing constantly, even though the stream of music was so constant that it might feel like it wasn't changing. The trick of that music was that it allowed the attention to form around a series of successive events that became almost unnoticeable—around the function of listening to something that seemed as if it were not changing, but was actually changing all the time.

In terms of the new dimension added to the music by amplification, it might best be described as a simple question of form and content, or surface and structure, from a sculptural point of view. The structure was there in the rhythmic phrases, and the surface would have been the sound. These ideas of form and content/surface and structure were at that time very much current in the world of art and performance.

With the third of the three pieces, "Music in Similar Motion," I discovered a completely different kind of development that provided a new compositional opening. "Music in Similar Motion" proceeded very much like "Music in Fifths" and "Music in Contrary Motion," with the difference that when the line of music reached its greatest length, it then began to shorten, phrase by phrase, until it arrived at the original length. At that point, by fragmenting the original phrase and using only a small part to build a new musical structure, based, as before, on an additive process, a new development could take place.

Effectively, I now had two systems: a closed system and an open system. "Music in Contrary Motion" represented the closed system, in which the compositional process reached a point where it was unable to offer any new musical development. This is like having a table filled with glasses and at a certain point, there would be no room for any more glasses. The open system, represented by "Music in Similar Motion," would be like adding a new table when the first table is filled.

Interestingly, this description of open and closed systems does not exist in any book on theory that I've ever seen. In this way, it became evident to me that I was working with a new language of structure. This new strategy would become an important underpinning for the works that immediately followed—*Music with Changing Parts* and *Music in Twelve Parts*. Furthermore, it would become the common practice of the additive music composed for *Einstein on the Beach*.

My first big public concert in a big museum occurred in January 1970 at the Guggenheim Museum. It consisted of those three pieces— "Music in Fifths," "Music in Contrary Motion," and "Music in Similar Motion"—which we played in the 120-seat recital hall. Almost the entire audience was made up of my friends, who were naturally enthusiastic. Each piece was close to twenty minutes long, so we would play a piece and then take a break. The music was amplified, but there wasn't very much to mix because the music was still very transparent. It was a very good program because the pieces were related, and it was the first time that the ensemble could really show off its highly developed style of playing.

SINCE RETURNING TO NEW YORK, I HAD SPENT SOME FREE EVENINGS with Richard Serra helping him at his studio. He couldn't really afford a studio assistant, so when I got home from my day job, I would help him with his work whenever additional manpower was required.

Sometime after the Cinematheque concert, in the winter of 1968–69, I had a call from Richard. Leo Castelli, who was recruiting a whole generation of up-and-coming artists for his gallery, had put him on a stipend and invited him to make a one-man show in Castelli's uptown warehouse. Richard was already known for doing floor pieces as well as for working with neon, rubber, and whatever of interest could be found in the streets of lower Manhattan. There was expectation and interest among art critics and people in the art world to see what he would do next.

Richard asked me to help him get ready for the show as his studio assistant. I always liked working in Richard's studio, but I also was making a decent salary at the time working for Sandy Rheingold. I remember telling Richard, "I'd love to do it, but I'm making two hundred dollars a week now working for a plumber."

Richard said that the money was no problem, but that we needed to start right away. That was fine with me and I began practically the next day. I worked full-time with Richard for almost three years. I enjoyed the work and it was a great parallel activity to my composing for the ensemble, not to mention the theater work that I was also doing with Mabou Mines. There was enough flexibility in his schedule so that I could still tour with the ensemble and perform in and around New York as the opportunity arose.

The first big job was to get ready for the warehouse show, which would take months of preparation. Much of the show would be Richard's early prop pieces, yet to be made. Also, there would be some rolled-lead pieces and even at least one freestanding piece, *The House of Cards*. This was very new work that few people had seen. As I came to understand, there were two elements that would have to come together—the materials and the process. I had no training in sculpture or art, apart from the occasional evenings spent with Richard in his studio. However, I had a good layperson's understanding of contemporary art, and I soon began picking up what Richard was doing. In fact, from the beginning he took over my art education quite seriously. He realized right away that for me to be useful he needed to talk to me and I had to understand what he was talking about. He would give me books to read and study, and we often went on museum and gallery visits that sometimes took up a whole day. In fact, I never knew what we would be doing on any day, because, apart from the mornings, there were no typical days.

The days began with coffee and breakfast at a cafeteria in Tribeca on West Broadway just above Chambers Street. Working artists live very regular lives, rising early and working all day—a fact almost completely unknown to most people. The cafeteria, in an area with a high density of artists' lofts nearby, was frequented by many of our friends—Susan Rothenberg, Richard Nonas, Chuck Close, Keith Sonnier, and Joel Shapiro, to mention only the first few that come to mind—a group of young people who were becoming very successful very quickly and who, almost overnight it seemed, became the leaders of a new art movement focused on working with materials and process.

These breakfasts were not leisurely meetings. Everybody was off and running very quickly. For Richard and for me, the beginning of the day offered three possibilities. Either we went out looking for materials to work with—found on the street or bought in different kinds of supply houses; or we went right to work in his studio nearby on Washington Street; or as mentioned, we spent the day in museums and galleries. A lot of these museum and gallery visits were for the benefit of my education, though Richard clearly enjoyed them himself. He was a born teacher, and he knew and thoroughly understood art history and practice. Richard likes to discuss things and analyze them, and he does so logically and intuitively. That is part of his dialectic method, so that he always has a chance of bringing in something new, something surprising. He has a well-educated sense of history, a highly developed sense of quality and what constitutes innovation in the arts, and he also has a great sensitivity to the difficulties of comprehension and the kind of complex world we live in.

During one of our working days together, I said to Richard, "You know, Richard, I wish I could draw. I can't even draw a tree."

"I can help you with that."

"Really? How?"

"I'll teach you to 'see' and then you will be able to draw."

I was completely stunned by his suggestion. Straightaway I had the following thought: Drawing is about seeing, dancing is about moving, writing (narrative and especially poetry) is about speaking, and music is about hearing. I next realized that music training was absolutely about learning to hear—going completely past everyday listening. And that was, for Mlle. Boulanger and Mlle. Dieudonné, the core of their training.

I never did get my "seeing" lessons from Richard, so I never did learn to draw. We were always busy with seeing his work, which I learned to do quite well. But the ability to see creatively, the way a visual artist could, always remained beyond my abilities. However, my future work in opera—using text, movement, image, and music—would place me in an active relationship with other "seers" and became a great source of growth and satisfaction.

———

ONE DAY, RICHARD SAID, "By the way, Chuck is taking pictures of people and painting their portraits. Will you let him take your picture?"

I had first met Chuck Close when I was living in Paris and he was on a Fulbright grant to Vienna. Now Chuck had a studio in the building next to Richard's.

"Sure," I said.

We went next door to Chuck's. It wasn't a very elaborate setup. There was a camera and a chair to sit in—like getting your passport picture taken. He might have clicked the shutter more than once, but it seemed I sat for him for less than a minute and it was done.

Chuck told me, "You know, in the past, portraits were paid for by patrons. They were very famous people, and this was how they had their likenesses done. There was no other way to do it. They were usually dukes or kings or queens or whatever they were. I'm taking pictures of people who are completely unknown." Ironically, it turned out that almost everyone whom Chuck took a picture of that day would become famous, something we would joke about.

In fact, what Chuck was actually doing was something much more radical: he was making portraits in which the process of painting became more important than the subject. He was able to do that through his highly developed technique as a painter.

Chuck had gone to Yale, as had a lot of other very good painters—Brice Marden and Richard Serra among them. They were all at Yale at the same time, and they all became very well-known. The painting of me was later sold to the Whitney Museum. When my daughter, Juliet, was seven or eight years old, she was taken to the Whitney with her class from school one day, and when she saw my picture on the wall she said to someone, "That's my daddy."

"Yeah, yeah, sure," was the reply. But it was, indeed, her daddy.

Those portraits were very distinctive works, and Chuck began elaborating on the images very quickly, sometimes painting with dots, sometimes with fingerprints, and even using wads of white and gray paper. He found ingenious ways of reproducing that image of me in even more variations—lithographs, prints, and whatever he could dream up. He made over a hundred different works from that one image. He told me once that the reason he liked the image was because of my hair. I had naturally curly hair, and I had a hard time growing it long, because it never grew down, only up—it would get down to my jaw and then start to turn up and grow upward. It wasn't as big as an Afro, but it was a very wild, oceanlike head of hair. That's what you see in the pictures, and it seems that Chuck enjoyed the technical challenge it presented.

TO BE WORKING WITH RICHARD was an irreplaceable experience. In the end, I believe Richard benefited from me as well. For one thing, since I was not an artist or sculptor myself, I "had no dog in that fight," as the expression goes. I had not a drop of envy, jealousy, or feeling of "ownership" in anything Richard did. I especially loved his talent, eye, and skill. My own work was in another domain apart from all that, so I was completely free to help and participate and actually enjoy the time in his studio.

The curious but not at all surprising fact was that the development of my own musical language, at least conceptually (not at all a small point!), had a relationship to Richard's development. How could it be otherwise? The two elements involved in Richard's work, the materials and the process, were the same issues I was addressing as they presented themselves in music. Certainly the music I was composing from 1967 to 1976 was steeped in just those same two essential issues.

But there is more to it than that. I was also inspired by two artists whose work Richard and I knew quite well. My personal response to Jasper Johns's *Flag* paintings was that the paintings of the flag and the flag itself were identical, and I couldn't see it any other way. By conflating form (the flag) and content (the painting of the flag), I saw them as separate and the same in a single moment of perception. That is similar to Johns's *Number* paintings and *Target* paintings. But the *Flag* paintings (including the astonishing triple flag) are more striking because the flag itself, as an iconic image with its own emotional baggage, is more loaded. Once the identity of form and content is understood (or "seen"), then this other emotional baggage drops away almost immediately.

With Robert Rauschenberg, I understood a similar idea at work with a radically different solution. It is well-known that Jasper and Bob knew each other very well as young painters, and were constantly looking at each other's work. And that went on for years before Leo Castelli took them both into his gallery in 1957—when I was just twenty, a good ten years before I had any idea what they were up to. It looked to me as if Bob was working out the same problem (form and content) but perhaps in an even more radical way. It was as if he was redefining painting in terms of how much he could put into the work and still keep it a painting. A door? A lightbulb? A goat with a tire around its middle? For all his efforts, it was a while before people, critics, and even other painters took his work seriously. So, if Jasper was poking around with images and canvases and their limits from the inside, then Bob was upsetting the whole apple cart by dragging things into the painting from the outside. Their strategies were wholly different, but it looked to me like they were fighting the same war. For me, a musician at the beginning of his own road of discovery, these two painters were monumentally important. And then, when you threw the work of John Cage and Merce Cunningham into the equation, everything made sense and lifted right off the ground.

For Richard's show in Castelli's warehouse, I made one small, but in the end, significant suggestion.

"Why don't you try lead?" I told him, when he was looking for materials to work with.

The root of the word "plumbing" is "plumb," and *plumbum* in Latin means "lead." Lead has had a long role in the history of plumbing, and now it was about to have another history in sculpture. I took

Richard to the plumbing supply store on Eighth Avenue where Sandy Rheingold had often sent me to buy materials. Bringing him there was actually all I did. Richard saw rolls and rolls of lead, as well as various implements and rigs for cutting and melting lead. He was unbelievably excited and happy and couldn't wait to get his hands on the lead. On the spot he ordered hundreds of pounds of lead and heating equipment to be delivered to his studio.

"I'll take some of that, and I'll take some of that, and I'll take some of that," he said. It was a big order, but it wasn't something out of the ordinary. Richard looked as if he could have been a building contractor, or the head of a construction team. He was strong, muscular, and clear-eyed. He didn't tell them why he wanted it, and they didn't give it a second thought. If we had been working for a construction company, we could have easily bought that much.

The next day the lead arrived. Fortunately there was an elevator, though a very slow one, and we managed to get the load up to Richard's studio. I spent a little time showing him how to cut, bend, and "wipe" (join together two pieces) lead, and also how to set up a small pot to melt the lead. After that, he was up and running. A lot of the work (rolling and cutting the lead) could be done better with four hands than with two, so I was still an important part of the process. In almost no time, Richard got around to throwing hot lead against a concrete wall or corner. I became an important part of these "splash pieces" by just keeping the lead liquid and plentiful while Richard was throwing the lead into place. He especially loved making those pieces, and I got a big kick out of it, too. For the next year or so, I accompanied him—and kept the lead flowing—whenever he installed the splash pieces.

While we were working together, Richard was invited to be part of two group shows in Europe scheduled to open in the spring of 1969, one at the Stedelijk Museum in Amsterdam and the other at the Kunsthalle in Bern, Switzerland, with a one-man show in Cologne at Rolf Ricke's gallery right in between. This would all happen in a two-week period, and Richard wanted me along to help prepare the lead for the splash piece on the exterior of the Stedelijk Museum as well as the normal installation of some of the prop pieces, which would be for all three locations. I worried about being away from home, family, and music that long, so I asked Richard about the possibility of my playing some concerts along the way. I already had a program in mind—*Wavelength*, a film by Michael Snow; then *Come Out*, a tape piece of Steve Reich's; and concluding with a solo performance of my own "Two Pages." Richard was happy to help with that and suggested he could arrange a concert in each of the same venues as his exhibits. These would be my first concerts in Europe with the new music.

It turned out to be a very good tour for Richard and myself. The lead splash piece made a big impression on the artists and art public, as did the prop pieces. This was Richard's early work from today's perspective, all of it really challenging. For me, this would be my first time among the new European artists and musicians, many of them older artists and well known from the generation before us. I met Joseph Beuys from Germany for the first time and also Mario Merz from Italy. Beuys, who had settled in Düsseldorf, was by then a huge icon in the art world in Europe and was becoming known in the States. Richard and I were doing a big splash piece outside the Stedelijk Museum, but we would go inside and see Beuys making his own installation. I was completely taken by him and his work, which was also process work where the materials became the subject. Beuys was easy to spot because he had a work costume—trousers with suspenders over a shirt open at the collar, boots, and a hat, which he wore all the time, making him seem like a cartoon of himself. After the outdoor splash piece was completed, Richard and I were given a room to work in. One day Beuys came and sat on the floor with his back against the wall opposite us, watching us for a long time. He didn't say a word while we were working, but later, as he was leaving, he came over and shook our hands. I don't remember whether he came to my concert the next day, but he was a very kind man, gentle in his manner, famous for being dedicated and very single-minded in terms of his art. The work was very radical. Sometimes it was hard to even tell what it was. This was during the time when he was making art out of huge pieces of margarine melting on the floor. Richard and I knew his work from books, and we were impressed that he had come and spent so much time observing us. I realized very quickly—and Richard did as well—that Richard was bringing something new to Europe, something that they hadn't seen before. And there was obviously great respect for Richard and his work.

Over the next decade I was often in these kinds of museum shows that brought together artists and, soon afterward, performers from all over. In 1974, at Project 74, a big festival in Cologne, I met Jack Smith, the legendary underground filmmaker and performance artist, and saw for the first and only time one of his big slide shows with the Hawaiian music he loved. Later, I did see some of his smaller pieces in New York, but far too rarely.

The concerts that Richard had arranged for me were, on the whole, enthusiastically received, though there were also, at times, enthusiastic rejections, which could lead to downright rowdy encounters. In the concert at the Stedelijk Museum there were whistles and catcalls during the showing of *Wavelength*. The film was a forty-minute single zoom from outdoors, through a window, onto a photograph on a wall, and finally ending on a tiny detail of the photograph. *Come Out* by Steve Reich was an early and beautiful extrapolation of a vocal phrase, re-recorded and pulled out of phase with itself. There was ample audience support, too, but the show's detractors' attempts to disrupt the performance and deny the audience the opportunity to see and hear these works was almost achieved. Clearly, the music deniers had had enough by the time I began playing "Two Pages." Before I had gotten even halfway through my performance, I noticed someone had joined me on the stage. The next thing I knew he was at the keyboard banging at the keys. Without thinking, acting on pure instinct, I belted him across the jaw and he staggered and fell off the stage. Half the audience cheered and the rest either booed or laughed. Without a pause, I began playing again, having lost the momentum of the music for not much more than five to six seconds. My assailant didn't come back and I was able to complete the performance. Meanwhile, Richard was sitting in the front row the whole time. I was a little annoyed with him after the concert, and I said to him, "How come you let that jerk climb up on the stage?"

"I think you did pretty good," he laughed.

That was the first time someone actually tried to stop a concert of mine, but not the last. That kind of outrage from audience members went on for years. I've never been entirely sure what the outrage was all about. The reason might have been that I didn't "sound" like what they thought new music was supposed to sound like. I think they thought I was teasing them, trying to make fun of them, which was a ludicrous idea. Why would I go all the way to Europe to make fun of a bunch of yokels there who didn't know anything about world music or even new music? They hadn't spent time with Ravi Shankar. They hadn't gone to India. They hadn't made the journey I had, opening myself to all different sounds of music. They didn't know anything. Still, even though Amsterdam was our first stop, nothing like that happened again on that tour. This was really the beginning of my European touring and, thanks to Richard, I immediately became part of the art world, just as I had in New York.

One of the last weeks I spent working with Richard was also the most memorable. Jasper Johns invited Richard to install one of the splash pieces in his home, a former bank building at the corner of Houston and Essex Streets. Richard and I spent a week there, more or less. I remember that one day I was downstairs for some reason, and when I looked in a room that had been the vault of the bank, I saw that it was full of Jasper's paintings, including one of his famous *Number* paintings, still on an easel.

I knew that it had been made years before, and I asked Jasper, "Are you still working on those *Number* paintings?"

"Oh yes, I'm still working on them," he replied.

The painting I was looking at was probably seven or eight years old, but he was still painting on it. It impressed me greatly that he was able to focus his attention to that degree.

At that time John Cage was Jasper's houseguest, and Jasper had lunch prepared for us every day. For that hour, we all stopped work—Jasper, John, Richard, and me—to eat together. It was very good company.

THROUGH A SERIES OF LUCKY EVENTS, by the end of 1971 my ensemble was able to make its first recording. It came about in this way. Carla Bley and Mike Mantler, two well-known jazz composers, were in Martinson Hall on the top floor of the Public Theater recording a new work, *Escalator over the Hill*. They were using a mobile studio, packed into a van owned by Steve Gephardt and Bob Fries, who worked under the name "Butterfly Recording Studio." Carla and Mike and I had become friends as active composers in New York and they offered me their setup, free, for two days on a weekend when they wouldn't be working. The work to be recorded was music I had written in 1970, *Music with Changing Parts*, an evening-length work we had been playing in Germany, London, and New York for most of 1970 and 1971.

I was in the habit, in those days, of sending in six copyrights together, because one could send in the form and register up to six pieces and only pay a single fee. Musicologists later would find paperwork that showed that a piece was written at a later date, but it wasn't *written* at a later date, it was only *copyrighted* at a later date. I did that to save the six dollars. One writer published in a book the copyright of a certain piece, just to prove that it was written at a later time. He thought I had backdated it, but actually, I just didn't get around to registering the copyright until later. I also had the mistaken idea that if I postponed the copyright date, the copyright would last longer, which isn't true because the term of copyright goes from the death of the composer, not from the birth of the composition. I didn't know that at the time, so I often made my dates later, thinking I would have more control over the rights. I was very aware at that point that the ownership of the music was mine. It didn't belong to a publisher or to anybody else. As I told my mother on her deathbed, I never gave copyrights away. Later, working on film music, it turned out not to be always true.

In *Music with Changing Parts*, the players improvised, within prescribed limits, extended long tones. At times, clouds of notes would emerge that formed harmonic clusters, as if surfing through the ongoing ocean of rhythm. Because I was using a much larger musical structure, it became possible to make a very extended piece. There were certain things that remained the same: a constant beat would always be there—a steady stream of notes. Within that, the texture could change and the melodies could float throughout. There could be a wash of sound, places with just a little bit of rhythm, and places with barely more than long tones. It could sound like a cloud of music that would shift from being structured to amorphous. At moments, just as the rhythmic structure became audible, the long notes had a way of overriding it, adding a depth to the music. The only other times I would use this technique would be in Part 4 of *Music in Twelve Parts* and in "Building" in *Einstein on the Beach*.

We played *Music with Changing Parts* straight through for the recording, but problems remained. Martinson Hall wasn't set up as a studio at all, so we didn't have the possibility of isolating the players. There were nine of us in one large room playing together. In addition, we had never done a recording before and had to spend time learning how to set up the microphones and how to balance the instruments correctly. Above all, we had to be able to hear ourselves, and at the same time avoid feedback from the monitor speakers. In spite of these complications, and others that we hadn't anticipated, it was an exhilarating two days—something I think you can hear in the recording.

Even though we were getting the studio for free, I still needed money for musicians and manufacturing costs. It wasn't anything enormous, and I had some cash, but not enough, so I went to an office on Second Avenue. I can still recall the sign on the door—"Hebrew Free Loan." I met a gentle, sympathetic gentleman who explained to me that they made small, interest-free loans. I told him I was starting a record company, Chatham Square Records (we were no longer rehearsing on Twenty-Third Street, but in Dickie Landry's loft in Chinatown). I explained that I had recorded my music at the Public Theater and had gotten the studio for free, and now I had the master tape and the only thing that stood between me and making the record was about a thousand dollars.

"What are you going to do with the thousand dollars?" he asked.

"I need it to print and package the records."

"How much will you sell the records for?"

"I'll make five hundred records to start with and I'll go out and play music and I'll sell them at my concerts, probably for five dollars a record."

"We started this place for immigrants," he said, looking at me thoughtfully. "People who came from the old country. If they wanted to start a business, they came here and we could give them enough money to get started. So we really started this for them. But it doesn't say anywhere that I can't do this for you. You're as qualified as anybody else."

"That sounds good to me," I said. "How do we do this?"

"Well, I'll give you a thousand dollars and you pay me a hundred dollars a month for ten months."

"All right," I said.

I had a check by the next afternoon. He asked for very little documentation and no collateral—he just trusted me. He had my address and my phone number. He didn't even ask if I was Jewish. I think he liked the idea that I was a young man who was born in America and needed his help. He practically stuffed the money in my pocket, and I paid it back just the way he asked.

I SAVED WHATEVER CLIPPINGS, PROGRAMS, and announcements I had gathered from the European tour with Richard and, after getting back to New York, began sending out letters to schools, art galleries, and museums. "I will be with my ensemble in your area, and I would be happy to present a concert," said my letter, written so that it could be used for any recipient, the idea being to communicate that I could do the concert at a very low price because I would be already on the road. In my mind, I figured the fee they would offer would be five hundred dollars, but I never asked for that.

I sent out 120 letters with copies of all my programs up until then: I had programs from the Cinematheque and the Guggenheim Museum in New York and from Europe, but I didn't have any reviews that I could show to anybody. I received nine replies and organized a twenty-day tour for the ensemble and myself, renting a van for three hundred dollars from Lee Breuer. Two of us drove the van, and the rest followed in a beat-up station wagon I'd bought. All of our sound equipment would be in the back of the van, along with our personal baggage.

This first real tour in the spring of 1972 began at the University of California at Irvine and continued through Pasadena and Valencia, California; Portland, Oregon; Vancouver, British Columbia; Seattle and Bellingham, Washington; Minneapolis (two concerts); and St. Louis. The promoters had to provide housing, usually in the homes of music supporters. I believe I paid the ensemble members six hundred dollars each for the whole tour. When I got home I was in debt for a couple of grand, which took me several months to pay back. However, within a few years of this initial touring, there were enough performances for the ensemble each year to allow me to pay the players a minimum of twenty paychecks per year. By registering the ensemble as a company, filing the necessary paperwork, and paying the employer's share of the premium, the players qualified for unemployment insurance for the weeks when we had no performances. With the financial basis of employment stabilized in this way, it guaranteed a consistent membership in the ensemble, which in turn allowed us to reach an amazingly high level of performance. Most of the players have remained with us for periods of between fifteen and forty years.

I traveled without any money whatsoever for promotion or advertising, but I had LPs with me, and not just to sell at concerts (though we did that, too). There was, I soon discovered, especially in the States, a network of college radio stations operating everywhere. There was always some bleary-eyed college kid with an all-night radio program. It was dead easy to get on the program, especially with a new LP, which they were always happy to play in its entirety. One such young man I met in that way was Tim Page, who had an all-night radio program on Columbia University's WKCR. Tim would grow up to be a highly respected new music radio personality, a well-known critic, a writer, and a lifelong friend. I was also quickly learning how to talk about music, art, and travel. Without the usual "new music" institutional support, which I never had, I was really on my own, touring and making records. For the next few years and really up to *Einstein* in 1976 I was inventing the tools I would need to make a place for myself in the music world.

WHEN I LOOK BACK, THE BIGGEST INFLUENCE on my music has been in fact the energy system known as New York City. The city is in the music, especially the early ensemble music. The concerts that I did at the Guggenheim Museum, *Music in Twelve Parts*, *Music with Changing Parts*, and even *Einstein*—all of them right up until 1976—come right out of the guts of New York City. I had grown up in Baltimore, but New York is a 24/7 city. Paris goes to sleep at night—the métro shuts down, the sidewalks are rolled up—but New York never goes to sleep. That's why I came here.

The artists I knew and worked with weren't part of the entertainment world, but were all part of the New York experimental art world, often *very* experimental. You would see Jack Smith walking down the street in the East Village and you might think he was a homeless person. Or you might meet someone like Moondog (whose real name was Louis Hardin), a very funny and completely unconventional grown-up.

My friend Michel Zeltzman had first met Moondog where he hung out on the corner of Fifty-Fourth Street and Sixth Avenue. "C'mon, I want you to meet somebody," Michel told me one day. He took me to see Moondog, who was about six foot three or four, blind, and dressed like a Viking, with a big helmet with horns that came to a point and made him look like he was seven feet tall. He wore robes and boots he had made himself and walked with a spear. If you bought a poem from him for twenty-five cents, he would sing and play a little music on drums that he had built himself.

I got to know Moondog a little bit, and when I read in the paper that he was looking for a place to live and sleep, I went up to see him.

"Moondog, I've got a house down on Twenty-Third Street. If you want to, you can room in one of the upper floors."

"That's very kind. Can I come and visit you?"

"Yes, come any time."

"Tell me the address," he said. "I'll come and see you."

A week later I was looking out the window when I saw a Viking walking down Ninth Avenue. It was Moondog, moving very confidently and fast, crossing Twenty-Sixth Street, then Twenty-Fifth Street, then Twenty-Fourth. As he reached each corner, he stopped to wait for the light to change before crossing the street. When he arrived I asked him, "Moondog, how did you know when to stop for the light?"

"That's easy. I stand where the light is, and I can hear the electricity when the light changes, and I can feel the traffic. If it's going to the right, it's going across town. If it's going downtown, I can tell. I wait until after it's gone, then I hear a click, and then I walk."

I took him upstairs up to the big room on the top floor and I said, "This could be your room, if you like it."

"Where are the walls?" He was trying to reach out and touch the walls.

"Well, it's kind of a big room."

"No, no, no. Do you have a small room?"

"Right next to it there's a small room."

"Take me to the small room."

I led him there, and when he reached out toward the walls, he easily could touch them.

"I'll take the small room. If I get the big room, I'll lose things in it. In the small room, I can figure out where everything is."

As it turned out, Moondog stayed with us for a year. The biggest problem—and there were several problems—was that he would always eat takeout, usually from Kentucky Fried Chicken or something similar, and he would put the trash down on the floor, forget it was there, and never pick it up. He simply didn't know where it was. I discovered this right away, so I would go upstairs once he had left for the day, clean up after him, and take the trash out.

At that time, the ensemble was having rehearsals at my place once a week, and before too long Steve Reich and Jon Gibson and I began playing with Moondog, rehearsing together once a week as well. The four of us sang his songs, usually in the form of a round. Jon and I occasionally played flute, with Moondog on the drums. Steve recorded five or six of the songs on his Revox tape machine and held on to those tapes for a long time. Recently, a book was written about Moondog, and those recordings were included with the book.

After a year, Moondog was given a small property somewhere in the Catskills and was ready to move on. He was a modern Pied Piper of sorts, often surrounded by young people, and a number of them went with him to the country to help build his new home. He was still staying with me while the construction was going on, and I asked him what his house was going to look like. From his description, I understood there was one central room, small enough that he could touch all its walls with his arms extended. Five long hallways, each of which led to another small room, extended out from the central room. From above, it must have looked like a five-legged spider. Strange perhaps, but perfect for a blind man.

Moondog had a contract at one point with Epic Records and made a couple of records with them. He was an artist, and a very individual one. He told me that he had lost his sight when he was sixteen, in a Fourth of July accident when some blasting caps blew up in his face.

After that, he said, "I was sent to a jerk-water conservatory to become a piano tuner." He never did become a piano tuner—by that time, he had acquired his Viking persona, and he would cross the country playing music. He showed me his scrapbook, which was filled with articles about him. He became famous, and he came to New York and took up his place at the corner of Sixth Avenue and Fifty-Fourth Street, near the entrance of the Warwick Hotel.

Moondog could write counterpoint, and he could sing, but he especially liked classical music. Listening to my music, he said, "You know, I like your music, it's interesting. But you have to spend more time with Bach and Beethoven. Those are the two I learned from."

When I asked him, "What did you learn?" that was when he told me, as I mentioned earlier, "I really was trying to follow in their footsteps, but they were such giants, that to follow in their footsteps I had to leap after them."

That was Moondog, a giant Viking of a man so typical of some of the great characters who haunted New York in that era, leaping from footstep to footstep after Bach and Beethoven.

I STILL THINK OF NEW YORK CITY as a powerhouse of a place in which human energy, imagination, and spirit are nourished. The work of artists who live here is inextricably bound up with the city. I think this was true for me at least until my fifties or sixties.

"What does your music sound like?" I'm often asked.

"It sounds like New York to me," I say.

It is alchemy that takes the sounds of the city and turns them into music. If you've lived here, you know that.

In the 1970s and '80s, when I went to Paris or London, or Rotterdam or Rome, people's eyes would pop open when they heard my music, because they were hearing something that they wouldn't have heard from Europeans. The music that I was playing and writing in those early years, that I was importing to Europe, was quintessentially New York music in a way that I always hoped it would be. I wanted my concert music to be as distinctive as Zappa at the Fillmore East, and I think I ended up doing that.

In this very same way, I was drawn to the jazz of Ornette Coleman's and Lennie Tristano's music, as well as to the sound of Bud Powell and Charlie Parker. During my last years at Juilliard, on many nights I would go to hear John Coltrane at the Village Vanguard. If he wasn't there, I'd go over to the Five Spot and hear Thelonious Monk and Ornette. I considered all of them to be fellow alchemists, taking the energy of New York and transforming it into music.

There was a huge explosion going on in New York in the 1960s when the art world, the theater world, the dance world, and the music world all came together. It was a party that never stopped, and I felt like I was in the middle of it.

CAPE BRETON

URING THE TIME WHEN JOANNE WAS PREGNANT WITH JULIET, the idea of finding a place outside the city to spend the summer months began to occupy me. In those days, concert work was still so sporadic that I could really take two months off. All I had to do was have enough money to eat, so I was looking for a place to go for July and August, since concerts happened mainly in the fall, winter, and spring, the opposite of today with summer festivals dominating everyone's schedule.

My partner in this search was my friend Rudy Wurlitzer, whom I had met in 1954 in Paris. We had been friends from his days at Columbia University and mine at Juilliard. Rudy was one of the first writers I knew who had a successful book. His first novel, *Nog*, had just been published and he was writing a new one and also doing some work in film. He, too, wanted to find a place to work and get away from New York.

I'm sure the idyllic summers I spent at camp in Maine influenced me to head north, but the coast of Maine, or any part of the United States east coast, for that matter, was already too expensive. So on our first trip north, in the fall of 1968, Rudy and I drove into Canada, just south of Halifax, but we didn't find anything we liked. The next spring, I was doing some plumbing work for the photographer Peter Moore—putting in an air pressure system so that he could clean his negatives before he printed them—in exchange for publicity photographs. When I asked Peter if he knew of any place where we could go, he said, "A friend of mine has a place up in Cape Breton, Nova Scotia. It sounds to me that's what you're looking for."

Cape Breton had been an unattached island until the 1950s, when a short one-mile causeway was built to connect it to the mainland of Canada. This little causeway turned into one road that followed the entire coast of the island. To me, that meant one thing: there would be very few people actually living there, and that would make it afford-able for us.

So in the summer of 1969, JoAnne and I drove up to Cape Breton with Juliet, who was about eight months old. Once there, we rented a house with no heat or running water for eighty dollars for the whole summer. I wasn't working that much, but I did write some music, and JoAnne was reading Beckett and thinking about his plays, and both of us picked and ate blueberries, which were everywhere nearby. That was the summer that Neil Armstrong set foot on the moon. JoAnne and I were lying on a blanket with Juliet outside our cabin, looking straight up at the moon, listening to the CBC broadcast on a transistor radio as Armstrong said his famous line, "That's one small step for a man, one giant leap for mankind." It was completely surreal.

"JoAnne, he's up there," I said. We just couldn't believe it.

Going around Cape Breton, looking for property, talking to people, I met a man named Dan Huey MacIsaac who told me, "There's a place down on the other side of Inverness, an old campsite, but no one's been there for a while."

Dan Huey had been one of the carpenters who built the camp—fifty acres with a big main house and eleven A-frame cabins, right on the shore. There had been a dispute between the American owner and some local people about the property, and the American shut the place down. The following spring, I persuaded Rudy to come with me to check it out, and we agreed to make an offer. I had some cash from a small share of a property I inherited from Uncle Willie, who had recently died, and Rudy had some cash from a film job, so when we found out the owner of the camp, Mr. Coulter, was actually in New

York, we drove back home, met with him, and made the whole trans-action for twenty-five thousand dollars right there in his office across from Grand Central Station.

We would spend our first summer on the new property in 1970. The whole Mabou Mines theater company came up to rehearse *The Red Horse Animation*, and I was able to finish composing *Music with Changing Parts*. It was the first of many productive summers. Along about June every year I would buy a used station wagon, usually a Ford Falcon (preferably white), which almost always was good enough for the road trip from New York City to Cape Breton and back. That first year it was just JoAnne, Juliet, and myself. The next year we had Zack with us, plus a border collie named Joe.

Right away our artist friends began to visit. We had taken down three of the eleven A-frames and put them back together at one end of the land for Rudy's house, still leaving eight for guest housing. Over the next few years, the video artist Joan Jonas, the painters Robert Moskowitz and Hermine Ford, the writer Steve Katz, and Richard Serra all came to visit us, and within a few years they all had places of their own nearby. The photographers Robert Frank and June Leaf found a house a little farther away near the town of Mabou, and Peter Moore's friend Geoff Hendricks, the artist from the Fluxus movement who had preceded us there by several years, was nearby on Colling-dale Road. There were enough of us for a poker game or a beach party and, at the same time, we were separated enough so we could be left perfectly alone to work as we pleased.

Cape Breton, for those who are open to it, is a somewhat austere but deeply beautiful place. There, you are truly in the north. That little finger of land reaches up and above the greater mass of North America, pointing almost directly toward the North Pole. It is not unusual to see the northern lights on a summer evening, and the sky is still light until well after ten p.m. The nights can be cool and the days never more than warm.

Inverness, our nearest town, had a co-op grocery store, a post office, a few gas stations, several churches, a high school, a pharmacy, a drugstore, and a racetrack for harness racing every Sunday afternoon and Wednesday evening. It also had a waterfront lined with boats and lobster traps. It was home to two or three thousand people and eventually had a hospital as well. After a number of summers there, when I first arrived at the co-op to go shopping after being away for nine or ten months, the townspeople, who by then were used to seeing my family and me, would say, "Welcome home, Philip."

One of the best things about Cape Breton was my neighbors. John Dan MacPherson had the farm on the main road, just behind our place. In fact our fifty acres had been part of his farm before he sold it to the people who were thinking of it as a home and campsite for tourists. It had never had a real season, however. The place had been shut down for eight years until Rudy and I came along and bought it.

John Dan, I believe, was happy when we came along, thinking that perhaps the campgrounds would finally open, bringing instant prosperity to the little parish named Dunvegan. That didn't happen but, as it turned out, he liked us pretty well anyway. It wasn't long before I got to know his life story. He came from a big family, a dozen or so brothers and sisters—quite common in that part of the world. As one of the youngest, he left home early. He told me that he had traveled all over the world, working from place to place. At the age of fifty, he returned to Cape Breton to marry, settle down, and have a family, and over the next thirty years he had twenty-one children. I met him when he was in his midseventies and several new ones came along after that. He made his living fishing, farming, and cutting trees for pulp, and in the course of a long lifetime he had accumulated an astonishing amount of knowledge and wisdom.

I saw him quite often working in the woods between our two houses. One day he was pinning a tree he had cut down to the ground with wooden pegs. He had taken off all the limbs, but it still had all its bark. He was getting ready to build Rudy's house, he said, and needed some poles, which he called "round lumber."

"What are you doing, John Dan?" I asked.

"Getting ready for the full moon. That will be in a couple of days."

He answered all my questions with the soft Scottish-inflected accent common in Cape Breton.

"What does the full moon have to do with the trees?"

"I need to take the bark off to make the pole clean all around. When the moon is full, it will pull all the sap in the tree to the surface and I can pull the bark right off."

I tried to get there to see him when he would next be working again, but I missed that moment. When I got back to that spot a few days later, I found six to eight poles stacked there, all free of bark and ready for use.

Another time, walking with him in the woods, I had a question: "Tell me something, John Dan. I've been coming up here for a number of years now, and I notice that on the twenty-second or twenty-third of every August there will be a big storm. Why is that?"

"That's the day the sun crosses the line."

"The line?"

"Yes, the line. That's when fall begins."

I now understood that he was referring to the equinox and the "line" must be the equator. From that far north, the sun would appear to move toward the equator a little earlier than we're used to farther south in New York.

"And?"

"That's the day the sun begins to get weak and will allow a corruption to come in from the southeast."

Apart from the natural poetry of his language, I would ask myself, Are these the kinds of things that grown-ups are supposed to know? I knew none of them.

Again, one day we were walking in the woods. We came to a big tree with a sizable trunk and branches reaching up through the natural canopy. We stopped there for a moment of silence. Then he said, "Now that tree there. A millionaire could come up from New York and try to buy that tree. But he would never have enough money."

He paused for a moment as we contemplated his thought.

"And those children of yours. They're little now, but it will seem like tomorrow when, one day, they will be driving up here in a big car," and then with a sweep of his hand which took in our surroundings, "and all this will be just a dream."

With that he turned and walked off into the woods, leaving me standing there alone and speechless.

John Dan wasn't the only one I hung out with. Father Stanley MacDonald was my immediate neighbor. Angus MacClellan had about one hundred acres next to me and had given one acre to Stanley, where he built a small house, right on the water. It was a beautiful spot and Stanley, in the days before he retired from the Church, would manage to be there every week. He was a great reader and had by far the best library on the road, and that included Rudy's library and my own. He had taken up an interest in Jung and had even gone to the Jung Institute in Switzerland for a summer course. The archbishop in Halifax didn't care for him much. Probably he was too much of a freethinker.

Stanley was from around there, but the family had moved to Sydney, on the other side of Cape Breton, where his dad had opened a bakery and where all his kids—a baker's dozen or so—had worked. Stanley had been the priest of St. Margaret's Church just up the road from us, at Broad Cove. He had been there for years and knew everyone on the road for miles around. The archbishop couldn't get rid of him, but he assigned him to a very small parish in North Sydney, about ninety miles away, and it was there that, at his invitation, I visited him one Sunday morning. There were only ten or twelve people present, and they were sitting in small groups up and down the center aisle. I was somewhere in the back. After the regular service, Father Stanley gave his homily (sermon). It was very simple and straightforward. The theme was the pervasive suffering of life from which no one escapes. He began speaking (and not from notes) at the small pulpit in front of and below the altar. Leaving the pulpit, he began to walk down the aisle, stopping in front of each of his parishioners, pausing in his movement but not in his speech. He spoke to each one of them in turn, then, reaching the end of the aisle, he turned around, and continued talking, pausing, and speaking until he arrived back at the pulpit. His timing was exquisite and he ended his homily exactly at the moment he finally turned to again face his entire congregation.

Stanley recently retired from the Church and is working part-time as a Jungian therapist, as well as spending the coldest part of the winter as a chaplain to a convent near Antigonish, about one hundred miles away on the road to Halifax.

I also became very friendly with Ashley MacIsaac, who, because of his name, always has maintained that he is from the lost "Jewish clan." Ashley is an astonishingly talented fiddler in the Celtic tradition, with an encyclopedic memory of Cape Breton and Scottish fiddle tunes. At dances and concerts he can easily play three or four hours at a time, accompanied only by a piano. In those concerts, often in barns and pubs in Cape Breton, he is as hot as a pistol. I've often seen a barn full of people just stop dancing and gather around him while he played. JoAnne discovered him before me, in the summer of 1990, and wanted to bring him to New York City to perform in a production of *Woyzeck* she was directing at the Public Theater. I was the composer of the music and, accordingly, met him at my house in Dunvegan. His father, Angus, brought him over to meet me. He was seventeen years old at the time and, after hearing him for only a few minutes, I accepted him on the spot to be one of our musicians. Shortly after, he came to New York and stayed at my house during the rehearsals and the entire run of the play. Later, from time to time, he was on tour with my ensemble. He also became very friendly with my son Zack, who is himself a gifted singer and songwriter. They are the same age, in their early forties now, and these days Ashley comes to New York and plays in Zack's concerts and records with him as well.

After all these years, more than forty now, I have deep friendships in Cape Breton. The people there have a remarkable and deep connection to the sun, moon, stars, ocean, and land. On my side, I have composed many—for me—significant pieces and parts of symphonies and operas and concertos there. I was even featured one year as a "resident" composer at an annual music festival that takes place in Halifax.

Having a home in Cape Breton has meant that the kids and I could be outside of New York for a whole summer, in a place where I could have real writing time. Along the way, Cape Breton has become an irreplaceable part of my life.

NEW YORK'S
EAST VILLAGE

ON SUNDAY AFTERNOONS MY ENSEMBLE BEGAN OPEN rehearsals at a loft I rented in 1971 for $150 a month from Alanna Heiss's Idea Warehouse, a program that was partially supported by New York City. It was on the top floor at 10 Elizabeth Street, right at the corner of Bleecker, and for a time we played there every week on Sunday afternoons. I had found some old theater seats that I used to line the perimeter of the loft, and there were rugs covering the floor, collected from the sidewalks of New York on the Sanitation Department's rug collection day—Thursday nights. The advertising was done with leaflets taped to the walls and doorways in SoHo.

Mainly, our audiences were lying on the floor. They could have been sleeping for all I knew, but, at any rate, their bodies were there— maybe twenty, thirty, forty people at those early rehearsals. Over time, people began to be aware that I was developing a long-form piece, which was *Music in Twelve Parts*. I was writing at the rate of about one part every three months, three or four parts a year, and in three years, I had written the complete piece. I was aiming to get people curious about what was going to happen next, so on the days of the concerts when I was going to play a new part, such as Part 6, I would put flyers around SoHo—"Premiere of Part 6, *Music in Twelve Parts*, by Philip Glass, this Sunday at 3 o'clock at 10 Elizabeth

Street"—and there would be a build around those days when we did the premieres. I was attracting a following, very slowly, but had only a vague idea of who the audience was.

The origin of this piece was a single page of music that I composed and called *Music in Twelve Parts*, referring to the vertical stack of twelve lines of music—twelve music staves. Four keyboard players could play eight of the parts, plus three winds and one singer playing the other four, making a total of twelve parts.

I took a recording of this first piece to a friend, Eliane Radigue, a French composer of electronic music.

"I have a new piece," I said. "It's called *Music in Twelve Parts*. Would you like to hear it?"

"Of course," she said.

Afterward I asked her, "How did you like it?"

"I liked it very much," she said. "What do the other eleven parts sound like?"

She basically had misunderstood the title, but as soon as she said that, the plan to make eleven more parts occurred to me. I knew about collections of pieces—when I studied with Boulanger, we had done the first set of the twenty-four preludes and fugues of Bach—so now I had to write eleven more parts.

"I'll keep working on it," I told her.

In this way, *Music in Twelve Parts* came into being, made up of twelve pieces each about twenty minutes long. Professionally, I was in the midst of an extended period of experimentation in which my ultimate goal was to integrate all three elements of music—melody, harmony, and rhythm—into one overall structure. This had gone on from 1967 to 1974, and *Music in Twelve Parts* was the culmination of this exercise. By the time it was complete, it was an encyclopedic work.

After the driving rhythms of "Music in Similar Motion," I felt the need to do something new, so in writing Part 1 of *Music in Twelve Parts*, I had composed a slow, stately adagio. It's not a waltz, not being in three-quarter time, but a slow, stately waltz would give you a feeling of the music.

Part 1 turned out to be a long prelude to Part 2, which quickly picks up speed and presents the idea of cyclic music—short phrases of three or more notes that repeat until a new note is added or subtracted. This series of cycles, played over a steady six-note cycle—the kind of cyclic rhythms I learned from working with Ravi Shankar and Alla Rakha—is sometimes described as "wheels within wheels," which gives a good idea of what it sounds like. With Part 3, I began using pulsating rhythms—a kind of musical Morse code. In addition, in the middle of the piece, the listener hears a "drop" where the dominant keyboard's left hand—a deep bass sound—suddenly appears, an effect that had appeared first in "Music in Similar Motion."

Further musical exploration led, in Part 4, to the development of psycho-acoustical phenomena (notes that no one is playing, but that arise from the activity and density of the music). In Part 5, a two-note melody swings through numerous addition and subtraction of beats in the cycle, producing a constantly changing melodic/rhythmic shape. Part 6 continues the processes of Part 5, but now using a three-note phrase, producing something resembling a true, recognizable melody. With Part 7, there is a return to the process of Part 4, but instead of reinforcing one note at a time, whole phrases of three, four, and five notes begin to "pop up" out of the rhythmic-harmonic stew, which itself is constantly changing.

Halfway through Part 8, the whole edifice of "minimalism" gives way, as the ascending and descending scales shift to a superfast foxtrot-tango-samba. Any way you want to describe it, it comes down to a fast, stomping dance piece. In Part 9, I combined alternating ascending and descending diatonic (seven-note) and chromatic (twelve-note) scales in an indirect but explicit reference to the practice common to Indian ragas (melodies), but here resembling the sound of a thundering waterfall.

By the end of Part 10, which basically is an everyman's introduction to ornamentation—it contains most of the baroque options, including trills—I had really completely covered the review of the music processes that had occupied me since my time in Paris. However, I had unexpectedly discovered a new musical issue: it turned out that the breaks between one part and the next were highly dramatic moments. The shifts that occurred between two adjoining sections revealed an exquisite intensity that I had simply not anticipated until Parts 1 through 10 had actually been composed and performed. I had left these features of adjoining tonalities, rhythms, and texture entirely unprepared in the compositional process. On reflection, I seem to have understood that these joining moments between adjacent parts would be best left bare, so that the new musical-dramatic events would be heightened, rather than hidden. Therefore, I used the idea of these dramatic transitions as the entire basis of the composition of Part 11, which also served to introduce the strategy of "root movement" (or "harmonic movement") to the previous techniques.

In the final piece, Part 12, I used everything in the previous eleven parts, with even a twelve-note tone row embedded in an ever-expanding transitional middle section, in this way summing up the melodic option in one sweep that provides a concluding wild ride.

For the first complete performance of *Music in Twelve Parts* I rented Town Hall, a concert venue on Forty-Third Street near Sixth Avenue. It probably cost me seven or eight thousand dollars, but I didn't pay all the money up front. I was counting on selling tickets, since I was responsible for the rental fee. Town Hall holds somewhat more than fourteen hundred seats, and I had never seen more than forty or fifty people in my loft on any particular Sunday afternoon. The biggest audience I had ever drawn at a gallery or museum was one hundred and fifty, and at a college or university concert maybe three or four hundred.

Yet, somehow, we sold out the concert, the last ticket being sold the day of the show. I had no idea how it happened. I think we might have taken out one or two small ads, and I got some help with listings in *The Village Voice*, but there must have been a lot of word of mouth. Somehow, over those three years, the idea had begun to grow that there was a piece of music being made, and that on June 1, 1974, there would be a world premiere of that music—the complete *Music in Twelve Parts*.

The concert was a four-and-one-half-hour marathon, with a short break after Part 3, an intermission after Part 6, and another short break after Part 9. People were wildly enthusiastic, because no one had heard anything like it. They'd heard *parts* of it at a time, maybe three parts, but no one had heard the whole piece. The idea that all the parts would make up a whole piece was kind of astonishing. It had a musical trajectory of its own, and the audience was experiencing this trajectory as the architecture of music that revealed itself over a period of four and a half hours. If you were paying attention, you would hear how it worked, and evidently some people were paying attention. It was, I would say, pretty much of an unprecedented event to make a piece that long with an ensemble of seven players playing together with amplified sound equipment. It actually looked like we knew what we were doing, and we did. We had been practicing it for three years, part by part, adding it together, until finally, for the first time, we played the entire work.

I LOVED WORKING FOR RICHARD SERRA, but in my midthirties, I wanted more time for my children and for my composing and performing. I was looking for some kind of work that gave me the independence I would need, would not be physically too tiring, and would keep my hands in a "safer" environment. So, after my long association with Richard, I began taxi driving.

Driving a cab was never a problem for me. I liked driving in New York and I got to know the city very well. In the course of one night I easily drove a hundred miles: in Harlem, up to the Bronx, out to Queens, all over Brooklyn, and of course mostly in Manhattan. I never found New York boring when I was driving. I unfailingly saw the city as entertaining. The passengers could be exasperating—the variety of people and the outrageous kinds of behavior that happen in taxis are known only to people who have to spend a hundred miles a night in a taxicab three or four times a week. The good thing was I didn't have to work that many hours, because in three or four nights

I could make enough money to live on. That was in the days where the cabdriver made 49 percent of the meter, paid in a check every two weeks, and kept all of the tips (maybe thirty dollars on forty to fifty rides a night). We didn't pay for insurance, gas, or tires. I remember many nights making a hundred or one hundred twenty dollars, and in the 1970s that was good money. If I worked three nights a week, I had enough to pay my rent and living expenses.

I worked out of the Dover Garage on Charles and Hudson Streets in Greenwich Village. On a typical day I would get there around 3:00 p.m. Sometimes my painter friend Robert Moskowitz and I would hang out with some other drivers we knew. At a time when a lot of artists, writers, and musicians still drove cabs, Dover was known as an artists' taxi garage. We'd throw our hack licenses in to the dispatcher—literally, you'd throw them into a little tray under a glass window—and theoretically they were put in the order in which the dispatcher had received them. We suspected that the dispatcher would arrange them in any way he liked. If the dispatcher liked you, you could get a car by 4:30, but if he didn't like you, you might not get out until 6:00 or 6:30, at the end of the day-shift change. It was very hard to butter up the dispatchers, because they didn't seem to care. They'd call out your name—"Glass! Moskowitz!"—and you'd better be there. If you weren't there, you went to the bottom of the pile and you might not get out. It could happen that they ran out of cars and you didn't go out, but this never happened to me.

You wanted to get your car as soon as possible, because the earlier you got on the street, the earlier you could come home. If I had to wait until five or six o'clock to get my car, I'd be out on the street until 3:00 a.m., and that wasn't so good, because I hated to pick up the drunks, who were really a problem: they got sick in the car, they didn't remember where they were going, they couldn't find their money. I didn't want to work with drunks, so that meant I had to be off the street by 1:30 or 2:00.

Usually, when I got home at 1:30, I would write music until 5:30 or 6:00, so I would be up all night, then take the kids to school. After that, I would sleep until two in the afternoon and get over to the garage by three. A lot of *Einstein on the Beach* was written at night after driving a cab. The days when I didn't have to drive I had time to write music in the daytime and also to clean up the house and attend to business, such as trying to arrange tours.

Back then, not all the cabs had protective partitions between the driver and the back seat, and that could be dangerous. I was almost killed a couple of times. Once, I was taking a woman up to 110th Street on the East Side, a dodgy area at that time, with numerous abandoned and burned-out buildings. I'd picked her up downtown on First Avenue, and that was a good fare because in the evening you could go up First Avenue and get almost the whole way there without hitting a red light. But I was a little worried about a woman alone going up there, and I was a little worried for myself.

When she gave me the address, I asked, "Do you know where you're going?"

"Oh, yes," she said. "It's okay, there's no problem."

"I'll take you to this address, but do you know anybody there?" I was really concerned about leaving her in that area. I didn't want to be there either, but at that moment, I was thinking about her.

I drove to the street she was going to, keeping my eyes open for any sign of trouble. At that time, in the early seventies, drivers were regularly getting killed in their cabs. I would say five to ten cabbies got killed every year. One thing that could happen was that if you pulled up and stopped behind a double-parked car, another car could come up and park behind you, trapping you. That was a death trap, and I knew that.

The street looked empty, but as soon as I stopped in front of the address she had given me, out of nowhere four guys leaped at the car, two on the front doors and two on the back doors. Luckily, right before I had picked up my passenger, I had stopped to get a coffee, and when I came back to the cab, I had remembered to lock the front doors, which you always mean to do but sometimes might forget. This time I hadn't forgotten, and the front doors held, but the back doors flew open. The girl ran out, I floored it, and I was a block away within seconds. I don't doubt that if they had gotten me—if they had opened the door and pulled me out—that I would've been dead. That was what was going on then. Some people thought cabs were banks on wheels.

But not all experiences were so scary. The fact was, you never knew what an evening behind the wheel would bring. One night, for example, I picked up Salvador Dalí on Fifty-Seventh Street and took him to the St. Regis Hotel, not that far away. It was really him, moustache pointing straight up—the whole picture-perfect Dalí. I was flabbergasted. I only had him for a few blocks, and I was dying to say something to him, but I was completely tongue-tied. He paid me, tipped me, and a doorman came to sweep him away.

The trouble with cab driving was that you never knew what was going to happen. Strictly speaking, you have to take anybody who gets in the cab anywhere in the city they want to go. In New York that's the law. The worst part was that adrenaline rush when you thought this would be your last night alive—and the rush occurred almost every night. But the other parts I liked. I liked driving the streets of the city, and the conditions of the work were perfect for me—I needed temporary work where I could just go in and do a day's work and get cash at the end of the day. The job didn't require steady employment. There was no commitment. You could go in three or four days a week, you could go in twice a week, you could miss three weeks and no one noticed. At that time I was touring about every six weeks, so I'd go out on tour for three weeks, and then come back. I always lost a little bit of money. I didn't get paid on those tours in the early years but I paid the players, so the first thing I had to do when I got back to New York was to pay off the debts of the tour. In about three or four weeks I could pay off what I owed.

When I came back after three weeks away, I would throw in my hack license and the dispatcher would say, "Hey, Glass, where ya been?"

"I've been busy taking care of my mother."

"Yeah, yeah, yeah, yeah," he'd say, and it was left at that.

We had some real strange people working there. There was one driver who was the spitting image of Jesus Christ. We don't know what Jesus Christ looked like, but he must've looked like this guy: skinny, with long hair, a beard, and a kind of astonished look in his eyes all the time. He was writing a book called *Seven Years Behind the Wheel*, and he said he was there getting material for the book. Of course, he was like the rest of us: he was there getting a pretty good piece of day work.

After five years, I finally quit driving a cab in 1978 when the commission to write *Satyagraha* for the Netherlands Opera came through. In a gesture that I hoped carried some finality, I gave all my cab-driving equipment—the clipboard that I used to hold the Taxi and Limousine Commission sheet where I had to write down the time and location of every pickup and drop-off; the cardboard Dutch Masters cigar box that sat on the front seat next to me and held the coins and dollar bills to make change (the big bills were always stuffed into your pants pocket safely out of reach—not kept in your shirt pocket, where someone could reach in and snatch them on summer nights when it was too hot to have your driver's side window rolled up); and my old-fashioned windup pocket watch, which was attached by a string to the clipboard—to my writer friend Stokes Howell, who was just beginning his ten-year stint of driving at Dover.

"Here," I said. "Take these. Maybe if I give them to you, I'll never have to do this again."

And I never did.

BY 1973, OUR PROFESSIONAL LIVES HAD TAKEN ROOT. JoAnne was working full-time with the theater and doing her other work part-time, while I was also occupied full-time, what with driving a cab and composing and touring. We had moved to the East Village to an apartment at Fourteenth Street and Second Avenue that was much closer to where we worked. The Mabou Mines company was still at La MaMa and I was busy also with my ensemble performances and composing music to keep up with my objective of having a new concert program every year.

The children were a constant source of enjoyment and amazement and despair—if you put it all together, that's what being a parent with little kids is about. It's joyous, it's amazing, and sometimes despairing because there's no time to do anything anymore. You're constantly up in the middle of the night taking care of the children and having to work in the daytime. If you were in the traditional wife-at-home-with-the-kids family, maybe that wasn't a problem. Daddy went off to work, Mommy stayed home and took care of the kids, then Daddy came home and he still wanted dinner at seven o'clock. That model was still very common then.

In our world—the world of experimental art, music, theater, and culture—that was not an acceptable model, and we wouldn't do it that way. What we did was the following: we got together with ten or twelve other families and rented a storefront on Avenue B, right by Tompkins Square Park. We hired a young man full-time, with an assistant, and we could leave our children there and go to work. We went to one of the child care agencies in the city and said, "We have a day care center, it's called Children's Liberation." Actually, of course, parents' liberation is what it was. The children were already liberated. *We* needed to be liberated. I think we were one of the first groups that got funded by the city.

One parent per family had to spend one day a week there, so JoAnne and I would take turns. There would be two parents there at a time, from two different families. We as parents had meetings very often and we talked about everything: what the diet should be (some people wanted there to be a vegetarian diet); what kind of language should be used (good language, no vulgar language); what kind of behavior would be allowed (some people asked, "Can they take their clothes off?") and so on. It was a whole grab bag. I went to all those meetings, and sometimes I was the only man there. On the whole, it was a women's group that had empowered themselves as women, and they were really angry at the men, and they were angry at me.

"Wait a second," I said. "I'm the only man here. It's those other guys you need to be mad at." I insisted on going to the meetings because I wanted to know what was happening with the kids, but I didn't like that aspect of it. I thought that that was very unfair.

At a certain point, JoAnne and I began living in separate but nearby apartments, sharing the care of the children on a fifty-fifty basis. Our lives had begun taking on different directions. We continued working together—and our working relationship and friendship has continued for the next forty years—but our home life had become difficult. In a situation that is fragile already, when you throw in another person, like a young man or young woman, the apple cart just goes down. In this case, it was a young woman. I wanted to pursue that relationship, which didn't last very long, but that was enough. That became the sufficient cause for my marriage to end.

So when it was my days to have the children, I would be home with them. On driving days when I was in the neighborhood I would stop by JoAnne's house and take them for a ride in the taxi. I found out many years later that those night rides in my cab frightened them. Juliet was sure that I had stolen the cab and that we were all going to be arrested.

Apart from such misunderstandings, we all seemed to be doing okay with our family arrangements. JoAnne had found a house on Houston Street near Avenue A, and I kept the place on Fourteenth Street, where I framed up a two-story bed for Juliet and Zack out of plywood and two-by-fours, and built the kitchen counter where we took our meals and where I worked when I wrote music. I myself slept on the floor on padded moving mats, and we had wooden crates for our clothes. I didn't have any furniture, but I didn't think I needed any. I actually thought I was living the proverbial life of Riley. I had formed an ensemble, I was giving concerts, and I thought I was doing really well. I thought I was a successful composer because I had time to write, I had musicians happy to play the music, and I had an audience. I could go to Europe sometimes and I went on small tours everywhere. I didn't make any money, but there were people who liked the music, and I had fans, people who were waiting for the next piece to come out. *Music in Twelve Parts* was like a cliff-hanger for them: every two or three months, a new part.

I had confidence about what I was doing. I didn't have to teach school. I didn't have to talk to anybody I didn't want to. I never got any money from grants—once I got three thousand dollars from the New York State Council on the Arts, but when they found out I was working, they asked for it back, so I never applied for any grants after that. I lived on my cab earnings, plus occasionally Ellen Stewart would send me some money, or Richard Serra or Sol LeWitt as well. Sol was nine years older than me, a successful artist who was making money already at that time. An extremely generous man, he began buying scores from composers—a way, actually, of giving us money. Eventually the scores ended up in the Wadsworth Atheneum Museum in Hartford, Connecticut.

Still, my perception was that I always did well. I never thought I was doing poorly. I thought, I've got a nice, two-bedroom rent-controlled apartment on Fourteenth Street and Second Avenue. I have two kids and they have food to eat. They have clothes. I've got a day job and a night job. I have a band, an audience, and a record company. I thought we were doing great, though my children were aware that they were living a different kind of life than most of their friends. I was never embarrassed by our circumstances.

My first consideration was to put the kids into a good school. I made just enough money to get them into Friends Seminary at Sixteenth Street just off Second Avenue. At that time the tuition was about three thousand dollars a year, and I somehow had enough. I wasn't making any money from music at all, so it was all day jobs. The Quakers had had a strong influence on education when I was in Baltimore, so I enrolled Juliet and Zachary at Friends Seminary with complete confidence that their educational, social, and emotional needs would be taken care of. The split week worked out well: when the children were with me, I could give them my complete attention, and when they were with JoAnne, I devoted myself to cab driving and music.

I had a little trouble with the school at first. They wanted me to take out a special "school loan" from a local bank. That way, the school got paid upfront and I would hopefully pay the bank back on a monthly basis. The trouble was none of the banks I spoke to would have anything to do with me, not even the bank that had dreamed up the whole deal with the finance people at the school. I had to go back to the school and see the bursar.

"Joe," I said, "they won't give me the loan."

Joe at first was shocked, but, thinking it over, he came around to understanding their viewpoint. After all, I hadn't had a "regular" job in years and, worst of all, whenever I would identify my occupation—itinerant musician and composer—to bankers or real estate people, their first reaction would be hoots of laughter. Thinking it over, Joe suggested I just come by the school at the end of every week and give him whatever cash I could spare, and that's what I did. I loved that man.

Once returning from Holland I came by Joe's office with one thousand guilders.

"That's it, no more foreign money!" he pleaded.

I never asked for a scholarship, and not out of pride. I just thought that I could probably manage it myself and scholarship money should be for people who really had no alternative. Now, here is a remarkable fact. Of course, every year the tuition would increase, and, miraculously, my income increased at exactly the same rate. By the time Juliet went off to college at Reed College some twelve years later, I was earning enough to pay her tuition there, too, at 1987 rates. Moreover, I was living on music earnings alone by then.

IN THE SPRING OF 1984, I HAD JUST FINISHED writing *Akhnaten* and I was getting ready for a double opening at the Houston Grand Opera and at the Stuttgart Opera. I had already used up all the commission money to pay for the preparation of the conductor's score and the piano reduction used by the singers for rehearsals. In addition,

I had to pay for copying the parts from which the musicians in the orchestra would play, and for that I needed about fifteen thousand dollars. Before computers, this work, an intense amount of labor, had to be done by hand, requiring three or four copyists. Out of the blue I got an offer to do a print ad for Cutty Sark, and, miraculously, they offered me fifteen thousand dollars. I was overjoyed and didn't hesitate. A photograph was taken of me holding a glass of Scotch whisky with musical notes floating in it. I took the money and had the parts done for the opera.

I thought that was a pretty good deal, but some people, even "downtown" people, called it selling out. I called it "selling in," because the money went into my work. I thought this selling-out idea was a bizarre notion. It seemed to me that people who didn't have to sell out, or in, must have had rich parents. Or they taught music, which I also wasn't willing or able to do. Otherwise, how did they do it? When someone said they didn't do commercial work, I just thought these were people who somehow already had money.

I never had any trouble with the idea of selling music. When my brother was twelve and I was eleven, we were already working for Ben selling records. From an early age, I saw that a customer would hand him five dollars and he would hand them a record. I saw that exchange innumerable times: money—music, music—money. It seemed normal to me. Oh, that's how the world works, I thought. It never occurred to me that there was anything wrong with it.

S UE WEIL, WHOM I KNEW FROM HER DAYS AS THE DIRECTOR OF the Performing Arts Program at Minneapolis's Walker Art Center, invited me to go with her one evening in 1973 to see a new work at the Brooklyn Academy of Music, where Harvey Lichtenstein was starting to bring big, ambitious pieces. This was before BAM's groundbreaking Next Wave Festival had begun, and there was real speculation about whether people from Manhattan would make the long trek out to Brooklyn at all.

Sue would later become director of the dance program at the National Endowment for the Arts, and after that she worked with the great Russian dancer Mikhail Baryshnikov at the White Oak Dance Project, but this night we were going to see Bob Wilson's *The Life and Times of Joseph Stalin*. Bob had already been making a stir in the theater world, but this would be the first of his works I had seen. It was to be an all-night event, starting at about seven p.m. and running almost twelve hours. I was already very interested in "extended time" in concert pieces—*Music with Changing Parts* had been a work that had the potential of lasting for hours, which in some cases it actually did, and *Music in Twelve Parts*, in a complete performance, could not be performed in fewer than four and a half hours—but Bob's work was more than an extension of "normal" theater duration. It was intensely visual and completely caught up with movement of all kinds.

To see it for the first time was an unexpected and exhilarating experience. If Stalin was on stage, I missed him, though from the outset I hadn't expected to see him. With dawn breaking over the city the next morning, we, the audience, followed Bob back to the Byrd Hoffman rehearsal space on Spring Street in Manhattan. There had not been a full house that night, with perhaps two hundred people in attendance, and it looked like a fair number of the audience was at this post-performance party.

I met Bob that morning and we got along from the first moment. On my side, I already had a strong premonition that there was work for us waiting to be done. We agreed to have lunch at a little restaurant on MacDougal Street. We had no real agenda for that meeting or for the next few that followed. We were just getting to know each other, our backgrounds, mutual friendships, and interests.

Bob is a tall, handsome man who is always gentle in his speech and kind in his attention. When you talk to him, he leans in and listens to you and he looks at you. Sometimes, if he's not looking at you, he might be drawing at the same time. It's very common to be speaking with Bob and, before you know it, he's doing some drawing that may have something to do with what you're saying, or it may not. Overall, though, I was drawn to him by the quality of his attention.

We began meeting regularly, every Thursday for a year, whenever we were both in the city. What I saw from the beginning was that Bob understood how events worked in time. It was very clear that we were working in parallel ways. We both had very strong connections to the dance world, Bob through choreographers Merce Cunningham, George Balanchine, and Jerome Robbins, and I also through Merce as well as John Cage. Bob knew the artists that I knew, so we were clearly living in the same world and had been nourished by the same generation of people that had preceded us.

There were other similarities. Neither Bob nor I were from New York. He was from Waco, Texas, and I was from Baltimore. We were people who had come to New York to find a world of high culture and the kind of stimulating people who belonged to it. We'd both had our training in New York, Bob at Pratt Institute in Brooklyn and I at Juilliard, and both of us were working in the theater. I was the musical version of what he was doing, and he was the theater version of what I was doing.

Soon after these initial meetings, we began to talk about a music-theater work that we would undertake together. It had no name at first, but that soon came. One early suggestion from Bob was to work with Hitler as a theme—Bob had already done Stalin, so this was not a far-fetched idea. My memories of World War II were more vivid than Bob's, I being four years older, so I had countered with Gandhi, which meant little to Bob. He came back with Einstein, to which I readily agreed.

As a boy I had been caught up in the Einstein craze that followed the end of World War II. I had read many books about him and even one (for laymen) written by Einstein himself. Science had always been a boyhood hobby of mine in a general way and I had developed a taste—though not such a sophisticated one—for mathematics and astronomy. I had even been part of an astronomy club at a very young age—ten or eleven—where the members built telescopes, including grinding a concave six-inch mirror for a reflecting telescope. From that age and until now, music and science have been my great loves. I see scientists as visionaries, as poets. In having composed operas about Kepler, Galileo, and Einstein—three outstanding scientists—I've probably written more operas about science than any other composer. I've also written music for a film about Stephen Hawking, and collaborated on a theater piece with the famous string theorist Brian Greene.

What interests me is how similar these visionaries' way of seeing is to that of an artist. Einstein clearly visualized his work. In one of his books on relativity, trying to explain it to people, he wrote that he imagined himself sitting on a beam of light, and the beam of light was traveling through the universe at 186,000 miles per second. What he saw was himself sitting still and the world flashing by him at a really high speed. His conclusion was that all he had to do—as if it were a minor matter—was to invent the mathematics to describe what he had seen.

What I have to do when I compose is not that different. All I have to do after I have the vision is to find the language of music to describe what I have heard, which can take a certain amount of time. I've been working in the language of music all my life, and it's within that language that I've learned how ideas can unfold.

I was immediately thrilled with our Einstein project. The original title, which I have on the cover of a book of drawings that Bob gave me, was *Einstein on the Beach on Wall Street*. Somewhere along the way the "on Wall Street" was dropped, but neither Bob nor I remember when. "On the Beach" referred to the Nevil Shute novel from the 1950s, which takes place in Australia, when the world has experienced a World War III nuclear apocalypse. In the penultimate scene of *Einstein on the Beach*, there is a spaceship and a huge explosion that Bob wanted, and I wrote a piece of music to go with it. We were aiming for a big finale that was apocalyptic, which, by the way, is followed immediately by a love story written by Mr. Samuel Johnson, the actor who played a judge and also the bus driver at the end. Bob juxtaposed the most horrible thing you could think about, the annihilation that happens with a nuclear holocaust, with love—the cure, you could say, for the problems of humanity.

Of course, from the outset it was clear that Bob would be the image maker. When we talked he always had paper and pencil. His thinking automatically became pictorial. On my side, I was good at structure. We both were comfortable in a "time-binding" medium that takes place on a stage, but Bob liked to feel time in his body, whereas I like to measure and map it. I've seen Bob countless times at auditions ask a dancer or actor to just walk across the stage. Bob would gaze intently at them during this exercise. I came to understand that he could see something that I would never see. He could "see" them moving through time and space. It would only take a few minutes and he would know, decisively, whether he could work with that person.

My abilities worked in different ways. For example, once Bob had decided on his three "visual" themes—the Train/Spaceship; the Trial; and two Dances in a field—he handed them to me and asked me to organize them into four acts. With barely a pause I wrote down the structure of the work. Using the letters *A*, *B*, and *C* for the three themes, it would follow this pattern: A-B for Act 1, C-A for Act 2, B-C for Act 3, and A-B-C for Act 4. Bob looked at the scheme and immediately added five knee plays—short, connecting pieces that came at the beginning and the end and in between each of the four acts. Oddly, but precisely, Bob had indicated the same "interstices" that, a few years later, Beckett would point out as the places for which I would then compose music in the production of *Company*, which Fred Neumann, working with Beckett, would direct and produce at the Public Theater. I don't remember ever mentioning this coincidence to Bob. At this point, after maybe six months of verbal exchanges, we didn't speak much about *Einstein*. We were beginning to work very closely and things began to fall into place.

Time would be the common material with which we would be working. The first thing we did was talk about lengths of time. Each act would take about one hour. The knee plays would be six minutes each, as they were little interludes (the knee being a connecting section between two larger parts). There would be a chorus throughout; a dance company for the dance sections; two judges—an old man and a young boy—for the trials; two additional performers for the knee plays; and a violinist (Einstein) who would be sitting on a small platform midway between the stage and the orchestra pit, where my ensemble, with Michael Riesman conducting, would be set. It had taken quite a while to get to this point, I would guess more than half a year.

During that first year, 1974, when the blueprint of the work was evolving, Bob brought Christopher Knowles to lunch. I grew to like him very much, but he took some getting used to. He was an autistic boy whose education Bob had taken on with the encouragement and blessings of the Knowles family. At our first lunch meeting, I barely understood anything he said. He could as easily, in those days, take a plate of food and try to balance it on his head as to eat from it. However, in the end, with two notable exceptions, he became the writer of the texts we hear spoken throughout *Einstein*. One exception is the love story mentioned above that ends the opera, and the equally brilliant text that our judge, Mr. Johnson, delivers at the end of the trial scene. The other speech was Lucinda Childs's "supermarket" speech, which she delivers during the second trial scene. Lucinda became one of the two women in the knee plays, as well as the choreographer for her "diagonal" dance in Act 1, scene 1 (the "Train"). Sheryl Sutton became the second woman in the knee plays—the only actor from Bob's previous work who was in *Einstein*. Paul Mann, at the age of nine, was the little boy judge, and Bob Brown, fully costumed and wigged, was our violinist playing Einstein. The chorus of twelve came from open call auditions and, besides singing, eight of them also had to be the dancers in Dances 1 and 2. That was it. It was conceived and the cast settled by the spring of 1975. I started composing the music to Bob's drawings and my "time outline" that summer in Cape Breton. When I came back to New York after Labor Day in September, I had already made a good beginning.

After the completion of *Music in Twelve Parts* I had begun right away with the series *Another Look at Harmony, Parts 1, 2, 3, and 4*, which was meant as a straightforward announcement that I was beginning the second "phase" of this extended cycle of work wherein the remaining element—harmony—would finally be addressed. *Einstein on the Beach*, if you look at it scene by scene, is a very clear presentation of a melodic-rhythmic cycle interacting with a harmonic progression—first one chord, then two, then three, and so on as the piece progresses. The spaceship at the end represents the culmination of this "unified field" of harmony, melody, and rhythm, and itself ends with a cascade of chromatic descending and ascending scales by way of a final gesture.

Another Look at Harmony, Parts 1 and 2 became the source for two important thematic units of the work I was doing for *Einstein on the Beach*. Using them, I was able to compose all the music for "Train 1" (that would be our A section) and "Dance 1" (that would be our C section). Through writing *Einstein*—but beginning with writing *Another Look at Harmony*—I continued the integration of rhythmic and harmonic and cyclic music into one coherent system.

I was looking at a reconciliation of harmonic movement and rhythmic cycles. It can be heard right after "Knee Play 1," in the "Train" music in Act 1. It became, in my mind, a unified theory, and the whole writing of *Einstein* was dedicated to that end.

In classical music, there are allegros and prestos in all kinds of pieces, but they were usually presented as contrast to other parts. There would be slow music, then fast music. I have done that myself many times, in string quartets. But with *Einstein*, the idea of an unstoppable energy was all there was. There was no need for a slow movement. Even in the scenes like the two "Trials," the push of the music remains, slowed down somewhat, but if you listen, there's a forward push that's always there. Same with the "Bed" in Act 4.

Part of our music rehearsals were given over to teaching and memorizing the music by our chorus of twelve singers (six women and six men.) Only a few of them could actually read music, so learning the music and memorizing it happened at the same time. Here I borrowed a teaching method from Alla Rakha, and used it with our singers with great success. The method was to take a three- or four-note phrase and repeat it with the whole chorus until they had it by heart. Then I began with a second phrase, which they also had to memorize. Next, phrases 1 and 2 were performed together, which now had become fairly easy for them to do. We practiced this first combined phrase until it was solid, and then added a third phrase following the same system, ending up with a combination of 1, 2, and 3. This was the basis upon which more extended music could be memorized—for example, in the Knee Plays, which were six minutes long.

For variety, I used two kinds of lyrics. One was based on numbers—1, 2, 3, 4, and so on, up to 8. This outlined the rhythm and became another mnemonic device. The second was based on the solfège system of "do-re-mi-fa-so-la-si-do," which are the names of the notes they were singing and which therefore aided in memorizing the melody.

One morning Bob came by to hear the chorus and was listening to one of the Knee Plays. By then the singers were doing quite well with the numbers and the solfège. At a moment when we were taking a break, Bob asked, "Are those the words they will be singing during the performance?"

That hadn't been my intention at all, but with only the slightest pause I replied, "Yes." And that is how the lyrics for the choral music in *Einstein* came to be.

The music for the five Knee Plays was actually composed last. They are all based on the same music, the seeds of which were in the other parts of the opera. By extracting the salient points and using them for the Knee Plays, they, and the larger segments of *Einstein*, were organically combined.

THE FINANCIAL AND ADMINISTRATIVE STRUCTURE for the *Einstein* production began to take shape during the winter of 1975–76. I was working with Performing Artservices, a not-for-profit organization formed by Mimi Johnson, Jane Yockel, and Margaret Wood, which was dedicated to the work of emerging performance art and had a solid background by that time in managing music tours with my ensemble. They were in turn linked to Benedict Pesle's company, Arts Services, our European office in Paris. Bob had an experienced team with the Byrd Hoffman Foundation, which had helped him build and produce his early body of work, already a substantial undertaking. But between us, we still didn't have real experience in touring a large music-theater production.

Einstein should have had a traveling opera company, which— especially for work like this, which would be highly progressive and avant-garde—as yet didn't really exist in the theater world. There were large-scale models operating at that time with Peter Brook, the Poor Theater of Grotowski, and the Living Theater. But what Bob and I were doing in music-theater was deeply ambitious and the earlier models would not be of much help. When Peter Brook did something like his stage version of *The Mahabarata*, what was missing was a driving musical idea that would carry you through the piece. Something I have known from the beginning of my work in theater is that music is the unifying force that will take the viewer-spectator from the start through to the end, whether in opera, theater, dance, or film. This force doesn't come from images, movement, or words. If you watch television and put on different records, with different music, the same images will look different. Now, try it the other way around. Keep the music the same and change the channels. The integrity of the energy remains in the music and changing the image doesn't alter that fact. People in the theater very rarely understand that, but Bob Wilson does. Both of us had a keen appreciation of the power of music to lift up a work. Any good theater piece, even one from Shakespeare or Beckett that wouldn't seem to need much lifting, would benefit from a good score.

Bob and I were two authors representing either side of the music-theater equation. We were mature enough—both of us in our mid- to late thirties—to have developed independently our own personal language. As I think about it now, it was that fact—that each of us had years of experience perfecting an easily recognizable and highly personal "style"—that set *Einstein* apart from other ambitious work. I had a well-trained team of technicians who came with me and he had the same from the theater side. I believe it was this equality that each of us brought to *Einstein* that allowed us to move forward together so comfortably. We had tremendous confidence in ourselves and in each other—a strong statement to be sure, but not in any way overstated.

The trickiest part, and it is always true of new performance work, was finding the money to make the work—that is rehearsing, building the décor and costumes and developing the lighting, and, in the case of *Einstein*, the sound design. It's traditionally one of those chicken-and-egg problems. The work cannot earn money to finally pay for itself (which is always a big question) until the piece is built, and you can't build the piece with money that has not yet been earned. This is where the "angels" and backers come in. Though we didn't have anything like a Broadway show with commercial potential, we effectively had the same problem. However, we did have friends with the means to help, including various members of the de Menil family. Christophe and François de Menil stepped forward to help. Then there were credit cards that we used shamelessly to buy plane tickets and whatever else that "plastic" could buy. The financial side was a little shaky, but good enough for us to get started.

I was still in the cab-driving phase of my day jobs, and from then until the spring of 1976, when we began rehearsing, I was finishing the music, mainly working at night after my nine-hour driving stint was complete. But when the rehearsals began in earnest in March 1976, in Bob's studio on Spring Street, I put the day jobs aside. We divided the day into three rehearsal periods of three hours each. We would begin with a vocal rehearsal at nine a.m. After the noon break, we had a dance rehearsal, and after a midafternoon break we had a staging rehearsal. I was the rehearsal pianist all through the day, and also the vocal coach for the morning rehearsal. I could see, therefore, how the music was working throughout. I could, as well, help the chorus who, in many cases, were also the dancers, form a solid basis for memorizing the music—not at all an easy task. Andy de Groat was, in this first production, the choreographer for the big dance pieces, and Lucinda Childs made all her own solo dances herself. Bob Brown also began playing some of the violin parts at this stage. Bob Wilson and I were asking a lot of our company. In later years we had a separate corps de ballet and chorus, which made it far easier. By then, Lucinda was responsible for all the dance choreography. The texts by Christopher, Mr. Johnson, and Lucinda would appear during these early staging rehearsals in the late afternoon. These texts have remained through all subsequent productions.

We put the whole thing together in about a two-month period and had a run-through performance at the Video Exchange Theater in Westbeth, a building fronting the Hudson River in the West Village that had been set aside for artist housing and rehearsals. It was done as a partially staged work but without any of the sets and drops that Bob had designed. Not all the music was ready for the ensemble, but there was enough for that early run-through. It was really our first glimpse of the work. It was rough in one way, but the *Einstein* energy was already beginning to surface, even in this partial version.

It was a "friends only" showing with our support team and a few older colleagues as well. Virgil Thomson, then the only American composer of opera whom Bob and I took seriously, was there, and our friendship began at that time. He had made a wonderful piece, *Four Saints in Three Acts*, with the texts of Gertrude Stein. Several generations before us, he had experimented with the idea that opera could once again become a popular art form, as it had been in the nineteenth century. *Four Saints in Three Acts* actually ran on Broadway, so Virgil knew something about the theater. Jerome Robbins, already a good friend and confidant of Bob's, was there as well. Jerry, known to the general public from his choreography for *West Side Story*, was a major choreographer for the New York City Ballet, and as one of the elder statesmen of the dance world, he understood the theater, and was very interested in what Bob did. Eight years later, in 1984, Jerry would choreograph his ballet *Glass Pieces* for the New York City Ballet to music from my 1982 album *Glassworks*, as well as the opening funeral music from *Akhnaten*.

One important development was the commission for the work, from the French government. The monetary value was small, but the recognition for the work was very significant for us. This was 1976, our bicentennial year in the United States. Our National Endowment for the Arts and any number of private and public foundations were commissioning new works of all kinds and genres—literally hundreds upon hundreds of new music, poetry, film, and dance events for that year's celebrations. I think Bob and I were too busy with the birth of *Einstein* to even notice what was going on, and in any case, neither he nor I had been contacted by any arts organization. I think we were too far below the radar for any official arts institution to notice what we were doing. That's pretty much how arts funding on an institutional level works, and it was no surprise to us. But someone at Bob's foundation did take notice and the Bicentennial Arts Commission was informed that *Einstein on the Beach* was the official gift from the French government to the United States of America in honor of its bicentennial. A few weeks later we received an American flag in the mail.

The head of the Festival d'Automne in Paris, Michel Guy, had come to a music rehearsal at Dickie Landry's loft as early as 1973. Dickie, in a fit of design perversity, had painted the entire studio black. The only lights in the room were our music stand lights. The room was very dark and the music very loud and, for some reason, we liked it that way. We must have been rehearsing the last parts of *Music in Twelve Parts* that evening. I was told that someone from Paris would be there, but even so I was a bit surprised when a tall, elegantly dressed Frenchman emerged from the shadows at the end of the rehearsal.

"I am Michel Guy from Paris, and I will bring you to the Festival d'Automne this coming year," he said.

"Sure thing, Michel," I said, and I didn't believe him for one second.

But that is exactly what he did. And when, soon after, he became the French Minister of Culture and learned that Bob and I were collaborating on *Einstein*, he jumped on it, securing the world premiere for the Avignon Festival, where he had also, until a few years before, been the director. I'm sure he was involved with the *Einstein* commission. He was always a man of independent thinking with a highly developed taste for new work. Josephine Markovits was his assistant at that time, and later, in 1992, she brought a revival of *Einstein* back to Paris.

Now we had a beginning date, July 25, 1976, in Avignon, and an ending date in Rotterdam. Ninon Karlweiss, our European agent, quickly put together the tour: Avignon, Paris, Venice, Belgrade, Hamburg, Brussels, and Rotterdam. All in all it would be about thirty-three performances in seven cities.

———

WE ARRIVED IN AVIGNON two weeks before opening night. Between music rehearsals, staging rehearsals, and dance rehearsals, the company was working unbelievably hard. At the same time, the sets and drops had arrived from Italy where they had been fabricated and had to be loaded in. Then the lights had to be set and focused. That and miscellaneous technical details made for a short, intense work period. Bob had never teched the show before—coordinating the technical aspects of lighting and movement of scenery, movement of props. None of that had been tried out. Even the spacing of the dancers, who now had to fit into a stage that was much bigger than the stage on which we'd been rehearsing, had to be adjusted. Bob was still setting light cues the day before the premiere. And, in fact, the Philip Glass Ensemble had yet to play through the music with the singers or even the solo violin. All these things had to be taken into account, but I wasn't worried. I was excited to be seeing the piece for the first time. Since I had been the rehearsal pianist, I hadn't really been able to see Bob's work until then.

In fact, we never had a proper dress rehearsal—opening night, July 25, was our first actual run without stops and fixes. It was only the second time that the performers had heard the ensemble playing with them, and we were not really sure how long the piece was. Typically, I played the "walk-in" prelude by myself at 6:20, at 6:30 the doors were open and at 7:00 "Knee Play 1" began. "Knee Play 5" would end at 11:00 p.m., so in the end it came to almost five hours long, counting the walk-in music. Over the thirty-three performances of the first tour, the overall time changed surprisingly little, never more than an overall difference of two or three minutes.

The excitement was so intense on the night of the piece that I feel I was probably outside of my body most of the evening. Neither the *Einstein* company, and certainly not the audience really knew what to expect. The five hours that it took went by like a dream. Everything happened as it was supposed to. We started with the first Knee

Play and before I knew it, we were in the "Night Train" scene. Again, before I knew it, we were in the "Building" scene. And before I knew it once more, we were in the "Spaceship," the next-to-last scene, with Bob on stage doing "the flashlight dance." It passed breathtakingly and quickly.

The audience was totally enraptured, both throughout and afterward. No one had seen anything like this before. It was a very young audience. Let's say you were twenty or twenty-five years old: you'd go to the Avignon Festival and you'd walk into *Einstein on the Beach*. You'd have no idea what it's going to be, and it goes on for five hours. People were out of their minds. There was an uproar. People couldn't believe it. They were screaming and laughing—practically dancing. We were near exhaustion. We'd had two weeks of intense work. We hadn't eaten. It was like the euphoria that accompanies childbirth, followed by ecstatic relief and, then, deep fatigue.

Then it was over. We knew we had done something extraordinary. And it wasn't just us. Everybody knew it.

All kinds of people who were involved in the production were there, and all kinds of people who I'd never seen before. Almost everybody seemed happy. Michel Guy, of course, was overjoyed. This was his baby—he had commissioned it. He must have felt like Santa Claus and he had delivered the present. Without him, there wouldn't have been an event. He gave us the money that helped us get it going.

There were four other performances in Avignon after the premiere. In the afternoons, Bob and I had conversations with the press and members of the public who wanted to talk about the work. We had debates and discussions and misunderstandings. We had huge support and rowdy dissent. We had everything:

"What the hell do you think you did?"

"How dare you do this?"

"What was that supposed to be?"

But the other thing we heard was "That was the most fantastic event I've ever experienced."

Some of the questions were inane and some interesting. The best questions were *both* inane and interesting. For example, the question "Is *Einstein* really an opera?" was both stupid and intriguing at the same time. Neither Bob nor I had any special preparation for these meetings. In the end, I don't think either of us really cared what people thought.

There were many writers from the press who now had their first chance to meet Bob and myself, since we hadn't been doing press conferences before. Some of the reviewers had even refused to review it. They said this is not real music making. The French left-wing publications, including *Libération*, loved it, while the right wing hated it. Just like today. Some things never change.

These kinds of public meetings followed us throughout the European tour. And how could it have been otherwise? One of the "problems," or possible grounds for misunderstanding, was the truth that *Einstein* had never had an "ideological" or "theoretical" basis. Very un-European. However, I believe that neither Bob nor I felt we needed to have one. For example, the fact that to produce *Einstein* required a proscenium stage, fly space, wing space, a lighting bridge, and an orchestra pit made using an opera house a necessity. In other words, an opera house was the only place where *Einstein* could be produced. That simple fact is what made *Einstein* an opera and that was good enough for us.

It feels as if *Einstein*, in its innocent and radical heart of hearts, had suddenly and unintentionally put Bob and me in a place where we were expected to explain a work that had emerged from our very lives and separate histories in a wholly organic, uninhibited, and unpremeditated way. It wasn't a work that either asked for or needed an explanation. And we never tried to make one.

TOWARD THE END OF THE TOUR we were in Hamburg, where Jane Herman and Gilbert Hemsley came to see *Einstein*. Jane and Gilbert worked for the Metropolitan Opera House, producing the Special Events series. Already being dark on Sundays, the Met wanted to do special events on those nights, and it was Jane's job to do the programming. Jerry Robbins, who had seen the piece in Paris and at the Video Exchange Theater at the preview of it, had urged them to go to Hamburg.

Bob and I knew someone from the Met had come to the show, but we didn't know why they were there. Afterward, when we met with Jane and Gilbert, they said that they wanted to stage it, and that they were going to bring it in. Bob and I smiled and said that was a great idea, but we didn't believe it.

They left a few hours, later after we talked it through. Once they were gone, Bob and I looked at each other and said, "This is not going to happen." Up to that point, the only concert hall north of Fourteenth Street I had played in was Town Hall in 1974. Mostly I had been downtown, in galleries and lofts, so the idea that we would go to the Met seemed a fantasy. Couldn't happen.

And yet, the Met booked us for a Sunday night in November 1976. We had an agreement with them that we would get a certain amount from the box office to pay our crew and so forth, and they would supply the theater and their crew. If you look at the billing on the program for that night, it says, "Presented by the New York Metropolitan Opera and the Byrd Hoffman Foundation." Over the years many writers, including professional journalists, claimed that Bob and I had rented the Met, perhaps thinking that it was astonishing that two young artists from downtown would have such a fantastic idea. But any way you looked at it, the idea that we rented the Met is absurd. For one thing, we didn't have the money. Besides that, we couldn't have put a show on at the Met without the Met's electricians, lighting people, and stagehands. There's no way we could have four-walled it—come into an empty theater and put the show up—in nineteen hours. Something on the scale of *Einstein* couldn't have been done by outsiders. The fact is, the Met wanted the show, they were willing to produce it, and Gilbert was already making the plans.

When the tour was over, Bob and I flew into JFK from Europe. Paul Walters, an old friend and patron of Bob's, met us at the airport.

"The first night is sold out," he told us.

"What?" we said.

"You are sold out at the Met."

The last ticket was sold eight or ten days before opening night. Right away they added a second Sunday night for the following week.

We only had a week before we moved into the Met. The problem was getting the piece set up in time for a six o'clock opening. The night before, they were doing *Die Meistersinger*, which ended at eleven. So we had from eleven o'clock Saturday night to six o'clock Sunday evening: nineteen very short hours. We usually took three days to load in, but we were able to do the turn around so quickly because Gilbert had figured out every minute, a tremendous feat of planning. He worked with the crew from the Met, who were fantastic and who worked all night until about five the next afternoon, when the doors opened. I don't think we even had a minute to spare.

My family was beside themselves about *Einstein* coming to the Met. Some relatives came up for the premiere, and many more would have come had there been tickets available. For my mother, it was completely different from what had happened eight years before, when she came to hear me at Queens College in a virtually empty auditorium. Now she was coming to the biggest opera house in the world, and it was sold out.

I don't know what she thought. We never talked about it.

As I mentioned before, Ida was sitting in the same box as Bob's father, and I know that they talked to each other about what was going on. One story I heard is that my mother said to Bob's father, "Mr. Wilson, did you ever have any idea what your son was thinking about, what was going on in his head?"

"No, I had no idea at all."

Basically, you have two people who weren't really similar—one was from Texas, one was from Baltimore—but they each had a son who had done something extraordinary, and they were clueless about what it was about. That doesn't mean that she didn't value it. I do know that Ida sent my brother, Marty, outside to find out what the tickets were being scalped for. I think they were going for about fifty or a hundred dollars, and that impressed her. It impressed her that you could sell the tickets right on the street for much more than the box office price. For her, it wasn't about judging the art or the music. It's not that she didn't care. She just didn't know, whereas Ben knew a lot about music, but he was gone by then. What Ida *did* know was that it was a big event, and that the city had turned out, and that it was going to be done again. And that somehow, in a miraculous way, this son of hers—whose career she must have more or less given up on after seeing the debacle at Queens College eight years before—had, at the age of thirty-nine, seen his ship come in. It must have been an astonishing moment for her.

The Met holds roughly three thousand eight hundred people. Even standing room was sold out, adding another one hundred and seventy-five. There isn't any other opera house that size in America, and we sold it out twice. What was surprising to Bob and me was that there was no indication there had been such a huge swell of enthusiasm for either his work or mine. Neither of us had a big promotional team. There was no wind pushing the sails, as far as we knew. Possibly a thousand people from downtown came, but I think the audience that filled the Met came from all over New York.

As soon as the two performances at the Met were completed, the last on November 28, 1976, Ninon Karlweiss invited us to her apartment on the East Side and informed us that, the great success of *Einstein* notwithstanding, the tour was $100,000 in the red. Bob and I were, of course, deeply shocked. A truism of the opera world—that operas lose money—was unknown to us. We were that naïve. We didn't realize that no opera house pays for itself, whether it's Paris or London, Moscow or New York. Huge fund-raising efforts go on all year long, every year, to pay for the deficits of those houses. For example, some years later when we were playing in Stuttgart, I was told that every seat in the house was subsidized with something like eighty *deutschmarks*. We hadn't realized we were going to lose money that first night at the Met, and the next week as well. None of the thirty-five performances of *Einstein* had played to an empty seat, and still the tour had ended up in debt.

Both of us said to her, "Ninon, how did that happen? How could you do that to us?"

She was calm and obviously unrepentant. After we had gotten over our shock, she told us very simply, "Let me tell you something. You were both really unknown, and I knew that *Einstein* had to be seen. So I had no choice. I booked every performance below costs and you took a loss every night. Not so much, maybe two or three thousand for each showing. Over the four months, it just added up. I knew you would be in debt at the end, but I also knew that it would make your careers. Both of you."

In the end, Ninon was right. But an immediate problem still faced us. To address it, we began by selling everything we could—drawings, music scores, equipment, the works. Some of our artist friends held an auction to raise money to help, but the *Einstein* debt dragged on for years.

In the aftermath, Bob worked in Europe and seemed to be making theater pieces everywhere. I stayed in New York and continued my work, but now as a "successful" opera composer, who still had to drive a cab for two more years. Neither Bob nor I was interested in becoming a partnership in the manner of the famous ones in music-theater—Brecht and Weill, Rodgers and Hammerstein, Lerner and Loewe, etc. In any case these kinds of partnerships—businesses, really—were far less common in the opera world.

Bob and I continued differently. From then on, every six to eight years we would do a work together, with other collaborators and other people in between. Our next work together would come in 1984, when I became one of six composers who worked with Bob on his *CIVIL warS: A Tree Is Best Measured When It Is Down*. I composed the *Rome* and *Cologne* parts. We would come together from time to time, bringing with us new experiences and independent ideas. Some of my favorite works with Bob, *White Raven* and *Monsters of Grace*, came about in that way.

I've always thought of *Einstein* as the end of a cycle of work that had begun with the highly reductive, repetitive music which characterized the early days of the compositions for my ensemble, a period that began in earnest in 1969 with *Music in Fifths* and *Music in Similar Motion*. For that reason, the music I wrote for *Einstein* didn't surprise me as much as those earlier pieces, when I had found myself unexpectedly writing music that had so much energy, discipline, and power. I was feeding off of my own music. The energy system that I was involved with was like a maelstrom, with *Einstein* as its fullest realization.

The years from 1965 on were overflowing with the sound of a new musical language that I shared with a number of other composers of my generation—a sound that was broad enough in scope, and intense enough in its urgency, to allow for all manner of individual expression. Several generations of composers were able to develop highly personal styles on that basis, and that has made it possible for the present generation of young composers to coexist so comfortably in a new music world of diversity and heterodoxy, where the means of expression—acoustic, electronic, various forms of global and indigenous music—can be equally broad and diverse. The generation I grew up with in the 1960s had to bear the brunt of another, older vision for the future of music that was narrow and intolerant. I think that kind of tyranny, for the moment, is behind us.

Einstein on the Beach rounded out an eleven-year period for me. The recognition that came from it made it easier to get work, but it didn't make any difference to the music. The pieces that came afterward would represent a new chapter, and, in reality, the disappointment felt by some diehard fans with the music after *Einstein* has more to do with their unfulfilled expectations than with what I was actually doing. *Einstein* was, indeed, over, completed. With the next opera—*Satyagraha*—I would be on the threshold of a new body of work.

PART THREE

PHILIP GLASS WITH GELEK RIMPOCHE AND ALLEN GINSBERG.

ANN ARBOR, MICHIGAN, 1989. PHOTOGRAPH: ALLEN GINSBERG.

OPERA

FTER *EINSTEIN*, *SATYAGRAHA* AND *AKHNATEN* FOLLOWED FAIRLY quickly, forming a trilogy of "portrait operas" of men whose lives and work changed the world. Einstein, the man of science, Gandhi, the man of politics, and Akhnaten, the man of religion, transformed the world they lived in not by force of arms, but through the power of ideas.

The commission for *Satyagraha* came in 1978 from Willi Hoffman, director of De Doelen, a concert venue in Rotterdam. Hans de Roo, as the head of Netherlands Opera in Amsterdam, was the actual producer. It wasn't a lot of money, but by the late 1970s taxi driving had become so dangerous that I knew I would have to quit as soon as possible. The success of *Einstein* had led to the Dutch commission, so in a sense I was saved, quite literally, by opera. In any event, it was the end of my day jobs, which had begun when I arrived in New York in 1957 and followed me even during my Paris years in the mid-1960s. All in all, not so bad. I even consider myself lucky.

Around the same time that the commission for *Satyagraha* came, another event took place that would eventually establish the basis for some future financial security. Barbara Rose was an old friend whom I had known from the summer of 1954 in Paris. She and I met again when I arrived in New York in 1958, and then, almost twenty years later, in 1977, she was the writer on *North Star*, a film about Mark di

Suvero and his work, for which I provided a score. Now she was married and wanted me to meet her husband, Jerry Leiber.

I liked Jerry right away. He was from Baltimore and even had gone to the same high school as myself.

"So, you're from Baltimore?" Jerry asked. "That's good. And your name is Glass?"

"Right."

"Wait a second. Was your mother the librarian at City?"

"That's right."

"I knew your mother."

"Really?"

"That's right. I knew her real well. She was the librarian and she saved my life every day I was there."

"What do you mean?"

"Well, I was this little Jewish guy and there was a gang waiting for me outside of the school—waiting to beat the crap out of me as soon as I was out of the building at the end of the day. Your mother, Mrs. Glass, let me hang out in the library for an hour. I would work for her, putting books back on the shelves."

"That's right. She always had kids helping her in the library after school."

"You know what? I'm going to do something for you that's going to change your life!"

"How's that?"

"I'm doing this for you for what your mother did for me. Come over to my office tomorrow. I'm in the Brill Building."

Everyone knew where the Brill Building was, on Broadway at Forty-Ninth Street. It was home to music publishers, record producers, and recording studios. Also everyone, at least in the music world, knew who Jerry Leiber was. He and Mike Stoller were "Leiber and Stoller," the songwriting team who were responsible for countless hits of the fifties, sixties, and seventies. They had written "Hound Dog," "Jailhouse Rock," "Stand by Me," "On Broadway," and on and on, Jerry writing the lyrics and Stoller the music. They had been two of the principal songwriters for Elvis Presley, the Coasters, and the Drifters, among others.

I was at the Brill Building the next morning and, once in the Leiber and Stoller office, walked down a long hallway lined end to end with framed gold records. It was most impressive. Jerry was waiting for me in his office, his feet up on his desk, relaxed and at home. There was a chair opposite him, a small spinet piano against one wall, and a couch with a coffee table. Jerry was four years older than me, still had a Baltimore accent, and was very energetic. He was the only person I knew who lived a life in Tin Pan Alley—the world where popular music was written, singers worked with writers, and songs were made famous.

After our hellos, he pointed to a side door and said, "Take a look over there." I walked over and opened the door. To my surprise I was looking into a large room with rows of desks, perhaps six rows and four desks deep. At each desk was a woman, occasionally a man, with a typewriter and wearing headphones.

"What do you think they're doing?"

"I have no idea."

"They're finding money under stones. When Mike and I write a song, someone will often make it famous. When that happens, other singers will make their own version of the song, called a 'cover.' We're the publishers and they have to pay us, that's how it works. Now here's what I want you to do. Go downtown to the county clerk's office at 60 Centre Street in the basement and register your publishing company. Do you have a name for it?"

"Yeah, I'll call it Dunvagen music. That's the name of the place I go in Canada in the summertime."

"Fine. You can get a DBA for almost nothing. It means 'doing business as.' Or you can register it with the State of New York for a few more dollars, then you have a fully professional company. I recommend that you do that."

The next morning I went downtown and that's exactly what I did. The registration fee was about two hundred dollars. I then registered myself and my company with ASCAP, a member-owned society that collects the rights money in the States and, through affiliates, in Europe.

When I was working on *Einstein*, I also met Harold Orenstein, who completed my education as a "publisher." Not only did he help Bob and me make agreements about *Einstein*, he also began helping out with the opera and film work that came in during the years after. It was a slow beginning, but by the mid-1980s I already needed to rent an office and hire a couple of people to look after it. Harold had been a Broadway lawyer and producer for years and had been the attorney for some big Broadway composers and writers, including Frank Loesser, and he brought that perspective to the opera world for the first time, as far as I know. He expected, and fought for, all kinds of monetary concessions from opera houses that, until then, had only been given to Broadway shows. For example, when I began to write operas after *Einstein*, he made the opera houses pay for the cost of music preparation—copying and producing all the scores and parts. It was common, up until then, for opera composers to pay for it themselves out of their commissioning fees. That meant that usually they ended up with nothing.

I liked the publishing business and became very familiar with it over the years. At least once a month, I would meet Harold at the Russian Tea Room on Fifty-Seventh Street and hear his stories. I soon had to hire a real business person to run the company, but it was still my company, and though I was spending all my time as a composer and a performer, I tried to keep up with the publishing, too. Of course, Ornette had told me years ago, "Don't forget, Philip, the music world and the music business are not the same." I learned that he was absolutely right, but I really liked both and had no problem in being active in both of them, as far as time allowed.

SATYAGRAHA AND THE SCORE FOR Godfrey Reggio's film *Koyaanisqatsi*, which was composed about the same time, in the late 1970s, were my first works in which social issues became the core subject. This had been a topic of discussion I had been having with composers throughout Europe and the United Kingdom for some time. Generally speaking, my colleagues abroad were very radical in their views. Mao's *Little Red Book* was then very popular among European artists, and some of them were actually Maoists. I was astonished by this, because I couldn't understand where it was coming from. It was unclear to me what their social activism was rooted in. In many cases, especially in the 1970s and '80s, these same artists were supported directly or indirectly by their governments. This was certainly true in Holland and Germany, but also to a lesser degree in Italy and Spain. Scandinavia also seemed well disposed to take care of their artists.

For Americans, it was and remains an altogether different matter. We have known little or no public support for the arts. Our museums and opera houses have received institutional support, but that was about it. The American artists, apart from the famously political Living Theater, were hardly political at all. As a result, we had a most curious situation: in countries where the arts received government or public support, the artists took up very radical politics; at the same time in the United States, where public support barely existed at all, artists were more often nonpolitical. However, when I got involved with the opera treatment of Gandhi, I saw a deeper side that I could relate to completely.

I came to understand that I had a social responsibility, which I could not avoid, but I also had a personal responsibility, which I was entitled to. From the personal point of view, I could do an opera or a movie in which I could address such things. For me, the moment of authentication came with *Satyagraha*. I knew why I was writing it, I knew what it meant, and I knew why it was important. I was in my forties before I was able to express, in musical terms, ideas that belonged to the world of social change. When I was younger, I hadn't taken on any kind of active role. But when I was older, I became involved with social issues and took part in charity concerts of all kinds, as well as working with the ACLU—just in the nick of time, I would say, because now there is a large part of our society that thinks that it is defending the principles of America whereas, in fact, it is destroying them.

Satyagraha—a Sanskrit word that means "truth force"—was a thoroughly conceived piece. I had been on the trail for a good ten years, reading Gandhi and thinking about America in the 1960s, and how it related to South Africa in the 1890s, when Gandhi went there and began his nonviolent movement for social change. As I conceived the work, it became part of a continuous meditation that had been going on for almost a decade. I wanted to focus on Gandhi's work in South Africa because I wanted to portray him when his ideas were new, when he was finding his own way. I had discovered that when he arrived in South Africa in 1893, wearing a pinstripe suit and a bowler hat, he had boarded the train with a first-class ticket, and they had thrown him off. He was profoundly shocked that a man of his education and his position could still be considered an inferior human being. This was a moment of revelation, of self-knowledge, where he said, "Oh! I'm not the person I thought I was, I'm the person they say I am, and what's happening to me is not right."

When Gandhi found himself in the dust, holding on to his first-class ticket after being bodily ejected, his whole purpose in going to South Africa became clear. He made a vow that night and immediately opened up law offices to organize a struggle against racial discrimination by Europeans against Indians. The opera spans the period from the moment he arrives in South Africa up to the moment he leaves. During those twenty years, he invented and developed the tools of social change through nonviolence. There is a misnomer that is sometimes used: passive resistance. It's not that at all. It's active resistance. It's just not *violent* resistance. For Gandhi, it starts with being tossed off the train and realizing that in fact he did not have the rights of the white population.

Each of the three acts of the opera is presided over by an historical figure: Act 1, Leo Tolstoy; Act 2, Rabindranath Tagore; and Act 3, Martin Luther King Jr. The culture of India emphasizes the system of

the "three times" (past, present, and future), so I was actually building into the piece much of what I had learned since I had begun to
study yoga in 1957. The past is represented by Tolstoy, the older man
who was in correspondence with Gandhi and referred to him as "our
brother in the Transvaal." The present is presided over by Gandhi's
contemporary, the Indian poet and Nobel Literature Laureate Tagore,
who accompanied him on marches and fasts. The future is represented
by Martin Luther King Jr., who adopted Gandhi's methods of nonviolence in the civil rights struggle in the United States.

The opera is a series of tableaux in which I was looking for events
that articulated very clearly moments in Gandhi's life. I wanted it to
seem as if you were looking through an album of family photographs
of your own life: you in kindergarten; your high school graduation;
your first job; you with your children. I wasn't interested in telling
a narrative story—the events did not have to be in sequence—but
there was an attempt to make them seem to have a causal relationship.
The words sung by the singers are taken from the *Bhagavad Gita*, the
Hindu sacred text that is part of the epic *Mahabharata*.

The first scene of *Satyagraha* reenacts the major debate of the *Bhagavad Gita—The Song of the Lord*—which takes place between Prince
Arjuna, who is about to go into battle on the Kuru Field of Justice,
and Lord Krishna, who appears as one of the combatants. The subject
of the debate is whether the proper conduct of a virtuous man should
be based on action or non-action. In principle, according to the scrip-
tures, both action and non-action can lead to liberation. However, in
the debate, the course of action is considered superior because it creates
positive karma. *The Song of the Lord* is one of the great pieces of religious
writing of humanity. Not only was Gandhi a devotee of the *Bhagavad Gita*, he knew it by heart. It is my belief that when Gandhi found
himself embattled with the South African government, the words of
the *Gita* could easily have come into his mind. So, in answer to the
question, "Do I take action or non-action?" he decided to take action.

Subsequent scenes are "Tolstoy Farm (1910)," the first community Gandhi organized that was dedicated to social change through

nonviolence; "The Vow (1906)," in which three thousand Satyagra-his raise their hands and vow in the name of God to resist, even unto death, the proposed discriminatory Black Act; "Confrontation and Rescue (1896)," in which Gandhi, upon his return to South Africa from London, is met by an angry crowd and rescued by the wife of the police commissioner; "Indian Opinion (1906)," showing the print-ing of the newspaper of the Satyagraha Movement; "Protest (1908)," which portrays Gandhi and his followers burning their identification cards, symbols of discrimination since whites were not required to carry them; and "Newcastle March (1913)," which takes place on the eve of a thirty-six-mile march from the Transvaal to Newcastle by two thousand people protesting, among other injustices, laws that made the marriages of Indians illegal.

Satyagraha opens with a sequence of notes commonly heard in fla-menco music. I had been aware for some time that there were hidden connections between the music of India and the music of Europe, and I had found evidence for this in the flamenco music of Spain. Thirteen years earlier, JoAnne and I had been in Mojácar, a small town on the southern coast of Spain, where the Gypsies, or Romany people, are to be found. I had taken great pleasure in listening to their music. The Gypsies are a people who have for centuries traveled between India and Europe. One part of the culture they brought with them was their music, and this music fit perfectly with how I wanted to begin *Satyagraha*. Melodically, the flatted second going directly to the tonic tells the whole story. In my case, I had reversed the Gypsies' jour-ney: while they had traveled from India to Europe, I had gone from Europe to India, listening to music all the way on my little transis-tor radio. I had been listening to what we now call world music from day one, and what I took away with me from that visit to the south of Spain was the flavor and sound of flamenco music, which became the seed of *Satyagraha*.

This was the first large-scale piece for which I had produced a full score in close to twenty years, since my Juilliard and Pittsburgh years. I was just forty-three and was, after almost twelve years with

my ensemble, about to reenter the world of concert music and traditionally presented opera. I hadn't forgotten orchestration or the
hand/finger positions of the violin or how people played the trombone. I hadn't forgotten anything. But the amount of work and preparation it took to get the music ready for rehearsal was new to me. I
spent that summer of 1980 in Holland working through all the stages
of learning and rehearsing a new work, an exercise I have repeated
many times since. My years of work with Mabou Mines had been
good training, though working with singers was a new discipline
unto itself. I had an understanding of choral writing because I had
sung a lot of it. But in addition, I was eager to make the solo vocal
parts singable and was constantly pestering the singers for suggestions. I skoon learned that if you ask a singer how a vocal part works
for her, she will definitely tell you.

The first to see the score to *Satyagraha* was Dennis Russell Davies.
We had met briefly through his wife Molly, an artist and aficionado
of new music. They were living in Minneapolis, where Dennis had
been leading the St. Paul Chamber Orchestra. He had won that job
shortly after graduating from Juilliard and had made a name for
himself and the orchestra in those early intense and creative years.
He was about to become the music director of the Netherlands
Opera in Amsterdam when I met him again at their summer home
in Vermont. He was interested in the opera right away, and I went
there to show him the score. We immediately got along very well.
Dennis had begun at Juilliard as a pianist and, along the way, had
also become a conductor. When I met him, he was already a highly
energized, engaged and passionate advocate for new music, and has
remained so to this day. He also had a taste for motorcycles, which,
of course, also pleased me.

Dennis had barely gotten through the score when he told me he
knew Hans de Roo in Holland and wanted to conduct the premiere
there himself. As it turned out, Dennis was about to have a great success in Bayreuth with Wagner's *The Flying Dutchman* and was then
offered the post of general music director at the State Opera House

in Stuttgart, so he had to give up the Dutch premiere of *Satyagraha*, which would be taken over by Bruce Ferden. But Dennis promised to present the German premiere in Stuttgart, which was to be a completely new production under the direction of Achim Freyer, the German painter and opera director. After I let Achim know of my plans for a trilogy, he also undertook the *Akhnaten* opera and eventually a new *Einstein on the Beach*. The trilogy would be presented in 1986 with all the operas—*Einstein*, *Satyagraha*, and *Akhnaten*—presented on three successive nights, beginning with Achim's complete and remarkable re-visioning of *Einstein*.

This really was only the beginning, but a most impressive one, of Dennis's involvement in my music output. Over the next three decades he would commission operas, concertos, and symphonies from me. The symphony commissions alone accounted for nine out of ten symphonies and number eleven is already in the planning stage. Though, of course, there is a lot of orchestral music in large-scale operas, the fact is that I didn't even begin my first symphony—the *Low* Symphony—until I was fifty-four. That surely must make me one of the all-time late starters among symphony composers. After years of writing for theater and opera, it was a real jolt for me to drop all of the extramusical content and make the language of music and the structure unfolding in time the sole content.

At one point I asked, "Dennis, why are you commissioning all these symphonies?"

"I'm not going to let you be one of those opera composers who never wrote a symphony," he replied.

THE PREMIERE OF *SATYAGRAHA* WAS IN ROTTERDAM. At the first rehearsal, the first hour of playing the music was so distressing that Bruce Ferden, an excellent conductor, stopped everything. "Anyone who would like to leave is welcome to leave," he said. About fifteen of the forty string players stood up and walked out. When Bruce started up again, the piece suddenly began to sound very good.

At the dress rehearsal I was sitting with Bob Israel, the production designer. Bob and I had gone with Constance DeJong, the librettist, to south India to the Kathakali Kalamandalam, and Bob had dressed up Krishna and Arjuna in typical Kathakali costumes. When the piece begins, Gandhi is seen walking upstage, and then behind him, these two characters come out in their chariots.

I leaned over and said to Bob, "What if people laugh?"

He just looked at me, kind of surprised, and didn't say anything. But no one ever laughed.

The reception of the piece on opening night depends on whom you talk to. I thought the audience liked it; it was pretty much all applause. But, as with *Einstein*, it made some people extremely angry. The new head of the Netherlands Opera, the successor to Hans de Roo, assured the public that *Satyagraha* would never be played in Holland again. He thought I had done something bad, that I had somehow sinned against music. There were some people in the press who didn't like it, and some professional musicians definitely didn't like it. If they were angry about *Einstein*, they were doubly angry about this. So not only did I get them mad about *Einstein*, I got them mad about something that was completely different from *Einstein*. They were going to be mad at me no matter what I did. But luckily I have a wonderful gene—the I-don't-care-what-you-think gene. I have that big-time. I actually didn't care then, and to this day I still don't care.

For some people, it was a tremendous disappointment. They really wanted something else, but I knew what I had done. "Did you really think I was going to write *The Son of Einstein*? Or *The Return of Einstein*?" I said. "Why would I do that?"

What *Einstein* had demonstrated was a style of rhythmic composition that I had been developing for ten years, and which was not carried over into *Satyagraha*. I was looking for a way of radicalizing the music again, and sometimes that can mean doing something that people already know. Recently I wrote "Partita for Solo Violin," which could be mistaken for something written a hundred years ago. What I'm interested in are my own abilities to think of things, to express, to use a musical language, to make it listenable. I had always felt there was a public that would like this music, and over time, the audiences, so small in the beginning, have only gotten larger.

WHILE LOOKING FOR THE THIRD PART of this trilogy of operas, I was thinking about the three estates: science, politics, and religion. I had been stuck in the twentieth century with Einstein and Gandhi, and now I began looking for a subject in the ancient world. I knew about the pharaoh Akhnaten from Velikovsky's work *Oedipus and Akhnaten* and, in fact, in my first pass at a libretto, I was going to do a double opera: Oedipus would be upstage and Akhnaten would be down-stage, and I would do the two operas at once.

But when I began researching Akhnaten, he became much more interesting than Oedipus. We think of the ancient world as Greece, but the ancient world was really Egypt. The Greeks were the heirs to the Egyptian culture. The more I got involved with the story, the less interest I had in Oedipus. What I was interested in was social change through nonviolence in the three estates, so to look at Oedipus as a psychological casualty didn't help my argument very much. Finally, I was rereading Freud's *Moses and Monotheism*, which I had read origi-nally at the University of Chicago, and it convinced me that Akh-naten was the person I was looking for.

Akhnaten was an Eighteenth Dynasty pharaoh whose name, wherever it appeared, had been eradicated from all public records. We didn't even know he existed until the city he founded, Akhet-aten (near present-day Amârna), was excavated in the nineteenth cen-tury. Then in 1922, when the tomb of Tutankhamun was uncovered, references to his father, Akhnaten, were found. There was a very big missing part of their history that the Egyptians, who had been so traumatized by the ideas of Akhnaten, had exorcised in a kind of a forced amnesia. Akhnaten had overthrown the traditional religion of Egypt in favor of a new monotheistic religion that he expected every-one to follow, and he was punished for that. He was pharaoh for seventeen years, but his punishment was to be erased from the record of kings for eternity.

It's hard for us now, I think, to appreciate how radical the idea of a monotheistic religion must have been. However, even today in indigenous societies around us, there are still multiple deities connected with the sun, the moon, and the forces of nature. This idea has historically preceded the development of an individual godhead. Some might ask, "Did the Egyptians really believe in their gods, or is it just poetry?" I don't think it was poetry, and I think when Akhnaten dethroned all those gods, he was acting like a murderer, and the Egyptians of his day couldn't tolerate it. Basically, it destroyed his reign, and he himself was dethroned and forgotten for thousands of years. Thinking back on it, it seems improbable that one man could change the whole society, which at that point had been governed by a polytheistic religion for two or three thousand years. In fact, he didn't succeed, though some credit him with the origin of monotheism. Freud's idea was that Moses was one of the priests of Akhnaten and that the Aten religion went underground and later formed the basis of Judaism, an idea that still presents some factual challenges.

The texts used in *Akhnaten* were found by my associate writer, Shalom Goldman, a scholar of ancient Hebrew, Aramaic, and ancient Egyptian. The singers sing in those languages, plus Akkadian and a fifth language, which is always the language of the local audience, be it English, German, or another. I gave myself the benefit of a narrator, thereby allowing the story to be more easily understood by the audience. I used the original ancient languages for two reasons: first, because I liked the way the words could be sung, and second, because I wanted the overall experience of the opera to come through movement, music, and image. However, "The Hymn to the Sun" in Act 2, scene 4, is singled out as an exception. Here, Akhnaten sings in the language of the audience for the first and only time, and at that moment they suddenly understand everything he is singing.

This aria is followed by an offstage chorus singing Psalm 104, in the original Hebrew. This Hebrew text has striking similarities to

"The Hymn to the Sun." In the productions we used projections of the English or German translations on the walls of the stage, which I had also done for the Sanskrit text sung in *Satyagraha*.

The sound of the music in *Akhnaten* developed in a way that was unexpected. It was commissioned by the Stuttgart Opera, but unbeknownst to us, they had scheduled a renovation of the opera house for the year we would work. Dennis Davies called me and said, "We don't have the opera house, but we're going to do the opera—don't worry."

"Where are we going to do it?"

"In the Playhouse. But you have to come over and look at the Playhouse, because it's not very big."

I went to Stuttgart and we asked to see the Playhouse. When we got inside, we discovered that the orchestra pit was tiny.

"What do you want to do?" Dennis asked.

Every once in a while, I have a really good idea, and I don't know where they come from.

"Get rid of the violins," I said.

Without the violins, half the orchestra was gone. What was left was a very different orchestra in which the highest string instrument was the viola. The violas became the firsts, the cellos became the seconds, and the double basses became the cellos. Now the orchestration was very dark and rich. Once I had established that texture, it became the sound of the prelude. To lighten it up, I added two drummers, one on either side of the stage, because I thought, It's kind of dark, I'd better add some juice. With the drummers in place, and the addition of the chorus and soloists, the sound of *Akhnaten* was complete.

If the theater hadn't been making that renovation, I would have had a full orchestra complete with violins, and *Akhnaten* would not have achieved its unique sound. Finally, the part of Akhnaten would be sung by a countertenor, a high male voice. His first note doesn't come until the third scene of the first act, and when he finally opens his mouth and the audience hears him, out comes the sound of a mezzo-soprano. I wanted the audience to think, at that moment, Oh my god, who can this be?

THE TRILOGY OF *EINSTEIN/SATYAGRAHA/AKHNATEN* was completed by 1984, and finally performed in 1986 twice as a complete cycle by the Stuttgart Opera. My life as an opera composer had really begun by the early 1980s, and opera composing remained thereafter a regular part of my work. During those years I undertook another practice which was meant to protect and even facilitate the life of these new works. Once an opera was completed, I arranged for it to have two different productions in the same year. I had noticed that generally it is difficult, if not impossible, to judge the quality of a new opera apart from its initial production. In fact, they are not at all the same. A mediocre opera can have a brilliant production and the reverse is equally true. It's for that reason that it might take decades for the quality of an opera to be fairly understood. My solution was to have two productions of a new work done more or less at the same time, or at least in the same season. I didn't expect that the same people would see them both. But, at the least, it would double the chances of having a successful "first night" and might provide a better vantage point from which to judge the work.

Still, surprising things could happen. *Satyagraha* had two good productions in 1980—one directed by David Pountney and conducted by Bruce Ferden in Rotterdam, the other directed by Achim Freyer in Stuttgart, conducted by Dennis Russell Davies. Not many people saw both, but I did and it was an important learning experience for me. I began to understand how the variables of a production—design, direction, casting, and performance—could so decisively impact a work. But knowing more didn't automatically lead to greater success. *Akhnaten*, for example, was a big roller-coaster ride, first with the production directed by David Freeman and designed by Bob Israel that was well received in Houston, generally dismissed as a failure in New York, but hailed as a huge success in London. *Akhnaten*, in the memory of English operagoers, was a big success. In the memory of New York operagoers, it was a complete disaster. On the other hand, the Achim Freyer production in Stuttgart was a success from the first night and stayed that way thereafter.

This is what I know about new operas: the only safeguard for the composer is to have several productions. Of course, the score—and that includes the libretto—has to be strong. Then the matters of directing, designing, casting, performing, and conducting come into play. With these many variables, the results can vary tremendously. However, if the work survives, say, its first decade (and most operas will never get that far), we might begin to form an idea of the quality and stature of the work in its third or fourth production. If we think through the process carefully, that is exactly what has always happened in the history of opera. Take *Carmen* or *Madame Butterfly*, or even *Porgy and Bess*, all of which had very shaky beginnings. And yet, all three have had thousands of productions since. What has happened is the following: at some point, when the productions have reached a very, very high number, the work itself has separated from *all* the productions and has taken on an independence of its own. It has now achieved a kind of platonic reality, as if it now can exist all by itself. Of course, that is an illusion as well, but an illusion that has become consensual and, therefore generally shared. I doubt whether any composer has lived long enough to have seen that happen to his or her work, with the possible exception of Verdi, who did live a very long time and happened to be, besides, an outstanding genius composer.

DURING THE YEARS WORKING ON *SATYAGRAHA* and *Akhnaten*, I had begun reading Doris Lessing's work, starting with her first novel *The Grass Is Singing* and continuing with *The Golden Notebook*. After that I read the entire five-volume *Children of Violence* series, ending with *The Four-Gated City*. When the *Canopus in Argos: Archives* series, which has been erroneously labeled as her science fiction novels, began coming out, I read them practically as she was writing them. These new books immediately struck me, and right away I began thinking of work that

I could make with them. In one way they were close to the work on social and personal transformation that had occupied me with the first opera trilogy. Especially in *The Making of the Representative for Planet 8* and *The Marriages Between Zones Three, Four, and Five*, I found the characters both more fragile and, ultimately, more resilient. I knew I had to meet this remarkable writer.

As it turned out, John Rockwell, a well-known writer and critic in the cultural world, knew Mrs. Lessing's work and how to reach her, and he made the first contact through Bob Gottlieb, her editor at Knopf. I then wrote to her directly and asked if I could meet her. I didn't say anything about an opera, just that I was a composer. She agreed to meet and suggested I let her know when next I would be in London.

"I'll be there next week," I immediately replied.

This was during the time that Ida was in the nursing home in Baltimore. Recently she had been in and out of a coma. We had no idea how long she would last, but I took a chance and flew to London. The morning after I arrived, she passed away, and I called Mrs. Lessing and told her I wouldn't be able to meet her for lunch as planned. However, she thought that since I had a few hours left in London, we should go ahead and meet anyway.

Doris was then in her midsixties, a woman with gray hair gathered in a bun. She had bright eyes and was lively in her movements. She did not have a matronly appearance, but more the look and dignity of an academic or an intellectual, which she decidedly was. There was nothing sharp or mean about her. She could easily be anyone's favorite slightly elderly aunt or cousin. From our first moments together, we slipped quickly into an easy, firm friendship.

"I'm glad we could meet, but why have your plans changed?"

"A death in my family. I'll be taking a plane late this afternoon."

"Who?"

"My mother."

"Oh. . . . Did you know her very well?"

I was completely stunned by her question. We spent the next several hours, until I left for the airport, talking about my mother. She was a good listener and, though she was younger than Ida by ten years or more, I already thought of her as a woman of my mother's generation.

On later visits we eventually got around to talking about doing an opera based on *The Making of the Representative for Planet 8*. Doris had a house in West Hampstead where she lived with her son Peter, a man about ten years younger than me. From then on, when I came to London, I would stay with her. Her home was full of books and paintings. Some might call it bohemian. For me it was always just comfortable. I knew she had lots of friends in London, but I hardly knew them.

One of our favorite things was to take a cab to nearby Hampstead Heath and walk around the flower gardens. We often had lunch in the little restaurant there, or sometimes in one of the Indian restaurants near her house. We spent our time talking about books, theater, opera, politics—everything and nothing. When I was visiting her shortly after she was given the Nobel Prize in Literature in 2007, she told me she had no idea it had even happened and was coming home one afternoon to find her street filled with press and police. She thought there had been a robbery of some kind in the neighborhood and was taken completely by surprise to find out they were all there to see her.

During the 1980s and '90s, when Doris was in New York, she would spend part of her visit with Bob Gottlieb and his family and part at my home with my family. On one visit, she arrived with a sprained ankle and only got around with great difficulty. During her stay with me I was in the midst of rehearsals and recording and had to leave the house each morning. Doris was sleeping on a couch in our downstairs living room and said she would be fine there all day, but she would be happy to have a few books to read. I knew Doris was famous for being a speed reader who always knew everything that everybody else was writing, so I left her a stack of at least ten to twelve books—all young American fiction writers.

When I got back about four that afternoon, Doris was sitting up reading a newspaper.

"Doris, did you get through those books?"

"Oh yes. Read them all. Some pretty good stuff in there!"

The premiere of *The Making of the Representative for Planet 8* took place at the Houston Grand Opera in 1988, and Doris stayed in Houston for quite a lot of the rehearsal period. The local Jaguar dealer had lent me a white convertible, and after rehearsals Doris and I would load it up with as many cast members as possible and head out to look for local Tex-Mex food. We ended up in some rough neighborhoods, but I think our Jaguar somehow afforded an unexpected protection. No tourists would be dumb enough to travel around Houston the way we did, so we must have seemed very smart, well connected, or both.

At some point during the rehearsal, real friction began developing between the opera director and our designer, Eiko Ishioka, whom I had worked with only a few years before on the Paul Schrader film *Mishima*. I told Doris during one rehearsal that I was very concerned that these difficulties were getting in the way of their work.

After not making any comment for some time, Doris said, "Can't you see what's going on?"

"No. What do you mean?"

"Those two are having a lovers' quarrel."

"What are you talking about?"

"The director and the designer, of course. They are obviously coming to the end of a romance, and Eiko will not be pushed around by him."

"No, no, Doris, you're making that all up."

"Oh, you can't see anything!"

"No, you're making it up, just as if it were happening in one of your books."

"You're hopeless!" she countered.

I never found out whether Doris's suspicions were correct, but in any case things got worse before they got better.

Doris and I would work on two operas together, based on her

novels *The Making of the Representative for Planet 8* and *The Marriages Between Zones Three, Four, and Five*. She loved spending time in the theater, and, as long as she was able to travel she came to as many rehearsals and opening nights as she could. That could also include auditions and discussions with designers. She didn't say much about the music, though I do think she liked it, and she trusted me to work with her words. In 2008, when she was in her nineties and wasn't leaving her house much, she came out to the English National Opera to see *Satyagraha*. She was still getting around by herself then and even refused to let me leave the theater to help her get a cab to take her home.

I saw Doris for the last time not long after that, and then in 2013, she died. Because I met Doris the day my mother died, she is, in my mind, still somehow connected to Ida, though I don't have the words or insight to unravel that connection.

During the almost thirty years of knowing Doris, besides the two operas we had completed, we had begun talking about a third based on *Memoirs of a Survivor*. The main character of the story, an older woman living alone in postapocalyptic London, was perhaps a little too close to her. Still, we were slowly moving ahead. Up to this point, however, it appears that these words are my "Memoir" and I have become "the Survivor."

AS MENTIONED EARLIER, the elements of music-theater and opera are music, image, movement, and text. These are the earth, air, fire, and water of performances, all of which will have some of the four. But only in music-theater, film, and opera do all four exist in a more or less equal way. Over the past forty years I have now written twenty-five operas, among them: *Mattogrosso* (1989), by director-writer Gerald Thomas, with designer Daniela Thomas; *The Voyage* (1992), commissioned by the Metropolitan Opera for the five hundredth anniversary of Columbus reaching the Americas, directed by David Pountney, with a libretto by David Henry Hwang; and *Waiting for the Barbarians* (2005), directed by Guy Montavon, with a libretto by Christopher Hampton.

The joy of working in the world of opera is impossible for many composers to put aside, and I am no different.

MUSIC AND FILM

N THE MIDDLE OF WORKING ON THE SCORE FOR *SATYAGRAHA*, I GOT A
phone call from a filmmaker named Godfrey Reggio.

"Hello, Philip. I'm a friend of Rudy Wurlitzer's. I'm calling you about a film I'm working on. I've spent the last year listening to all kinds of music and I've decided that I need your music in my film."

"Thanks, Godfrey. I would be happy to meet you, but I don't write film music."

That was true, with the exception of the film about Mark di Suvero, which I had recently completed, in 1977.

The next day I got a call from Rudy himself.

"Phil, this guy has come here from Santa Fe and he's not going to leave New York until you look at his reel. So just go look at it, say no, and he'll go back home. Besides, I'm sure you'll like him."

A day or two later I met Godfrey at Jonas Mekas's Cinematheque on Wooster Street. Godfrey had a film montage about ten minutes long that would eventually become the opening of his film, *Koyaanisqatsi*. He told me that he had made two versions, one with an electronic score from Japan (he didn't mention the composer's name) and the second with my music. After viewing both reels he said, "As you can see, your music works much better with the picture than the electronic score."

I agreed with him that my music worked better with the film, not realizing at that moment that I had tacitly accepted the assignment.

Rudy was right. I liked Godfrey right away. He's quite a tall man, six foot seven, with a gentle demeanor and a soft voice. I found out later that he had lived in a Catholic monastery in the Cajun country of Louisiana, starting as a fourteen-year-old boy and remaining there until he was twenty-eight. It looked to me as if the combination of strength, focus, and reserve, which one could easily associate with the contemplative life of a monastic, had never left him.

What appealed to me from the beginning were the two major themes of the work. The first was a series of beautifully photographed moving images of the natural world. The film began with an opening part Godfrey called "The Organic"—from the American West and, in particular, the area known as the Four Corners, where Arizona, Utah, Colorado, and New Mexico meet near Monument Valley, with its enormous landscape sculptures that were made by Mother Nature herself. Then, toward the end of the film, in the fifth reel, we would see "The Grid," the hyperactive life in our big cities—in this case New York, Los Angeles, and San Francisco. The oversimplified interpretation of the film is that technology run amok is the perpetrator and the natural world is the victim. Godfrey himself has never accepted this black-and-white interpretation, but he does use "Life Out of Balance" as a descriptive subtitle for *Koyaanisqatsi*, a word in the Hopi language. Living in Santa Fe, Godfrey had gone to a Hopi settlement nearby for inspiration and wisdom and had become close to some of the elders of the tribe. The ideas he picked up from them became the place where he began.

The second theme of the film is embodied in a series of film "portraits" of ordinary people in which the camera does a very long shot coming in very close on their faces. The perspective he brings to his subjects is intense and moving and is as powerful as the images of nature.

During our work on the film, I often met with Godfrey to hear directly from him how his ideas were developing. He has described this process as a dialogue between us and has credited it that way in the films we have done together: *Koyaanisqatsi*, *Powaqqatsi*, *Anima*

Mundi, *Naqoyqatsi*, and, most recently, *Visitors*. The truth is clear and simple. Godfrey would talk to me about his ideas for the films and about the context of the films themselves, and I would listen. Godfrey's views were powerful and, though they are generally known now, were unique at the time of their conception. They are far from the formulaic version that technology is bad and indigenous life is good, though he is constantly reflecting on the interaction between modern technology and "traditional" ways of living. In fact, I find his work much more free of judgmental posturing than most of us are capable of in matters of this kind.

In my film work, I continued, to the degree it was permitted, the collaborative approach I had arrived at in my theater and opera work. I made a point of being present through the entire process of making a film, and that included extensive visits on location as well as many hours watching the editing process. My overall strategy was to set aside as much as possible the "normal" role of the composer in the traditional filmmaking process, where the music is considered part of post-production and one of the very last ingredients to be added before the work is completed. In fact, through the 1980s and '90s, I was experimenting with the role of the composer in the overall work scheme. Godfrey was especially interested in this kind of innovative thinking and he welcomed all suggestions.

For the beginning of the film, Godfrey decided that he wanted to use NASA footage of a rocket launch.

"What kind of music do you think we should use there?" he asked.

"Look," I said. "You're going to be showing this film in big movie theaters. The history of film is also the history of theater, and the history of theater comes from the cathedrals. That's where theater began, with the mystery plays. Let's go back to the idea that when you go into the theater, you're entering a huge temple, and the instrument you would hear in there would be an organ. Maybe it's no coincidence that when theaters were built for silent movies, organs were installed and ready to be played."

The opening music begins as a classic baroque passacaglia in which the theme is stated in the deep pedal tones of the organ. The counter-point is then filled out by the two upper keyboards, and we hear one deep voice singing the name of the film—"Koyaanisqatsi." The idea of the piece was to prepare people for a performance that would be similar to what they would see in a mystery play. I went to the Cathedral of St. John the Divine, on Manhattan's Upper West Side, where I knew Dean Morton, the administrative head, and I asked, "Can you arrange for me to play the cathedral organ?"

"Yes," he said. "I'll get someone to open it up for you."

I went there and, in a few hours, I wrote the piece right on the organ.

As the opening music ends, there is a moment of silence, and then a long, low tone slowly appears. The very next image, filling the screen, is Monument Valley, with the big sky and open landscape, in a very slow pan—a pristine, untouched environment. If what we are seeing is the beginning of landscape, what we are hearing is the beginning of music.

There are two ways that I could have composed the music: to *comment* on the image, or to make the music *identical* with the image. I chose the latter. Apart from a sustained pitch, which increases and decreases in volume, the music hardly changes for a minute and a half. Then the saxophones begin playing one note on an off-beat rhythm, suggesting that we are going back to the beginning of time, to something very ancient. As the music begins to build and the landscape begins to change, we are clearly no longer in the church.

The post-production work on *Koyaanisqatsi* took place in Venice, California, and, as I was New York–based, the kind of participation I was looking for was only partially realized. The next four films I would work on—*Powaqqatsi, Anima Mundi, Naqoyqatsi*, and most recently, *Visitors*—were edited in New York City, often within walking distance of my own studio. I had seen very quickly that the earlier the music came into the film, the more it would help to determine the work process. Godfrey was very encouraging and allowed that to happen.

Some of my proposals, according to traditional filmmaking practices, were really radical. *Powaqqatsi*, the second film in the trilogy, begins in the Serra Pelada gold mine in northern Brazil. Godfrey had some film footage previously shot by Jacques Cousteau. Using that as a reference, I composed a short ten-minute piece of highly rhythmic music for brass and percussion. Then I traveled with Godfrey and his film crew to Brazil to Serra Pelada itself, an open-pit gold mine that at its high point had ten thousand miners working side by side. By the time we arrived in 1986, it was down to about four thousand miners.

This was quite a bizarre place. It could easily have been mistaken for a prison set in a jungle, but in fact it was a startling display of capitalism at work. Every man there was an owner of part of a six-by-nine-foot plot. They all belonged to the *cooperativo* and, though there were soldiers and wire fences all around the site, the miners were, in fact, all owners of the mine. When we got there, Godfrey immediately began walking down into the pit, a huge crater that was the work of six or seven years of miners digging straight down into the earth. When we got to the bottom, we just sat down and watched the men digging and hauling bags of earth up bamboo ladders to the surface. Once there, they would dump the earth into a large wooden sluice that was fed by a rivulet of water from a nearby stream. The water carried away the dirt, leaving behind gold nuggets.

I had been traveling to Brazil for several years for a winter composing retreat in Rio de Janeiro and could manage to speak Portuguese reasonably well with the workers. Down below I talked to the men. They were consumed by gold fever. I had never before seen anything like it. Moreover, I realized how young they really were. I guess none was older than his early twenties and some were younger still.

"Hey man, what are you doing here?" I asked.

"We're here finding gold."

"Where is it?"

"There's gold everywhere, all over here"—this with a broad sweep of his arm all around the horizon.

"So how are you doing?"

"I've been finding a few nuggets. But when I get a good big one, I'll cash it in and go home." In fact, there was a Banco de Brasil at the top, right next to the pit.

"Where are you from?"

"A small town near Belém" (275 miles to the north).

"And what will you do when you get home?"

"I'll either open a restaurant with my family or maybe buy a VW dealership and sell cars."

What they really did, when they found a nugget—the nugget could be worth five or six thousand dollars—was to sell it to the bank, take a plane to Manaus, and in one weekend, spend all the money. Then they would come back to work. There was one fellow who had a little restaurant there, just a tent and some tables and a fire. He said, "I don't know what I'm doing making food here. This place is probably right over gold. I could dig right down here and find gold."

The people there were obsessed with gold. They were convinced they were going to make a fortune, and some of them did, but they also spent it. Every morning when you woke up and walked outside, you saw a line of men in front of the Banco de Brasil, trading gold dust for *cruzeiros*, the Brazilian currency at that time. They were making money every day.

A little while later Godfrey and I climbed up the bamboo ladders to the surface. It was a good five hundred feet up and the ladders were only about twenty feet long. When you came to a ledge cut into the wall, you had to change over to another ladder, and once you got in the line moving up there was no stopping—the men behind you just pushed right on up. They were thirty years younger than us—tough, strong, and in a hurry.

We began filming that afternoon. The music I composed was on a cassette and Leo Zoudoumis, our cinematographer, was set up with headphones to hear it on a Walkman while he was filming. The filming got started and went on for a while. Finally, one of the miners noticed the headphones and asked, "What are you listening to?"

"The music is for here. You want to hear it?"

Of course they did, and, for a while, the Walkman and headphones were passed among the small circle that had formed around us.

"*Muito bom! Muito bom!*"—"Very good!"—was always the response.

The music for Serra Pelada is driven by highly percussive drumming. By this time I had listened to the *baterias* (drummers) in Rio de Janeiro often during *Carnaval*, where you would hear two or three hundred players playing different drums in synchronization with one another. It was a tremendously powerful sound. If you were lucky, and you were sitting in the right place, it would take eight or ten minutes for that group of people to parade past you, and you would hear nothing but this drumming. There were some cross-rhythms, maybe some twos against threes, threes against fours, but most of it was just straight-on drumming that you hear in a marching band, except that it was like a marching band on steroids. It was really loud and fast and that's what I put into the score, along with shrill, strident whistles that fit in perfectly in that piece.

When I came back to New York, I played this music for some of the people working on the film. They watched the footage, and they were shocked.

"Is that the right music?" they asked.

"Yes, it's the right music."

"But is that what it was like for those people?"

I said to one of them, "Did you think I should have done a piece like 'Yo-ho-heave-ho'? Is that what you think was going on there?"

Later, when I was actually making the film score, I added the voices of a children's choir to the brass and percussion already there, in order to capture the childlike energy and enthusiasm of the miners. To me, they were children, and I wanted to evoke that feeling with the children's choir in the score. That became a memorable musical moment.

Godfrey and I went to all the venues together, whether they were in South America, Africa, or somewhere else. I went because he wanted me to be a part of the work and he urged me to come with him. The reason the music came out the way it did was that I had been there. I could have made it up, but I would have definitely missed something. If I hadn't seen what it was like, not just on film but actually *seen* it for myself, I wouldn't have known to put the children in. I was trying to make a sound track that lived in the muscle and blood of the people who were there.

In this case, I had managed to completely change the traditional order of filmmaking. Instead of waiting for the music to be added at the end, during post-production, I had moved it up to the front, before the cinematographer had even shot the film. I wasn't out to prove anything, except that the "normal" conventions of filmmaking were just that—conventions. Over the next ten years, I made all kinds of experiments of this kind. I was, in a few rare instances, even able to carry over some of my procedures into commercial film work. The main problem is that filmmakers already think they know how to make a film, so changing their procedures would almost always be out of their reach.

When I work with Godfrey, I don't spend a lot of time looking at the image. I look at it once. *Maybe* twice, but not more than twice. Then I depend on the inaccuracy of my memory to create the appropriate distance between the music and the image. I knew right away that the image and the music could not be on top of each other, because then there would be no room for the spectators to invent a place for themselves. Of course, in commercials and propaganda films, the producers don't want to leave a space: the strategy of propaganda is not to leave a space, not to leave any question. Commercials are propaganda tools in which image and music are locked together in order to make an explicit point, like "Buy these shoes" or "Go to this casino."

The strategy of art is precisely the opposite. I would describe it this way: When you listen to a piece of music and you look at an image at the same time, you are metaphorically making a journey to that image. It's a metaphorical distance, but it's a real one all the same, and it's in that journey that the spectator forms a relationship to the music and the image. Without that, it's all made for us and we don't have to invent anything. In works like Godfrey's, and in works, for that matter, like Bob Wilson's, the spectators are *supposed* to invent something. *They* are supposed to tell the story of Einstein. In Godfrey's movies *Koyaanisqatsi* and *Powaqqatsi*, the words in the title are the only words there are. The journey that we make from the armchair to the image is the process by which we make the image and the music our own. Without that, we have no personal connection. The idea of a personal interpretation comes about through traversing that distance.

ACCORDING TO GODFREY, in the Hopi language, *powaqqatsi* is a conjunctive word: the word *powaqa*, which refers to "a negative sorcerer who lives at the expense of others," and *qatsi*, which means "life." Most of the film was shot in South America and Africa, and one of the ideas of the film is that the Northern Hemisphere is consuming the Southern Hemisphere. At a certain point, much of the Southern Hemisphere has become industrialized like the Northern Hemisphere. It has become a mirror of it.

When we were in Peru, twelve thousand feet up near Lake Titicaca, we walked toward the mountains of Bolivia, where we were told there was a ceremony going on. After hiking for a mile in the high desert, we came to a church that faced a walled courtyard, twenty-five yards square. It was the time of year that the statue of the Black Virgin was being taken from the altar, carried around, and put back, followed by a crowd of perhaps two hundred people. In two diagonally opposite corners of the courtyard there were two bands playing, each trying to outplay the other. I stood in the middle, listening.

The musicians were village people from that area. Some of them had come back from the army, and they had brought instruments back with them. There were trumpets with some of the pistons not working, or maybe clarinets that didn't have all the notes, and drums with only one side of the drum left. Basically, these were broken instruments that had been thrown out by the army and taken back to the villages by young men who then formed small bands.

When we listened it was truly difficult to hear what was going on. After all, there were two bands and they were trying to play louder than each other. I tried to record it but I didn't succeed. When I came back to New York, I wanted to get the sound of what they were doing, so I tried to imagine that instead of hearing two bands, I had heard one band. And what if they had been playing real instruments—instruments that were not broken—and what if they could actually play them? What would I have heard? I tried to remember what I had actually heard, which was the failure of the music to sound like anything because of the distress of the instruments and the ignorance of the players. But if I accommodated for that, what would it be?

From this came the music that would become the anthem of *Powaqqatsi*, which was based on an imaginary music that never really existed. But I conjured it in my mind, and in a real way, it came right out of the experience. Without having been in that place, with those two orchestras playing in the courtyard, I never would have written that music. I never would have even tried.

A lot of the pieces for *Powaqqatsi* were done that way. I traveled in different countries, and I brought home instruments that I could barely play myself: flutes, trumpets, drums, whatever they were using. I looked at the instruments and made up pieces that sounded like they might have come from there, but they really didn't. I just used that as a point of departure. However, I can say absolutely that I wouldn't have written that piece of music unless I had heard what I heard.

After the work in Brazil and Peru, Godfrey and his crew went on to Africa to continue the photography for *Powaqqatsi*. This time, instead of traveling with him, I went ahead to the Gambia on my own. Robert Browning of the World Music Institute introduced me to the Gambian griot Foday Musa Suso. Foday Musa is one of the most widely known and accomplished singers and kora players of the Mandingo tradition. He became my guide, friend, and eventual collaborator through Godfrey's insistence (in line with my own enthusiasm) that I include the sound and heart of African traditional music in the score for *Powaqqatsi*.

We spent about three weeks in the Gambia, Senegal, and Mali just driving around and listening to music. Foday Musa was a superb guide because he not only knew so much of the music himself but was a product, and a very famous one, of that very tradition. I went with him to the home where he lived in the Gambia, a compound with a wall around it and one door to get in and out. Inside was a large open space with houses built around it with balconies and stairways and windows. Everything faced in toward the courtyard— if you were standing in a window and looked down, you'd see the whole courtyard. The food was cooked there. Children were raised there. If the father was away working—maybe in Belgium or elsewhere in Africa—no one would worry, the children would be raised by a group of women. Four or five families—cousins and uncles and relatives—lived there together.

Foday Musa told me he began his music studies at about the age of six. Part of the learning was to build his own kora, a harplike instrument with twenty-one strings made with a gourd. The gourd sits in your lap, as big as your belly, and then there is a stem. The strings line up along the stem, and each string has to be tuned separately. His teacher was his uncle. If you're a griot, you are descended from a line of griots, but your own father cannot be your teacher, so Foday Musa went to live in his maternal uncle's house quite a distance away in a different village.

He told me a story about how, when he was living there, his uncle told him one day, "There's a man in a village that I want you to go to. He owes me some money. I want you to go and get the money."

Foday Musa took his bicycle and rode on a path through the jungle, taking two or three days to get there.

"What did you do at night?" I asked.

"At night I would climb up into a tree and I would tie myself to the tree. I couldn't be on the ground. Sometimes the tree would be surrounded by hyenas and they would call out to you. They would try to get you so nervous and upset that you'd fall out of the tree and then they would destroy you. You have to resist. You have to tie your-self on tight."

"How long did it take to get there?"

"About three days."

"It sounds like you could have died there."

"Well, I didn't, but when I got to the village, I had no money. I found the man who owed my uncle the money and he said he didn't have it."

"What did you do?"

"I didn't have any money to go home, and I had no food. But I found a dollar in the street"—he meant a dollar in the Gambian money—"and it saved my life. I bought some food, and I could eat a little bit, but I didn't know how to get home without having some supplies. I sat there about two days and I thought I was going to die in the street."

"Didn't anyone take you in?"

"No, I wasn't from there. They didn't know me. No one was going take me in. Then another uncle of mine came by and saw me and gave me enough money to go home, and I went back the same way."

"Climbing and sleeping in trees?"

"Yes."

"How long did the whole thing take?"

"About a couple of weeks."

Foday Musa was laughing, because I was having trouble believ-ing this story.

"This is what life was like in the Africa that I grew up in," he said.

Griots are the keepers of the history of the people. Foday Musa told me that the history of the Mandingo people that he sings about goes back eight or nine hundred years, and that he had to learn 111 songs. In Africa, it is an oral history done through songs, some of which can last two or three hours, about all the kings and the people. It's not like learning 111 five-minute songs. It's a huge amount of material.

"How do you know when you've finished your studies?" I asked.

"When I got to be a teenager, my uncle sent me out to sing in peoples' houses. So I went out to sing, and when they told my uncle that I knew the songs, it was done. I went out a couple of times, but some people had to spend years before they were graduated. They graduated the same way—you just go to somebody's house and they tell you whether you sang the songs correctly."

I spent three weeks with Foday Musa, going from place to place and listening to music.

"Where will we find the music?" I asked.

"We don't have any concert halls here," he replied, "so we have to go out on the street."

We would find a wedding where there would be music, or a dance celebration, or just someone sitting at the market playing. On my last day there, as we were getting ready to leave the Gambia that evening, Foday Musa said, "Come on, I want to take you to hear something."

We went to a place in Banjul, the capital, where there was a huge street fair that Foday Musa had arranged, to celebrate us. There were people singing and dancing, and Foday Musa said, "Okay, now you have to dance. You can't leave here until you dance."

Everyone was standing in a circle, and they pushed me into the center of it, and I had to dance. There were men and women, and I was dancing with them, and they pulled me and pushed me around until they said I had finished my dance.

FODAY MUSA PLAYED KORA AND COMPOSED two important solos toward the end of the score for *Powaqqatsi*. He and I continued to work together, our next important collaboration being a score for Genet's *The Screens*, a play about the occupation of Algeria by French colonialists. We composed separately and together about fourteen compositions. He did the African parts and I did the European parts, although he also played in my parts and I played in his. By that time we had learned how to play together. The production took place at the Guthrie Theater in Minneapolis in 1989, the director being JoAnne

Akalaitis. We then began touring with *The Screens* music as the basis for our repertory. We also added percussion, keyboards, saxophone, and violin along the way. We didn't travel all the time with such a large group, but it became for a time another performance ensemble I worked with. We continue, even these days, to add new pieces that we compose together. *The Screens* has become the name for the collection of music that Foday Musa and I have jointly made, a collection that, as far as I can tell, has yet to be completed.

It is really through working with Foday Musa that I began to have real insight into the relation between our Western notated concert music and the music of indigenous sources and people. Working with Raviji and Alla Rakha had opened the door for me. But it was really Foday Musa who pushed me through the door. On the first day that he and I began to compose together, we were in my studio on Broadway at Bleecker Street. We didn't know where to start, so I suggested that we should first tune the kora to the piano. Like the harp, the kora has a string for each pitch. So we began.

"Foday, play your lowest note."

He played the A below middle C. I played the A on the piano and he tuned his kora to the piano A.

"What's the name of that note?" I asked.

"The first note."

"Oh. Okay, play the next note." He played the B above the A. I played the B and he again tuned his string.

"Foday, what's the name of that note?"

"The next note."

"Oh." I was getting a little nervous, but I pushed on.

"Okay, play the note after that." He played the C. I played it, and he tuned his third string to the C.

I hesitated to ask, but I did anyway.

"And what is the name of that note?

"It's the note after that."

I almost fainted. I suddenly understood that, for Foday Musa, the notes did not have names. I was feeling a strange vertigo and I hung on to my chair. In my very first flute lesson, fifty-four years before at the Peabody Conservatory, Britton Johnson had placed my index finger and the thumb of my left hand on two keys of my flute, pressed the keys down with my fingers, and said, "Blow across the hole."

I managed, after a few tries to get a sound out.

Mr. Johnson then said, "That is a B."

At the same time he pointed to a note on the middle line on a page of music paper with a G clef written at the left side. In far less time than it takes to tell, he had locked together a sound, my finger position, and a written note on the page. Now, fifty-four years later, Foday Musa had *unlocked* them. In a flash I finally understood that the whole system of music I had learned, starting with Mr. Johnson and going right through to Mlle. Boulanger, had been just that—a system, consensual in its very language and no more eternal than the human beings that contrived it. It didn't make it less beautiful. Perhaps it was now even more beautiful. And as impermanent as an afternoon shower, ever so lightly moistening the air we breathe.

We might consider a fourth in Foday Musa's playing a little flat, or a second a little sharp, and so on, so that the actual intervals of African and Western music are not identical. What he has done is retune his instruments to fit a Western scale. He told me that a lot of the players who come from Africa will not retune their instruments.

"What happens then?" I asked.

"They can't play with anyone because they're never in tune. If you want to come to Spain or England or Germany and you want to play, you have to retune your instruments and most of them won't do it.

"Do you have any problem with it?" I asked.

"I have no problem at all."

What happened to Foday Musa was similar to what happened to Ravi Shankar. When Raviji first came to America and then went back to India, he was criticized for the success he had. He would have to calm the critics who thought he couldn't play anymore. He would put on a big concert in New Delhi or Bombay and play the traditional music fantastically well. He had to prove to them that he could still do it. That stopped after a while—they knew that he was able to do both. When Foday Musa would go back to the Gambia, because he had changed the tuning on his Western recordings, they thought he had lost the music. But when he returned to the original tuning of the kora, they were satisfied that he could still play the traditional music. Foday Musa and Raviji were able to move between musical cultures, and the real entry for them began with retuning their instruments.

Through my contact with both of these men, I learned to adapt my playing to music that was not part of Western traditions. Recently I made a record with some indigenous Wixárika musicians from central Mexico. I didn't know what they would play, but I knew whatever it was, I would manage it. I listened to the music and said to myself, "Where is the music? Where does the music go? What can I play?" And then I began to play.

The work with Godfrey opened up a world of music for me, because it meant that in the end I could go and play with almost anybody. I've experimented widely with musicians—Raviji; Foday Musa; Mark Atkins, the Australian didgeridoo player; Uakti, a group from Brazil; Wu Man, the Chinese *pipa* player; and the Wixárika musicians. All of this music has been performed live or been recorded. Traveling with Godfrey for the film shoots had made it possible for me to have regular encounters with skilled musicians in other traditions. The time I spent with them gave me the confidence to pursue new directions, and my forays into global music—Indian, Himalayan, Chinese, Australian, African, South American—have widened and deepened my understanding of my own musical roots. And not only that, over the years and as I ventured further and further away from my musical "home base," I have come to understand that all music, without exception, is ethnic music.

In 1990 I became the artistic director for the annual benefit concert for Tibet House US, which had been established in New York City in 1987 at the request of His Holiness the Fourteenth Dalai Lama. It followed his stated wish for a long-term cultural institution to ensure the sustainability of Tibetan culture in exile and to create an awareness of Tibet's contribution and relevance to the world's cultural heritage. The founders of Tibet House US included Robert Thurman, Richard Gere, Porter McCray, Elsie Walker, Elizabeth Avedon, and myself. The first concert was held at the opera house at the Brooklyn Academy of Music and included Allen Ginsberg, Laurie Anderson, Spalding Gray, and me. Having lived and worked in New York since 1967, I had developed, with the help of a committee from the music world organized for this purpose, a large pool of talent to draw from in making the evening's lineup. I discovered that almost none of the players I knew had ever played in Carnegie Hall, and that seemed to have been a major attraction for them.

Perennial performers have been Allen Ginsberg, Patti Smith, Laurie Anderson, and myself. Guest performers have included Angélique Kidjo from Benin, Caetano Veloso and Marisa Monte from Brazil, Ashley MacIsaac from Cape Breton, Pierce Turner from Ireland, and Foday Musa Suso from the Gambia, as well as such Tibetan musicians as Nawang Khechog, Yungchen Lhamo, Tenzin Choegyal, Dechen Shak-Dagsay, and Techung. In addition the concert has featured hugely popular performers like Paul Simon, David Bowie, Debbie Harry, Lou Reed, Ray Davies, Michael Stipe and REM, David Byrne, Richie Havens, Iggy Pop, Shawn Colvin, Emmylou Harris, Taj Mahal, Rufus Wainwright, Sufjan Stevens, Rahzel, the National, the Black Keys, New Order, and the Flaming Lips.

This extension into the pop-commercial-folk world has become the living confirmation for me that talent is among our most universal qualities, appearing where it will regardless of gender, race, age, or nationality.

When I studied with Nadia Boulanger, she was basically teaching central European art music. That was her tradition, and that was what she taught. She was not interested in teaching anything else, for the very good reason that that was really what she knew. When I finally left her, I possessed an important skill and the tools with which to adapt music to different needs. I learned to move with ease from one tradition to another. Now, when I'm conceptualizing music on my own, it's easier for me to leave Western music behind. Piano was my instrument—that's where I started—but I had come to see that it was just a small part of the world of music. It wasn't the whole world.

SHORTLY AFTER *KOYAANISQATSI* HAD BEEN COMPOSED and had come to be known, Paul Schrader, the director and screenwriter, called me and we began talking about his film *Mishima*, about the life and work of the controversial Japanese author Yukio Mishima. This would become the first studio film on which I worked. Paul was filming in Tokyo in November 1983, when I was there performing with the ensemble, and I was able to be on location a number of times. Besides being on the set, I spoke extensively with Paul about his ideas for his film. I also met Eiko Ishioka, whose visual imagery for the film was so beautiful and who would work with me on the Doris Lessing opera *Making of the Representative for Planet 8.*

The music had an important role to play in the film. The score I composed was not meant as a musical decoration of the film. It was, in fact, used to help articulate the film's structure. Of course this approach grew directly out of working with Godfrey, and in that way, and particularly with *Mishima*, I think that integrating the composition of image and music into a unified endeavor can provide the most powerful tool for a filmmaker.

With *Mishima*, Paul had a clear idea. There are three threads that run throughout the film. The first is the last day in Mishima's life, which begins with him putting on his uniform to lead his private army in the attempted takeover of an army base. This last day is distilled into music—a snare drum and strings—that provides a military aspect. This march will become a march to his death.

The second thread is stories from Mishima's life: the young boy, the young man. We see him becoming a writer, becoming famous. The music of a string quartet is generally considered to have an introspective quality, and here it is used for these autobiographical passages. Schrader chose to shoot these sections in black and white, further separating them from the fictional aspects of the film taken from his novels—*The Temple of the Golden Pavilion, Kyoko's House, Runaway Horses*. This, the third thread of the film, contains the most lyrical and sumptuous music.

At the penultimate moment of the film, Mishima, looking out from the cockpit of a plane, receives a profound revelation about his work and his life. The string quartet music now takes on the orchestral colors of the music associated with the novels, and leads him to the confrontation that is about to take place at the army base. His life and the stories he has told have merged and will culminate in his *seppuku* (suicide).

There may be no writer more autobiographical than Yukio Mishima. Everything he wrote was about himself. The film *Mishima* is a portrait of the writer Mishima, and the music of *Mishima* is meant to add a further dimension to the film. With the Mishima material I used my total immersion strategy, reading every book in English I could find. I was very impressed with his writing. It was passionate, it was modern. In his life he had arrived at a transcendent experience that was at the core of what motivated him to be a writer. For all the writers I personally know, writing is a way of accommodating themselves to the world, of making the world a bearable place in which to live. Mishima became a writer in order to make the world understandable to himself.

That's very different from having an agenda, let's say, an existentialist agenda that has an ideological or theoretical basis. Mishima's solution derives from his experience, and in that way, he resembles Céline and Genet, writers who were not political writers but who were working out of the crisis of being alive, the crisis of experience itself. This applies to the whole postmodern generation, of which we have to say we are a part. That which authenticates our work is the genuineness and spontaneity of our intuitions. In this way, the activity of writing makes the world meaningful. It has no political status, and I would say it has no real social status. That's precisely the way it is transcendent—it goes beyond the visible world into a world in which being alive makes sense. For the postmodernists, writing becomes the remedy. One of Allen Ginsberg's T-shirts said, "Well, while I'm here, I'll do the work. And what's the work? To ease the pain of living. Everything else, drunken dumbshow." That's at the core of the postmodernist movement, and even now, nearly two decades after Allen's death, we respond to his poems immediately. They need no explanation.

WHEN I HEARD IN THE MID-1990S that Marty Scorsese was making a film, *Kundun*, about the life of the Dalai Lama, I was immediately interested. I had previously had some contact with Marty in the 1980s through Thelma Schoonmaker, his longtime film editor. She was married to the filmmaker Michael Powell, director of *The Red Shoes*, who wanted to make a film out of my opera *The Fall of the House of Usher*, based on the Edgar Allan Poe story. Michael was quite an elderly gentleman by that time and there was some concern among the producers that the film might get started and he might not be able to finish it. Thelma asked Marty whether he would be the back-up director, in case something happened. We met, and we talked about it, and he said he was willing to make that commitment. The idea then was that there would be a contract that would involve Michael Powell, and the back-up director would be Marty, so that the people in Finland who were producing the film would be guaranteed a completed film. But before we finished the agreement with Marty, Michael Powell passed away, and the project never materialized. But it had put Marty and me in touch with one another, so that later I was able to call Marty and he took the call.

"Marty, I'd like to talk with you about this film that Melissa Mathison has been working on with you."

"Come on over and let's talk about it."

When I saw him, I told him that I knew Melissa, the screenwriter for *Kundun*, through Tibet House, where we were both on the board of directors, and that I had had a long association with the Tibetan community. He must have known my music, because we had spoken before about the *Usher* project. He never told me he had heard it, but I don't think he would have agreed to be the stand-in for Michael Powell if he hadn't known something about the music. Also, by that time *Mishima* had been done, and Paul Schrader was one of Marty's favorite writers, having written the screenplays for *Taxi Driver* and *Raging Bull*.

I was passionate about wanting to work on the film, and Marty accepted my request. At that meeting I proposed that I do "advance" work on the score—actually sending him music while he was shooting. At first he was a little puzzled and hesitant. Industry films normally do not tolerate innovations of this (or scarcely any) kind. Finally I think he just succumbed to my enthusiasm and acquiesced, and it became one of the few times I was able to follow my preferred working methods with a film made by a major studio and with a well-known and highly regarded director.

When Marty was in Morocco filming *Kundun*, I was sending him tapes of music for the scenes he was shooting. I knew that Thelma was there making a rough "assemblage" of the film, staying perhaps no more than a day or two behind Marty's shooting schedule. At one point, he found that I had fallen behind on my film composing, and he urgently needed the music for reel 5, the "Escape to India" reel of the film. I had a few days off from my concert tour in Europe, so I flew to New York and quickly sketched out the music for the scene. The score I was composing included contributions from Tibetan musicians, some of them known by the actors, who themselves were Tibetan men and women whom I knew from my work with the Tibetan community in New York City. They were able to hear the music that would eventually become the sound track of the film, and I'm told that the music was very warmly received.

Working with Marty, I became interested in everything he did. I would go to the editing room in New York almost every day that he and Thelma were working. Marty is famous for his knowledge of film history, and, for almost every scene that we worked on, he could elucidate something about that scene from the history of filmmaking. When I looked at his script, I found he had put in the camera positions when he was writing. He knew how he was going to shoot it, and he knew how it was going to look. He talked a lot about his own films and how his working methods were developed for them.

At one point, he had been talking about *Taxi Driver* for a while. I didn't say anything—I just was listening, which I normally did—but something must have piqued his interest.

"Wait a second, have you *seen Taxi Driver?*"

"No, I didn't see *Taxi Driver.*"

"You didn't see *Taxi Driver?*"

"Marty, I *was* a taxi driver. During the time when you were making that film, I was out driving a hundred miles a night in New York City. On my night off, the last thing I was going to do was see a movie called *Taxi Driver.*"

"Oh my god, we've got to fix that. I'm going to have a special screening for you."

Before the special screening took place, I happened to be in an airplane on one of my music tours and, by luck, they were showing *Taxi Driver* and I watched it.

The first thing I thought was Good lord, it's exactly like the people I knew who worked at Dover Garage!

SCOTT RUDIN, THE PRODUCER of *The Hours*, asked me if I was interested in writing the score for that film. I already knew that there had been two other composers but I didn't know who they were. Scott asked me if I wanted to see the movie with the scores he had rejected, and I said, "No, I don't want to hear it. Give me your rough cut without any music in it at all and let me write the music."

The Hours, based on the novel by Michael Cunningham, is the story of three women living in three different eras: the writer Virginia Woolf, played by Nicole Kidman, who is seen during her life in the 1920s and then at her suicide in 1941; a 1950s Los Angeles housewife and mother played by Julianne Moore; and a woman played by Meryl Streep who is living in New York in 2001 and is preparing a party for her friend who has AIDS.

I saw right away that the issue with the movie was that the three stories were so distinct from each other that, like a centrifugal force, they pulled you away from the center and made it difficult to keep your attention on the movie as a whole. It seemed to me that the music had to perform a kind of structural alchemy. Somehow, it had to articulate the unity of the film.

The job of the music was to tie the stories together. What was needed were three recurring musical ideas—an A theme, a B theme, and a C theme. The suicide of Virginia Woolf, for example, was always the A theme. That was always her music. The B theme was always the music from Los Angeles, and the C theme was always New York. The movie progresses A, B, C, and all six reels follow that plan. Basically, it was as if a rope had been threaded straight through the film. It was a conceptual idea, and it could be realized by the music. It worked, but it wasn't so easy to accomplish.

I don't think there was really any other way to do it. I never heard the other scores, so I don't know what the previous two composers had tried. Being the third composer on a film is very common in Hollywood. Often two composers, or sometimes three or four, will get fired and other people are brought in, until the studio decides it's the right music. Fortunately for me, and for the film, I think, Scott Rudin saw right away what I was doing. He liked it and he stuck with it.

Scott is extremely intense and very opinionated, but, as abrasive as he could be in terms of presenting his ideas, the films in fact got better because of him. That was true on every level.

Very often when I worked with him he would say, "That's wonderful. I loved the music. But there's one little thing that bothers me."

As soon as he said that, I knew I had to rewrite the whole thing.

He would press his point, but he began from a point of appreciation, which I liked. He always listened to me, and I always got a fair hearing for what I wanted to do. I wasn't commanded to do something, I was persuaded to his point of view and, most of the time, his ideas were right. They prevailed not because he was the producer, but because his ideas improved the movie. And that was not only in the music, it was also in terms of the editing, storytelling, and acting.

After *The Hours*, I did *Notes on a Scandal* with Scott, another film on which he was, again, a very hands-on producer. But unlike a lot of producers who are hands-on, he knew something about film. He knew what made films work.

At one point, I asked him, "Scott, why don't you just be the director? You do everything anyway."

"Oh no, no, no," he replied.

He insisted he could never be a director, and yet he often seemed to usurp that position. In any case, as the producer he had a very decisive role in the two films I made with him. I liked the films and I liked working with him.

I HAVE NOW MADE CLOSE TO THIRTY SOUNDTRACKS. There were others that I enjoyed working on, though perhaps not as well-known. David Gordon Green's *Undertow*, Neil Burger's *The Illusionist*, and *Taking Lives*, directed by D. J. Caruso, are among them. My all-time favorite is perhaps the least known of these—Christopher Hampton's *The Secret Agent*. I thought Hampton's adaptation as well as his taut, nononsense direction totally captured the obsessive and sinister aura of the Joseph Conrad novel.

Another favorite is Errol Morris, with whom I worked on three films—*The Thin Blue Line*, *A Brief History of Time*, and *The Fog of War*. I found Errol to be one of the most brilliant directors, extremely funny at times and terribly eccentric. Like Godfrey in many ways, Errol has redefined the relationship of the viewer to the subject matter, and as I feel about Godfrey, I'm always ready to work with him. The experience, though confusing and sometimes trying, is always rewarding.

The director I found the most surprising was Woody Allen. I worked with him on *Cassandra's Dream*, and he completely left me alone to place the music in the film. He welcomed my suggestions as to the temper of the music as well. In fact, that is very much the way I work with my opera, theater, and dance collaborators. My sense is that if I believe in their ability and talent, the best thing I can do is get out of the way and let them do their work. Woody seems to work in much the same way.

THOUGH FILM SCORING HAS NOT BEEN THE MAIN THING I was doing for the last thirty years, I have generally found it interesting. The writers, directors, actors, and a few of the producers can be enormously talented. Even though the marketplace mentality is always present, it is still possible to make films of real quality and integrity. That they are mainly "industry" films does not mean they are necessarily made in Hollywood.

I have often compared film scoring to opera composing. I've done a fair amount of both. More than other performance practice, films combine elements of image, music, movement, and text. Skills acquired in one easily translate to the other. I will add to these reflections about film work just a few points:

The first is quite simple. If the movie or opera is actually telling a story, I've learned to leave it alone or, at least, not get in the way. If there is no story, I will not impose one, but instead allow another of the performance elements to assume a larger role.

Second, I've learned how to "underscore" the voice—either spoken or sung—by letting the actor or singer assume the central role at that moment. Sometimes that requires the instrumental parts to play a secondary or tertiary part. However, it's also quite possible to double up the vocal parts with solo or accompanying instruments and, in this way, to actually extend the range and depth of the sung or spoken parts.

The third point is the hardest to describe. It has to do with that imaginary "distance" I mentioned before that exists between the spectator-listener and the film or opera. I've found that the music can absolutely define that space. In the end, it is a psychological space. The closer the spectator-listener is to the "image"—sound or visual—the less choice he has in shaping the experience for himself. When the music allows for a distance to exist between the spectator-listener and the image, then she will automatically bring her own interpretation to the work. The spectator travels the distance to the image herself, and by moving to the image, she has now made it her own. That is what John Cage meant when he said that the audience "completes" the music. Modulating that distance precisely is an acquirable skill. Talent, experience, and some innate sensitivity will still be needed.

D URING THE TEN YEARS WE WERE TOGETHER, CANDY AND I ALWAYS felt that something was going to separate us. We didn't know what it would be, but we both knew that somehow we would become separated.

We would speculate about it. "Maybe you'll be on a boat or plane some place, or I'll be, and the boat will disappear, or the plane will crash," we would say. We thought it would be a kind of incidental tragedy of modern life, like a car accident. This feeling bothered us, and we talked about it not frequently but not infrequently either. It was something that would come up, like a shadow that we lived with.

I first met Candy Jernigan when I was flying from Amsterdam to New York in 1981. I had been working in Europe, and she was changing planes on her way back to New York from Berlin. Candy was already sitting down in the plane when I got to my seat next to hers, and she seemed preoccupied with reading a magazine, pretending not to notice me at all.

Over the next ten years I would sometimes ask her, "How was it that you were sitting next to me on the plane?" but she never would tell me. Apparently what had happened—related to me later on by people to whom she told the story—is that she recognized me, and when she found out I was on the plane, she went up to the person whose seat was next to mine and said, "Mr. Glass is a friend of mine, would you mind changing seats with me?" As I was sitting on the aisle, the seat next to me was not a seat that was hard to swap, because people never want to sit in the middle. Not surprisingly, that person switched seats with her, and by the time I sat down it was a fait accompli.

It was a rather daring thing to do, and as I got to know Candy I could not imagine that she was that kind of person. But she knew my music, and she wanted to meet me. Once I met her, I never wanted to let her out of my sight.

In a funny way she never wanted to talk about how we met, and yet the meeting itself was remarkable, because it was a meeting of two people who somehow knew that they wanted to be together, and she knew that before I did. Why she knew that, I can't say, but we began talking and there was an immediate rapport, as can sometimes happen. There was a flow of intelligence, an almost poetic way of talking, that we fell into almost immediately, so we didn't need to talk about very much. It turned out that she had recently separated from a man she had lived with for a long time, so she was alone. I was not alone, but from the moment I met her, I was suddenly in a place where something very unexpected but profound had happened in my life, and that was the presence of a person with whom I would spend the next ten years.

Candy's hair was long and raven dark when I met her. Later on, at different times, she might dye it orangish, or purplish red, but that was a passing thing. She wasn't tall, maybe five foot two, and she wore glasses with black plastic frames. She liked to wear vintage clothing, a lot of black, with black tights and big, wide black or red belts. Her style showed a sign of taste but not of wealth. She was always able to look distinctive without spending very much money.

Candy's grandmother on her mother's side was from China, a fact that no one in her family talked about for some reason. Candy only discovered this when she found her mother's passport and learned that her mother was born in Shanghai. She also found a photo of her mother as a little girl being carried in a palanquin with her grandmother. If you knew about Candy's Asian ancestry, you could see hints of it in the shape of her face and in the quality of her skin, which had a kind of porcelain transparency.

By the time our plane reached New York, we were reluctant to part, though I was really in no position to make any arrangements to see her again, because at the time I was married, and it wasn't something I wanted to get out of or change in any way. But it became impossible for me to think about *not* seeing this young woman again. I happened to have an apartment downtown in the East Village that I had used as a studio, so instead of going home, I went to that apartment on Fourteenth Street between First and Second Avenue. Candy happened to be living on First Avenue and Eleventh Street, so I was just around the corner from her. That wasn't planned, but that's how it was.

Candy was twenty-nine and I was forty-four, which doesn't seem like such a great obstacle, though at that time it seemed she was very young. Many things might have bothered me, but nothing to the degree that could dissuade me from immediately pursuing this friendship, and in fact, from then on we were hardly separated. There were some very uncomfortable and unhappy moments when my marriage fell apart, without my meaning it to, but without my being able to stop it. It did take a little time to straighten things out. It wasn't very easy, and it wasn't very happy for anybody.

Candy was a painter, and her friends were painters, writers, dancers, and musicians, the same kind of people I had worked with all my life. That was her world, too, one that sustained her and seemed to fill every minute of the space and time that she had. Her day job was working for Paul Bacon, a celebrated book cover designer. When I met her, she was working in figurative oil painting, but soon thereafter she went into different kinds of painting and art making. Her work was part of a different art movement than the one I grew up with, which was abstract, heavy-duty masculine artists like Mark di Suvero and Richard Serra, who were making large powerful pieces in public places.

Candy was making art that was much closer to the casual inclusion of materials that you'll find, for instance, in Robert Rauschenberg's work. With Rauschenberg, he always asked the question "Can this fit into my painting?" and the answer was always yes.

Like Rauschenberg, Candy also followed the gesture of opening up the canvas or the artwork to anything that you could put in it, but she did it in a different way, so that her work became a form of documentation. She would find objects, which could be as unalike as a cooking pot that had been run over by a truck, crack vials she found on the street, and a dead rat she had stuffed and mounted, and then she would ask the question "Is this art?" In her case, the answer she gave was "Let's just put a frame around it."

We were living together very soon after we met. I had the kids, Juliet and Zack, plus two cats, and she had two huge blue-and-gold macaws who were fiercely loyal to her and just fierce to everyone else. She became very close to Juliet and Zack right away, and the four of us spent a lot of time together. For a couple of years, we lived in a kind of haphazard way. She had an apartment a block and a half away, where she would go to change clothes, and I had my own apartment, a small place where the four of us managed to live together.

By 1984 we were actively looking for a bigger place. Candy and I had been looking in SoHo for a loft or apartment, but wherever we looked, the prices were out of our range. Then my friend Richard Savitsky, an attorney in entertainment law and real estate, called me excitedly and said he had found a home we could afford, a redbrick town house in the East Village. I was so doubtful about the possibility that we waited several weeks before even bothering to look at it. The house was off Second Avenue and not so deep in the East Village as to make it a long walk to the subway. But it was clearly at that time a drug-infested neighborhood, with the entire street teeming night and day with drug sellers and users. The owner lived in Texas and had, under the circumstances, given up looking for a sale.

We loved the house and, for Candy and me, by that time both practically East Village natives, the neighborhood was not an unmanageable problem. Because the area was then so undesirable, the seller was expecting only a 10 percent down payment, but even so we didn't have the cash. I had ten grand from Sony as an advance on my album *Glassworks*, and I borrowed five grand each from Juliet (sixteen at the time) and Zack (thirteen), which had been gifts to them from their Akalaitis grandparents. The last ten grand I borrowed from an old friend, Rebecca Litman, on a 60-day loan, which I actually paid back in 120 days.

The plan was that we would live in the upper two floors and rent out the lower two as a duplex. I registered the duplex with a real estate agent on East Fourth Street, but there was not even a single inquiry during the next three months. However, somehow I had made the first three mortgage payments on time. Accordingly, I removed our listing with the agent and we took over the whole house.

It was a perfect home for us. The downstairs was a kitchen and living room, and the floor above it had a painting studio for Candy and a music studio for me. On the third floor were a bedroom, a bathroom, and a library with empty shelves on all four sides, leaving only space for three windows. The top floor belonged to Zack and Juliet, where they also had their own bathroom and even a small kitchen. Candy's two vicious parrots, Jack and Carol, by general demand, had to stay in her studio.

Our house became the center of our lives. Candy would come home from work and we would have dinner with the kids. We took turns cooking, ultimately making a list of sixteen or seventeen meals that we taped to the refrigerator door. Each night we would look at the list and pick a meal, saying, "Okay, let's make number seven." As a vegetarian, I was good at making pizzas with homemade dough— potato pizza was a specialty of the house—and I also learned to make lasagnas and all kinds of pasta. I was also good at home-fried potatoes and a dish I called Martians in the Himalayas, mashed potatoes with green peas mixed in. Candy, in turn, enjoyed Southern dishes like sweet potatoes with melted marshmallows on top. I used to tease her about that because that's something you find in Jewish homes. I couldn't believe that she was cooking sweet potatoes with marshmallows: it's much too sweet and can't possibly be good for you.

After dinner and homework, the children would go to bed and Candy would go to her studio. The room she painted in, every inch of it, was an extension of her, with drawers and cabinets filled with her artwork and the materials she had collected to use in her work. Our studios were separated by two sliding doors, and both the music room and the painting room were filled with our personal artifacts. Candy would buy a six-pack of beer and a couple of packs of cigarettes and she'd paint until one or two in the morning, this being her regular painting time. We were together almost all the time, except that she would stay up late and I would go to bed early. She liked to work at night, and I liked to sleep at night—I had to get up with the kids, so I was on a different schedule. She wasn't interested in having children of her own, but she was very close with mine.

Even before we met, Candy was a completely articulated personality, and yet when I look at her work now, I realize it underwent a very big change almost from the day we met. Suddenly, she had a whole new community of friends. My friends became her friends, and her friends became mine. I was told that she changed personally as well. One of her friends who had known her before said she could be mean and sarcastic. He was always afraid she might say something cutting. But she was never that way with us. It was almost as if, when I met her, she found a home. She felt so comfortable that there was nothing to be mean about. We all loved her, and she was part of our life, and it seemed to happen overnight.

Above all, Candy was passionate about her work. In almost all of her paintings, there is an element of humor, and a slight distance, which is always interesting, that separates her from the work itself. It was this slight angle that she was coming from that gave all her paintings their tremendous humor and quality. *Ten Kinds of Beans*, a painting of ten different varieties of Goya-brand canned beans, is subtitled

Homage to Goya. A single square of pink toilet paper from a bathroom in the Louvre is mounted, framed, and labeled *April in Paris.*

She liked my music and she designed album covers for a number of pieces—*The Photographer, Dance,* and *In the Upper Room* among them. She was particularly curious about writers. She had many friends who were writers, some of whose book covers she designed, and she collected first editions, which are still today upstairs in my library.

During those years, Candy could often arrange a leave of absence from Paul Bacon's studio and travel with me when I had a music tour. She assembled a whole series of travel journals on our trips: Mexico, Brazil, India, Africa, Italy, the American Midwest—fourteen of them in all. She carried with her all the things that she needed for collecting specimens: glue, containers, wax envelopes, labels, pieces of string. She was a professional cataloguer, and she traveled with a bag full of the things she picked up along the way: bottle caps, postcards, pop-tops from aluminum cans, matchbooks. She even collected dust in little plastic bags—dust from the Louvre, dust from the Vatican. The travel books were usually being made in the planes or the cars or the taxi while we were traveling. She would take out the things she had collected the night before, and she would take two open pages, and those things became her journals, which in addition to being priceless diaries of our travels became works of art in themselves, all of them archived and preserved.

We took numerous trips with our friends Stanley and Elyse Grinstein, the art publishers and collectors who founded Gemini Press, which produced so many lithographs, prints, and books by Rauschenberg and Johns, among other well-known artists. Stanley and Elyse had been hosts for the Mabou Mines theater group when we first performed in Los Angeles way back in 1970. Our trips together to India, Italy, and Brazil were documented by Candy in her journals. One journey took us from Quito, Ecuador, to Manaus, Brazil, a five-day boat trip down the Amazon. In India, a country she found incredibly colorful and exhilarating, we visited Kalimpong in the northeast and went south to Kerala to see the Kathakali.

Some of the travel could be quite rough. When I was working on *Powaqqatsi*, we took a memorable trip to Africa. At one point we were in the Gambia and supposed to go to Mali. We went to the airport to catch our flight, but there we learned that the president's wife had decided to go shopping in Paris. Our plane was gone and there was no other plane to take. We were told we could go by land from Banjul, the Gambia, to Bamako, Mali, but first we had to cross the estuary of a river so wide it reminded me of the Amazon. To make the crossing, people used peanut boats, maybe twenty-five or thirty feet long but only four feet wide—no wider—with a motor that went *putt-putt-putt-putt*. You could count the *putts*, it was really that slow. The boats were *filled* with peanuts, not even in bags. It was just a boat filled to the brim with loose peanuts.

Foday Musa, my Gambian musician friend with whom we were traveling, said, "Just get up there and sit on the peanuts." So Candy and I got in the boat, and Zack, who was traveling with us, got in, as well as Michael Riesman.

Kurt Munkacsi and his wife, Nancy, however, said, "We're not getting in the boat."

"What are you going to do?"

"We're going to go to another city, we'll take a bus, and we'll get to Mali," Kurt said. They had already found an alternate route. "We'll be there in about three days."

All we had to do was get over to the other side of the river and we would get there a lot quicker.

Soon after we got on the boat, it started getting dark. A young fellow with a can was sitting in the center of the boat, and as soon as we left the shore, he began bailing out water. He had a permanent job, as far as I could tell.

When we got to the middle of the river, I couldn't see the shore behind me and I couldn't see the shore in front of me. I knew that if that motor stopped, we would sink like a stone. The only thing that kept us going was that little motor—*putt-putt-putt-putt*—that kept us moving through the water.

Because I was taking Zack, who was about fifteen at the time, JoAnne had said to me before the trip, "Now you be sure you bring him home."

It took us about forty or fifty minutes to cross the water, and the whole time I was thinking, Oh my god. What if I lose Zack? She'll kill me. And what if I lose myself? She'll kill me, too.

But somehow we got to the other side and scrambled off the boat.

Land travel in the Gambia was generally shaky. When we traveled overland, we'd rent a car, and we'd also rent a mechanic to go with us. The mechanic sat up front next to the driver, and there were two rows of seats behind them where we sat. The car would go for a while, maybe ten or fifteen miles, and then it would stop. The mechanic would get out and fix it somehow, then he would get back in, they would start the car, and we'd get moving again.

We managed to get around pretty well, but the form of travel was extremely primitive, and accommodations could be sketchy. In one small town we stayed in a place that called itself a hotel, which meant basically that the room had a bed, and the bed had a sheet on it. The sheet looked like it hadn't been washed in a while. Kurt took one look and said, "I think I'll sleep standing up in the corner tonight." Candy called that particular lodging "the bucket hotel," because the bucket in the room took the place of running water.

Candy wasn't fazed by the travel conditions we encountered, because for her these trips were a way of collecting material for her art. This was a woman who affirmed her existence by collecting what she called "evidence." In fact, she was *always* collecting. When we went off the beaten path, we got very exotic stuff, and you couldn't get more exotic than the countryside of Africa.

Candy liked the music in Africa, she liked the people, and she could eat more of the food than I could, given my vegetarian diet. Foday Musa once took us to a butcher shop that was a kind of lean-to with a cement floor, with parts of an animal laid out on the floor. You didn't know how long that animal had been there, but there was an ax, and if you wanted something, the butcher chopped it off with the ax and gave it to you. I saw the men who were going hunting carrying what looked to me like muskets—really old-fashioned-looking guns. They had gunpowder and everything. It was like hunting in the nineteenth century.

"Where they going?" I asked Foday Musa.

"They're going hunting."

"They're going hunting with those things?"

"Oh, yeah."

EVERY SUMMER, WE PACKED CANDY'S PAINTING and drawing supplies into the car, and with the two kids we drove a thousand miles north to Cape Breton, often staying there for two months. Usually friends came throughout the summer, so the cabins around the main house were full and the kitchen was never empty. The first thing I had to do was get under the house and fix the pipes, because they would always break over the winter. There were a lot of other repairs needed to keep the house going, but somehow I had time to write music.

The main house was very big, and I had one studio apart from that, an A-frame in which I'd write. The front room was Candy's studio. Sometimes she brought her dance-theater group, the XXY Dance/Music Company, for which she designed sets and costumes. They worked in a boathouse down by the water that later on would become Zack's house. Everyone worked in his own cabin during the day and met at the big house at mealtimes. It wasn't unusual to have fifteen to twenty people gathered around the picnic tables in the evening sharing a good home-cooked meal after a day spent making art or taking day trips to the many rivers, beaches, forests, or to Cape Breton Highlands National Park.

Candy made many artworks in Cape Breton: a series of drawings of insects that became an accordion-style book called *The Dead Bug Book*; a small wooden case filled with rocks—*99 Blue Rocks*; a box of drawings of twigs; and innumerable landscape paintings of the hill leading to the cliffs by the ocean shore and the island across the sound from our house. We spent ten glorious and wonderful summers there.

On a family trip with Juliet and Zack to the Yucatán in the summer of 1990, Candy made her usual travel journal. Upon our return, we went to Cape Breton, and at the end of the summer we came back to New York to our house to settle back into the routine of work and school for the kids.

At this time, Candy began not feeling well. She said she felt tired. A visit to the doctor eliminated Lyme disease and parasites, and she was prescribed vitamins and told to stop smoking, which she did, trading in her Marlboros for packs of Nicorette gum.

Later in the fall she felt somewhat better, and a few weeks before Christmas we flew to Santa Fe to stay for ten days with Rudy Wurlitzer and his wife, Lynn Davis, the photographer, who had rented a house for a month. At night we sometimes went to the outdoor hot springs, where you could sit in the warm water and look at the stars, thinking it might be therapeutic. We also thought the change of environment might help, but some days Candy had a hard time getting out of bed. We were still operating on the belief that her problems were related to some kind of fatigue syndrome, which could have a long recovery time.

We returned to New York for Christmas, but then in the New Year Candy began feeling worse. She kept working and painting, but she was not well at all. Then, at a certain point, her skin turned yellow almost overnight, and it was thought that hepatitis was the cause. The Dalai Lama's doctor happened to be in New York, and he was available for diagnosis. I knew enough people so I could get him to come to my house, and when he came, he did an analysis. He asked her for a urine specimen, took it into the next room, and came back. He didn't say anything about what it was.

"Take these pills," he said. "Chew them up." He gave me maybe twelve pills, and said to take one every week.

"What do I do when we run out of pills?"

He gave me a very strange look. "You'll get in touch with me when that happens."

I realized later that he didn't expect her to outlive the pills.

Soon I received a call from the Tibetan doctor's assistant and was given the analysis: "We've spoken to the doctor, and he says she has cancer of the liver."

I talked to someone later about this and asked, "How would he know that?"

"What they used to do," I was told, "is they would taste the urine. If there was sugar in the urine, it meant it was a disease of the liver."

Our Tibetan doctor was very experienced and his analysis was completely accurate. He also knew that she would only live another six weeks. He didn't tell me that, but right afterward we got the diagnosis from her New York doctor, who had also done tests, who confirmed that in fact it was liver cancer. Hepatitis was something that maybe she could have survived, but not cancer of the liver.

With the help of my friend Rebecca, who herself had survived lymphoma a year earlier, we found Candy the best oncologist, and she was admitted to Sloan-Kettering to begin chemotherapy. She would go in for a few days or a week at a time, then come back home. She began to have a syndrome where she would walk around at night. At the hospital she would go for walks, walking and walking around the corridors. It's a known reaction to chemotherapy. When she came home, she would stay up all night painting.

In such a life-threatening situation, you always want to think that there will be a positive outcome, but in our case, it was wishful thinking. If I had been thinking clearly, I would have realized, "No, this isn't working." But I didn't think that at all. Nor did I think, until many years later, that her illness was, in fact, the realization of our fear of being separated, that it had finally come true, only not in the way we expected. That thought, This is the thing we were afraid of, never occurred to me.

The last few weeks of her life, Candy came back home, stayed for maybe two weeks, then went back to the hospital for the last time and never came home again. During those two weeks at home, she painted nonstop, producing something like eighty paintings, at the rate of five or six a night. She would paint, and then she would come upstairs and go to sleep. I would come down in the morning to see what she had done, and all these new paintings would be there, eight of them at a time hung on the wall in two horizontal lines, four above and four below.

She called the series *Vessels*. The paintings were watercolors on paper, eighteen inches wide by twenty-four inches tall. Each painting was of a bowl, glass, cup, or pitcher. Some resembled ancient Greek vases. The "vessel" was situated on a horizontal line toward the bottom part of the painting, as though sitting on a stage. Many of the paintings had what looked like pulled-back theater curtains in the upper right and left corners, often with streamers of paint dripping all the way down to the "stage." The background might be smooth or tumultuous, most often a single color that could be solid or washed-out—red, blue, yellow, gray, or green.

Clearly, these were very personal paintings. The vessels became a stand-in for herself. I'm talking about the function of a symbol, how an object can become filled with the personality of a person. It becomes easier to paint the object than to paint the person, so the object becomes a stand-in. All the qualities of a person are in the painting, but it takes the shape of a vessel. We can ask, "Is it a womb?" or "Is it the chest?" but it's easy for us to imagine it as the human form.

What Candy did—and she was very good at this kind of thing— was to take an ordinary shape or form and use it symbolically. It would become a presence, a kind of artifice, a substitute for a person. It's easy to say that these were portraits of herself, but they were more than that. The painting she was doing was an extraordinary exercise that she was going through. It was almost as if the bowl or the vase represented an organic unity of some kind that *was* her. And of course, it was a feminine image, not a masculine one. She didn't talk about this at all. She just continued painting them.

One morning I came down, and she had done four or five more paintings as she did every night, but one painting was empty. She had done all the background, with the stage and the curtain, but she didn't paint the last vessel. There was no object. It was gone. It seemed that as long as she could paint a vessel, she would stay alive. Then one night she could no longer paint it. She had gone up and gone to sleep, and when she got up the next day we took her back to the hospital and she never came home.

I called Juliet, who was twenty-two and at Reed College, and said, "Juliet, you have to come home now." And she came home.

"How could this happen?" she asked.

Candy was only thirty-nine. It didn't seem possible that someone could be that young and die. We had been in complete denial about what was happening right in front of us. We never thought we were going to lose her. We didn't think that the universe was so badly arranged that someone like her could be taken away from us. We just couldn't believe that could happen. And we were totally wrong.

When Candy died, I was sitting with the children in the hospital room. I wanted everybody to leave the room but Juliet and Zack and me, and we sat there together. Anyone who has sat with people who are dying will know—it's not a mystery—that after the last breath, after the heart has stopped beating, after what common medical practice recognizes as the physical death, there is still an energy in the body. Until that energy leaves, the body doesn't relax, if I can put it that way, and this can go on for some time. In Candy's case it would last two or three hours.

"Let's wait here until she's gone," I said.

An intense passage was taking place, both for the children and for me. We stayed there for a couple of hours, and at one moment—it was the damnedest thing—it was as if a film director had changed the lighting. Somehow, the whole appearance of the body changed. The *actual* physical change was slight, but it was unmistakable. It was as if the body had just gone limp.

"Did you see that?" I said.

"Yes," Juliet and Zack both said.

"She's gone."

And that's what it was.

I think this was the first time we understood the fact of impermanence and the inevitability of death. It became very clear to us. Until then, we had no idea. We were strangely out of touch with the simplest reality of life, which is that death doesn't keep score of our years. It moves at will, and it takes who it wishes to take.

Candy had carried on until she wasn't able to do any more. Artists very often do that. They work up until the last minute. There's no time when they're not engaged in the work. With that last painting, there was no vase, no vessel, and when I came down and saw this, I knew it was an omen, a sign, or a message. It was very clear.

I actually had the incredibly foolish idea that I could will her life to continue—I was sure that I could do that—but my will had nothing to do with it. Will is okay for writing music, or for writing books, but not when it comes to the great matters of life and death.

When Candy died in 1991, she left close to six hundred paintings, objects, combines, books, and other pieces, a lot of them made in her last few years. We were able to make books and publish her work, which continues to be shown at the Greene Naftali Gallery in Manhattan. In the last year, the Whitney Museum of American Art in New York City and major collectors have purchased her work.

IT TOOK US ALL SOME TIME to put our life back together. It was especially hard for Juliet and Zack. Our ten years together had flown by and, without warning, had come to an end. To them, and me too, it was unimaginable.

I took some time off and went to stay in the country with Tomo Geshe Rimpoche at his place in the Catskills. I was in a little house by a lake, just walking in the woods, listening to the wind in the trees, looking at the night sky. He was in the main house, a mile away, and

I would walk down the hill in the evening to have dinner with him. We didn't talk much about it.

One afternoon, Geshe Rimpoche caught up with me walking around the lake. He patted me hard on the back and with a quiet smile said, "That was a big lesson on impermanence."

I smiled slightly and nodded.

NOT LONG AFTER CANDY'S DEATH, DURING A SIX-WEEK RETREAT in Rio de Janeiro, where since the late 1980s I had been spending parts of January and February composing, I began writing *Orphée*, the first of a trilogy of operas (*Orphée*, *La Belle et la Bête*, and *Les Enfants Terribles*) based on the films of Jean Cocteau.

Orphée is based on the well-known Greek myth of Orpheus as told by Virgil, Ovid, and many others. It is the story of a man who, when his wife, Eurydice, dies and is taken to the Underworld, descends to try to bring her back from the dead. Hades and Persephone, the god and goddess of the Underworld, are so moved by the music of Orpheus that they allow him to take Eurydice back with him to the upper world, on the condition that she walk behind him and he not look back at her until they have both reached the world above. In his anxiety, Orpheus forgets these instructions, and as soon as he sets foot in the upper world he turns to embrace Eurydice, who vanishes back into the Underworld. He loses her again, this time forever.

It's hard for me to believe now, but at the time I was working on *Orphée* I had no idea I was reproducing my own life.

"No, it has nothing to do with Candy," I said, when I was asked about it back then.

But thinking back on it, how could it have been otherwise? In the story, the wife dies, the poet-musician Orpheus tries to save her, he almost succeeds, and then he loses her for eternity. I was in denial, and it wasn't until much later on that I realized it.

The story of *Orphée* may be the most famous and widely set story in the history of opera. Monteverdi, Gluck, and Offenbach are the first few that come to mind. There are plenty of modern ones besides. Harrison Birtwhistle has a famous one—*The Mask of Orpheus*. There is a long list that goes on and on. The themes of love, life, death, and immortality are, for theater composers and authors, just about irresistible.

One of the things that drew me to these films of Cocteau is the pacing of his writing. If you look at it, it is truly Shakespearean. He knows when to introduce a character, he knows how to develop him, and he knows how many characters are needed. The real secret of writing operas is having a good libretto. Composers know that, because operas are not easy to write. I have, in fact, done operas without great librettos, but they are operas that don't require librettos. *Einstein on the Beach* didn't really require one, nor did *Satyagraha* and *Akhnaten*. For a number of years I avoided the issue of librettos entirely, but at a certain point I wanted to see what it was that I was avoiding, so I began to write narrative operas. I chose the films of Cocteau because his sense of dramatic development was impeccable. For the mixture of the tragic and the comic in one opera, *Orphée* is the perfect example—it's a romantic opera, it's a comic opera, and it's a grand opera. It's all three together. And very few artists have the ability to combine all three.

When I began composing these operas, it was always clear that Cocteau could be found in the characters he invented. In *Orphée*, Cocteau *is* Orphée. At the beginning of the film, sitting at a café, Orphée, the poet, encounters a well-known critic. None of the avant-garde crowd at the café is paying attention to Orphée. Everyone is busy lavishing attention on the young "poet of the day," Cégeste, who, at a nearby table, is surrounded by a crowd of young admirers.

"No doubt they think I'm old hat," Orphée says to the critic, "and that a poet shouldn't be too famous."

"They're not overly fond of you," the critic replies.

"What you mean is they hate me. And who's that rude drunk over there?"

"It's Jacques Cégeste. A poet. He is eighteen and adored by everyone. The Princess finances the magazine that just published his first poems. Here's her magazine."

The critic hands the magazine to Orphée, who opens it.

"But every page is blank," Orphée exclaims.

"That's called 'nudism,'" the critic replies.

"Totally absurd!"

"No excess is absurd. Orphée, your worst fault is knowing how far one can go before going too far."

"The public loves me," Orphée/Cocteau says.

"*Il est bien le seul* (The public is alone)," says the critic.

As depicted in *Orphée*, Cocteau's reaction to being seen as an aging lion, from having once been a brilliant young genius, overflows with humor. It is as if Cocteau can't wait to roll out this scene, placing it at the very beginning of the film. We don't see the critic again until toward the end of Act 2, when he returns with the League of Women leading a rabble that surrounds Orphée's home, goads him into coming outside, and then murders him. That, I take it, is the measure of the role of the critic in the eyes of Cocteau.

The scene pretty much sums up how Cocteau must have felt when he began *Orphée* only a few years after World War II had come to a close. In 1949 Cocteau, who died in 1963, was sixty years old, and he was no longer treated as the young artist, writer, and filmmaker genius he was taken to be in the twenties and thirties. He had clearly been pushed aside. He knew that he was a great creative personality, yet nobody was any longer paying attention to him. He was regarded as someone who no longer had to be taken seriously.

The situation that Cocteau found himself in interested me, and when I told my French friends that I was basing operas on Cocteau's work, they said, "Why would you do that?" They didn't ask even what it was that I was planning to do.

"He is one of the great writers of France," I replied, recalling how intrigued I had been when I first saw his films in the Hyde Park theater when I was a student at the University of Chicago.

"No, he isn't."

"Yes, he is."

"*Mais non!*"

"*Mais si!*"

In their opinion, Cocteau was a populist and a dilettante, because he did drawings, he wrote books, and he made movies.

"You're absolutely wrong," I said. "What he was doing was looking at *one* subject—creativity—through different lenses."

In Cocteau's version of the myth, in the film's last act, after Orphée has been killed and returns to the Underworld, he declares his love for Death, whom we met in the first scene of the movie in the guise of the Princess, the poet Cégeste's patroness and companion. But Death has already decided on a course of action that will free Orphée to become an immortal poet: to restore Orphée and his wife Eurydice to life, Death/the Princess reverses time back to the moment before Eurydice's death. Heurtebise, Death's chauffeur, tries to dissuade her from the forbidden act of reversing the arrow of time, but her answer is astonishing and final.

"The death of a poet requires a sacrifice to render him immortal."

When Death is asked what will happen to her now, she replies, "It is not pleasant."

But we know that the price Death will pay is her own death—her own immortality will be taken from her. We know this beyond a shadow of a doubt, and we have known it from the beginning. Shakespeare's rendering of this idea appears as the last line in his famous Sonnet 146, written more than 350 years earlier:

"And Death once dead, there's no more dying then."

Only a writer as remarkable as Cocteau would have known to take a sentence of Shakespeare and make it the key that turns the lock in his film. The skill of Cocteau is to lead all the threads—Orphée's political, social, and personal obsessions, many of which reflect Cocteau's own—to a resolution and clear expression. One of the autobiographical aspects of Cocteau's treatment of *Orphée* is that Orphée, the consummate poet and visionary, is trapped in an ordinary domestic life that, for an artist of his caliber, is intolerable. The real issue for Orphée and, by extension, for any artist is to escape his earthly fate and make the jump into immortality. Cocteau has made the route to immortality abundantly clear. Only Death herself has the key to immortality.

WHEN I BEGAN WORK on the Cocteau trilogy, the first idea that governed my work was to bring out the underlying themes of the three films. They are best described as a pair of dualities—life/death and creativity being the first; and the ordinary world and the world of transformation and magic being the second. These topics are at the core of all three works and are explicitly put forward in the films. Whereas the first trilogy of operas (*Einstein*, *Satyagraha*, *Akhnaten*) was about the transformation of society through the power of ideas and not through the force of arms, this second trilogy from the 1990s revolves around the transformation of the individual—the moral and personal dilemmas of a person as opposed to a whole people or society. A corollary to this is the way in which magic and the arts are used to transform the ordinary world into a world of transcendence. These three films of Cocteau are meant as a discussion, description, and instruction on creativity and the creative process.

My second purpose in making the trilogy was to effectively rethink the relationship of opera to film. The simplest statement of the idea, though not a complete one, is that instead of turning an opera into a film, I would be turning films into opera. In doing this, it would be necessary to turn around the conventions common to almost all filmmakers. The normal flow that guides the threefold process of pre-production, photography, and post-production is far from eternal truth, and the processes of filmmaking and opera writing offer powerful alternatives to conventional thinking. It is important to note that the accepted conventions have a good reason for being there. In that they are universally accepted, film production is made far easier for the large number of people who will be working together. The process does not need to be explained. It works well enough, and the film business can carry on efficiently just being what it wants to be— that is, a business. However, once that way of thinking is set aside, all kinds of other possibilities quickly appear. But this will happen well outside of the commercial framework, where the rules are set by the marketplace and the conventions of working are well-known.

Each of my approaches to the three films was different. For *Orphée*, I took the film script and treated it like a libretto. The movie is not shown—simply, the scenario of the movie is used to stage an opera, with singers, sets, and lighting. The stage director doesn't reference the film at all. The staged version is fifteen minutes longer than the film version because it takes longer to sing a text than to speak it. Since I didn't have to worry about fitting the libretto to the picture, I could let it be any length needed. Every line from the movie is included in the libretto, every scene from the movie is in the libretto, so in a real way, the libretto for the opera was by Cocteau.

Fittingly, almost every piece of music I wrote for *Orphée* comes directly out of each particular scene of the movie. For instance, in the opening scene in the café, Cocteau has someone playing a guitar, but that was much too tame for an opera. What was needed was a honky-tonk piano. I thought of it as if some piano player who plays honky-tonk music was sitting in the café and someone said, "Hey, play the piano for us!" because that's the music you would hear if you were sitting in a café. The music provided for going to the Underworld has a bit of a funereal sound, but it's also almost boogie-woogie music. For the two romantic duets for Orphée and La Morte (Death), one in Act 1 and one in Act 2, I was thinking of Puccini and Verdi, composers who wrote operatic love music. I thought, If I were a real opera composer, and I was about to write a romantic duet, what would it be? I wanted to write a modern love duet, and that was my version of it. I think the reason this opera is so popular is that the music composed for it was directly inspired by the film, and not by the myth.

Edouard Dermithe, who as a young man played both the role of Cégeste in *Orphée* (1949) and Paul, the male lead in *Les Enfants Terribles* (1950), was an elderly gentleman when I met him in the early 1990s. At that point, he was representing the Cocteau estate, and it was he who made the financial and legal arrangements for the rights that I would need to make the adaptations I had in mind. Though I took great pains to let him know, both in French and English, what I was intending to do, I'm not sure he really understood what the outcome would be. He was mainly concerned that the actual words were kept intact, which is what I did in both *Orphée* and *La Belle et la Bête*.

Since my work would be in French, no translation was needed. Finally, after a long three-hour lunch, we had an understanding, opened yet another bottle of wine, and toasted to the success of the new adaptations.

A few months later he sent me a typescript of the scenario of *La Belle et la Bête*.

"Please underline all the things that you cut," he wrote on the cover.

I made a copy of the scenario with not even the slightest changes or marks and returned it to him the next day.

"It's not necessary," I wrote back. "Nothing from the movie was cut. No changes were made."

I didn't hear from him again for about a year. Early in 1994, he wrote me that he would be attending a performance of *La Belle et la Bête* during one of our European dates, but his car broke down en route and he never got there. As far as I know, he never did see any of the productions. Nor did I hear from him again.

AS A TRADITIONAL FAIRY TALE, *La Belle et La Bête*, the second opera of the trilogy, was an ideal vehicle for Cocteau's symbolic-allegorical film. In Cocteau's telling, La Bête is a prince who has been bewitched and transformed into a fearsome creature who can only be returned to his human form through the power of love. The young and beautiful

Belle comes to live in La Bête's chateau in order to save her father, who had stolen a rose from La Bête's garden, from death. The first time Belle sees La Bête, she faints out of fear, but over time she becomes fond of him, though she still refuses his proposals of marriage. The plot progresses through a series of events involving the rose, a golden key, a magic mirror, a magic glove, and a horse named Magnifique. In the end, Belle is allowed to leave La Bête's chateau to save her ill father, but she returns when she sees through the magic mirror that La Bête is dying of grief over losing her. When, through death, La Bête is transformed back into a prince, she flies away with him to his kingdom to become his queen.

My treatment of *La Belle et la Bête* was the most radical of the three works. I began by projecting the film as the visual aspect of the opera but turning off the soundtrack—music and speech—completely. I replaced the speech with singing parts, with all the other music also replaced. Technically this was not that hard to do, but it took a little time. I used the scenario from the film, timing every syllable, scene by scene. In using this method, the singers would only have the same amount of time to sing as the actor on the screen has to speak. Then I set up the music paper with bar-lines and metronome markings, also scene by scene.

After that, it was like hanging clothes on a clothesline. I began with the instrumental accompaniment, which was scored for my own ensemble. Now I knew where the vocal line needed to be and also, referring to the instrumental accompaniment, what the actual notes could be. After that was completed, we made a "demo" tape of the music in my studio and played it against the actual screen image. It seems my time working on *doublage* in Paris in the 1960s, almost thirty years before, had been more useful than I had ever anticipated. I knew from those years that the synchronization of image and sound did not have to be 100 percent throughout. In fact, all that was needed was a good moment of synchronization every twenty to thirty seconds. After that, the spectator's own mind would arrange everything else. This gave a lot of flexibility in placing the sound on the lips. I also knew that words beginning with labial consonants such as *m*, *v*, or *b* in English and associated with the lips being closed were the best for those "synch" moments. Using these technical aids and the computer to adjust the sound to the image, Michael Riesman and I were able to fine-tune the vocal lines as needed. This was especially helpful because this score would be performed live with the film, and Michael would be the conductor.

At this point, in the mid-1990s, Michael had conducted Godfrey's *Qatsi* films many times over the past ten years. It had quickly become clear that the live performances were more interesting and powerful when the synchronization of music to film was achieved visually—without the mechanical aid of a metronome or "click track" to guide the music. When the conductor visually matched the flow of music to the film, the effect was identical to a live performance (with the usual ebb and flow of the tempo) because it *was* a live performance. Over the years Michael had become so skillful with Godfrey's films that I often noticed that these synchronized live performances were better than the pre-recorded version that one might see in a movie theater or at home on a DVD. From our point of view, the live performance raised the bar in terms of our expectations.

La Belle et la Bête was set up with the ensemble sitting in front and below the screen facing Michael, who was standing facing the screen with his back to the public. The singers stood behind the ensemble, their heads just below the screen, also facing Michael. They were in concert dress, not looking at all like the actors in the film. They were lit from in front, but not so bright as to "white out" the screen image. At the beginning, the singers read the music from music stands, but after a few dozen performances, they hardly looked at the music.

This presentation had some surprising and unexpected results. We soon discovered that the audiences, for almost the first eight minutes, simply didn't understand what was happening. They could see the film and the singers, but it took that long for them to understand that the voices of the singers had become the voices of the actors on the screen. There was a learning curve taking place and it happened without fail at every performance. Then, at almost exactly eight minutes into the film, the entire audience actually "saw it." There could often be a collective audible intake of breath when that happened. From that instant on, the live singers and the filmed actors had merged into a double personae and stayed that way right through to the end of the singing and the last image of the film.

Before that last image, there is even a more intense moment when La Bête appears to be dying. At that moment, the audience is watching both Jean Marais, the onscreen Bête, and Greg Purnhagen, our singer, singing his words. I've watched that a hundred times and, at that moment, it is as if the two performances had perfectly merged. I have to admit I had no idea that this would happen, and it never fails to surprise me. But there it is—a merging of live and pre-recorded performances, both unexpected and powerful.

With *Orphée*, the music comes out of the scenes of the film, but for *La Belle et La Bête* I wanted to use some of the techniques found in traditional operas whereby a musical theme is linked to a person: when a character appears, their music is heard. This is the traditional operatic system of leitmotifs. There was a theme for Belle and a theme for La Bête. There was a theme for when they are together and another for when they're traveling toward each other. As the opera progresses, those themes return. That was the chosen musical strategy of the film.

The leitmotif for La Bête starts low in the orchestra, and as it rises, turns into a melody. The theme associated with Belle occurs for the first time when she enters the chateau and walks through the hallway of candle-holding arms that have emerged from the walls. It is delicate music, but it's constantly being interrupted by growls and other sounds being made by La Bête. Her music is also heard when La Bête enters her room to watch her sleeping. As the opera proceeds and La Belle begins to return his love, her music becomes intertwined with the music of La Bête. It is his music that becomes the love music of the opera.

In the scene when Belle begs La Bête for permission to visit her father, La Bête, moved by her plea, decides to let her go, but requires her, at the cost of his own life, to return in a week. He explains to her that his magic exists by the force of five power objects—the rose, the key, the mirror, the glove, and the horse. These five are the root of La Bête's creativity and magic.

The point is, if a young artist were to ask Cocteau directly what he would need to pursue the life and work of an artist, these five elements would be the answer. The rose represents beauty. The key represents technique—literally, the means by which the "door" to creativity is opened. The horse represents strength and stamina. The mirror represents the path itself, without which the dream of the artist cannot be accomplished. The meaning of the glove eluded me for a long time, but finally, and unexpectedly, I understood that the glove represents nobility. By this symbol Cocteau asserts that the true nobility of mankind are the artist-magician creators. This scene, which leads directly to the resolution of the fairy tale, is framed as the most significant moment of the film and is the message we are meant to take away with us: Cocteau is teaching about creativity in terms of the power of the artist, which we now understand to be the power of transformation.

FOR COCTEAU, PLACE HAS A SPECIAL SIGNIFICANCE related specifically to creativity. In the three operas, the place or site of creativity is a central idea. The site of creativity for *La Belle et la Bête* is the chateau. In *Orphée*, the site of creativity is the garage where Orphée's car is parked and where he hears the communications from the other world. In the third part of the trilogy, *Les Enfants Terribles*—adapted for the screen by Cocteau from his 1929 novel of the same name but directed by Jean-Pierre Melville—the site of creativity is "the Room," where almost everything in the film plays out.

For this third opera, which premiered in 1996, I chose a different approach to the resetting of the film. If *Orphée* was a romantic comedy and *La Belle* an allegorical romance, there is no doubt that *Les Enfants* is a grand tragedy, ending with the death of Paul and Elisabeth, the brother and sister who are the two principals. The film follows the lives of Paul and Elisabeth from when Paul is recovering from an injury and Elisabeth is nursing him back to health in their shared bedroom. It is here in the Room that they invent "the Game," in which the winner is the one who has the last word, leaving the other frustrated and angry. After their invalid mother dies and they have become young adults, they move together into a mansion left to Elisabeth by her deceased husband, where they reconstruct the Room. The Game is now played much more seriously, involving two other young people, Agathe and Gerard. The love, jealousy, and deceit that develop between these two star-crossed couples lead at the end of the movie to the deaths of Elisabeth and Paul.

In my rethinking of this film as an opera, I sought to introduce dance into the mix. Dance was the only modality of theater that had not yet been addressed in the trilogy and was the one with which I had had the most direct working experience. I asked Susan Marshall, the American choreographer and dancer, to be both director and choreographer, and to bring her dance company into the production. Besides that I would need four singers for the two couples. The original score for the film was the Concerto for Four Harpsichords by Bach, and I decided to continue the main musical texture with a multikeyboard work by using three pianos as my music ensemble.

Susan and I spent months of preparation mapping out how the vocal quartet and her company of eight young men and women would, in music and dance, translate the film into a live performance work. In this way, at least we had a preliminary plan for the division of the work into scenes and an overall idea for the staging.

In *Les Enfants* the Room itself is where almost everything plays out. It is here that the Game is played which, transparently enough, becomes "the world as art"—here actually replacing the ordinary world completely. The voice-over in the film (which is the voice of Cocteau himself) makes it absolutely clear that we are to understand Elisabeth and Paul not as just twins, but really two sides of the same person. The total immersion in the Game has now led to something not unexpected but almost familiar: the obsession of the artist in this narrow context, shared, as it were, only between themselves, as a heightened form of narcissism.

Cocteau assures us that the ones who seek transformation put themselves at great risk when their energy is applied to themselves. In *Les Enfants Terribles*, though the artist must, and will, risk everything in the game of inner and outer transformation, this interaction with the ordinary world can be dangerous and decisive. The ultimate subject of Cocteau's work is creativity. He was greatly concerned about being the one who transcends the ordinary world, about being immortal in his work. The bargain he struck was to give up the bourgeois life in order to live the life of an artist.

These alternative realities—the ordinary world and the world that the artist either is creating or creating from—result in the artist's having his feet in two different worlds at the same time. In the case of poets, they are obliged to use the language of the quotidian world, the daily world. This is one of the curious things about poetry: the currency of poetry is the currency of everyday language. They are truly the alchemists who are turning lead into gold—and that is, above all, what makes poetry such a high art form.

Painters, dancers, musicians, composers, and sculptors, on the other hand, live in two worlds. In my case, one is the ordinary world and one is the world of music, and I'm actually in both at the same time. There are special languages we use in that other world—the language of music; the language of movement; the language of image—and they can exist independently. We live in these different worlds, though at times we may not even see the connections.

When a composer is asked "Is this the right note, or is it not the right note?" or if a painter or a dancer is asked "Did you mean that?" the artist will try to go back to the moment of creation to find out.

"If I can remember what I did," he might say, "I can tell you the answer."

The problem I have—one shared by almost everybody—is that in order to write that piece of music in the first place, or to write almost anything of quality that is both abstract and moving at the same time, the artist has to arrive at new strategies of seeing—or in my case, even to hear clearly what I think I have heard. It can be a very slippery business: "Am I hearing a triad? Am I hearing a tritone? Am I hearing a fifth?" To finally know what I'm actually hearing takes an extraordinary function of attention. In other words, the artist has to gather up his ordinary ability to see or hear, and he has to see better, farther, and more clearly than he ever did before. With this we are now moving out of the ordinary perception into the extraordinary perception that the artist has when he is writing. In order to do that, what we do routinely is to gather together our entire attention.

Weight lifters, the ones who lift the five-hundred-pound weights, sometimes stand in front of the barbell for thirty seconds, or a minute, or even a minute and a half. When they are finally in the right frame of mind, they execute the clean and jerk—they pick the barbell up and then throw it up above their heads. They are able to do this because of their passage from their usual ordinary attention to the extraordinary gathering of attention that is required to accomplish something that is unbelievable.

In order to do that, a sacrifice has to be made, as Cocteau, speaking through Death/the Princess, says in *Orphée*. In fact, something has to be given up. What is given up is the last thing left that we are holding on to: the function of attention we use when watching ourselves.

In the ordinary world, we see ourselves essentially all the time—walking down the street, looking at ourselves in the mirror, sitting in the subway and seeing the reflection of ourselves in the window. This function of seeing ourselves is a form of attention. It's like the trapped miner who is trying to get out of the mine. He'll do anything he can to break through. In the same way, in order to break through that moment of frustration—to grasp the abstract and bring it into our own mind—what we have left to sacrifice is that last aspect of attention, the ability to watch ourselves.

The reason I know this is that I often have a great deal of trouble remembering what I was thinking when I wrote a piece. What I do is to take all my sketches and number them, like an archivist, or almost like a scientist, so that I can look into my own past and find out what I was thinking.

Although these notes provide me with *evidence* of a thought, they don't, however, provide me with the thought *itself*. Sometimes a player will say to me, "Is this an A or an A flat?" and I'll say to him, "I don't know."

"How can you not know? You wrote it."

Well, that's the point. I wrote it, but I wasn't there. The "I" that was watching wasn't there. The witness of my life at that moment had been sacrificed. The witness had to go, because I needed every increment of attention that I could muster in order to visualize the music. I believe that what happens at that moment is that I've lost awareness of myself. That awareness is now part of the attention and with that attention I can continue the work.

"But what was it like when you wrote *Satyagraha*?" someone might ask.

"I don't know."

"But you were there, weren't you?"

"Are you sure?"

Because I'm not sure that I am there at that moment. The ordinary witness has been lost—the artist Philip has robbed the daily Philip of his ability to see himself. That's very clearly what happens when people say "I wrote it in a dream," or "I don't know where the music came from." They'll say all kinds of things: "It must have come from God," or "It must have come from a past life," or whatever. All they're really saying is, "I don't remember how I did it," and they may make up an outside source. But the real source is not any of those things. It's a process that the artist has learned. He has tricked himself into gaining that extra attention that he needed to do the work.

There was a teacher named Krishnamurti, born in India in 1895, whom I wasn't particularly close to, but who had a number of ideas I liked. Krishnamurti, who lectured all over the world and authored many books, including *The First and Last Freedom*, before his death in 1986, always talked about the moment of the present being the moment of creativity. He tried to press on you that if you really understood that creativity was opening up to you at every single moment of time, the experience of that would be the real moment of awareness. I never really understood it very well, and yet I felt that it was a very powerful idea. What he was talking about, as far as I could tell, was a truly spontaneous experience of living. He wasn't my teacher—I heard him speak once and I read some of his books—but what was interesting about what Krishnamurti said was that it was about a spontaneous unfolding of life. There was nothing routine about it, there was nothing repeated about it: it was continuously new.

When you have one foot in this world and one foot in the other world, the foot in the other world is the foot that takes you into the world of clarity and of power. The problem with recall is that when I return to the world of the witness, I'm not sure if I'm remembering correctly what I wrote, because I'm not using the same tools to remember as I used to write. The world of the witness is less powerful than the world of the writer, because the function of writing will eventually rob the witness of his energy so that the writer will be able to conceptualize the "art" work.

When I'm making a sketch, I'm hearing something, but I don't know exactly what it is. A lot of writing is the effort made in trying to hear. The question for me always is "Is that what I'm hearing?" I've heard so much music in my life that it's now easy for me to recall it. I can remember Beethoven's Ninth, Bach's and Vivaldi's concertos— they're all available to me. Outside of my memory, they're written in books, they're in recordings. I can hear them whenever I want to. But when composing, this new music doesn't have the benefit of having had a prior existence of any kind at all. A particular piece has zero existence until the moment of its creation. Therefore, the question comes back to "Can I describe what I heard?"

I've had dreams where I dreamed music and saw it as having width, length, breadth, color: a visual object. Once I was having a dream about a piece of music, and I came to a modulation, and what I saw was a door on a hinge. It was a perfect image of modulation. You walked through a door and into another place—that's what a modulation does. What I did in the dream was to create a shorthand to represent the modulation by seeing it visually. It offered me an alternative way of thinking of modulation—my idea of modulation was enhanced to some degree by this image of the hinge found in a dream.

As a composer, I think we develop techniques in a kind of desperation to find a way of making something new. My sense of what happens next is "Where is the paddle that's big enough and strong enough to power me through that moment?"

Perhaps I've wandered into a discussion that's too abstract, but the truth is that, though these ways of thinking about music may seem abstract as I write them, I think about such things all the time.

O PENINGS AND CLOSINGS, BEGINNINGS AND ENDINGS. EVERY-
thing in between passes as quickly as the blink of an eye.
An eternity precedes the opening and another, if not the same, follows
the closing. Somehow everything that lies in between (the events of
this book included) seems for a moment more vivid. What is real to
us becomes forgotten, and what we don't understand will be forgotten, too.

So I save this closing not for thoughts but for images, memories
which, by writing them down, are no longer mine alone.

I had met Allen Ginsberg many times after I returned from Paris and
India in 1967. He, of course, was close to William Burroughs whom I
knew from the *Chappaqua* film work when I was assisting Ravi Shankar. We had shared the stage quite a few times at music-poetry events
and at the Nova Convention in 1979 in New York City, a celebration
of Burroughs's work. But we didn't do any work together until 1988.
It then happened that a theater group that emerged from the Vietnam
Veterans Against the War was organizing a fund-raising effort that
had, as its major event, an evening at the Shubert Theater on Broadway. Tom Bird from the theater company called me and asked if I
would participate. I agreed but really had no idea what I would do.

A few days later I was in the St. Mark's Bookshop and Allen happened to be there, in the poetry section. I was inspired to ask him if

he would perform at the event. He immediately accepted. I then asked if we could perform together, using a poem of his and new music which I would compose. In a flash he picked up a copy of his *Collected Poems* off the shelf, deftly opened to the section "The Fall of America" and in a few seconds his fingers pointed to the lines, "I'm an old man now" from "Wichita Vortex Sutra." I went home and, starting with that line, in a few days had composed the music, stopping after the line "Stop for tea and gas." We only had a few weeks before the Shubert performance and we rehearsed at my house, where I had the piano. This, our first collaboration, came together quickly. After that, we began to see each other often, and since we lived not far from each other in the East Village, our regular visits were no problem.

The first performance went very well and we were beginning to think about a longer work. I suggested an evening-length event for my own ensemble with a small vocal group. He agreed and we took up the challenge of selecting the poems from his *Collected Poems*— itself a colossal body of work. For the next half year, we had frequent sessions in which he read poems to me that he wanted to consider for our "song" opera. By then we were talking about staging, design, and décor. Allen was very excited by the prospect, as was I. While he didn't read every poem in his *Collected Poems*, he read a lot of them, and we also considered other poems written after its compilation. Allen suggested *Hydrogen Jukebox* as the title. It was a phrase from *Howl* and worked perfectly for our project. The work, when completed, was a collection of twenty songs for an ensemble of six singers, including "Father Death Blues," and "Wichita Vortex Sutra," which I left as a spoken piece and which Allen and I performed together when he could manage to join us on the tour.

We began to meet often in Allen's apartment, along with Jerome Sirlin, the designer, and Ann Carlson, our director. The six singers eventually were set as six archetypal American characters—a waitress, a policewoman, a businessman, a priest, a mechanic, and a cheerleader. The themes of the poems reflected a good range of Allen's favorite topics, including the antiwar movement, the sexual revolution, drugs, Eastern philosophy, and environmental issues. Jerome's designs were colorful, powerful, and sometimes almost stark in their directness.

I had already been presenting some solo concerts in the 1980s, but in the 1990s I became serious about piano playing and began devoting some regular practicing and composing time to it. In a way it grew out of my performing with Allen, because after *Hydrogen Jukebox* had run its course, we began presenting music-poetry concerts. We did a fair amount of work together and that meant new music for some of the poems that had not been part of *Hydrogen Jukebox*. "Magic Psalm" was one such poem, as were "Footnote to Howl" and "On Cremation of Chögyam Trungpa, Vidyadhara." I also composed new piano solos for these concerts, which included Allen's solo readings as well as poems with which he accompanied himself on a small Indian harmonium. He considered Bob Dylan his teacher in this area of performance. He said he learned everything he knew about music composition from Dylan.

My Tibetan friend and teacher, Gelek Rimpoche, who lived in Ann Arbor, Michigan, had founded a center there called Jewel Heart, which was devoted to traditional instruction in Tibetan Buddhism. When he asked me to do a fund-raising concert in 1989, I invited Allen to come with me and help out at the benefit. I knew Allen had an interest in the subject and had had a famous teacher, Chögyam Trungpa, who had died two years before. When Allen met Gelek Rimpoche soon after, they immediately became close friends. From then on, he was at all the teaching sessions that would happen in New York and traveled frequently to Ann Arbor. During those years, Gelek Rimpoche's Jewel Heart organized two retreats a year—one in the winter and one in the summer—and Allen and I went to both every year. There were usually three of us sharing a room, the third person being either Stokes Howell, another writer friend of mine, or Kathy Laritz, Gelek Rimpoche's assistant at that time. During the retreats I often saw Allen wake up at night, turn on a flashlight, and begin writing poetry.

One summer Allen and his lifelong friend Peter Orlovsky came to visit me in Cape Breton. I remember many evenings after dinner when Allen would recite poetry. There was no TV near us and the radio offered very little of interest, but Allen knew volumes of poetry by heart. He could recite hours of poetry by Shakespeare, Blake, and Tennyson, to list just a few. He told me that his father, Louis Ginsberg, himself a poet of some recognition, had gotten him and his brother Eugene as children to memorize poetry. At times there were readings when both Allen and his brother read poems, a performance I found both moving and beautiful.

Allen was outspoken and honest to a fault up to the very end of his life. From time to time I witnessed his encounters with people who knew him only by name, but had no idea what a warm and spontaneous person he truly was. I remember a dinner in the 1990s at the house of Hank Luce, the publisher of *Time* and *Fortune* magazines. Hank was a big loud guy and part of the Luces—a powerhouse family in New York and throughout the country. Hank didn't really know Allen, but at dinner began poking around conversationally, clearly looking for trouble. But Allen, at that moment, was not interested in getting riled up. He answered Hank amiably enough. Finally Hank said, "I hear you write pornographic poetry?"

"I do."

"Let me hear some."

At that point Allen let loose with some real hair-curling, pornographic poetry. Not only was it pornographic, it was really vulgar, too. I could see that Hank was deeply impressed. Finally, when it looked as if Allen might be slowing down, he said, "Well, well, well . . . that certainly is pornographic."

After that they fell into a lively and very friendly conversation. In fact, Hank and Allen had a very good time together.

During the last ten years of his life, Allen didn't take care of himself very well. He was diagnosed with diabetes and heart disease. He saw a specialist in Boston for his heart and another in New York for the diabetes, but I didn't notice him paying any special attention to his diet. Toward the end he spent more time in hospitals, but his general good spirits were not dampened. A year before he died, he sold his archives to Columbia University, where he had gone to college. He paid his taxes, gave his archivist some bonus money, and bought a beautiful loft that ran through the whole block from Thirteenth to Fourteenth Street between First Avenue and Avenue A. He was dying, and several times he talked to me about it. These were difficult conversations for me. I had lost Candy only six years before and I wasn't ready to lose him. He did tell me during that year that he had always been afraid of dying, but now for the first time, the fear had left him.

Early in April 1997, Allen was at Beth Israel Hospital for some sort of checkup. I was supposed to have lunch with him on the coming Wednesday, but I stopped by the hospital on Monday to visit him. While I was there, and just before I was to leave, he said to me, "Do you want to read my last poem?"

"No."

"C'mon I want you to read it."

"No, Allen. I don't want to read your last poem."

"Here, read it."

It wasn't long. Not even a whole page long. I don't remember it or even reading it at all. I think I just stared at the page.

"Allen, you're supposed to be home tomorrow evening, so I'll see you on Wednesday for lunch as planned."

He got out of bed and walked me to the door of his room. I didn't know what he was up to, but I didn't like it. As I was about to leave he turned me around and kissed me on the cheek.

"I am so happy I knew you," he said.

At that point I was actually getting angry.

"Stop it, Allen. I'll see you on Wednesday." And I ran down the hall to the elevator.

He did in fact go home the next day and he spent that evening calling up friends and saying good-bye. I heard about a number of those calls later in the week, when we were all together at his house.

That same Tuesday night he had a stroke and went immediately into a coma. Gelek Rimpoche sent six or seven monks to stay at my house and he came, too.

Allen's loft was filling up with friends. His bed was placed almost in the center of the room near his Buddhist altar. He was still alive, but in a coma. On Wednesday night, the monks slept in a row on my parlor room floor. By Thursday they were all sitting near Allen's bed, reciting Buddhist texts. Gelek Rimpoche told me that he had been working with Allen for some time, preparing him for his last hours. I knew some of the texts, but only in English. I followed along in English anyway. It was the best I could do. More and more people were coming but mostly people who knew him well. Patti Smith was there. Bob Thurman, the head of Tibet House, too. And, of course, Peter Orlovsky. I had to leave on Friday for a solo concert nearby. When I got back on Saturday, Allen had already stopped breathing, though he was still there in his body. Gelek and the monks began the final recitations, and a few hours later, he was gone.

To say that Allen "passed on" or "died," which of course he definitely had, does not capture for me the emptiness that his leaving has left behind. Still, as I'm writing about him now, years after he is gone, I think of him with great pleasure. And to be truthful, even now I do not feel he is very far away.

OPENINGS AND CLOSINGS, BEGINNINGS AND ENDINGS. Everything in between passes as quickly as the blink of an eye. An eternity precedes the opening and another, if not the same, follows the closing. Somehow everything that lies in between seems for a moment more vivid. What is real to us becomes forgotten, and what we don't understand will be forgotten, too.

In my first year at the University of Chicago, the question I asked myself was "Where does music come from?" The attempt to answer that question led to the composition of my first piece of music.

More than a dozen years later, still pondering the same question, I asked Ravi Shankar where music comes from. His reply was to bow toward a photo of his guru and say, "Through his grace, the power of his music has come through him into me."

Over time, for me, the question has evolved into another question: "What *is* music?"

For a while, the answer I found was that music is a place. By that, I mean a place as real as Chicago, or any other place you want to think of, that has all the attributes of reality—depth, smell, memory. I'm using the word "place" poetically in a certain sense, and yet what I want to convey is the solidity of the idea. A place is a way of outlining a particular view of reality. You can mark a particular view and call it a place, and you can go back to it. When I say music is a place as real as Chicago, what I mean to say is that in our minds it exists in very much the same way. I can take the plane to Chicago, and I can also imagine Chicago, but either way, I know Chicago is a place for me. In the same way, that same place can exist in a painting, in a dance, in a poem, or in a piece of music.

Place is both abstract and organic. It's completely organic when it is something we can see as connected to ourselves—as an extension of an organic being in an inorganic world. But at the same time, place also has the quality of being abstract, in that it has the fluidity of scale and movement. One of the things that we learn to do is how to return to that place, which is at least as real as anything else you can imagine, including yourself.

Recently I've been thinking about music in yet another way, less allegorical and more in terms of what really happens. Now when I'm writing music, I'm not thinking of structure; I'm not thinking of harmony; I'm not thinking of counterpoint. I'm not thinking of any of the things I have learned.

I'm not thinking *about* music, I'm *thinking music*. My brain thinks music. It doesn't think words. If I were thinking words, then I would try to find music to fit the words. But I'm not doing that, either. In working with mixed media, I have to find music to go with the dance;

I have to find music to go with the play; I have to find music to go with the image or music to go with the words. And I have to find the music from *music itself*.

The only way to do that, I eventually learned, was that, instead of trying to do it from the outside, I would have to work from the inside. I would have to hear the music *in* the place. In other words, when I'm looking for what that music would be, I find the music by looking at the subject itself.

When someone says "How do you write music for a film?" I say to them very truthfully, "I look at the film and I write down the music." I don't make music to go with the film, I write the music that *is* the film.

As for the pieces I'm composing now, I wouldn't have been able to write them ten years ago. Not that I didn't have the musical means— I didn't have the ability to *hear* music in that way.

In an opera I recently composed based on Franz Kafka's *The Trial*, the main character, Joseph K. is in the office of his lawyer. He is waiting to meet the lawyer, and also in the office is a man named Block, another client.

K. says to Block, "What's your name?"

"Block, I'm a businessman," the man replies.

"Is that your real name?" K. asks.

"Yes, why wouldn't it be?" Block answers.

That's a wonderful response: "Why wouldn't it be?"

In the same way, now when I'm writing music for a theater scene, film, or dance event, I can truly say "Why wouldn't it be this?" One can only say that from a place of understanding or even of knowledge about one's relation to that particular theater scene, film, or dance event. This alignment is made through a conscious, nonverbal, contemplative activity. Once the alignment between oneself and the dramatic material is established, a link is made on a deep, nonconceptual level between the material and one's inner musical voice. That link is the key, and when it is achieved, it is no longer necessary to make the music fit the scene, because the scene will fit the music automatically.

In other words, the specifics of the scene will naturally accommodate themselves to the music because the music is already there.

From this point of view, the brain is the prism through which the music appears. When I say "I'm not thinking *about* music, I'm *thinking music*," the music *is* the thought. The modality in which the brain is operating *is* music.

Tomo Geshe Rimpoche told me once that there is not just one universe, there are three thousand universes.

Right away I asked him, "Is one of them music?"

"Yes," he said.

"Could I go there someday?"

"Hopefully," he replied.

When he told me that, fifteen years ago, I thought that he meant "in some future reincarnation." But perhaps he didn't. Perhaps he was thinking that in this very life I would be in that world. And now I'm thinking that *is* what he thought, and I feel that I'm closer to the realization of that than I've ever been before.

OPENINGS AND CLOSINGS, BEGINNINGS AND ENDINGS. Everything in between passes as quickly as the blink of an eye. An eternity precedes the opening and another, if not the same, follows the closing. Somehow everything that lies in between seems for a moment more vivid. What is real to us becomes forgotten, and what we don't understand will be forgotten, too.

It is 1943 in Baltimore, a summer Saturday afternoon. My sister, Sheppie, is eight years old, and I am six. We've left our house on Brookfield Avenue and we walk down the sidewalk to North Avenue with my mother, Ida, and my big brother, Marty. We cross North Avenue and take a right toward Linden Boulevard. The #22 streetcar stops there, heading downtown on its iron rails. I will come to know it better because it is the same #22 that will take me to Mount Vernon Place and the Peabody Conservatory, where I will take my music lessons. But that is two years away and still unimaginable.

Halfway up the block we come to the barbershop. It's like all the barbershops in every town in America, with the red, white, and blue striped pole spiraling downward. Inside we take our seats. The barber, a little fellow with a thin mustache, grins at us. This will be his show, he seems to say. And we know it, too. Sheppie takes her seat in the barber's chair. There's a little seat for her that fits into the big seat. Otherwise the barber wouldn't be able to reach down to cut her hair. Marty and I watch intently. The barber dips his comb in a bowl of water and begins to comb her hair straight down. And slowly, slowly, her hair gets shorter. We know it's a trick. He must be cutting her hair at the same time with the scissors in his other hand. But, try as we might, we can't catch him doing it. So the haircut becomes an act of magic. He pretends the watery comb is shrinking her hair. It's marvelous and we love it but, at the same time, we want to catch him tricking us.

Now, another Saturday six years later, Marty and I are downtown working in Ben's record store. I'm twelve and he's thirteen. Because it's Saturday, the bank is closed. That means the money collected from radio repairs and records from the end of the week can't be deposited that day. There is, though, a night deposit box, and if you have a business on Howard Street or Lexington Avenue, you may not want to leave cash in your store over the weekend. Really only Sunday, but still. . . . So what you have to do is make out a deposit slip and put it in an envelope with the cash and slip it down the opening of the night deposit box. Ben will get it all ready. He does that part in the back of the shop where John, the radio repairman, is fixing radios. Ben can fix radios, too, and he will start to teach Marty and me how to do it later when we're a little older.

Now he does an absolutely astonishing thing. He fills out the deposit slip, stuffs it into the envelope with the cash (all bills), puts it in a brown paper bag, and hands it to Marty and tells us to take it to the bank. I ask Marty, but in a whisper, how much money is there. I'm sure he doesn't know but he pretends to.

"Two hundred and seventy-five," he says.

I'm terrified. But Marty has it all figured out.

We're outside the store now. Marty gives me the paper bag (so nobody can see the official bank envelope and know we have cash). I walk ahead of him maybe three or four feet. My job is to not look nervous and just walk straight to the bank. This is the plan, this is how we always do it. He tells me not to worry, he will be watching me and will make sure nobody tries to rob me. I walk west on Lexington Avenue. Marty is right behind me. At Eutaw I take a right, and cross the street. The bank is now only half a block away. When we get there, Marty takes the bag from me and puts the bank envelope through the slot.

We breathe easy again. We both feel great and hurry back to the store. A little later Ben will take us to the deli near the corner of South Howard and Lexington for corned beef sandwiches and a root beer. He drinks seltzer.

Now it's winter and Sheppie, Marty, and I are downstairs in the basement at Brookfield Avenue. We, all three, are standing in two concrete tubs. Usually this is where our clothes are washed. But it's also where we get our baths. Maud is there, taking care of us. She helps Mom while Ben is away, serving as a private in the Marine Corps. It's the war years and I must be five, Marty six, and Sheppie seven. Mom is upstairs making oatmeal for breakfast. The water in the tub is a little cold but it feels good.

And then, I'm sitting with Mom at my grandparents' house. It's only a few doors away from our house at 2020 Brookfield Avenue. We sit at a big table in the dining room. The house seems dark to me and, like my grandparents, very old. They are talking together, but not in English. Later I learn that it is Yiddish. If I pay attention I can easily understand them. But it's just talk about work and relatives and a little about the war. That's when they stop talking for a few minutes, just looking down at the table.

One weekend Ben is home from the Marine Corps. He doesn't like to wear his uniform on leave and is wearing his regular clothes and no coat, just a jacket. We're walking up to Druid Hill Park. It's not too far from our house. Marty and Sheppie are back with Mom at home. Ben and I walk on up to the reservoir. There is a cinder-stone track all around it, and kids and parents go there to ride their bikes. I see some families nearby trying to get a kite in the air. Ben rents a kid's bike for me. It doesn't have training wheels, so he has to push it to get it going, and then, for a few seconds, it feels like I'm really riding it all by myself. He runs after me and we do it again, him pushing and running, me with my feet looking for the ground, and sometimes touching the pedals.

ACKNOWLEDGMENTS

There were two people, both with extensive experience, who provided critical help in the task of writing this book.

First I owe a special thanks to Stokes Howell, who lent his highly developed literary skills by helping to organize and shape the actual written material that I composed. This allowed the book to achieve its final narrative form.

Second, I owe my deep gratitude to Bob Weil—my main connection to the W. W. Norton and Liveright book companies. He combined a sharp, critical overview with a steady flow of encouragement, which was essential in crystallizing my growing writing skills.

I would also like to offer a special thanks to the following people: Sheppie Glass Abramowitz, Mort Abramowitz, Marty Glass, Cevia Highstein, Norman Highstein, and Beverly Gural; Jim Keller, Rebecca Litman, Charlotte Sheedy, and Drew Smith; Joanne Akalaitis, Kyra Borre, Linda Brumbach, Don Christensen, Richard Guerin, Kaleb Kilkenny, Claire Lampen, Katy O'Donnell, Tim O'Donnell, Alisa Regas, Carla Sacks, Drew Smith, and Jim Woodard; Trent Duffy, Elisabeth Kerr, Phil Marino, Drake McFeely, William Menaker, Peter Miller, Anna Oler, Don Rifkin, Bill Rusin, and Albert Tang; Marcus Raskin, Gelek Rimpoche, Mr. Sarup, Phintso and Pema Thonden, Bob and Nena Thurman, and Saori Tsukada.

INDEX

Page numbers in *italics* refer to illustrations.